Duty to Dissent

Personal Note:

Henri Bourassa & W.W. 1 would have been my Ph.D thesis had I pursued my studies at that level in 1970. RI.

Duty to Dissent

*Henri Bourassa and
the First World War*

Geoff Keelan

UBCPress · Vancouver · Toronto

© UBC Press 2019

All rights reserved. No part of this publication may be reproduced, stored in a retrieval system, or transmitted, in any form or by any means, without prior written permission of the publisher, or, in Canada, in the case of photocopying or other reprographic copying, a licence from Access Copyright, www.accesscopyright.ca.

28 27 26 25 24 23 22 21 20 19   5 4 3 2 1

Printed in Canada on FSC-certified ancient-forest-free paper (100% post-consumer recycled) that is processed chlorine- and acid-free.

Library and Archives Canada Cataloguing in Publication

Title: Duty to dissent : Henri Bourassa and the First World War / Geoff Keelan.
Names: Keelan, Geoff, author.
Description: Includes bibliographical references and index.
Identifiers: Canadiana (print) 20190156856 | Canadiana (ebook) 20190156864 | ISBN 9780774838825 (hardcover) | ISBN 9780774838832 (softcover) | ISBN 9780774838849 (PDF) | ISBN 9780774838856 (EPUB) | ISBN 9780774838863 (Kindle)
Subjects: LCSH: Bourassa, Henri, 1868–1952 – Political and social views. | LCSH: World War, 1914–1918 – Canada. | LCSH: World War, 1914–1918 – Québec (Province) | LCSH: Journalists – Québec (Province) – Biography. | LCSH: Politicians – Québec (Province) – Biography. | CSH: Canada – Politics and government – 1911–1921. | LCSH: Canada – English-French relations – History – 20th century. | LCSH: Devoir (Montréal, Québec) | LCGFT: Biographies.
Classification: LCC FC556.B68 K44 2019 | DDC 971.061/2092—dc23

Canadä

UBC Press gratefully acknowledges the financial support for our publishing program of the Government of Canada (through the Canada Book Fund), the Canada Council for the Arts, and the British Columbia Arts Council.

This book has been published with the help of a grant from the Canadian Federation for the Humanities and Social Sciences, through the Awards to Scholarly Publications Program, using funds provided by the Social Sciences and Humanities Research Council of Canada.

Printed and bound in Canada by Friesens
Set in NewBaskerville and Galliard by Apex CoVantage, LLC
Copy editor: Dallas Harrison
Proofreader: Lauren Cross
Cover designer: Michel Vrana

UBC Press
The University of British Columbia
2029 West Mall
Vancouver, BC V6T 1Z2
www.ubcpress.ca

Contents

Acknowledgments / vii

Introduction / 3

1 Fais ce que dois! / 21

2 The Duty of Canada at the Present Hour / 46

3 What Do We Owe England? / 68

4 The Soul of Canada / 93

5 The Possibility of Peace / 118

6 The Wall of Deceit / 144

7 Silenced / 166

Conclusion / 190

Notes / 211

Selected Bibliography / 267

Index / 271

Acknowledgments

I HAVE READ MANY ACKNOWLEDGMENTS and realize that they are strange and unique things. Some are funny for the stories that they tell, others are interesting for the names that they mention, while most are generically bland. A special few are touching; one or two are tragic. It is only after you finish a work that you realize thanking people is the most important part of the work. How you write your acknowledgments is not as important as making sure you convey the enormity of writing a book. It is by necessity a group effort. So many people have helped with this book that I am certain I will not name them all – so know that the work before you is a testament to countless acts of support big and small.

This work would not have been possible without the financial support of the Social Sciences and Humanities Research Council, the University of Waterloo, Western University, and the Laurier Centre for Military, Strategic, and Disarmament Studies. As well, I have to thank the University of Toronto, Microsoft, and the Internet Archives for providing access to many digitized documents that improved this work.

Its quality would not have been possible without the hard work of the team at UBC Press as well as two anonymous reviewers. One, whom I can only assume is Québécois, offered an invaluable French review that provided worthwhile insight into Quebec literature on the war and corrected many minor errors. If I have not addressed the breadth of the suggestions, it is entirely my fault. A special thanks to Dallas Harrison, whose copyediting undoubtedly improved this work. I also gained a much clearer understanding of academic publishing through a stint at Wilfrid Laurier University Press, which truly helped to spur this book onward, and I still value my short time there with Lisa, Clare, Siobhan, Catherine, Murray, and Rob.

Numerous professors have guided me on my path as a historian. A second-year course with Robert Hanks was the first time that I became seriously interested in the craft of history. During a fourth-year seminar,

Jasmin Habib exposed me to vigorous and enjoyable academic discussion. In another undergraduate seminar, and later a master's seminar, Susan Neylan showed me that studying historical works could be engaging and exciting. Both Alan Gordon and Ken Coates offered careful direction in my doctoral fields as I learned the difference between a student of history and a historian. Cynthia Comacchio was also an invaluable teacher during my master's work. Her comments in class and on my written work helped me to evolve as a student and historian. I have also had the great pleasure to work with one of the most insightful scholars whom I have met in my academic life, Geoff Hayes, and I remember many times walking out of his office in awe of his perceptive remarks.

I do not think that any graduate student at the University of Waterloo could have survived without the constant support and help of our administrative assistant, Donna Hayes. She was there at the worst of times and the best of times, and she was always willing to help us or cheer us on. I am glad to call her my friend. The most formative and fruitful connections that I have made as a student of history have been at the Laurier Centre for Military, Strategic, and Disarmament Studies. Jane Whalen inspired me as a young student. Kellen Kurschinksi always reminded me of the scholar whom I strive to be, and I respect him greatly as a colleague and historian. I met Jazz Groarke there; he did some very useful work indexing Bourassa's articles in *Le Devoir*, and I am delighted to see him again as my new life in Ottawa begins. Mike Bechthold, Vanessa McMackin, Kate Rose, Marc and Joan Kilgour, Matt Symes, Caleb Burney, and all the others – thank you! Many hours have been spent enjoying your company.

Numerous friends have helped me throughout this process – stretching back to my undergraduate studies. Estelle Hjertaas generously provided me with a place to stay and many hours of conversation during research trips to Ottawa. I spent a lot of time with Matthew Wiseman and Marjorie Hopkins, both of whom were invaluable sources of relaxing and academic conversations. Trevor Ford, a source of constant disagreement over political views, was a steady companion through this process. Kirk Goodlet is an amazing colleague and friend, and through our discussions of academia, history, and many other topics I am undoubtedly a better historian. Nick Lachance, who somehow lived with me for three years of this process, generously devoted countless hours of his own time playing video games with me when I needed to do so. He is truly a great friend.

Terry Copp, director of the Laurier Centre for my time there, was an invaluable mentor and friend. He guided, inspired, and shaped the scholar and person that I am today. Since my first undergraduate class with him, I have been greatly honoured to be his student, his research assistant, and his colleague. This work is proof of his generosity and influence as an educator and a historian. Without his pushing me to test my potential, I would likely be working at a Starbucks in downtown Waterloo (or hopefully managing it by now).

Whitney Lackenbauer was just as generous with his time and help. I could not have asked for a better scholar to guide me through my years as a graduate student. He invited me into his classroom and his home, and I never failed to leave a conversation with him inspired to be a historian and to work harder. It is difficult to express how valuable such inspiration has been, but it is why this work is before you. Whitney helped me to become a better writer, a better student, and a better historian, and I am thankful to have his support throughout my academic career and my current endeavours.

My family has also been incredibly supportive. Alan, Richard, and Paul all provided me with moments of relaxation and enjoyment. Meghan and Bill opened their home for a weekend away, as have Bill and Liesel. My grandmother Jean inspired me with her energy. My parents, Bryan and Val, offered constant support, encouragement, and food and drink. Years of their love helped me to endure this process, and I greatly appreciated their generosity in offering a place to edit my work peacefully. I also cherished my moments with Mary-Jo, Ashley, and Brydon in Alberta since I began visiting there with my partner.

More than anyone, though, this work owes its existence to her. I met Jocelyn while writing this work, and the long arduous hours spent at a computer were worth it because she was there when I was done. Writing this work and falling in love with Jocelyn will be forever etched in my mind as one incredible journey. As one part of that journey ends and another begins, I am extremely thankful to have her at my side.

Duty to Dissent

Introduction

CANADA WAS AT A BREAKING POINT during the "old-fashioned" winter in the final month of 1917. Weather stations logged record low temperatures, and snow swept across the continent.¹ Amid the deep freeze, Canadians went to the polls to pass judgment on Sir Robert Borden's wartime government. After more than three years of unrelenting industrialized warfare, the country was immersed in one of the most bitter electoral campaigns in its history. On the one side, Prime Minister Borden and a coalition of Conservatives and former Liberals sought to convince Canadians that the government had directed a successful war effort and that only the imposition of conscription could ensure its continued success. Sending more Canadian soldiers to the battlefronts of Europe was the only way to bring about victory in the ongoing world war. On the other side, Liberal leader Sir Wilfrid Laurier believed that there had to be a referendum on conscription to keep the country united during the increasingly fractious war. Borden's Conservatives had failed to preserve the unity between French Canadians and English Canadians, and their short-sighted efforts to win the war could cost them the country born only half a century earlier. National unity was the only way to win the war, Laurier had reminded Borden during the debate on conscription six months earlier, a warning dismissed as typical political grandstanding.² But it was not a typical time for Canadians. The war had changed their country and the world – and not for the better. Millions had been killed, wounded, or traumatized, and there was no end in sight. It seemed as if any sacrifice could be justified. Amid such extremes, the "party-truce" declared at the outbreak of war in August 1914 was a distant memory as both sides accused the other of treason.

The election over conscription could be seen as a microcosm of the war itself. For Canadians immersed in the political turmoil, the life-and-death struggle in Europe was mirrored by a brutal and unforgiving election battle at home. The future was at stake, or so it seemed to those living through the turmoil, as the fabric that held them together was ready to tear. The nation was cracking along familiar lines, split between French and English, conservative and liberal, imperialist and nationalist. Conscription in Quebec, historian Béatrice Richard wrote, was a matter of life and death for many young men that year and became an issue that would decide the life and death of the province.[3] All believed that Canada's place in the world was changing, but they differed on what price they owed for that change. As the world fought over whether a German hegemony would emerge triumphant against an Anglo-Saxon one, conscription reflected the same fundamental question: who would shape the future of the world?

The war had transformed everything from daily life to the international balance of power, and it had left an indelible mark on Canada's government and people. Hundreds of thousands of Canadians had fought and continued to fight in the trenches of France and Belgium for a war of which the outcome remained uncertain. New government powers had expanded the state's role in private and public life. Although the enthusiasm that marked the beginning of the war in 1914 had subsided, the country could not escape the urgency that it demanded. Canada, like the rest of the world, had not had the time to adjust to the new reality of warfare between modern industrialized societies. Social schisms that predated the conflict were exacerbated, and the once familiar political playing field for Canadians was upended and shaken.

In the midst of this tumultuous election campaign and worldwide conflict, French Canadian nationalist Henri Bourassa advised readers of his newspaper *Le Devoir* that no party in Ottawa was worth trusting fully. He counselled French Canadians to reject Borden's conscription policy, but he admitted that Laurier was little better. The Liberal solution of a referendum on conscription still ignored the fundamental problems of the war. Neither Conservatives nor Liberals could claim to have the Canadian nation's best interests in mind, for they had mindfully discarded the careful considerations that had slowly improved the dominion since Confederation fifty years earlier. Bourassa instructed his readers on the great perils of the election, but eventually he caustically endorsed the Liberal leader after great deliberation:

> The unionist program is the antithesis of everything we love, everything we believe, everything we want. It is the synthesis of everything we hate – men, ideas and trends – in both parties ... As determined opponents of the coalition ministry, its entire policy, and its staff, we accept Mr. Laurier's program

where it moves closer to our principles and ideas; we reject it wherever it virtually matches that of the ministry.[4]

Bourassa was clear that Laurier was the lesser of two evils. An English Canadian majority dictating the conduct of a British war posed a far greater threat to his native province of Quebec, the country, and Canadian society itself. French Canada could not afford to resign control over its fate in a world where old institutions were crumbling and those replacing them were not yet fully formed.

Bourassa feared English Canadians, many of whom continued to support – or at least accede to – a seemingly unlimited war effort. War supporters believed that victory in Europe outweighed the war's growing cost and that Canadian soldiers necessarily protected the British Empire and their allies against the menace of a triumphant Germany. Only more men could prevent an ascendant Germany from stealing Canada's and the British Empire's places in the world. Against this certainty of belief, Bourassa stood in the national spotlight of 1917 and proclaimed his total opposition to the war. It marked him as a prominent voice but one in the wilderness away from Canada's political metropole and out of step with the debate between Laurier and Borden that winter.

While the two party leaders argued over how to enact conscription as a path to victory, Bourassa alleged that it represented self-destruction on a national scale. He feared a country where so many of its citizens were willing to hurt its whole. Canadians' approval of conscription demonstrated an insidious acceptance of militarism that could supersede Canada's normal democratic culture. The journalist no longer saw any allowance in wartime Canada for his liberal nationalist values that enshrined the rights of the individual, adherence to law, and equality between French and English. Instead, conscription forced Canadians to fight in a war that they did not support. In the December election, Bourassa hoped that Laurier would win in order to protect the country against the "brigands" who threatened both its unity and its purpose.[5] It was a holding action in stark contrast to the idealistic vision of a unified Canada that Bourassa had held when war had broken out. By 1917, he wished only to avoid greater fissures in Canadian unity, the breakdown of social order, and any further transformation of the Canadian dominion that he had known in 1914. His condemnation of the largely English Canadian Unionist Party was no surprise, nor was his reluctant support for Laurier, a man who, Bourassa had once alleged in the pages of *Le Devoir*, had betrayed his liberal principles and the country. There were few options in the increasingly narrow political spectrum of Canada at war.

Bourassa's polemic during the harsh winter of 1917 reflected his experience of the war. From its outset, he had cautioned against the consequences of an overreaching war effort while promising his readers that he would conscientiously examine the issues of the war to provide a complete picture. His duty as self-appointed protector of the public good demanded that he resist the wave of popular enthusiasm found in newspapers across the country. When it became clear that the government had no interest in moderating its military and economic contributions, and as other Canadians refused to heed his warnings, he rejected participation entirely in January 1916. The following year Bourassa was the loudest voice against Prime Minister Borden's introduction of conscription. Facing a government that had no sympathy for French Canada and had ignored Bourassa's arguments for three years, the journalist urged his supporters to vote for Laurier's Liberals. Laurier still lost the election, since English Canada voted overwhelmingly for Borden's Unionist Party, but Quebec voted for Laurier. The country seemed to be irrevocably divided between the "two solitudes" of French and English.

It proved that Bourassa was right to worry that the pressures of wartime could split the seams of Canada's federation. Its French and English peoples separately avowed their ability to decide the country's direction as they accused the other side of disloyalty to the "true" Canadian nation during the 1917 election. To Bourassa, the division embodied the worst of the First World War's transformative intensity.

How did he reach that dismal point? It was a path mired in the upheaval of the First World War but one of his own choosing. Bourassa had long ago decided to stand against the wave and forge his own path in Canadian politics. The clearest distillation of the fire that fuelled Bourassa was the name of the vessel that carried his ideas to the public, *Le Devoir*. He explained his goal at the newspaper's founding in January 1910: to awaken Canadian citizens to a commitment to public duty, religious duty, national duty, and civic duty. In his first editorial, Bourassa wrote that "our ambition is limited to striving, as best we can, to do what we preach: the daily duty."[6] The tagline attached to every issue of his newspaper encapsulated this mission: "Fais ce que dois!" (Do what you must!).[7] His idealistic goals were somewhat undermined by his first editorial's belligerent title, "Before the Fight," as he prepared to enter a fierce political debate on the creation of a Canadian navy. From the beginning, Bourassa committed himself to public reflection without shying away from argumentative commentary.

His willingness to defy popular opinion was no less apparent in his writing during the First World War. As a result, Bourassa was rarely an innocent bystander to the country's discord. He extolled one-sided, uncompromising views of wartime Canada as much as his opponents did. Critics in English and French Canada accused him of treasonous disloyalty – to Canada or the nationalist movement that he had helped to create – and some repeatedly appealed to the government to censor his writing. Bourassa offered little to soothe their outrage. His inflexible stance denounced Canadians in favour of the war as immoral hypocrites, though they held their views as earnestly as he held his own. His opponents failed to convince him that political and social issues that predated the war had disappeared. Instead, Bourassa rejected their plea for new attitudes to confront Canada's role in the European conflict. To him, the Great War was an obstacle that required a reasoned response measured by Canadian interests and values. For better or for worse, he would stay loyal to his own principles, determined to do his duty for Canada as he understood it.

In this book, I provide a close examination of the wartime writings of Henri Bourassa, especially his articles in *Le Devoir*, with an emphasis on his understanding and analysis of international developments. I underline his Canadian perspective as part of an international discourse on the war, its impact on his unique vision of Canadian nationalism, and the force of his beliefs in shaping those views. Bourassa was a liberal who feared the rise of militarism, but he believed that the cure for the ills of war was the pope in Rome, not liberal society itself. The realm of mortal affairs was flawed without divine guidance, and the atrocity of the First World War proved that to Bourassa beyond doubt. As beneficial as liberalism was, it was merely a vessel for achieving humanity's benediction. Armed with his faith and political principles, Bourassa explored the domestic and international implications of the war with a uniquely liberal, Canadian, and Catholic perspective. That contradictory perspective makes him intriguing to a historian, especially since it is brought into sharp relief by the Great War. The war was a cataclysm undoing everything right in the world, at least in the eyes of Canada's most vocal dissenter.

The allure of Bourassa's writing and the contradictions that shaped his ideas on the war are not lost on me. I cannot help but be drawn into the tone and style of his work. It is somewhat unusual for an English-speaking Canadian historian to offer a detailed study of a French Canadian nationalist, but Bourassa described the war in a way that I had never encountered before, one that evoked its serious nature not only to him personally but for all of those involved. Unsurprisingly, this work emphasizes Bourassa over other sources of dissent in Canada and Quebec, a conscious choice that necessarily limits its scope, but it also speaks to the magnetism of his words even a century after he wrote them. There is a power in the way that he wrote and about what he wrote. Every editorial is steeped in the importance of the war years and what was at stake for Bourassa, for Canada, and for the world. I have also endeavoured to translate his words into English so that this book might be open to an audience in English Canada that often misses his most important work.[8] Both French Canadians and English Canadians ought to have the opportunity to understand the emotional resonance of the world's first industrialized war in Canadian and Quebec society, even so far from the trench battles traditionally offered as the most traumatic part of the war. The intensity of the war years back in Canada is readily apparent in his writing of 1914–18.

Bourassa spoke for a small audience, but his prominence was projected onto a national stage by the power and emotion of his writing. Like many others around the globe, he recognized that the war was causing irrevocable changes to his world. His articles were more than just opinions on his times; they were appeals to join him in resisting the tidal forces at play. Pushing back against changes that seemed to be overwhelmingly powerful imbues Bourassa with a tenacity of spirit that one cannot help but admire.

These traits did not endear him to his opponents, who must have read his work with horror. To see Canada's most pre-eminent French Canadian nationalist rally against the war or, at least before 1916, critique it weekly, would only have confirmed what they had believed all along: French Canadians were not loyal to the British Empire and could not be trusted to support it. Bourassa was disloyal and thus had no right to make arguments against the war – not because he was wrong but because of who he was. The mistake of English Canadians in their appraisal of Bourassa, epitomized in the conscription crisis of 1917, was that they refused to accept that French Canada could have logical and rational reasons to oppose the war and the means of fighting it. There was no room to disagree within the same community, not even a shared language to express that disagreement. Instead, the alleged failure of French Canadians to enlist and their failure to vocally support the war like English Canadians did, were results of being French Canadian rather than being free-thinking individuals with a different worldview. The mere fact that Bourassa and

French Canadians like him were different from English Canadians culturally, religiously, or ideologically was enough to dismiss their words. This obsession with Bourassa's identity as a French Canadian, nationalist, and Catholic has subsequently coloured much of the historical work on Bourassa, as it did the contemporary reaction to his writing.

Bourassa elicited much attention from historians, even before his death in 1952. His prolific career and far-reaching influence mean that he has been included in general Canadian histories.[9] Any textbook on Canadian history mentions him alongside Sir Wilfrid Laurier and Sir Robert Borden. A history of Quebec, or Canadian Catholicism, or Canadian nationalism, or the First and Second World Wars usually includes a discussion of Bourassa. The debates in which he engaged on the "solution" to the "problem" of French-English relations in Canada help to explain his prominence in Canadian history, but those debates led historians to critically examine his role as a domestic commentator first and foremost. As a result, the historical literature focused on Bourassa is unusually narrow. A few scholars have broken from this trend, but most consider him to have been an inward-looking French Canadian nationalist – a French Canadian actor, on a Canadian stage perhaps, but for French Canadian audiences alone.

Two contrasting views characterized early historical scholarship. One was Elizabeth Armstrong's *The Crisis of Quebec, 1914–1918*, published in 1937, the first major historical work to deal with French Canada during the war.[10] Bourassa played a large role in her analysis of the province. Her view of him was ultimately negative, but she did not fail to acknowledge his influence. Describing him as a "mixture of sincere patriotism and demagoguery,"[11] though not a "narrow bigot or a fanatical partisan," Armstrong believed that his contemporaries viewed him as "a real Frenchman in the cultural rather than the political sense of the word, one who combined grace with courage, logic with wit and deep learning with eloquence."[12] This does not lessen the criticism that she levied against him. Armstrong condemned his rejection of Ottawa's wartime policy and glossed over the detailed analysis that Bourassa offered.

The rise of extreme nationalism in the 1930s heavily influenced Armstrong's conclusion that Bourassa was a dangerous domestic threat.[13] In her words, he dreamed of a "French Canada as a proselytizing force ... [that would] bring the American continent back to the arms of Rome and to the glories of French civilization."[14] Armstrong used the terms "passive" and "active" nationalism to describe Quebec and argued that the war saw a brief flare of active nationalism spurred on by Bourassa. As a result, she treated him and his fellow *nationalistes* as anomalies in French Canada who preached moderation while breeding radical action. They were not representative of the true passive French Canadian nationalism. The "crisis of Quebec," then, was not a conflict of language, or culture, or even loyalty; it was a crisis of nationalism without restraint advocated by Bourassa.[15] He and his cohorts, she posited, could never live in harmony with English Canada. Instead, "[the] Nationalists were convinced that the great majority of French Canadians believed that Canada had done enough for the Dominion war effort and that their sole obligation was to fight for their own native country. To force them to fight against their innermost conviction was to make revolutionaries out of the population of Quebec."[16] For Armstrong, the only acceptable Canadian nationalism could not stray across the line between tradition and revolution. That would mean a denial of French Canada's history. By pushing across it, the *nationalistes* became more than aberrant in her view; they became abhorrent. French Canadian nationalism must be inherently conservative, she argued, couched in the safety of survival at all costs to keep it well away from the modernized, horrific fanaticism of her time. Armstrong's work was a shallow history in which Bourassa did not provide answers to political or cultural problems or react to unfolding events. He was a dangerous catalyst for French Canada but one without agency.

Robert Rumilly, best known for his voluminous history of Quebec, expressed a more positive portrayal of Henri Bourassa in a biography of the nationalist leader.[17] Almost hagiographic, the book essentially credited Bourassa with creating modern Quebec nationalism. It is a painstakingly detailed biography but contains little critical historical inquiry. Rumilly's analysis of Bourassa's role in opposing conscription is typical of his writing: "Bourassa developed a balanced thinking in a panicked world. He alone remained cold-blooded among the unleashing of passions."[18] Although offering incredible detail on his monthly accomplishments, there is no questioning of why Bourassa acted the way that he did. The instances of purple prose between quotations from him or the simple descriptions of what he was doing provide an invaluable narrative of his life but offer little analytical depth. Without investigating Bourassa's motivations, Rumilly failed to take a key inquisitive step.

Born in 1897, Rumilly was a committed nationalist and wrote extensively on the history of French Canada from the 1930s to his death in 1983. Both personal experiences and ideological leanings obviously influenced his work on Bourassa. Rumilly was one of the founding members of the

French Canadian Academy, formed to combat the colonial influence of both Britain and France on Quebec society.[19] He presented Bourassa as a heroic national figure in his monograph: "I know young French Canadians who, when the national situation seems discouraging to them, comfort themselves by thinking: 'There was Bourassa! ...' Thus Bourassa, the great Bourassa we have just lost, continues to protect us."[20] The conclusion consoled French Canadians that Bourassa's spirit would live on in a new generation. Rumilly's history had the air of being incomplete and superficial, but Rumilly "rediscovered" Bourassa after his death and made him as captivating a figure to Quebec as he had been in life.[21]

The contrast between Armstrong and Rumilly in their depictions of Bourassa shaped the historians who followed them, particularly their views of his role during the First World War. In one, he was a dangerous instigator; in the other, he was a stalwart saviour of the *patrie*. Although they described both his positions and his actions, they minimized their analyses of his ideas and the war's impacts on them. Instead, Bourassa was a simplified character cast in a predetermined role, more useful as an influential force on the known historical outcome than as an individual influenced by his experience. Written while Bourassa was still alive, both are more descriptive than historical, but they are key in comprehending the historiography on Bourassa marked by different understandings among French Canadian and English Canadian historians. Equally, they reveal the failure of literature that touches on Bourassa in the First World War. He was not simply a Quebec *nationaliste* discussing domestic issues but also a legitimate and powerful dissenter who discussed international events with the same clarity and fervour as Canadian ones.

Bourassa's death in 1952 and the centenary of his birth in 1968 produced brief flurries of academic interest in his career.[22] In English Canada, Bourassa was remade into a primarily pan-Canadian nationalist. Joseph Levitt's *Henri Bourassa and the Golden Calf*, published in 1969, largely ignored the impact of the Great War, focusing instead on specific aspects of Bourassa's career and the *nationaliste* program for Quebec.[23] By the 1970s, English-speaking historians had reclaimed Bourassa as an important predecessor to the bicultural and bilingual world of post-1967 Canada and its iconic prime minister, Pierre Elliott Trudeau. General histories, such as Robert Craig Brown and Ramsay Cook's overview of early-twentieth-century Canadian history, *Canada 1896–1921: A Nation Transformed*, portray Bourassa prominently as an antagonist to English Canada and an important catalyst for the development of a modern Canadian identity.[24]

Historians distilled Bourassa to his vision of a bilingual and bicultural Canada at the expense of his other views.

The works of Ramsay Cook throughout the 1960s and into the 1990s demonstrate the compelling nature of Bourassa's ideas on French and English Canada. In the midst of growing animosity between French Canadians and English Canadians, and as Quebec experienced the Quiet Revolution and a neo-nationalist separatist movement emerged, Cook published in 1966 *Canada and the French-Canadian Question*. Each chapter explored different elements of Quebec's history in Canada and its different forms of nationalism. Bourassa understandably played a large role in some chapters, mirrored in much of Cook's future work.[25] Cook compared the *nationaliste* Bourassa with his neo-nationalist descendants, such as René Lévesque and the Parti Québécois, as well as his "successors," epitomized in the bilingual and bicultural policies of the Liberal Party and Pierre Trudeau. Bourassa's antagonistic role during the war was minimized if not ignored. In another vein, Susan Mann offered several works on the history of Quebec to English Canadian audiences that mention Bourassa frequently. Mann's study of Quebec in the 1920s and the Action française[26] offers valuable insights into Bourassa's views on feminism and women, otherwise understudied in the literature.[27] Since the works of Mann and Cook, however, English Canadian scholarship on Bourassa stagnated.

French Canadian historians have discussed Bourassa more recently and in greater detail, often with greater interest and vigour than English Canadian historians. An article from René Durocher in 1971 focused exclusively on Bourassa's relationship with the Catholic Church during the war. He used Bourassa's correspondence to shed light on his disagreement with the church hierarchy, but he did not address other aspects of Bourassa's war experience.[28] Jean-Philippe Warren succeeded Durocher through an examination of Bourassa's ultramontanism, nationalism, and the position of the pope and could easily be read alongside some of the conclusions of this book.[29] Réal Bélanger's entry in the *Dictionary of Canadian Biography* furnished an in-depth study of Bourassa but understandably had to limit the journalist's role in the war to two paragraphs.[30] The entry was a preliminary version of Bélanger's two-volume biography of Bourassa. The first volume was published in 2013 and covers the years from his birth to the outbreak of the First World War in 1914, while the second volume is forthcoming. It is without a doubt the most comprehensive and detailed work on Bourassa since Rumilly.[31] Bélanger explores Bourassa's upbringing and the first half of his political career while including myriad other details throughout. Sylvie Lacombe's *La rencontre de deux peuples élus,* published in 2002, critically contrasts the religious nationalism of French Canada and the imperial nationalism of English Canada. Bourassa is the dominant figure used to analyze French Canada's "ambition nationale."[32] Although her specific discussion of the First World War is brief, her analysis of the "hierarchical relationship" between Bourassa's liberal political beliefs and conservative religious ones, and her concluding summation of his religious nationalism, offer sophisticated scholarship on Bourassa.[33] Lacombe further examined his contradictory beliefs and their transformation during the war, which she argued had a radicalizing effect on him.[34] Yet, even as Lacombe deepened our understanding of French Canadian nationalism and Bourassa as a nationalist, her work underplayed his role as a Canadian intellectual and commentator in the midst of the First World War.

Some general intellectual histories of Quebec have addressed Bourassa's ideas more broadly, notably the work of Yvan Lamonde, and offer French-speaking audiences more insight into the intellectual context of Bourassa's analysis than is available to English-speaking audiences.[35] A few other French-language works on Bourassa have appeared as popular histories, while the literature on the history of *Le Devoir* touches on his formative role in creating the newspaper.[36] As in English Canadian works, Bourassa is a dominant figure in French Canadian history, and there are references to him in many studies of Quebec and the twentieth century.[37]

This continuing focus by both French Canadians and English Canadians on his domestic role has hampered an all-encompassing historical study of Bourassa and diminished some of his most impressive writing on the Great War. Studies that touch on his thoughts during the war do so completely removed from the context of the events of the war. Since historians often focus on the domestic aspects of his editorials, it is understandable that they would not address his writing on the international aspects of the conflict. As a result, a reader of Canadian history has an incomplete picture of his life from 1914 to 1918. Few historians convey the exceptional nature of his reasoning and coherence on a wide variety of subjects during the turbulent war years. Bourassa was one of Canada's great wartime thinkers, and historians have not yet thoroughly examined the depth and breadth of his perspective.[38]

In this book, then, I ask what can we discover if we step away from the confines of traditional literature separated by English Canadian and French Canadian identities? Or at least open those boxes a little? Certainly,

Bourassa evokes such a study. Although he identified himself as a French Canadian Catholic nationalist, his ideas about Canada and the war were not so easily categorized. They were not always in line with what other French Canadians, nationalists, or Catholics were thinking. They were sometimes diametrically opposed to the majoritarian views in his province and his country. Bourassa was not like other Canadians during the war; nor was he like other French Canadians, nationalists, and Catholics. There is no easy box into which we can place him, especially in the context of those war years.

"People do not 'have' ideas," John Lukacs advises historians, "they choose them ... It may be important what ideas do to men, [but] it is often even more important what people do with their ideas."[39] The process by which Bourassa chose his ideas (and the beliefs that he held as a result) was a long one. In this book, I deal with the second part of the advice from Lukacs: what Bourassa did with his ideas. I examine his actions during the Great War and focus on the commentary that he offered to Canadians – primarily French Canadians because of the language in which he most often wrote. His beliefs compelled him to offer his commentaries through his chosen medium, his newspaper *Le Devoir*, even during the worst of the war's political maelstroms.

In trying to understand Bourassa's beliefs during the war, Mark Bevir's *The Logic of the History of Ideas* offers some useful guidance. Unlike Canadian intellectual historians, who have largely ignored the "linguistic turn" in favour of the cultural one,[40] Bevir roots his book in the philosophical debate on the meaning of language and texts for historians.[41] He describes the complex process of establishing an intellectual history of beliefs. It must put together what he calls a "spherical jigsaw" in which "each piece of the jigsaw, each belief, belongs where it does by virtue of the pieces around it. The puzzler completes the jigsaw by joining all the pieces together to form a single picture which then makes sense of each individual piece."[42] There is a growing literature that discusses Bevir's approach.[43] His advice that "historians should assume that people meant what they said unless there is evidence to the contrary" has an appealing simplicity to it,[44] but critics have not accepted his emphasis on believing an individual's words over an interpretation of their meaning with the benefit of hindsight.[45] It is clear that Bevir's webs of beliefs might be a worthwhile method of writing intellectual history, but they must be balanced by understanding the context of an individual's life and environment.[46] Examining individuals without that context risks their objectivity and can overwhelm the factual foundation of academic writing. Attention to both allows historians to attempt to reconstruct accurately a "history of beliefs."[47]

One of Bevir's conclusions is that by examining individuals who change or confirm their beliefs, we can examine what grants those individuals the agency of shaping their beliefs independent of an impersonal force or a model of history. This human element of history is at the core of José Miguel Sardica's defence of historical biography in *Rethinking History* that responds to several decades of criticisms from historians who had discarded it as a parochial and exclusionary vision of the past.[48] Its value rests in its ability to reflect on larger questions of history while combining a more literary and communicable style focused through the history of a single life.[49] This utility is only reinforced when confronted with the "all too fragmented and liquid present day societies and intellectual structures [as] the writing of past lives becomes a sort of necessary connecting thread, providing human sense and moral lights to map regular lives and model inspirations to inform future options."[50] Historical biography, though limited in scope, allows readers to immerse themselves in an individual's view of the world that is entirely biased. Although this narrow view diminishes the scope of historical analysis, in return it provides an individual's certainty about what was known and not known.

Thus, the following chapters are inspired by Bevir's philosophy of intellectual history and Sardica's affirmation of historical biography. They describe Bourassa's web of beliefs about the First World War and the dilemmas that Bourassa encountered that transformed him – dilemmas such as equality between French Canadians and English Canadians, the pervasive influence of imperialism, and the necessity of a liberal Canadian nationalism altogether different from the nationalism advocated by English Canadians. Wartime dilemmas also pushed Bourassa to examine international issues that he previously ignored in favour of domestic concerns. He devoted many pages to peace proposals, such as the diplomatic efforts of Pope Benedict XV to end the conflict or President Woodrow Wilson's neutrality and subsequent shaping of the peace accord that ended the war in 1918. Bourassa addressed events outside Canada such as the Easter Rising in Ireland in 1916, the American election in 1916, and the American entry into the war in 1917. Global affairs affected Canadians as they never had before, and Bourassa was one of the few voices in Canada who critically examined them as an active participant in national, continental, and transnational frameworks.[51]

Just as these global events changed the Canadian nation, so too did they affect Bourassa's ideas. His views on imperialism, French Canada and English Canada, religion, and international affairs informed his analyses of Canada's war experience. Each was the result of a long contemplative career, and the events of the war changed them. As we will see, the Bourassa who emerged from the war in 1918 was not the Bourassa who entered it in 1914. This simple and factual observation reveals nothing of his struggle to remain loyal to his beliefs; of the complex politics, desires, and fears of wartime Canada; or of the terrible power of modern war over the societies that fought it. Bourassa would know of these issues all too well by war's end, but in 1914 he carried none of those burdens.

I cannot fully describe in this book the life, beliefs, and times of Bourassa even within the short period of the First World War. There were many facets of his public life. Over the course of his prolific career, he wrote articles on political, economic, and social issues to a small but attentive audience. The sheer volume and variety of his work make it difficult to explore it in its entirety, and the war years were busy ones at home and abroad. The work published by Bourassa was understandably dense, so it is challenging for the historian to explain his influence on Canadians during the Great War. The polarized politics of wartime led Bourassa and his opponents to extremes, existing on the periphery of supporting or rejecting the war, often resorting to hyperbole if not outright intellectual dishonesty to assert their respective cases. Under the shadow of the Great War, Canadians treated solutions to old problems and new ones with an urgency that belied their complexity. The war did not initiate many of the issues that Bourassa raised; however, when cast in the light of a struggle for the survival of Canada and its European allies, debates on them became intensified.

I study the depth of Bourassa's public analysis and pay strict attention to chronology. The successes and failures of the home front, battlefront, and international diplomacy shaped the form, content, and tone of Bourassa's articles, with the understanding that his public work was attuned to an audience. Public commentary is reactionary in nature: writers commented on the events and issues of the war as it unfolded. It is impossible to consider newspapers as completely accurate pictures of their times; instead, they use constructed versions of events and considered opinions of journalists and present them to a public audience, and only rarely are they eyewitness accounts or personal views. News and editorials are indicative of opinions and biases, and an examination of Bourassa's public editorials does not comprise a comprehensive exploration of his thoughts, only the views that Bourassa presented to the world. In some cases, I do not explore domestic topics as other historians have already examined them in detail. Ultimately, I follow Bourassa's war, and it is within the structure and pace of his public analysis that I examine Canada and the First World War. An unintended consequence of this analysis is that it offers a glimpse of the political and international news that would have confronted any close reader of Canadian newspapers during the war and *Le Devoir* in particular. Though this is not a political history, it offers an account of what was most important to politics of the day.

Bourassa stands as one of the most intelligent figures willing to dissect the war for Canadians. A careful examination of his writing during the war connects him to an international dissident movement and reveals that he was more than just a domestic commentator. Bourassa presented a complex and detailed review of international events as well as his thoughts on them, reflecting his beliefs as a liberal nationalist, an ultramontane Catholic, and a French Canadian. Although he often advocated the same ideas as European dissenters, he remained firmly entrenched in a Canadian experience of the war. He was still a Canadian looking out to the world at war, willing to share what he thought of it even in the face of opposition, and above all he remained concerned with the future of his nation.

In Chapter 1, I review Bourassa's life before the war. I introduce the major events that defined his career. From his entry into federal politics as a member of Wilfrid Laurier's Liberal Party in 1896, I trace Bourassa's growing dissatisfaction with Laurier's treatment of French Canada. Bourassa did not accept Laurier's moderate stance toward imperialist ideology, particularly when Laurier allowed volunteers to fight in the Boer War. Bourassa believed that Laurier's acquiescence to Britain's request for aid set a dangerous precedent that forever committed Canada to British foreign endeavours. The growing influence of imperialism on Canadian politics pushed Bourassa to look for other allies within his home province. As an influential member of the French Canadian *nationalistes*, he began his role as a non-partisan commentator on Canadian politics. He was deeply involved in national debates on a Canadian navy, the election of 1911, and the role of French Canadians in Confederation. I also explore the intellectual and historical contexts of Bourassa's career that subsequently shaped his response to the First World War.

I turn to the first months of the war in Chapter 2. Bourassa initially supported Canadian involvement – asking for moderation and a limited war effort – and ultimately affirmed that the war was worth fighting. I detail the responses of his English Canadian and French Canadian critics, for their hostility played a crucial role in isolating Bourassa from the rest of the country. In the last months of 1914, he alone critically examined the war for a national audience. Not even fellow nationalist J.S. Ewart was prepared to contravene the developing dominant Canadian narrative of the war. Bourassa presented to his readers a detailed exploration of the causes of the war, which according to him were not simply the defence of Belgium but also reflected British interests in Europe as well as Russian claims to Constantinople. He urged his fellow Canadians to approach the war in pursuit of Canadian – not British – goals. Although some commentators agreed that Bourassa had a right to express his views, his attempts to communicate his thoughts on the war to an audience in Ottawa nearly caused a riot in December 1914. The year ended with Bourassa realizing that English Canada cared little for the substance and tone of his arguments.

In Chapter 3, I deal with Bourassa's search in 1915 for other voices in the world that opposed the war. Bourassa reviewed the work of Britain's anti-war group, the Union of Democratic Control, as well as the efforts of Pope Benedict XV to mediate the conflict. Events such as the Second Battle of Ypres and the sinking of the *Lusitania*, which convinced others of the necessity of the war, had little impact on the French Canadian journalist. Instead, he scorned the Canadian war effort, which only seemed to grow more extensive and encompassing. That December he published his first major book on the war, *Que devons-nous à l'Angleterre?* (What Do We Owe England?), which summarized his opposition to the conflict. Bourassa furnished a wide-ranging historical review of Canadian history to argue that Canada had no obligation to fight Britain's war. Britain was obliged to defend Canada, but there was no reciprocal relationship. By unquestioningly approving Canada's entry into the war, Bourassa believed, an "imperialist revolution" was taking place. Its transformation of the Canadian nation could not continue unimpeded, and Bourassa vowed to continue combatting its influence.

I explore in Chapter 4 Bourassa's growing dissent, epitomized in the correspondence with his cousin serving in the Canadian army, Talbot Mercer Papineau, in the summer of 1916. Bourassa had disavowed any support for the war in January at the annual celebration of the anniversary of *Le Devoir*. From that point onward, his writings became increasingly hostile to the forces supporting the war in both French and English Canada, including the Catholic episcopacy. He published another book, *Hier, aujourd'hui, demain* (Yesterday, Today, Tomorrow), that repeated his arguments from December. Bourassa expanded his views on the nature of the imperialist revolution to include its influence on the Catholic hierarchy in Quebec. He also envisioned what the end of the war might look like, and he emphatically supported future independence from Britain. His half French Canadian and half American cousin, Papineau, had joined the Canadian forces in August 1914. His time in the trenches profoundly affected his political beliefs about the war, and he wrote to Bourassa urging him to change his views. Bourassa dismissed Papineau's arguments since they paid no attention to his deep exploration of the war from the previous months. Papineau lectured Bourassa about the meaning and significance of the war without any knowledge that Bourassa had already set out a contrary position in great detail.

In Chapter 5, I focus on Bourassa's examination of international issues. Bourassa affirmed support for the worldly perspective of Pope Benedict XV in August 1916 and studied the goals and plans of the Union of Democratic Control. In December, he detailed the peace proposal from Germany and the Allied response to it for his readers, asking that it be considered honestly if only because it held the possibility of ending the terrible conflict. Likewise, he supported President Wilson's request that the belligerent nations clearly explain their war aims. In the early months of 1917, the United States gradually became more involved in the war and eventually entered it that April. Bourassa, who often visited the United States at this time, offered a comprehensive perspective on American politics and why the country had entered the war after three years of neutrality. He analyzed these international events in far more depth than any other Canadian writer at the time. In his assessment, the failure to achieve peace and the American entry into the war further emphasized its futility and the growing threat of militarism.

I return in Chapter 6 to the home front as Bourassa confronted Canada's enactment of conscription legislation in May 1917. Forced military service was an important element of a militarist society, and Bourassa opposed it at all costs. Prime Minister Borden's involvement in the Imperial War Cabinet, which nominally gave a voice to Canada in imperial affairs, was of little importance to Bourassa unless it was matched by a reasonable policy focused on Canada's national interests. The ineffectiveness of Borden's new role was clear when, on his return to Canada, Borden announced that there would be conscription. Bourassa warned that society could withstand only so much pressure before something broke. He foresaw violence and unrest if conscription was imposed on people who could not express themselves democratically. The journalist denounced the lacklustre debate in the House of Commons when few federal politicians turned against the war that made conscription necessary. Violence in Montreal that summer confirmed Bourassa's fears.

In Chapter 7, I cover the final months of Bourassa's commentary during the war. I analyze his reaction to Borden's election legislation in August and September 1917 as well as Borden's successful efforts to forge a coalition of Conservatives and Liberals in favour of conscription. Bourassa and Laurier reunited after almost two decades to oppose conscription, with both perceiving the dominance of English Canadians as a threat to Canada's national unity. If English Canadians controlled Parliament, then they could pass legislation without any concern for French Canadian views. After Borden won the election that December, Bourassa lamented the isolation of French Canada – isolated because it alone had remained loyal to the Canada of 1867, whereas the rest of the country had embraced militarism and total war. His writing became increasingly dissentious as he continued to hope for a peaceful end to the war. As men were called up for conscription in March 1918, riots broke out in Quebec. Bourassa urged calm, anxious that social unrest could turn into rebellion or revolution. The Easter Riots were quelled, but the federal government passed new censorship laws as a result. Bourassa voluntarily agreed to stop writing in *Le Devoir*, and his commentary effectively ceased from April 1918 to the end of the war.

By the war's end in 1918, Bourassa was not the same man as the one who had witnessed its beginning in 1914. His liberalism, once firmly entrenched in a classical British form, shifted as he aligned with the views of radical liberals and socialists in Britain opposed to the war – though perhaps he did not realize it. His nationalist dream of a Canadian identity that united French and English peoples seemed to be impossible after the crisis over conscription and the December 1917 election. His vision of a bilingual, bicultural, and liberal Canada that he had fostered for decades was dimmed. Bourassa emerged from the war doubting the capability of humanity to resolve the problems that plagued it. Instead, he turned toward his Catholic faith as the last bastion of rationality and hope for a broken world. It seemed to him that only the compassionate stance of Pope Benedict XV had survived the war uncorrupted. Elsewhere, the war's extreme sacrifices and the totality of the conflict left no space for moderation, sound judgment, or goodwill. Although Bourassa never set foot on the battlefields, his war was still a traumatic and haunting experience.

1
Fais ce que dois!

1868–1914

BORN IN 1868, HENRI BOURASSA was the grandson of famed Lower Canadian radical republican Louis-Joseph Papineau. As one biographer notes, he had politics in his blood, and it coloured every aspect of his life from an early age.[1] His father, Napoléon Bourassa, was an artist and married Papineau's daughter, Azélie, who died six months after the birth of Henri. His mother's death left a gap in his family, but his relatives stepped in to help raise the intelligent boy. His uncle Augustin-Médard Bourassa, an Oblate missionary, exposed him to his library at a young age. The young boy read the works of Catholic writers Louis Veuillot, Joseph de Maistre, and Jules-Paul Tardivel, all of whom would influence his intellectual development. Bourassa recalled that it was "in my uncle's library and in the reading of *The Universe* that I forever drew my notions about the role of the Church in society, about the relationships that must exist between the Church and civil leaders."[2] His early exposure to the ultramontane vision of Catholicism had a lasting effect, marking him with a deep faith.

Catholicism had played an equally powerful role in the history of French Canada. French colonists settled along the St. Lawrence River in New France during the seventeenth century before the British conquest in the Seven Years War in 1759. Known simply as "the conquest," British rule was relatively benign. Most of the ruling class of New France fled and left behind Catholic priests and bishops who took on the role of guiding the conquered *Canadiens*. Under their leadership, the former colony refused to fight alongside the Americans during their revolution against Britain or in the War of 1812 a generation later. French Canadians existed together with the neighbouring colony of Upper Canada and the Maritime colonies on the coast as part of the Second British North America.

In the aftermath of the failed rebellions of 1837–38 that advocated republican and secular control, the Catholic Church emerged as an even more powerful force in Quebec society and politics. The fading influence of the rebellions' republican *Patriotes* and the union of Lower and Upper Canada in 1841 marked a significant defeat for Quebec's liberal political elite. In place of the liberal national identity that the *Patriotes* advocated, a conservative nationalism was consolidated by the Catholic Church, which affirmed its moral and political leadership of French Canadians.[3] A French Canadian identity tied to the survival of Catholicism, the French language, and French Canadian culture soon emerged among the *Canadien* minority. Known by the term *survivance*, this connection of language and religion to their cultural and national purpose, or what Sylvie Lacombe terms "national ambition," became central to their identities.[4] So much so that Lacombe has termed French Canada (and Quebec in particular) not as a nation-state but as a "church-nation" during this time. The church's control over institutions such as education represented a merging of civil and religious society that, unlike in other parts of the Western world, only strengthened throughout the nineteenth century.[5] By the beginning of the twentieth century, the Catholic Church had become the dominant social and cultural institution of French Canadian society. The religiosity of its citizens likewise defined many of their political struggles.

Among the most fervent believers of French Canada's church-nation were ultramontane Catholics such as Henri Bourassa and his uncle Augustin. "Ultramontanism" was a term first used to describe the location of European Catholics north of the Swiss Alps as being "over the mountain" from Rome. Over time, it became a description of all European Catholics who looked to Rome for direction rather than the nation in which they lived.

French Canadian ultramontanists – such as Bishop J.J. Lartigue of Montreal, his successor Ignace Bourget, and Bishop L.F. Laflèche of Trois Rivières – believed that their sacred duty was to protect and preserve French Canadian Catholicism in North America. Laflèche released a booklet of articles in 1866, *Quelques considérations sur les rapports de la société civile avec la religion et la famille* (Some Considerations on Civil Society's Relationship with Religion and the Family), in which he outlined the role of Catholicism in Quebec society. He defended the "providential mission" that had formed and sustained the Catholic state in North America and proclaimed that French Canadian survival in North America was a solemn duty for Catholics.[6] Laflèche's ideas had a lasting impact on Quebec Catholicism as future generations of thinkers and practitioners adopted his views. By the twentieth century, papal infallibility matched by technological advances in transatlantic communication allowed Rome to reach Quebec City with relative ease.⁷ Quebec society reflected the observation of Nancy Christie and Michael Gauvreau: "Religion is not an identity, it is an ideological system ... [It is] a set of structured ideas that specific groups and institutions attempt to make authoritative in various historical contexts as the dominant formulator of social values."⁸ From that system, identities are shaped. For ultramontane Catholics such as the Bourassas, the Catholic Church's expression of those social values was beyond reproach. There was no power greater than God, and his representative on Earth was the pope, the voice of God in human affairs. Bourassa's initiation into these ideas would colour his political beliefs for his entire career.

Bourassa was exposed to less conservative strains of thought as well. His aunt Ezilda Papineau helped to raise him, and, even as she instilled in him a lifelong belief in ultramontanism, she introduced him to a wider world of literature that included non-French writers such as Walter Scott and James Fenimore Cooper. By the age of nine, Bourassa had read Émile Keller's *Histoire de France* as well as John Lingard's *History of England*. Often the young Bourassa listened to debates between his father and his father's friends about the social and political problems of the day. He excelled in his studies under the supervision of private tutors and as a student at various schools. For two years, he attended the Catholic Commercial Academy in Montreal, and briefly enrolled at the École polytechnique in 1885, then switched his focus to religious studies at Holy Cross College in Massachusetts, where he perfected his English. Bourassa drifted from career to career, even attending law school in the late 1890s, but he never settled on one profession. Instead, he gained wide-ranging knowledge of many subjects and a keen passion for debate and critical thinking. Eventually, he found his calling in the world of politics.⁹

On 22 November 1885, he was among the crowd that gathered to hear French Canadian politicians rally the province against the execution of Métis leader Louis Riel. Riel had brought Manitoba into Confederation in 1870 while securing the rights of its Métis and French Canadian Catholic peoples against English Canadian domination. Part of the deal was that he would be exiled from the young dominion for the murder of a Protestant, Thomas Scott. Fifteen years later Riel returned from the United States to lead a Métis resistance in the North-West Territories (later Saskatchewan) and proclaimed himself a messianic prophet leading his chosen people to freedom.¹⁰ This time authorities caught him, accused him of treason, and executed him. French Canadians were outraged. They believed that his madness obviated his responsibility and that the government had equal blame in rousing Riel to action. His unquestioned indictment in the English Canadian press alongside the subsequent show trial that sentenced him to execution demonstrated that the federal government had little interest in addressing the minority rights that Riel defended.[11] French Canadians publicly decried the decision as racially and religiously motivated, while the opposition Liberals gladly attacked Sir John A. Macdonald's Conservative government on the issue in the House of Commons and in public addresses.

One of the largest gatherings held by French Canadian politicians took place in November at Montreal's Champs-de-Mars. Future leader of the Liberal Party Wilfrid Laurier and future Premier of Quebec Honoré Mercier took the stage. The young Henri Bourassa in the crowd would have heard Laurier famously declare to a captive audience "Had I been born on the banks of the Saskatchewan, I would myself have shouldered a musket to fight against the neglect of governments and the shameless greed of speculators."[12] For French Canadians and the young Bourassa, those words cemented Laurier's place as a leader who would defend their rights in the Dominion of Canada.

The speeches convinced Bourassa to enter politics. He was elected mayor of his childhood hometown of Montebello in January 1890 at the age of twenty-one. By 1896, he was the Labelle riding's successful Liberal candidate in the federal election that brought Laurier to power with significant French Canadian support. The Liberal leader made sure to offer guidance to the young new member of Parliament, and the impressive young man quickly emerged as Laurier's protégé.[13]

But his early political life as an MP was difficult. Bourassa tried to reconcile the tumultuous world of politics with his deep-rooted religious faith and French Canadian ideals. After the election, Laurier appointed him as part of the delegation to resolve the crisis of the Manitoba schools, a result of the 1890 provincial government decision to remove funding for Catholic and Protestant schools. This decision restricted the right of French Canadians to learn their native tongue and threatened their religious schooling. The compromise in 1896 between Laurier and Premier of Manitoba Thomas Greenway, appropriately named the Laurier-Greenway Agreement, effectively enforced the status quo. It maintained a single public school system in Manitoba that included Catholic and French schooling but only allowed for schools with enough French-speaking students to offer French-language education. French Canadian Catholics appealed to the Vatican for an intervention as Laurier also sent a delegation to Rome. Eventually, the Catholic Church dispatched an apostolic delegate, Archbishop Raphael Merry del Val, to Canada. Del Val decided that, as long as the Laurier government made some administrative changes, it was best for Canadian Catholics to side with it.[14] In December 1897, Pope Leo XIII affirmed that, though the Laurier-Greenway Agreement was "defective, imperfect, [and] insufficient," it was a worthwhile remedy and might eventually lead to better legislation. Leo warned that "nothing would be more detrimental than discord: union of minds and harmony of action is required." This clearly rejected Quebec's opposition to Laurier's solution.[15]

The papal position did not prevent Bourassa from feeling unsettled by Laurier's refusal to defend the rights of French Canadian Catholics that Laurier had so eloquently championed at the Champs-de-Mars in 1885. Almost a decade later, in the midst of another school crisis (this time in the new provinces of Alberta and Saskatchewan), Bourassa reflected on his experience in Manitoba and denounced "the history of Manitoba and its disappointments, its abuses of power, its weaknesses and the deceit that it has recorded in our annals."[16] In 1896, however, he was still willing to work with his Liberal leader.

After a disappointing eight-day term as editor of the then radical liberal paper *La Patrie,* when Liberal Party members rejected Bourassa's ultramontane perspective on moderate liberalism that envisioned a liberal society guided by the authority of the Catholic Church, Laurier hoped to expose his protégé to the world of international politics. The prime minister appointed the young man as secretary for the joint Anglo-American commission meeting in Quebec to settle a dispute about the Alaskan boundary between the United States and Canada.[17] The talks collapsed within a year, and Bourassa returned to Ottawa. He left the commission convinced that Canadians could not trust the British to represent their interests in Washington and that Canada had to forge its own path in international relations.[18] Later in 1899, the British invasion of the Boer republics in present-day South Africa compelled Bourassa to express his views, increasingly divergent from those of the Liberal Party and his mentor.

French Canadians and English Canadians fiercely contested their nation's involvement in the British war with the Boer republics, and Bourassa was one of the loudest voices in the debate. At first glance, it seems to presage the domestic dissent of the First World War a decade and a half later, but Carman Miller has recently suggested that historians' approach to French Canada and the Boer War might require a reassessment. That war was not a prelude to the divisive issues and opposition experienced during the First World War. Months of increasing tension between Britain and the Boer republics preceded Britain's declaration of war on 11 October 1899. Canadians had had a long time to develop their own views of, and in some cases apathy toward, the conflict.[19] Attitudes among French Canadians shifted from opposition to cautious acceptance.[20] Although this might have been true for some French Canadians, it was not so for Bourassa. Canadian involvement in the British war not only irrevocably broke his loyalty to the Liberal Party, after he had served only three years as a Liberal MP, but it also served as the basis for his developing nationalist ideas.

Whereas imperial-minded Canadians believed that it was their duty to the British Empire to fight in the war, Bourassa believed that Canada had no reason to send troops to faraway Africa for British colonial interests. He argued in the House of Commons that any Canadian involvement in empire affairs that were not direct concerns of Canada set a dangerous precedent. With his typical flair for sharp comment, Bourassa claimed that "Mr. Chamberlain [the colonial secretary] wanted the African war to tear away from the colonies, at a time when the intoxication of pride and wild passions silenced reason, that first blood tribute they had refused him until then."[21] Bourassa distinguished two key problems with Canadian participation: a question of fact and a question of law. Not only was Britain's justification for the war incorrect, if not immoral and unjust, but also Canada had no legal obligation to join it.[22] In the age of Canadian political imperialism supported by Liberals and Conservatives alike, Bourassa's imposition of morality and legality onto imperial responsibility was a significant intellectual intervention.

His distinction between the act of committing Canadian troops and the legal obligation as a member of the British Empire revealed a critical aspect of his burgeoning sense of Canadian nationalism. Bourassa's rejection of the Boer War was rooted in a position against Canadian imperialism and in favour of Canadian nationalism, and it marked his first serious evocation of a fundamentally different conception of the country and its place in the world. At the other end of the political spectrum, imperialists believed that Canada's active participation in the British Empire was invaluable, but Bourassa could not accept such a worldview. He believed that Canada had its own interests and values entirely separate from those of Britain.

The political ideology of Canadian imperialism that Bourassa opposed had emerged in the late nineteenth century. It began as a British debate about the purpose and utility of the empire that eventually spread to Canada. "Constructive Imperialism," a term coined by W.A.S. Hewins in 1899, described "the deliberate adoption of the Empire as distinguished from the United Kingdom as the basis of public policy." Its adherents advocated "those principles of constructive policy on all constitutional, economic, defensive, and educational questions which will help towards the fulfilment of that ideal."[23] It is also termed "Conservative Imperialism," though opponents and supporters did not always divide along party lines. This brand of imperialism that championed "Greater Britain" and an imperial federation emerged out of the changing international context of the late nineteenth century as rising states such as Germany, Russia, and the United States ballooned into global powers. Britain was no longer the sole power spread across the world, and imperialists argued that the centre and the periphery of the empire required each other for future prosperity.[24]

Constructive Imperialism reached the peak of its influence in Britain and abroad during the two decades before the First World War. Some aspects, such as imperial preference regarding trade and tariffs, failed to gain traction among the empire's former colonies. Most of the dominions considered any changes to tariffs conditional on other political concerns, not inherently appealing as means of expressing imperial patriotism alone. Discussion of imperial defence was more popular as both Britain and its colonies sought solutions to growing defence costs while increasingly using military power to achieve international and collective security.[25]

This brand of imperialism was fiercely debated during the Boer War, and it was epitomized through Joseph Chamberlain's time as colonial secretary from 1895 to 1903. Chamberlain advocated an active British presence in imperial management and the creation of a moral and cultural framework that unified current and former British colonies. Until the last quarter of the nineteenth century, imperial governance had often been left to private concerns.[26] Under Chamberlain, an enlightened and united British Empire could benefit from its former colonies, as demonstrated by the enthusiastic contribution of soldiers to the Boer War by the self-governing dominions. Chamberlain encouraged the view that there was popular support for stronger imperial relations among them, and he was eager to use that enthusiasm to strengthen imperial unity. He believed that popular British support for the Boer War proved the possibility of support for imperial unity at home as well.[27] Paradoxically, the success of guerrilla tactics in the war and examples of British barbarism during the conflict also helped to discredit Chamberlain's particular vision of imperialism. The British failure to defeat the Boers and use of concentration camps proved to some that the empire was not as glorious and civilized as it claimed.[28] Perhaps as a result, enthusiasm for constructive imperialists' goals waned during peacetime, especially without the military necessity of defending the empire. In the end, the idea that "*general* support for the Empire could be translated into enthusiasm for a *particular* concept" proved to be false.[29]

The British Empire's response to the Boer War and subsequently the First World War demonstrated the compelling nature of a call to arms over a call to political unity. Rallying political and popular support was often most successful in a military context. Appeals to the empire's role in defending its members from potential threats, such as Germany, or the military value of defending prosperity, as in South Africa, rallied far more citizens to the cause. In Canada, it was no different. The policies advocated by Canadian imperialists were most popular during situations such as the Boer War, the naval crisis (when Britain called on Canada to help in the naval race against Germany), and in August 1914 at the outbreak of the First World War.

Canadian imperialism mirrored the grander British conception of imperialism, though obviously in a local context. As historian Carl Berger famously noted in his study of the period, imperialism emerged as a set of cultural values and a political ideology that was a form of nationalism unto itself in Canada.[30] Imperialists, in his view, comprised a crucial aspect of Canada's path from colony to nation and, though they stood in opposition to liberal-nationalists, proved that Canadian nationalism did not necessarily mean opposition to the British Empire. British writer Richard Jebb published *Studies in Colonial Nationalism* in 1905 after travelling through the British dominions and witnessing the emergent nationalist sentiments of Britain's former colonies. Colonial loyalty was giving way to national patriotism, and "the Empire [was] less valued for its own sake and more in proportion as it subserves the interests and ideals of separate nationalism."[31] For Canadian imperialists, imperial loyalty fulfilled their vision of the Canadian national community. They were perfectly situated at the end of the nineteenth century to envision a modern nationally imagined "community" tied to the British Empire, though often at the expense of non-English-speaking and non-British minorities.[32] These ideas were encouraged by men such as George Denison, G.M. Grant, G.R. Parkin, Stephen Leacock, and Andrew MacPhail, who in the late nineteenth and early twentieth centuries supported a Canada more closely connected to the empire. Organizations such as Canada First, founded in 1868 but dissolved in the late 1870s, pushed for the first organized creation of a national consciousness, again linked to the British Empire.[33] Its successor, the Canadian chapter of the Imperial Federation League in the 1880s and subsequently the British Empire League in the 1890s, cemented the connections between Canadian imperialists and the larger British discussion regarding the future of the empire. These "colonial nationalists" sought to enlarge Canada's position within the empire.

Other historians have qualified Berger's statement, arguing that imperialism cannot be reduced to a debate between liberal and conservative Canadians. Simon Potter notes that "few people used the terms 'nationalism' and 'imperialism' with either precision or consistency," and commentators used "nation" as a term with different meanings depending on constitutional or political contexts.[34] Douglas Cole separates patriotism – loyalty to the state – from nationalism – loyalty to the national idea. It is important to distinguish the difference. Although almost all Canadians were loyal to the state, there were many different shades of that loyalty. Britannic nationalists or pan–Anglo Saxon supporters demanded imperial connections, and existed alongside those who demanded colonial autonomy for the British nation of Canada, whereas others were Canadian nationalists who sought cultural as well as political independence.[35] In that respect, outside the committed adherents whom Berger outlines, most Canadians lay somewhere on a scale of imperialist and nationalist belief, regardless of their level of patriotism.

In a political context, Canadian imperialism aligned with Constructive Imperialism's goal of creating a unified British Empire, though imbued with a Canadian perspective: a close-knit empire assured the future prosperity of the Canadian nation-state. Unlike in Britain, where debates about the empire were focused on its implications for Britain's global power and economic success, in Canada the simple, abstract objective of prosperity and future greatness had a broad appeal to many on Cole's scale (and not just avowed imperialists). These were desirable goals for any patriotic

Canadian. Liberals as well as Conservatives could ostensibly support Canadian ascendance inside a global imperial institution.

Thus, devotion to a nationalism wedded to the Canadian nation, not a Britannic one, led Bourassa further away from his former Liberal compatriots but made him no less patriotic. That commitment was apparent in how strongly he opposed Laurier's Boer War policy and led him to leave the Liberal Party and sit as an independent in the House of Commons. Bourassa continued to define his brand of Canadian nationalism through his commentaries on political issues. Réal Bélanger observes that, after the Boer War, Bourassa was determined to communicate "informed public opinion by providing Canadians with a clearer understanding of Canada's relations with the Empire and the nature of the relationship between the Protestant English-Canadian majority and the Catholic French-Canadian minority in the country."[36] His role as a critic of all sides of the House of Commons was evident by the time the war ended in 1902. He turned to his native province to seek allies who agreed with his vision of Canada.

In 1903, Bourassa helped to found the Ligue nationaliste along with Olivar Asselin, Armand Lavergne, Jules Fournier, and Omer Héroux. Although he would never officially join the league, he served as its de facto leader. All of the men were rising young professionals, part of Quebec's established intellectual class, and already involved in the province's public life. Asselin, Fournier, and Héroux were journalists; Lavergne was a lawyer. Asselin and Fournier came from farm families. All were well educated and well trained in writing.[37] At the helm of the group was the now well-known federal politician Bourassa. The league used periodicals such as the aptly named weekly newspaper *Le Nationaliste*[38] to express ideas on provincial and national matters. Powerful rhetoric made Bourassa the most prominent of this band of French Canadian nationalists who argued for greater Canadian autonomy within the empire in opposition to Canada's imperialist movement.[39]

Nationalisme, as distinguished from other forms of Canadian nationalism, was a uniquely French Canadian ideology. It expressed a Canadian nationalism that included French Canadian and English Canadian nationalism, even though they did not always fall neatly into such defined categories.[40] Bourassa and the *nationalistes* did not support either of two dominant political parties, the Liberals and the Conservatives. Many of their ideas were deeply embedded in the intellectual currents of French Canada at the turn of the century, but their political ideology differed from that of their contemporaries – though there was some overlap of their social, economic, and political beliefs. Generations of French Canadian intellectuals and politicians informed the views of the *nationalistes*, stretching back to François-Xavier Garneau, but two notable contemporaries were politician Joseph-Israël Tarte and journalist Jules-Paul Tardivel, who directly inspired Bourassa to turn away from established political groups.

Tarte was a Quebec Conservative politician who served as the party's "conscience" during the 1870s and 1880s and kept the province loyal to John A. Macdonald's Conservative Party. By the 1890s, Tarte had left the party after growing dissatisfaction with its anglophone wing, which paid less and less attention to French Canadian problems. The Manitoba schools crisis in particular proved that the party was no longer the best option for Catholic French Canada, and when Wilfrid Laurier asked Tarte to join the Liberal cabinet he agreed. Tarte briefly opposed the Boer War, though he eventually accepted Laurier's argument that volunteers averted any future Canadian responsibility in a British war, but it was rumoured that he might lead an independent party in 1900.[41] By 1903, however, he had returned to the Conservatives over the issue of protectionist tariffs, and he remained there until he died in 1907. Historians have called Tarte a "francophone, Catholic, Canadian, and British subject," never quite a Liberal or Conservative, and certainly not a *nationaliste*.[42] Bourassa had helped Tarte to win his first election as a Liberal in 1893, and Tarte had inspired the young Bourassa, who described the senior politician as one of the most interesting men whom he had ever known.[43] Tarte was one of the prominent protectors of French Canadian identity within a united Canada in the years before the *nationalistes* coalesced, but undoubtedly he paved the way for later adherents in the decades after Confederation.[44]

Tardivel was a more extreme defender of French Canada than Tarte. Indeed, Tardivel was one of the first advocates of Quebec's separation from Canada. An ultramontane Catholic, Tardivel could not separate French Canadian nationality and Roman Catholic Christianity, and he believed that only an independent French Canada could protect the two. From the time of the Riel affair, Tardivel developed a vision of French Canadian autonomy that advocated a French Canadian nation distinct and separate from the English Canadian nation. In his view, French Canadians had been chosen by God to Christianize North America. Mathieu Girard summarized Tardivel's views: "Being separatist, for [him], is to be Catholic, it's an act of faith."⁴⁵ Tardivel established an independent newspaper, *La Verité*, in 1881 to communicate his religious and political beliefs that he edited until his death in 1905. During his career as a journalist, even though Tardivel never formally entered politics, he was an influential force on French Canadian political thought.⁴⁶ He worked closely with Bourassa and fellow *nationaliste* Omer Héroux (who married his daughter) before and after the establishment of the Ligue nationaliste. It was Tardivel with whom Bourassa consulted during his opposition to the Boer War as he debated whether to start an independent third party or find another solution.⁴⁷ He was a significant figure to the *nationalistes* even though they rejected his separatist perspective.⁴⁸

Instead, the next generation of French Canadian nationalists combined the passions of Tarte and Tardivel, wishing neither to support an English-dominated government like Tarte or separation from Canada like Tardivel. Their ideology combined elements of British liberalism, American progressivism, and a bilingual and bicultural Canadian nationalism. When the league formed in 1903, they presented a comprehensive program of their vision of Canada's future, which they continued to develop over the next decade through speeches and newspaper editorials.

The social concerns of the *nationalistes* were rooted in the tenets of social Catholicism, which deserves some explanation. Over the course of the nineteenth century, Catholicism modernized its approach to the social dilemma of industrialization and the demand for democratic rights.⁴⁹ As a result, liberal Catholics began to push for church involvement in social programs and through organizations such as the Society of Saint Vincent de Paul. In 1891, Pope Leo XIII issued the *Rerum Novarum*, a papal encyclical that addressed the growing influence of Marxism and individualism and served as a general Catholic reply to political liberalism. He defined for his flock "the boundaries of the rights and duties within which the rich and the proletariat ... ought to be restricted in relation to each other."⁵⁰ *Rerum Novarum* outlined a role for social Catholicism in the modern world. The Catholic Church and the state could address social ills without allowing private life to supersede public life or doing away with social hierarchies. Catholicism could preserve family hierarchy and private property, as well as the separation between rich and poor, even as individual concerns gave way to collective ones.

In Quebec, the Catholic Church underwent a similar transformation, though with great difficulty. Liberalism's demand for a clear separation of church and state continued to clash with Catholicism in Canada throughout the nineteenth century. It reached its peak in the 1870s when the Guibord Affair debated burial rights based upon religious affiliation and the *Programme catholique* demanded clerical political influence, highlighting attempts by Quebec ultramontanes to combat liberalism in their province. Only after 1877 did an uneasy truce emerge when young Liberal MP Wilfrid Laurier confirmed that "Catholic liberalism is not political liberalism" and that Canadian Liberals had no interest in degrading the powers of the Catholic Church.[51] Eventually, the church in Quebec accepted that in a democracy it was one voluntary association among many, but it could still balance its social role in regard to education and public charity without contravening the role of the state to intervene in public life as liberalism demanded.[52] By the turn of the century, the *nationalistes* could be strong advocates for social Catholicism in Quebec without contradicting conservative strains of Catholic thought.

The *nationaliste* vision of society was a social Catholic one and drew much from *Rerum Novarum*.[53] The church was to help create a stable and prosperous society so that Catholic values could be preserved within it rather than be at odds with it. This sometimes meant supporting unions, rejecting materialism, and improving the conditions of the poor. The *nationalistes* endorsed state action to fulfill the goals of social Catholicism, for instance addressing social problems such as poverty and class exploitation. Education also played a vital role in society. Schools, controlled by the church, could impart moral and religious values to society and allow Catholic societies to resist corruption and materialism. By allowing the Catholic Church to continue directing the province's educational programs, society would be able to confront the moral dilemmas of the modern age.[54] Like Pope Leo XIII's missive, the *nationalistes* presented a view of society that preserved French Canada's traditional societal values in the process of modernizing their state for the twentieth century.

The economic program of the *nationalistes* reflected their social beliefs. They envisioned a state that could intercede in the economy for the benefit of its people. Their position was rooted in the ideas of Quebec's leading economist of the era, Errol Bouchette, who lamented Quebec traditionalism that shunned the study of economics and social sciences and its disastrous impact on French Canadian capital.[55] Bouchette argued instead that French Canada had to use its own capital and people to exploit its natural resources, which depended on the ability of a French Canadian state to intervene economically.[56] Only then could French Canadians control their economy rather than leave its reins in the hands of English

Canada or the United States. The *nationalistes* were willing to adapt to the economic realities of the industrial age. They espoused an economic liberalism that did not want clerical interference in economic matters, but neither did they challenge church control in other areas.

Politically, the *nationalistes* sought ways to ensure French Canadians' survival in North America, as had generations of French Canadians before them. They desired greater autonomy within a bicultural and binational Canadian federation and independence from the British Empire. Describing the *nationaliste* perspective, Bourassa noted that "[our] homeland, for us, is the whole of Canada, a federation of distinct races and autonomous provinces. The nation ... is the Canadian nation, composed of French and English Canadians."[57] In their 1903 program, they demanded for the provinces "the greatest measure of autonomy compatible with maintaining a federal connection" alongside Canada's political, commercial, and military independence from British policy.[58] The constitutional promise of protection for minorities curtailed provincial power since French-language schools had to be protected in provinces where English-speaking Canadians had a majority, just as Quebec protected its English-language schools. A bicultural nation would allow both of Canada's peoples to prosper, and equally they argued that such a Canada could only be sustained if it was autonomous and not under the control of the British Empire, at least eventually. As Bourassa wrote in 1901, "the first necessary condition for the independence of a people is to be assured of inner and outer peace."[59] There was much work to be done, and a *nationaliste* Canada could exist only if it upheld its internal commitments to racial equality as well as possessed the ability to decide the manner and scope of its external commitments.

The *nationalistes* and Bourassa sought to establish a new national political ideology, though ultimately it remained limited to Quebec. Joseph Levitt argues that the *nationalistes* failed to create a Canadian nationalism because they could not convince English Canadians that their Canadian identity naturally ought to include both cultures. Although the *nationaliste* program intended to broaden the case for a Canadian nationalism to include both French and English, the chosen battleground of Quebec inherently restricted its influence.[60] The *Canadian* nationalism of the *nationalistes* can be contrasted with the *French Canadian* nationalism of Jules-Paul Tardivel. He believed that French Canada could only survive alone, not cooperatively with English Canada. He warned them that, "just as Mr. Bourassa is wary of those who are thinking of founding a great British Empire, so we are constantly on guard against those who are working to create a great Canadian whole."[61] Tardivel and older forms of French Canadian nationalism distrusted any encompassing movement that might weaken French Canadian identity. Notwithstanding their ambitions, the *nationalistes* remained a French Canadian movement and positioned themselves within provincial politics more than national politics. Bourassa transcended those boundaries more easily than his compatriots did.

In a broader Canadian context, *nationalistes* might be considered liberals but not Liberals. A conservative set of French Canadian cultural values, and for some of them Catholic ones, mitigated their liberal ideology. Still, historian Yvan Lamonde has termed their ideas as a "nationalist derivative" of Laurier's liberalism since they too supported collective national values of equality, democracy, and economic intervention.[62] They were mostly pro-clerical (though some were not) rather than simply not being anti-clerical like Laurier. Their liberal nationalism, Olivar Asselin explained in 1909, aligned with a wider American progressive tradition as well. He explained that they were "Liberals in the matter of minority rights, and Progressists [sic] in economic and social matters." He elaborated that "it is that opposition to both Imperialism and Annexation [by the United States], that Liberalism and that Progressism [sic], which makes up our brand of Nationalism."[63] The *nationalistes* existed in a national and continental context, as did their nominal leader, Bourassa.

Thus, even though the *nationalistes* were representative of a particular stream of French Canadian political thought, they also existed within an international reaction to liberal ideas. *Nationaliste* ideology was different from both social Catholicism and American progressivism because of their French Canadian circumstances. The *nationalistes* dealt with the problem of foreign corporate control, which Pope Leo XIII never addressed, since they faced a lack of French Canadian capital investment. Nor were they entirely American progressives, whose "frontier individualism" meant that all individuals were equal in modern society,[64] since they believed that social hierarchies were a component of stability necessary in modern life. Instead, the *nationaliste* ideology was a fusion of corporatism, liberalism, and social Catholicism. These "utopian corporatists" envisioned an ideal society that had ingrained economic inequality, state intervention, and no class distinction. The persuasive force of social elites informed by Catholic social philosophy, rather than by democratic voice or state power, guided their philosophy.[65] Inspired by social Catholicism and American progressivism, they still chose which ideas most suited their situation in Canada.

Historians have also drawn parallels between the *nationalisme* of Quebec and British liberalism. Bourassa in some ways was a classical British liberal of the nineteenth century, echoing the political tradition of the Whigs that minimized the role of empire and emphasized democracy, equality, and the rule of law.[66] He publicly admired its well-known disciples, chiefly British politician William Gladstone, who served as prime minister four times between 1868 and 1894.[67] Although this admiration undeniably shaped Bourassa's views of political liberalism, it is worth emphasizing that this does not mean Bourassa was a British liberal. He was a product of the political and cultural legacy of British liberalism that existed in Canada, as was Laurier, but unlike the prime minister Bourassa repeatedly rejected that Canada was bound to British traditions envisioned by Gladstone and other British liberals.[68]

James Kennedy sheds some light on the link between the *nationalistes* and Gladstone in comparing the French Canadians to the Young Scots, an early-twentieth-century nationalist movement in the United Kingdom. Both groups attempted to reconcile nationalism and liberalism, and Kennedy argues that they revealed the contrasting faces of nineteenth-century liberalism as they tried to resolve its emphasis on individual rights against the national (or collective) rights that they championed. The two groups resolved that dilemma differently. The Young Scots were nationalist *liberals*, whereas the French Canadians were liberal *nationalists*. Thus, the Young Scots nationalized classical liberalism, whereas the *nationalistes* liberalized their French Canadian nationalism.[69] Both co-opted classical British liberalism according to their political and social contexts while nurturing the national community that they sought to create.

Bourassa was the leading *nationaliste* and the best known on the national stage, before and after the creation of the Ligue nationaliste. At the heart of the *nationaliste* position lay the bicultural and autonomous Canada that he first articulated, where two peoples lived in equal partnership free from imperial responsibilities. In spite of parallels to American or British political traditions, Bourassa espoused a nationalist sentiment focused on Canada's uniquely French Canadian and English Canadian character rather than on its colonial heritage. His nationally imagined community did not attach itself to the former motherlands of England and France. "The French Canadians as a people have no other homeland than Canada," Bourassa wrote in 1903, and "they are ready to give it all that they owe it; but feeling no debt to England or any other country, they expect nothing from it."[70] He believed that Canada possessed a political culture that was a combination of French and English heritage and deserved expression in its own right. In his mind, the long history of French Canadians in North America left them best equipped to define this political culture and defend it versus their English Canadian neighbours who would have preferred their assimilation into a British-centric nationalism. Bourassa, unsurprisingly, often led the charge.

His efforts took him from federal politics in Ottawa to the provincial arena of Quebec in 1907. Although Bourassa lost the first by-election that he contested, against Minister of Lands and Forests Adélard Turgeon, he defeated Liberal Premier Lomer Gouin in the 1908 election. Bourassa's provincial campaign against Gouin sought to reclaim from the provincial Liberals "the old flag that they tore and soiled."[71] During his time in the Assemblée nationale, Bourassa concentrated on economic issues such as the colonization of Quebec's northern frontier and the management of its natural resources. This focus underlined the *nationaliste* belief that "industry and commerce were the keys to national power, that economic development was the weapon of this century and that only if it possessed economic strength would French Canada become an important nationality." Strengthening Quebec was an important step toward righting the power imbalance in the Canadian federation.[72] Equality was not simply a matter of the rights and privileges of a minority but also the equal ability to contribute to the progress of the dominion.

Although Bourassa spent several years in Quebec City, he left frustrated in 1912, feeling as if he had failed to accomplish his goals. During his time there, however, he had built the connections within provincial politics and with the Quebec wing of the Conservative Party that he needed to found his influential newspaper, *Le Devoir*.

Le Devoir began publishing in 1910 and quickly became Bourassa's preferred vehicle for developing ideas on national, provincial, and international politics. As its editor from its founding to his resignation in 1932, Bourassa offered his opinions in regular editorials to a limited but influential readership.[73] The size of his audience understates his influence. Bélanger describes Bourassa as the mouthpiece of the "petty-bourgeois elite" who spoke for a generation of French Canadians.[74] He certainly did not represent the views of all French Canadians, but he acted as a crucial spokesperson for many of the province's most passionate citizens, who debated French Canada's place in Confederation and Canada's place in the world. His public speeches drew hundreds of spectators, and he travelled extensively extolling his views. Nevertheless, it was always in the pages of *Le Devoir* in which Bourassa began formulating the bases and details of his arguments.

Le Devoir's first target was Sir Wilfrid Laurier's decision to create a Canadian navy in light of the ongoing naval crisis between Britain and Germany. In 1909, the British government realized that Germany had increased its ship production and could surpass British naval supremacy within several years. In theory, the German navy could eventually threaten British control over the North Sea and the Atlantic, impose an embargo, and win a war against the British Empire. New Zealand immediately offered to build or at least fund the construction of powerful battleships, the Dreadnought class, while it spurred debate on the matter in Australia and Canada. The opposition Conservatives demanded that Canada immediately make a gift of ships or money to Britain, but Laurier refused it as an expensive "imperial obligation."[75] After meeting with British authorities that summer, however, he became convinced of the need for some form of Canadian contribution, but the British demanded that any ship Canada built be under imperial control.[76] On 12 January 1910, the prime minister put forward the Naval Service Bill to the House of Commons in Ottawa that proposed a small fleet of ships to form a Canadian navy that only the Canadian Parliament could commit to action. Laurier walked a tenuous line between the two opposing forces of Canadian imperialism and Canadian nationalism. He famously told the House of Commons that, "when Britain is at war, Canada is at war; there is no distinction," though he carefully qualified his statement by noting that, "if Great Britain, to which we are subject, is at war with any nation, Canada becomes liable to attack, and so Canada is at war."[77]

Laurier's "tin-pot navy" of five cruisers and six destroyers satisfied neither imperialist nor *nationaliste*. Many Conservatives decried it as an insufficient contribution to the defence of the British Empire. Opposition leader Robert Borden, seeing an opportunity to weaken the Liberals, demanded that Canada acquire a voice in imperial affairs alongside its new navy.[78] Bourassa reiterated his fear from the Boer War that such a course would implicate Canada in future imperial conflicts, and he denounced Laurier as a traitor.[79] This marked the journalist's first foray into international affairs through *Le Devoir*, in which Bourassa dissected Britain's policy and Germany's rising prominence. The resulting furor over the Naval Bill helped to convince him and the Conservatives to work together to bring down Laurier despite their vastly different political perspectives.

The Liberals' shaky position in Quebec became clear with a by-election in the prime minister's old riding of Drummond-Arthabaska. The Quebec wing of the Conservative Party led by F.D. Monk had become dissatisfied with Borden's moderated support for the Naval Bill and found common cause with Bourassa and the *nationalistes*. In January 1910, the two corresponded regarding possible political cooperation in Quebec. By May, they had agreed to an alliance between Quebec Conservatives and *nationalistes* to pursue the goal of creating a third party, composed of conservative-*nationalistes*, separate from both Liberals and Conservatives.[80] Bourassa desired a counterbalance to the English- and imperialist-dominated federal parties in the House of Commons, and he believed that the Quebec Conservatives could provide it. When Laurier announced a by-election in Drummond-Arthabaska in August 1910, the new coalition was ready to present a candidate to challenge what was considered a safe Liberal riding. The Liberals nominated a little-known Arthabaska lawyer, Joseph-Édouard Perrault, who faced a *nationaliste* local farmer, Arthur Gilbert. The campaign was bitterly contested. All knew that it represented Laurier and Bourassa competing for control of the province.[81] Gilbert won the election by 200 votes, signalling to the nation that, after fourteen years in power, the Liberals no longer enjoyed unquestioned support in Quebec.

The Drummond-Arthabaska by-election set the scene for the 1911 federal election. In English Canada, the election focused on the issue of reciprocity, or free trade, with the United States. It was a shock to the ruling Liberals when President William Howard Taft suggested a free-trade agreement to Canadians in 1910. Previously, Canadians had always had to persuade Americans to enter into discussions. Laurier found it difficult to refuse, and a trip to western Canada suggested strong support for lowering tariffs among prairie farmers.[82] In January 1911, the Americans and the Canadians signed a final agreement. All Laurier had to do was pass it through Parliament. The Conservatives made every effort to impede its passage, and the debate remained unresolved when Laurier left for an Imperial War Conference in May. He was confident that the country stood behind him, but his departure gave his opponents time to organize. While Conservatives criticized the reciprocity agreement across the country, Bourassa expounded the dangers of imperialism in Quebec, and Liberals in Toronto became apprehensive about the effects of reciprocity on their businesses. These were all ominous signs for the Liberals as critics ably threatened traditional centres of electoral support. The reciprocity debate stagnated after Laurier's return in mid-July. By month's end, the government had announced an election for 21 September with far less confidence about the results than it had two months earlier.[83]

The election yielded a victory for Conservative Robert Borden. Historians have argued that reciprocity and imperialism turned Canadians away from supporting the Liberals, in English Canada and French Canada respectively, but more recent work suggests that the Liberal loss was razor-thin. Historians Patrice Dutil and David Mackenzie argue that the Liberals lost because the Conservatives convinced between a few dozen and a few hundred voters in a riding to switch their allegiance. Seventy-one seats, a third of the 221 in total, were decided by less than 5 percent of the vote.[84] The Conservative victory did not signify a sweeping change in the country's attitudes away from the Liberals, but it did produce a change in government.

Conservative victories in Quebec were undoubtedly unique compared with elsewhere in the country. Quebec's election was a judgment on the naval issue and Laurier's decision to cooperate with Britain's naval expansion. The Quebec Conservatives supported Bourassa as he attempted to bring a caucus of conservative-*nationaliste* MPs to Parliament. He spoke fervently against Laurier alongside Conservative candidates while insisting that Borden would not be much better as prime minister.[85] His goal was not to bring Borden to power but to ensure the election of conservative-*nationalistes*. Bourassa believed that they would be independent of the Conservative Party. In the end, however, most of the Quebec MPs elected as conservative-*nationalistes* joined the new Conservative government and followed the party line. Bourassa's push to unseat the Liberals had merely helped to place Borden and his imperialist allies in power.[86] The Conservative leader and his cabinet led Canada even further away from the nation envisioned by Bourassa and his *nationaliste* compatriots.

After the loss in 1911, Bourassa refocused his energy on the issue of French-language education in Canada. Ontario enacted Regulation 17 limiting Franco-Ontarians' access to French instruction. The politician-cum-journalist remembered well the imperfect solution of the Manitoba schools crisis through the Laurier-Greenway Agreement. Keeping a tenuous balance between minority and majority rights had been a difficult task for Canadians since before Confederation and certainly after it. As early as 1871, New Brunswick's banning of religious schools had violated section 93 of the British North America Act, which nominally recognized the educational rights and privileges of linguistic minorities but did not specifically mention French-language rights outside the province. The attack on Manitoban French Canadians' separate schools helped to spur the Franco-Ontarian minority of the province's eastern counties to protect their linguistic and minority rights.[87] Increased agitation of these French-speaking Catholics alarmed the Protestant Orange Order. A fiercely Protestant and pro-British organization, it held a significant presence in Ontario's Conservative Party, which had come to power in 1905. The growing hostility between Irish Catholics and Franco-Ontarians added to the tensions and culminated with Conservative Premier James Whitney passing Regulation 17 in 1912. The regulation severely restricted the use of French in the schools of the province and had a devastating effect on French-English relations in Canada.[88]

Ontario anglophones believed that they were protecting their cultural identity against a restless and allegedly dangerous minority. In 1907, Robert Sellar published *The Tragedy of Quebec,* which claimed that French Canadian Catholics were an insidious force bent on supplanting English Protestants in rural Quebec and eastern Ontario. "Nationalism," Sellar warned, stood for nothing more than "French-Catholic supremacy in the Dominion." The book went through four editions between 1907 and 1916.[89] Meanwhile, French Canadians viewed Regulation 17 as yet another English Canadian refusal to uphold the promises of Confederation. They perceived the Ontario government's legislation as part of a sinister decades-long trend in Canada to limit French Canadians to Quebec alone. French Canadians, and certainly *nationalistes,* understood the compact formed in 1867 primarily as an agreement to safeguard their cultural and religious identity in the country. By the twentieth century, they believed that a guarantee of French rights outside the province should always inform government policy, particularly in light of how well Quebec's English-speaking minority was treated.[90]

By the eve of war in 1914, Bourassa's political and journalistic career had shaped a set of ideas about the nature and purpose of Canadian nationalism. His Canada was one where imperial affairs did not supersede Canadian ones, a nation that respected and protected the pillars of French Canadian culture, its language, and its religion. Above all, his vision stressed equality between English Canadians and French Canadians. Canada as Bourassa saw it was neither English nor French but a partnership of the two languages and cultures. He perceived a grave threat in the dominant influence of imperialism that fundamentally placed the values and beliefs of "British" Canada above those of other "races."

Race was conceived differently in the early twentieth century compared with now. Today we would consider French Canadians (or Québécois more likely) as a cultural identity rather than a biologically separate race. In the nineteenth century, however, the term "race" carried societal connotations and was used to distinguish cultural identities. Race had been a concept in European thought for several centuries before Darwinian ideas of evolution were co-opted into social constructs, which then separated "races" by their historical accomplishments and how "civilized" they were. That some races were superior to others was a vital aspect of understanding larger historical developments, such as European superiority. The terms "nation" and "race" were used interchangeably to explain successful national accomplishments. For the British, race took on an especially cultural dimension in relation to their empire. Race delineated a set of national values and qualities, distinguishing the British people from their colonial subjects.[91] Emerging out of the context of its multiracial empire, the "British race" was on a civilizing mission to its various colonies and dominions, be it for Indians, Africans, or French Canadians.

In Canada, the concept of race mirrored European developments. Unlike in Britain, which approached race from a global perspective, Canadians were more likely to encounter it in local contexts as a descriptor of French and English peoples. The two dominant "races," or cultural identities, that would have been identified in Canada at that time had a long history of conflict. Since the Conquest in 1759, when the British conquered New France during the Seven Years War, Britain had tried to incorporate its new French-speaking subjects into a system of government with varying degrees of success. The Quebec Act of 1774 guaranteed the new population's Catholicism and use of civil law in private matters, defined the structure of its colonial government, and abandoned any structured attempt at "anglicization."[92] The establishment of a representative assembly with the Constitution Act of 1791 did not completely assuage the concerns of a growing number of republicans in the colony, and in 1837 the short-lived rebellion against the government erupted. Its failure led to an investigation by Governor General Lord Durham, who wrote in his report in 1839 that "I found two nations warring within the bosom of a single state: I found a struggle, not of principles, but of races."[93] He bluntly dismissed French Canadians as "a people with no history, and no literature."[94] The solution was to subsume French Canadians so that they could thrive as part of British North America. Other sections of Durham's famous report eventually led to the establishment of "responsible government" in the Canadian colonies of Lower and Upper Canada (Quebec and Ontario respectively), where the government was responsible to the electorate rather than to the governor general. It did not solve the "struggle of races" between Canada's two emergent cultures.

Instead, French Canadians proved Durham wrong by setting out to describe their unique North American history and writing their own literary works devoted to their "racial achievements." François-Xavier Garneau's three-volume *Histoire du Canada*, published from 1845 to 1852, focused on the accomplishments of French Canadians and their ability to survive while surrounded by Anglo-Saxon Protestants in North America. This early French Canadian historian emphasized the endurance of his people's language, laws, and religion.[95] Other French Canadian historians who echoed his theme of survival, though sometimes with a more positive view of the clerical or British contribution to French Canadian history, followed Garneau.[96] This cultural renaissance proved that they were not simply a subjugated diaspora but a vibrant and unique community. The idea of *survivance* was embedded in French Canada with aid from the Catholic Church. Cultural, religious, and linguistic survival was paramount, and implicit in that struggle was a dichotomy between Canada's "English" and "French" races.

By the beginning of the twentieth century, most Canadians accepted a difference between "English Canadians" and "French Canadians" and used the term "race" to describe them. Phillip Buckner has discussed Canadian "Britishness" in the context of race as a "form of civic nationalism that included the adoption of certain values and institutions defined as 'British.'"[97] In this vein, Bourassa envisaged a distinct "Canadian" civic nationalism, though it shared values identified as British, but contemporaries tended to focus on "French" and "English" races in Canada. French sociologist André Siegfried toured Canada in 1904 and wrote *The Race Question in Canada* based upon his experiences. Siegfried outlined a pessimistic view of Canada's political and cultural tensions that hinged on the religious and racial differences between its French-speaking and English-speaking peoples. "There is a pronounced feeling of jealousy between [Ontario and Quebec]," he reflected. "The dominant race suffers the presence of the French because it cannot do otherwise, but it sets up its own tongue and religion and form of civilisation against theirs. An open warfare is in progress, the bitterness of which it were useless to seek to disguise."[98] He dissected the forces shaping the two sides and their impacts on Canadian politics, concluding that, in "the absence of ideas and doctrines dividing electors into opposite camps, there remain only questions of collective or individual interests."[99] The cultural divisions outlined by Siegfried had a racial component, and, linking together race and progress, he believed that without resolving the crisis of Canada's two "races" its political development remained stunted.

Bourassa disagreed with Siegfried's conclusions but not his views. He too believed that French Canadians' and English Canadians' languages and religions were inseparable racial characteristics. Bourassa reflected on their fusion in a "Canadian" civic nationalism during a famous speech at the Twenty-First Eucharistic Congress in Montreal in September 1910 (an important Roman Catholic gathering of clergy and laity to practise their faith collectively and to reflect on Catholicism publicly). Various speakers addressed the audience in Montreal. Archbishop of Westminster Francis Bourne delivered a speech arguing that the English language was the future of Catholicism in North America.[100] In return, Bourassa offered an impassioned and eloquent defence of French-speaking Catholics in the New World. French speakers, he argued, were the true bastion of Catholicism in North America. Religion and language were engrained in French Canadians' identity, and Catholicism had to preserve the French language if it wanted to survive. Only then would a strong Catholic presence on the continent be assured forever.[101] Bourassa foresaw no acceptable future in which the religion and language of French Canadians would come undone, nor could they be subsumed within the concept of a "British" race. His understanding of Canadian cultural identities at the turn of the century had a deep impact on his political thought.

Despite Canada's racial strife, Bourassa was not as convinced as Lord Durham or Siegfried about the impossibility of unity between Canada's French and English peoples if each group preserved its identity. An excellent example of his optimism is evident in an address to Montreal's English-speaking population only a few months before the outbreak of the First World War. For decades, it had been the city's custom to elect a French-speaking mayor followed by an English-speaking one, but Médéric Martin's successful campaign in March 1914 broke that tradition. Bourassa wrote to Montreal's English-speaking population during the election campaign in the pages of *Le Devoir* as well as in a brief pamphlet. He counselled them in English that "they ought to take the lead in the crusade for the triumph of equal justice to all minorities, and the maintenance of the principle of equality of rights, for both races, all over the land. Upon that principle Confederation was built, old feuds were pacified. Upon that principle alone Confederation shall stand, and peace and harmony prevail."[102] Despite two decades in politics and much experience with an intransigent and sometimes hostile English Canada, Bourassa still believed on the eve of the war that French and English peoples could come together as Confederation had promised. There were differences, of course, but they were reconcilable. In Montreal, the most bilingual and bicultural city in the country, Bourassa saw a place where French and English cultures could fulfill their separate destinies together.[103]

His career before the war was marked by his perceptive and vocal discussion of the problems of national unity, Catholicism and Quebec, and the growing danger of imperialism. Together with his fellow liberal *nationalistes*, he shaped a new political ideology that differed from that of other French Canadian nationalists, such as Jules-Paul Tardivel, and from that of other liberals, such as Sir Wilfrid Laurier. Accordingly, prewar ideas and experiences led Bourassa to an understanding of the First World War different from that of many other Canadians. He was intimately involved in Canada's political debates either as an MP or as a journalist. Whether English Canadians and French Canadians accepted or understood what Bourassa was saying is less certain. His prominence on the national stage on the eve of war positioned him as a man who had a clear and well-developed set of ideas about Canada, Quebec, and the world, and he was willing to communicate them to his audience. Unfortunately, the war was unlike anything that the world had seen. Like others, Bourassa was unprepared for its intensity and brutality and its drastic impact on Canadians' perspectives, including his own. In the ensuing years, he offered novel arguments about Canada and the world unlike any others presented to Canadians. Yet, though the war led Bourassa down a different path than most, it was not one that he wanted to tread.

2

The Duty of Canada at the Present Hour

1914

BOURASSA'S WAR BEGAN under more dangerous circumstances than those of most of his fellow Canadians. Bourassa left on 21 May 1914 for a summer trip to Europe to ascertain British opinions on Canadian affairs and to explore the plight of linguistic minorities, especially in light of the Ontario schools crisis of 1912, which led him to research the situation among similar European communities.[1] Bourassa's intended destinations included Wales, Belgium, Switzerland, and the German-owned province of Alsace, annexed from France during the Franco-Prussian War more than forty years earlier. On 30 July, Bourassa arrived in the Alsatian village of Colmar to meet with Abbé Émile Wetterlé, a member of the Reichstag for Alsace-Lorraine since 1898, editor of the newspaper *Le Nouvelliste d'Alsace-Lorraine*, and a well-known opponent of German rule there.[2] Bourassa planned to speak with the abbé but quickly discovered that the prospect of war had forced many of Alsace's most fervent voices against German rule to flee. Wetterlé, accused of high treason, had fled to Switzerland that day as German authorities searched his home and office.[3]

Unlike many Canadians who experienced news of the war as a distant event, Bourassa was close to its dangerous reality. Since Bourassa had no place to stay on the night of 30 July, a young Frenchman, the secretary of Wetterlé's *Le Nouvelliste d'Alsace-Lorraine*, invited him to his home. With war all but certain, Bourassa and his host fled the next morning. The secretary joined the French army, whereas Bourassa hoped to return safely home. He reached a deserted, soldier-filled Strasbourg the next day and prayed with Alsatians in their cathedral.[4] On 2 August, he arrived in Cologne and took the train as far as the German-Belgian border, closed to railway traffic. Undaunted, Bourassa abandoned his luggage and crossed on foot, resigned to the "fortunes of war." Reaching wartime Paris, which he found had "almost the air of a religious city," he witnessed first-hand the *union sacrée* of France's bitterly divided politics. "Royalists, imperialists, republicans, socialists, all seem to have one heart," he wrote of his time in the capital.[5]

Back in Canada a week later, Bourassa immediately described what he had seen to fellow writer and *nationaliste* at *Le Devoir* Omer Héroux in his first published response to the war in late August. Bourassa told his readers of the ethereal, quiet French cities through which he had passed and reminded them that "those who lived those hours in France can say that they saw the soul of the French nation."[6] War, he noted solemnly, "is not hell ... It is the worst punishment on earth; it is also the most salutary of atonements."[7] He echoed a generation of Christian thinkers before him when he extolled this chance for Europe's – and maybe Canada's – regeneration. The sense of national purpose that bound the French together was palpable and something that Bourassa wished to see in his native land. His return home to Montreal on 21 August marked a moment when it seemed that the war's zeitgeist, which had subsumed many in 1914, captured his spirit as well. His first experience of the European war was a stark contrast to that in the months that followed in Canada.

The political landscape of *nationalistes* and imperialists that had dominated Canada during Bourassa's career still defined his understanding of Canadian political discourse. At the onset of the war, English Canada seemed to be replete with enthusiasm for "the great adventure," though this might have been the loudest urban voices crowding out those on the periphery.[8] Bourassa prepared to counter that rhetoric with a different understanding of the war. In the coming months, he would furnish a tempered response to supporters of the war, detailing both Canada's potential contribution to it and its causes. In August, however, he offered cautious support, and in September he had careful criticisms of Canadian involvement that revolved around the axis of his political life: Canadian nationalism.

Despite his historical position against Canadian involvement in foreign wars, in August 1914 the French Canadian journalist approved of Canada's role in the European conflict. Bourassa publicly agreed with joining the war but continued to offer sharp critiques in the pages of *Le Devoir* of how the government was waging the nascent conflict. The contrast between supporting the war while repeatedly denouncing the Canadian method of war seemed to implicate Bourassa as hypocritical or dishonest in his position. Endorsing the war but criticizing war supporters was the result of the pressure of early wartime enthusiasm on Bourassa, which equally affected all Canadians, as well as the belief that he could fulfill his vision of a unified Canadian nation. Rather than intentionally lying to his readers, Bourassa walked a fine line between support and rejection in 1914 as he tried to avoid opposing the Catholic Church, appease the *nationalistes*, and still pursue the idealistic future that the war seemed to offer.

First and foremost, Bourassa hoped that the war would bring about true national unity, which had been absent since Canada's creation almost fifty years earlier. He believed it possible to put on hold political arguments in favour of a national war effort, as he had observed in France, but it would require compromise from both sides – specifically from English Canadians in return for support among French Canadians for the war. In his first editorial response to the war on 29 August, Bourassa offered a truce to his opponents: make this truly a Canadian war, not an imperial one, and French Canada would support it.[9] Therefore, it had to be fought under the auspices of Canadian nationalism and not Canadian imperialism. If English Canadians sought to enter the British Empire's war alongside Bourassa and his fellow French Canadians, then the first step had to be a show of good faith. *Nationalistes* would compromise by supporting a war for Britain if imperialists would compromise as well. After all, French Canadians were at a disadvantage, so what reason did they have to support a British war when they themselves faced persecution at home?

Bourassa argued that the clearest peace offering by English Canada would be for Premier of Ontario James Whitney to end his discriminatory Regulation 17 against Franco-Ontarians.[10] This legislation had eliminated French-language schooling for thousands of Franco-Ontarians since 1912, opening a wound for French Canadians who had seen their linguistic and educational rights outside Quebec minimized since Confederation. If Whitney repealed Regulation 17, Bourassa insisted, then "this elementary act of justice and intelligent policy will do more to ensure the unity of the Empire and the Canadian nation than any donation of flour or money."[11] The contradiction of asking for national unity while demanding political concessions elicited sharp condemnations, but to Bourassa it represented a fair attempt at political negotiation and compromise. A Canadian *union sacrée* could form only if the Ontario bilingual schools question was resolved.

The premier ignored his request, revealing Bourassa's excessive optimism about the war's short-term transformative potential. After all, why would English Canadians in Ontario consider the request of their longtime opponent? French and English Canadians supported the war in 1914 and seemingly fulfilled an imperialist dream of widespread support for the British Empire and evoked a consensus under the banner of a "British race" fighting for its imperial motherland. The impassioned speeches of Prime Minister Sir Robert Borden and Liberal leader Sir Wilfrid Laurier during the parliamentary session of 19 August referred to the need both to defend Britain and to uphold Canadian honour and emphasized Canada's duty to join the war. Borden declared that the dominion had entered the war "for the cause of honour, to maintain solemn pledges, to uphold principles of liberty, to withstand forces that would convert the world into an armed camp."[12] In December, Borden more explicitly articulated to Canadian soldiers leaving for Europe his hopes for the war effort:

> There is only one respect in which we in Canada have not yet attained our full share of self-government in this Empire and that is with regard to foreign relations – the decision of those questions of alliances and understandings which in the end must determine the issues of peace and war ... I may see the day, and you young men will certainly see it, when the men of Canada, Australia, South Africa and the other Dominions will have the same just voice in these questions as those who live within the British Isles.[13]

Borden hoped that Canadians could earn the control of their own affairs but within the empire. As Canadians across the country rallied around the cause of defending European nations (particularly Britain and Belgium), in defence of British ideals against German ones, it seemed to be a natural step forward. In most of the Canadian press, there was no question about the necessity and legitimacy of Canadian involvement.[14] As in Britain, the invasion of Belgium and the atrocities there, alleged and real, significantly influenced Canadian public opinion in the first months of the war. Newspapers were replete with accounts of Belgium and the plight of its people.[15] In the light of Germany's aggression, imperialist ideas about Canada's role in the world and its relationship within the empire seemed to be justified if not triumphant.[16]

Imperialists had agitated for a larger Canadian role in the British Empire for decades. They had fashioned a national consciousness intrinsically linked to imperial values in the years before the war. For imperialists, Canadian domestic and international policies were best guided by an imperial connection that superseded national concerns.[17] The outbreak of war opened an opportunity to realize these objectives. The transformations that they desired from the war were far different from those that

Bourassa sought and easily ignored his vision of cultural unity. Instead, the imperialists wanted the war to ensure Canada's continuing importance to Britain and to bring together French and English speakers in a far different union than Bourassa envisioned.

The public reaction – largely unquestioning of the war's purpose – resembled the national unity that Bourassa had found so appealing in France, but it was not the transformation that he wished to see. With the outpouring of support for the war, he witnessed more Canadians than ever publicly supporting the supremacy of an imperial connection – not a national one. To him, any backing of Canadian involvement in the European war was invalid if it failed to consider and integrate Quebec's *nationaliste* view. If Borden or other Canadians subsumed in war enthusiasm could not distinguish between national interests and imperial interests, as Bourassa demanded, then they excluded the *nationalistes* and rejected what he considered true national unity.

His resistance to accepting an imperialist context for Canada's involvement in the war meant that Bourassa opposed the war narrative developing throughout the rest of the country, effectively making the journalist the largest obstacle to unity in 1914. Bourassa did not want to be a hindrance to the war effort, but he could not avoid this role without voluntarily censoring his opinions in his newspaper, at that time a step nearly unimaginable to the journalist. War supporters dismissed his rejection of imperialist positions as unpatriotic at best and traitorous at worst.

As Bourassa failed to bring about English Canadian concessions for French Canada, other French Canadians continued to express support for the war. In September, Montreal doctor Arthur Mignault offered the government $50,000 to form a French Canadian battalion. A recruiting rally, held at Parc Sohmer in Montreal on 22 October, featured speeches from Premier of Quebec Lomer Gouin, Sir Wilfrid Laurier, Conservative MP Thomas Chase-Casgrain, and Liberal MP Rodolphe Lemieux. "I have come here to tell you ... above all that our hearts will follow you to the field of duty and honour," Premier Gouin told his fellow Québécois; "when you return, covered with the glory of victory, you will not only have told, but have proven to the Empire and to the Province of Quebec, what you have done for them."[18] French Canadians appeared to be as committed to the war effort as English Canadians, at least if we judge their views through public expressions in urban newspapers and public meetings. However, despite its organizers' claims of success, by 5 November only 32 officers and 891 other ranks had enlisted in the 22nd Battalion, Canada's sole French-speaking battalion.[19] Lower recruitment numbers throughout Quebec belied popular manifestations of support for the war in public and in the press.[20] Public exultations aside, enlistment numbers belie the historical narrative that there was consolidated support for the war among ordinary French Canadians (and, it is important to note, by 1916 and 1917 among native-born English Canadians). Bourassa, however, who lived and breathed the ongoing debates of the public sphere, was most concerned with reacting to what was discussed in newspapers across the country.

The most serious divergence for Bourassa among the upswell of public sentiment was the position of the Catholic Church. The Quebec bishops' official Catholic newspaper, *L'Action sociale,* published a detailed refutation of Bourassa's tepid support on 11 September, grounding its stance in a moral obligation to fight in the conflict. Its editor, Abbé Joseph Prio Arthur D'Amours, penned the unsigned editorial for the official organ of the church even though Cardinal Louis-Nazaire Bégin had left for Rome to help choose the papal successor after the death of Pope Pius X. D'Amours thus represented the word of the church in Quebec. His support for imperialist arguments and his repudiation of Bourassa were absolute: "We have a duty to give England what they are entitled to claim from us, what is fair and just, for the maintenance and defence of the Empire of which we are a part as a British colony."[21] Law and tradition demanded that Canada come to the aid of Britain. Weeks later the bishops of Quebec released a pastoral letter, on 23 September, that made an emotional and moral appeal for prayers and contributions to the Patriotic Fund to supplement the money and men that Catholics had already "generously" offered. The bishops described the terrible situation in Europe for their followers and wrote that Canada must "turn this war to the benefit of justice and law ... It will be Canada's honour and glory ... for having contributed, through its pious pleas, to restoring peace in the world, and to alleviating, through its generous contributions, the evils from which humanity has suffered."[22] In October, the bishops affirmed that "Britain is engaged in this war, and who does not see that the destiny of every part of the Empire is bound up with the fate of her armies? She counts very rightly on our co-operation, and this co-operation, we are happy to say ... is being generously offered to her both in men and in money."[23] The upper echelons of the church hierarchy and many of its public organs moved in unison with the federal government, in stark contrast to the devout Bourassa.

He anguished over any perceived conflict with the Quebec bishops over the war. Historian René Durocher suggests that many members of the clergy privately supported the views of Bourassa.[24] Durocher argues that Bourassa's early support for the war was intentionally ambivalent and reflected a desire not to contradict the position of the Catholic Church rather than a desire to construct a cultural coalition between French Canadians and English Canadians. This would explain Bourassa's carefully worded editorials of 1914 that grounded his support in an appropriate *nationaliste* critique and a subsequent dissection of British policy. By crafting an argument that emphasized Canada's political autonomy, Bourassa could occupy a position between support for the war and *nationaliste* opposition to any imperial involvement without potentially setting himself up to contradict the church. This stance, which awkwardly placed him between favouring intervention and criticizing it, can help to explain some of the incoherence of his views in 1914. Bourassa supported the war, but he was critical of many aspects of Canada's involvement in it.[25] However, if his Catholicism forced him to moderate his reaction to the war, even though it went against his equally fervent political beliefs, it is difficult to find proof of it in 1914.

Durocher relies on letters written later in the war, when Bourassa sought to repudiate his former stance. He explained the difficulty of his position two years later in a letter to Bishop Georges Gauthier. Bourassa knew beforehand that the Catholic Church in Quebec would publish the pastoral letter and did not want to be in the position of publicly contradicting the episcopacy. Instead, he claimed that he offered a conciliatory view – though measured and limited – that endorsed participation in the war. In retrospect, he told Gauthier, he should have opposed any military intervention and stayed true to the principles that he had held for fifteen years, but "I still dared to believe that the bishops would speak as national bishops: I wanted to be as close as possible to their likely attitude."[26] Durocher's review of Bourassa's relationship with Catholic bishops during the war concludes that Bourassa was convinced that "an essential link between Catholicism and French-Canadian survival" demanded that the bishops be *nationaliste* in their position, so as to defend the rights of the minority.[27]

If his Catholicism forced Bourassa to moderate his reaction to the war, even though it went against his equally fervent political beliefs, then it seems to be more likely that he looked to Rome and the pope for guidance rather than Quebec and its bishops. The ultramontane Bourassa found solace in the position of the newly elected Pope Benedict XV, who condemned the war. While the Catholic Church in Quebec carefully avoided disagreeing with the neutrality of Pope Benedict XV, it still reminded its flock of Canada's obligations in Europe to its former motherlands of Britain and France. As the war continued, Bourassa espoused views aligned with those of Rome and not those of the spiritual leaders of his native province.

Still, regardless of Durocher's argument, Bourassa, like many Canadians in the early months of the war, nonetheless presented an idealistic picture of Canada's role in it. If his support was a façade, as Durocher claims, it was a convincing and well-reasoned one. Bourassa's first serious critiques appeared in early September as the fate of the Allied powers in Europe remained undecided. The German offensive in August had steadily pushed back the French army, and the French government had fled from Paris to Bordeaux in an ominous echo of the 1870 German victory in the Franco-Prussian War. The British Expeditionary Force, outnumbered and defeated at Mons in Belgium, had withdrawn to the Marne River, where the Allied forces made their final attempt to resist the advancing German armies. The "Miracle of the Marne" that saved Paris and the Western Allies in September 1914 was not certain when Bourassa wrote to his fellow Canadians of their imminent role in the war.

He turned his critical gaze to the events at home through *Le Devoir*. Bourassa wanted Canadians to understand some of the far-reaching consequences of the war beyond simply saving Belgium and France. "After the War, Famine," declared his headline from 2 September as he examined the massive food requirements for the newly formed Allied armies.[28] Quoting the imperialist Lord Milner, in charge of organizing coal and food production in Britain,[29] Bourassa warned of an impending food crisis and its implication for Canada. Since many farmers had joined the armies of Europe, and because almost half of the world's wheat grew in nations now at war, he expected a worldwide famine in 1915. Lord Milner called for a mobilization of agriculture alongside the mobilization of soldiers, and Bourassa used this declaration as a platform to question those Canadians devoted to the war effort. Echoing the advice of English Canadian millionaire Herbert Samuel Holt, Bourassa wondered "if it is necessary for England, directly involved in the European conflict, to triple its agricultural output at the risk of sending only a slightly larger army than the valiant Belgian phalanxes to the battlefields."[30] Bourassa translated Milner's unease about food production into fear about the potential for

Canada to succumb to a reckless war effort. Canada should contribute to the war qualitatively, not just quantitatively, as Britain did. Why devote manpower to a large – but still minuscule – Canadian army when those men could be plowing fields?

Bourassa repeated this argument more forcibly later, but in early September he used it to introduce an intellectual manifesto laying out his position on the war. Although alarmed by the potentially devastating consequences of the world war, he took heed of Borden's and Laurier's inspiring speeches in Parliament that August. Bourassa presented himself as ready to support the war effort, as they had, and he proclaimed that "it is not time for polemics" as he outlined the intellectual foundation that guided his writing about the war:

> Within my humble sphere of action, I propose to conscientiously research, in all loyalty, and to say, in all frankness, anything I believe urgent to foresee and do, and to avoid in Canada and, by implication, in the Empire, disasters that people talk about in the shadows, and to which very few seem to have the courage to draw the attention of their governments and the cooperation of good people.
>
> In this research and in the conclusions it inspires, I am firmly determined not to depart from the tone that circumstances have imposed on us. No provocation, no insult, no slander, no gutter will lead me from this path. I will not even examine the motivations behind the brutal or grotesque attacks to which I may be subjected.
>
> The grandiose and touching performances I have witnessed in Europe have empowered me to distinguish between selfless patriotism, true dedication to the public good, and the sordid exploitation of the most sacred things.[31]

This manifesto, which guided Bourassa's commentary over the next four years (though with significant exceptions), pledged to explore the unreported, the ignored, and the unpopular. In so doing, Bourassa aligned himself against the triumphant and positive rhetoric surrounding the conflict. In making the promise that he would discuss issues that others were afraid to address, regardless of the consequences, Bourassa revealed the essence of his wartime writing. He did not explain whether he was for or against the war; instead, he committed to uncovering the dangers that the war presented to Canada – and he made sure to include the empire as an appeal to English Canada. According to this rationale, his wartime opposition was not an expression of disloyalty, as his detractors were quick to claim. Instead, the French Canadian intellectual vowed to help Canadians better understand the war. If that meant examining its negative impacts, so be it. It was his *loyalty* to the nation of Canada that compelled him to dissect the conflict. Although later Bourassa regretted his position on the war or, as Durocher suggests, was forced to support it given the context of the time, a reader in 1914 would have read only of Bourassa's determination to discuss the most pertinent issues of the war.

A few days later, Bourassa thoroughly examined Canada's potential duty to the war effort and the legitimacy of its growing contribution. In the first article, aptly titled "The National Duty," he criticized Canada's war effort for overestimating the country's importance and ability. Canada could not, Bourassa argued, remain indifferent to the war raging in France, for it was an "Anglo-French nation, bound to England and France by a thousand ties ... [It] has a vital interest in the maintenance of France and England." But he lamented "the almost complete absence of a sense of Canada's real responsibilities as a nation – external responsibilities and even more so internal responsibilities."[32] Bourassa carefully qualified his support for the war with the caveat that Canadians remain realistic and measure exactly what the country could or could not provide. After all, he reminded Canadians, Britain demanded no less of its own policy.

Bourassa also took the time to respond to his supporters who asked if he now approved of Canadian participation in wars foreign to Canada as he had in 1899. He outlined the case for *nationaliste* support for the current war, arguing that the Canadian nation had an interest in the success of Britain and France in Europe based upon historical and cultural connections. Although he did not consider the Canadian character as intrinsically tied to Britain, since it could never fully accept Canada's French-speaking Catholic peoples, there were connections that obliged Canadian participation in the war. Bourassa emphasized that Canada had no moral, constitutional, or immediate interest in the conflict; rather, he spoke of a historical national responsibility. It was a worthwhile war for French and English Canadians, nationalist or not, even if it meant aligning so closely with imperialism. This reflected his belief that, as in France, the war could give birth to a national unity that superseded historical divisions.

Next Bourassa dissected Britain's entry into the war and justifications of its actions in a five-part series. Called "A Page from History," each editorial examined the British White Papers containing Foreign Secretary

Sir Edward Grey's communications with the great powers of Europe in the final weeks before the war. It was an account based purely upon his reading of the diplomatic papers, whereas the actual British entry into the war was more nuanced, but it was at least an honest attempt to understand unfolding international events.[33] Bourassa traced Britain's refusal to go to war for Serbia in July and its attempts to persuade Germany that Britain would stay out of an Eastern European war. As late as 2 August, he noted, the English were committed to defending their coasts from the German navy but not to protecting France or Russia. The English did not want to commit to a war if peace was still viable. Only the invasion of Belgium on 3 August and King Albert I's request for the intervention of Britain secured its entry into the war. By 4 August, Bourassa had concluded that war with Germany was unavoidable given British public sentiment and the threat that Germany posed to the English Channel. His outline of English efforts to sidestep the conflict exudes admiration for Sir Edward Grey, whose diplomatic machinations revealed a statesman who was "courageous, tireless, whose entire action is inspired only by one motive: the interest of his country."[34] In Bourassa's view, the foreign secretary's goal was the preservation of peace for the benefit of Britain, and it was only after all hope had been extinguished that Grey used the invasion of Belgium to rally public opinion for the war to unite the nation and enter the war under the most favourable circumstances.[35]

Bourassa couched his high regard for Grey in terms that did not endear him to Canadian imperialists. Bourassa evoked Grey's actions not as an example of English suavity in handling the crisis but as a blunt refusal to compromise on issues of national self-interest. This was not the sort of esteem that English Canadian imperialists embraced. Yet to Bourassa Grey was "faithful to the great British tradition, [and] he was first and foremost a man of his country." "It seems to me that Canada could not better demonstrate its 'loyalty' than by drawing inspiration from the examples of the great nation from which it has borrowed its political institutions," Bourassa wrote.[36] His articles portray the British as "perfidious seekers of peace," willing to play all sides against each other in the name of ever-important national self-interest. British entry into the war stemmed not from a moral obligation to defend Belgium, as most other Canadians believed in 1914, but from its failure to secure England's interests through a refusal to participate in the continental conflict. Only once it was clear that participation was necessary for British interests did England enter the war. Bourassa used the articles to repeat his support for the war, and he did so in such a way that stripped away the moral ambiguity (or perhaps the moral certainty) granted to it by English Canada's call to defend the British Empire. British entry into the war was an act of self-interest for Great Britain – a national policy that Bourassa wished to see at home as well.

He noted that the value placed on Britain's self-interest by Edward Grey was in contrast to many of the proffered justifications of the war, for it did not explicitly demand the defence of France or a resolve to contain German militarism. Canada as a nation, he argued, should equally have no interest in those European concerns. It should only wage war for the potential benefits to Canada itself. Implicitly, a war that was an ocean away in defence of an ally did not deserve a total Canadian war effort. The events of August 1914 did not lead Bourassa to reject the validity of the war, even if he questioned their impacts on Canada; instead, he believed that they denoted the need for Canada to mirror British policy and adjust its involvement according to its national interests. He argued that, like their British counterparts, Canadians should have a clear vision of those interests and which actions they prescribed.

This position had many critics. In November 1914, Bourassa categorized three forms of opposition that he had received for his views over the past several months: that they were unpatriotic, that "now was not the time to speak of such things," and that his arguments were faulty.[37] Bourassa encountered each criticism from a different audience. The first came largely from the fervent English Canadian war supporters, the second came from moderates in French and English Canada alike, and the third came from former allies or what he termed "reasonable people" who disagreed with the results of his arguments but not the acts of submitting them to the public. The opposition appeared in different forms, but most of it fell into one of these three categories.

His peers within the Canadian press did not help to convince Canadians that Bourassa had a right to his own opinions. They portrayed his articles of late August and early September as a *nationaliste* polemic that once again denounced the dangers of Canada's imperial ties, as he had so many times before. The reaction to this commentary meant that Bourassa had not been so prominent on the national stage since the Boer War. Across the country, newspapers responded to his arguments with scorn and derision. None addressed his promise of 2 September to loyally investigate the issues of the war or the details of his argument but attacked its implication that a *true* Canadian was a nationalist and must reject Canada's total support for an imperial war. Although the Quebec journalist lamented the mischaracterization of his arguments, in truth most of the popular responses rejected his position regardless of its rationale. His past political actions, such as his opposition to the Boer War and especially his support for the Conservatives in the 1911 election, suggested to many that Bourassa had always been self-serving and not above furthering his own political interests rather than Canada's political interests, as he claimed in 1914. During wartime, his *nationaliste* critique (or any critique) was deemed unpatriotic. Canadians' duty to fight, according to supporters of the war inside and outside Quebec in 1914, surpassed the petty political issues that Bourassa raised.

The most common rejection of Bourassa centred on his assertion that the current war effort did not serve Canada's national interests. Although his critics agreed that Canada's interests lay in the historical and cultural obligations to England (and perhaps France), they argued that those obligations superseded national ones rather than accented them, as Bourassa believed. Other than *Le Devoir*, the French-language press of urban Quebec had been in favour of the war in August. Accordingly, many commentators attacked Bourassa's evolving views in September.[38] *La Patrie*, the second largest French-language newspaper in Montreal now aligned with the Borden Conservatives, first responded to *Le Devoir* on 31 August and throughout the ensuing month. Its editors dismissed the idea that England was acting in its self-interest in July and August and instead argued that it was saving France and Belgium from the German menace. *La Patrie* also denied that the war required compromise between nationalism and imperialism.[39] Those ideologies represented positions no longer relevant during the war. Instead, its editors demanded that, in the name of patriotism, those divisions be put aside for the sake of political unity and that Bourassa abandon his partisan positions.

Editorials in smaller papers such as *Le Pays*, *Le Clairon*, *Le Soleil* (the Liberal Party newspaper), and others, mirrored those in larger ones. To these French Canadian editors, Bourassa seemed to be naively unaware of the seriousness of the European war and the consequences of defeat – he was a political agitator to be pitied.[40] Quebec's English-language newspapers, such as Montreal's *Daily Mail* and the *Montreal Star*, added their voices, though in far stronger terms than their French Canadian counterparts. In the pages of *L'Action sociale*, the bishopric press organ, Paul-Eugène Roy wrote that French Canadian Catholics had a duty to the mother country and owed it their cooperation.[41]

A few papers would temper their criticism of Bourassa later in September. *Le Canada* responded reasonably by undertaking another interpretation of Grey's diplomacy that rejected Bourassa's arguments, while *Le Pays* defended the *nationaliste* chief's right to offer his opinion.[42] Yet these exceptions were few compared with most newspapers, which continued their unequivocal support for the war and their attacks against its only vocal critic.

French Canadian commentators also delivered an emphatic appeal to English Canada that Bourassa did not represent them. A reminder that French Canada supported the war usually accompanied articles attacking the *nationaliste* leader. Thomas Chase-Casgrain, a French Canadian lawyer, Conservative politician, and imperialist, offered his interpretation of the French Canadian reaction to Bourassa's argument in a letter to *La Patrie* on 14 September. Chase-Casgrain asked how Bourassa could demand that Canada pursue its national interest when the war represented its most important interest: the defence of the two Canadian motherlands, France and England. "French Canadians," he wrote, "do not wish ... to stand aloof ... Duty, gratitude and self-interest unite them to the other members of the great family in this fight for justice and right." According to Chase-Casgrain, the majority of French Canadians did not support Bourassa. Instead, they remembered the French Canadians of 1775 and 1812 who fought for England.[43] The editorials of Quebec newspapers suggest that many French Canadians likely agreed with Chase-Casgrain in the first months of the Great War.

Outside Quebec, most major newspapers echoed these disputes. The *Winnipeg Free Press* wrote that Canadian and British interests in the war were the same.[44] Toronto's *Globe* and *Toronto Star* barely mentioned the French Canadian iconoclast, perhaps an equally damning condemnation of his seeming irrelevance to many Canadians outside Quebec.[45] Although some papers, such as the Kingston *Standard*, went so far as to demand the arrest of the "traitor," most were content to demand his silence.[46] A cursory examination of the other news that garnered headlines, since many of them did not mention Bourassa, reveals that the Canadian press did not understand the war through the lens adopted by the journalist. For most Canadian newspapers, there was no question that Canada had to enter the war and wage it wholeheartedly. Any discussion of the nature of Canada's entry or the scale of its participation was no longer worth debating during the struggle for Europe across the Atlantic.

One of the most common rejections of Bourassa in newspapers portrayed his editorials as a craven effort to draw attention and support to his own ideological beliefs. The editor of *La Patrie* denounced the man who "now [tells] us what we must think of the political platform he formulated, and that the first German cannon shot reduced it to dust."[47] For the *Montreal Daily Mail*, Bourassa was not a man but a "troubled spirit ... formed of suspicion, distrust, envy, malice, ingratitude and prejudice."[48] The *Winnipeg Free Press*, one of the most widely circulated papers in the country, debated with its local Catholic press, *La Liberté*, about its unquestioned support for Bourassa's desire for limited participation in the war. The *Free Press* lumped *Le Devoir* and *La Liberté* together as "ultramontane organs" in blindly rejecting England's and France's calls to arms to further their own political objectives. The *Free Press* hoped that Bourassa would "keep his nationalist theories to himself," for they had little to do with Canada's present circumstances.[49] These criticisms were not altogether unwarranted: Bourassa was as committed to his ideological positions as they suspected.

His grounding in the political views that he had nurtured for more than a decade was a weakness to his critics rather than a testament to his sincerity. They perceived the Great War as unlike any other situation that Canada had experienced. To debate political issues from before the late summer of 1914 was self-indulgent. The arrogance of Bourassa in demanding a concession from English Canada – the repeal of Regulation 17 – seemed to be an obvious attempt to use the war to push his own political agenda and gained him few friends. The worst of the English Canadian press believed him to be a traitor to Canada and the British Empire, whereas French Canadian newspapers thought that his belligerence undermined the unity that he professed to desire. Regardless, none believed that wartime was an appropriate moment to divide the nation over such concerns.

For French or English Canadians critical of Bourassa's views, national unity demanded that all political considerations be put aside immediately. Unity meant total, unquestioning support for Canada's war, not a discussion about concessions. His intransigence only seemed to be further proof that Bourassa was an impediment to national unity rather than an advocate of it. Commentators across the country presented his refusal to compromise in the face of the new wartime circumstances as ignorant and delusional. They did not accept that his *nationaliste* position demanded a critical examination of Canada's involvement in the war to discern the best possible course of action for the country. For a Canadian nationalist such as Bourassa, unity meant debating and agreeing on the best course of action.

Although the articles that denounced Bourassa proffered honest opinions of his criticisms, they did not shy away from dishonest or dismissive portrayals. Most newspapers quoted his words in the worst possible light. They told their readers that Bourassa believed that Canada had no obligation to fight in English wars while omitting his defence of its participation to the extent that it could afford to offer.[50] Other banal renunciations included that of the Canadian Club, which expelled Bourassa even though, he noted dryly, he was not actually a member.[51] His critics accused him of blind adherence to his own ideology and of ignoring the moral and political urgency of the war, but he could easily accuse them of the same narrow-minded focus.

The words of retired Major General Sir William Dillon Otter, who returned to active service for the war and was the first Canadian-born chief of staff for the Canadian army, exemplified the attitude of critics of Bourassa. In an interview with the *Canadian Courier,* Otter explained that "the public mind should not be allowed to dwell too much upon what is going on in Europe. That can be safely left to the military leaders of Europe."[52] Although one might never have encountered Bourassa's words at all unless one followed the newspapers closely, since they were overwhelmed with news from the front lines, most Canadians probably did not care about his *Le Devoir* articles other than noting brief mentions of them in small columns of their local papers. Apathy silenced Bourassa as effectively as any censor. As loud as his voice was in the national press, it was still a small world for most Canadians just beginning to understand the war. He and his detractors played out their dramas for each other. They communicated how Canadians understood the beginning of the war but certainly did not represent them in their entirety.

A few English Canadians, even though they did not support his perspective, believed that Bourassa should at least have the opportunity to express his views. One of his most fervent defenders was prominent Montreal lawyer Charles Hazlitt Cahan, who first encountered the French Canadian journalist in the naval debate. They exchanged correspondence and remained friends in the years leading up to the war. Cahan vehemently disagreed with Bourassa's arguments but wrote letters to editors of newspapers across the country (e.g., the Montreal *Gazette,* Halifax *Herald,* and *Toronto Star*) protesting their misrepresentations of those arguments.

Cahan argued that the French Canadian was neither unpatriotic nor against the war.[53] His defence of Bourassa was grounded in the same British ideals that war supporters used to justify British superiority over German militarism. As Bourassa noted in a letter to Cahan, "the best feature of English civilisation is individual liberty," which always allowed for the presentation of opposing perspectives.[54] Bourassa's belief in the inviolability of Britain's liberal values in Canada would not survive the war, but they remained a pillar of his position in its early years.

Cahan was an exception among Bourassa's opponents. The widespread condemnation of his views in newspapers across the country in September led Bourassa to denounce supporters of the war as hypocrites, a message that he continued to communicate as 1914 drew to a close. Accordingly, finding common ground with his opponents that autumn proved to be a difficult task. Although Bourassa tried to respond to his critics by citing British or English Canadians who agreed with his arguments, it was not a conversation. He simply accepted those who agreed with him and summarily rejected those who did not. Just as his detractors had little influence on him, so too his complete adherence to his beliefs minimized his potential influence on his critics. For many of the newspapers in Quebec and throughout Canada, Bourassa was the primary (if not the only) voice criticizing the war effort – but an unconvincing one. Critical comments only solidified his belief in the pervasiveness of imperialist ideas across Canada, while his own commentaries confirmed his opponents' view of him as a dangerous iconoclast. This mutual affirmation of the worst of each side narrowed the Canadian understanding of the war.

Those who cared most about Bourassa's acceptance of the war were his *nationaliste* allies. The journalist's position did not align with some of their own views on the war, revealing divisions within their political group. Armand Lavergne and Omer Héroux agreed with Bourassa and asked that Ontario repeal Regulation 17 in exchange for support for the war. On the other side, Olivar Asselin and Jules Fournier took an anti-clerical position and did not accept Bourassa's distinction that Canada could join the war on Britain's side as a nation without the strings of imperialism attached. They openly condemned the Catholic Church's and their leader's support for the war.[55] In their newspaper, *L'Action*, they called Bourassa's hesitation a bankruptcy of *nationalisme*.[56] Unlike Bourassa's equivocation about the church's position, Asselin went so far as to publish a series of articles condemning the Church's influence on Quebec and the war. They were collected under the provocative title *Les évêques et la de la propagande de l'Action catholique* (The Bishops and the Propaganda of the Action Catholique).⁵⁷ Asselin, who later joined the Canadian forces despite his criticism, was one of the loudest voices attacking the Catholic Church's abuse of power and imperialist rhetoric.⁵⁸ At the same time, Fournier attacked Bourassa's position repeatedly that autumn, demanding that Bourassa reconcile his principles of the past decade with his current attitudes.⁵⁹ The war separated their nationalist views: Asselin and Fournier turned toward a focus on Quebec, whereas Bourassa, Lavergne, and Héroux still believed in a pan-Canadian nationalism.⁶⁰ Ultimately, Bourassa's popularity superseded the other dissident voices within the *nationaliste* movement. From 1914 on, English Canadians identified Bourassa as the most active opponent of the war effort.

An unexpected but profound influence on him during the fall of 1914 was a British radical leftist, Henry Noel Brailsford. A noted left-wing British intellectual, Brailsford was a British political commentator whose career stretched from the Boer War in 1899 to the Suez Crisis in 1956. He believed "that the citizens of a democratic society would respond in enlightened fashion if political issues were properly explained," his biographer observes.⁶¹ Brailsford visited Macedonia and wrote about the tumultuous situation there, caught between various Balkan powers in the early twentieth century, and he subsequently co-authored the *Report of the International Commission to Inquire into the Cause and the Conduct of the Balkan Wars*, published by the Carnegie Foundation in 1914.⁶² He later used that experience to apply J.A. Hobson's view of British imperialism to other European powers in his own study of the "armed peace" of Europe, *The War of Steel and Gold*, published in May 1914. Brailsford condemned the British "balance of power" policy in Europe as intrinsically faulty. Its preservation, he argued, was not "self-sufficing" but represented a means to an end: the preservation of British national liberties.⁶³ According to Brailsford, Europe's problems in 1914 sprang from the corruption of that principle, wherein the balance of power became an end unto itself.⁶⁴ By 1914, he had made a name for himself as a left-wing commentator dissecting British imperialism and the complex Balkan crises. He joined the anti-war group Union of Democratic Control alongside other well-known British leftists, and he became influential enough to be included in A.J.P. Taylor's history of British "trouble-makers" – a group of political dissenters with whom Bourassa might have found common purpose, though not common ideology.⁶⁵

In his editorials, Bourassa does not refer to Brailsford as an outsider or radical but merely introduces him as a British writer. Building upon a recent article by Brailsford in the *Contemporary Review*,[66] unlike anything that Bourassa might have read in the pages of Canadian newspapers, he recites Brailsford's argument that Germany's invasion of Belgium did not cause the war. Instead, the Serbian alliance with Russia was a thorn in Austria's side that precipitated the July Crisis. Germany, in turn, responded to Russian aggression and launched a defensive war.[67] According to Brailsford, and consequently Bourassa, Russia was the isolated entente power and agitator that pitted Serbia against Austria, drawing the other great powers into a European-wide conflict for its own political machinations and economic benefits.[68] Ironically, Brailsford wrote, if the entente won and Germany, Austria, and Turkey were crushed, then Russia would control the Balkans, the Dardanelles, and Turkey and would sit on top of Britain's road to India. In this case, imperialists would have argued, only a strong Germany could balance the threat of Russia.[69] In its focus on the German aggression thesis to explain the war in Western Europe for a British audience, Brailsford's emphasis resembled Bourassa's challenge to the dominant Canadian narrative of the origins of the war.

Reviewing Brailsford's account fulfilled Bourassa's promise to interrogate issues that others ignored so that Canadians might better understand the European war. Neither Brailsford nor Bourassa simply sought to alleviate the blame of Germany for attacking Belgium; each discerned complexity in the political issues underlying the outbreak of the war rather than the monocausal emphasis presented in patriotic rhetoric. Bourassa had agreed with Brailsford as early as 29 August when he had written that many were responsible for the war and that it could not simply be in defence of Belgium.[70] Bourassa believed that Canadians deserved to know as much as possible so that they could make informed decisions about the scale and nature of Canada's contribution to the war.

One of the few Canadians to share Bourassa's position on national autonomy was J.S. Ewart, a well-known lawyer and English Canadian nationalist. Ewart had defended the rights of Franco-Manitobans before the Privy Council in the 1890s and wrote *The Kingdom Papers* in the years before and during the First World War, a voluminous examination of Canada's legal obligations to Britain that envisioned a future distinct from the British Empire.[71] Many of the prominent liberal politicians and academics of the day, including Bourassa, read Ewart's work on Canadian nationalism.[72] Like Bourassa, Ewart sought an independent and equal Canada that could nurture Canadian nationalism and remove it from European affairs and British wars. The only way to unify Canada's disparate peoples, Ewart argued, was to "make her a nation in name as well as in fact. Let her throw off her mean colonial wrappings and let her assume her rightful place among the nations of the world."[73] Ewart's "romantic" notions of nationalism presented it as a unifying and inevitable force of Canadian history.[74]

Unlike Bourassa, however, Ewart voluntarily removed himself from the debate about the war. In its early months, he supported the war, hoping that it would reveal the power imbalance of Canada's relationship with Britain.[75] One of the few instances that Ewart did venture into the public realm during the war years was 24 October 1914, when he published an article in the *Ottawa Citizen*. In it, he summarized the reasons behind the outbreak of the war and offered the same far-ranging causes that Bourassa had presented – though without the French Canadian's inflammatory invectives.[76] Bourassa translated large sections of Ewart's piece for a French-speaking audience and noted their agreement that Russian mobilization had pushed Europe into war, not the invasion of Belgium. Both distinguished between "predisposed" causes of the war, such as imperialism and national ambition, and "precipitating" ones, such as the invasion of Belgium and Russian mobilization.[77]

Ewart wrote little after the October article, and his silence strained the relationship between the two nationalists. Two years later he wrote to Bourassa to explain his silence: "I should not think it at all right at the present time to say anything that would tend to distract our people during the stress of war." "After the war is over," he went on, "all those interested ... will have much to engage their attention and quite possibly I shall not be amongst the silent when the right time arrives."[78] Although Bourassa and Ewart privately acknowledged the similarities in their views on the British Empire, Ewart refused to threaten Canadian unity with his public commentary aside from a handful of articles. In his mind, it was not the time to raise such issues.

By December 1914, Bourassa stood alone as the most public voice against the Canadian war effort. In the previous month, a People's Forum in Ottawa invited him to speak about his views, but opposition forced the organizers to rescind the invitation. A group of Ottawa citizens organized a second potential appearance at the Russell Theatre on 17 December. In the interim, Bourassa toured New England speaking to Franco-Americans,[79] though he looked forward to the opportunity to explain himself directly to English Canadians in their own tongue.

The architecture of the Russell Theatre at the corner of Queen and Elgin Streets in Ottawa reflected the talents of its creator, J.B. McElfatrick, whose beaux arts design echoed the Italian renaissance while incorporating new American techniques to perfect acoustics and the seating arrangement. Like the speaker that night, Bourassa, it fused Old World style with New World pragmatism.[80] The 1,500-seat venue was packed with journalists, citizens, and soldiers who awaited the intellectual and sometime polemicist Bourassa. He was the heart and voice of the *nationaliste* movement and had made a career out of challenging members of Parliament, a stone's throw away from where they gathered.

Some in the audience arrived solely to disrupt the proceedings. For days, pamphlets had been circulating in Ottawa decrying the appearance of the "arch traitor" and "rebel" Bourassa. "The Skull of Rebellion must be crushed," the pamphlets declared, urging "loyal citizens" to enter with or without paying the admission fee. The text promised readers that the police and the militia were on their side against "the rebels" who had invited Bourassa to speak on "the duty of Canada at the present hour" in the midst of the Great War.[81]

As Bourassa stepped onto the stage, the crowd erupted. Shouts and jeers drowned out the words of Dr. Anthony Freeland, who tried to introduce the night's speaker. Bourassa ignored them and spoke directly and fluently in English to the journalists who had gathered. This enraged his opponents in the crowd even further. A sergeant in uniform leaped to the stage with a Union Jack and demanded that the French Canadian wave the flag. Bourassa turned from the journalists and took the flag in his hands. The tumultuous crowd quieted as they listened to his words. "I am ready to fly the British flag of freedom, but I will not do it under threat," he affirmed, turning back to the journalists. When the sergeant repeated his demand, other soldiers rushed the stage, overwhelming the organizers and journalists who encircled Bourassa. Some French Canadians in the audience sang the Marseillaise. Amid the chaotic chanting and threatening invective of the crowd, Bourassa left to deliver his speech at the Château Laurier down the street.[82] Later he would write that "the only serious aspect of the situation is the marked growth of intolerant and arrogant jingoism. There is, for all true Canadians, a danger to be more dreaded than the expansion of German militarism in Europe: it is the moral conquest of Canada by Prussianism under false British colours."[83]

It was not the first time that Bourassa had referred to his fellow Canadians as Prussians, nor would it be the last, but the Russell Theatre debacle revealed the divide between the dissenter and the majority of English Canadians and French Canadians in 1914. Over the previous five months, Bourassa's editorials had repeatedly rejected the rhetoric that Canadians used to defend fighting for the British Empire in the First World War but not the war itself. Instead, he attacked the high ideals that justified the war for Canadians, which focused on British ideals, atrocities in Belgium, and upholding Canadian honour. Bourassa believed that this rhetoric was merely imperialism in disguise and, as a veteran critic of imperialist arguments, countered that Canadian self-interest took precedence over jingoistic contributions of money, resources, and soldiers. Both sides took deep offence at the other's position. Even before Canadian soldiers had reached the battlefield, the home front was dividing into a contest between Bourassa and the rest of the country.

The Ottawa event nearly devolved into a riot after his opponents aggressively campaigned against his presence, labelling Bourassa the "arch traitor" of Canada. He was prepared to face disagreement, as he had many times before, but the violent disruption of public order in response to his words testified to the wartime transformation of Canada. Later he offered a rejoinder: "[I] can well afford to laugh at the easy game played against [me] by all dealers in 'cheap loyalty' ... [I] survived it [during the Boer War], and will pass through this one, in the minds at least of those people whose opinions and sympathy [I care] for."[84] At the end of the year, Bourassa stood more isolated than ever on the public stage. French and English, Catholic and Protestant, and even other *nationalistes* rejected his equivocating position on the war. No one realized how long the war would last or the extent of the transformation about to be wrought on Canada and the world. However, the coming months underlined the transformative nature of the war for all Canadians, especially as it brought about a transformation of Bourassa's cautious position in favour of Canadian intervention.

3

What Do We Owe England?

1915

THE YEAR BEGAN with Canadians still enthused by the war but not yet having experienced its consequences. For the French Canadian dissenter, the shadow of Bourassa's experience at the Russell Theatre stretched throughout the year as all of the belligerents embraced the extremism of total war. Bourassa looked for other voices that explored the nuances of the war, but he found few allies at home. Pope Benedict XV and the Union of Democratic Control, far away from Canada, aligned with his religious and political beliefs. He praised their wisdom while criticizing the seemingly blind adherence of war supporters in Canada to what he increasingly saw solely as an imperial crusade. By year's end, Bourassa published his first major booklet arguing against Canadian involvement in the war, aptly titled *Que devons-nous à l'Angleterre?* (What Do We Owe England?). "We" applied to Canada as a whole but easily could have been French Canada and certainly Bourassa and the *nationalistes*. After the hostile reception that they had received in 1914, Bourassa and his followers owed England no compromise and no national unity for the sake of an unjust war. The coming year further emphasized the lesson that he had learned at the Russell Theatre: the war was deforming public discourse. Total war pushed everything to the extremes.

Alongside Bourassa, many French Canadians who welcomed the war in August 1914 began to question a prolonged Canadian war effort as the year progressed – or at least they were no longer as enthusiastic in their support for it. Equally, tensions between English Canadians and French Canadians did not endear the latter to an "English" war in Europe. The relationship became more strained as allegations of poor recruitment in Quebec and the debate about language equality in Ontario revealed that the two sides disagreed about the purpose of the war. English Canadian recruitment was higher because of the number of British-born Canadians, as opposed to Canadians actually born in the country, but Bourassa's dissident tone accented the belief that French Canadians were not "doing their bit." That accusation shaped perceptions of French Canada during the war, but it might not have been as justified as contemporaries and historians once thought.[1] Regardless, English Canada placed blame for the poor recruitment on Bourassa's criticism as well as on his interference in the bilingual issue in Ontario.[2] The neighbouring province's Regulation 17, which banned French-language education in the province, was scheduled to appear before the Supreme Court of Ontario to judge its legality in 1915. The *nationalistes* pursued a campaign to overturn or at least temper the law, and its lingering presence drained what little French Canadian enthusiasm there was, yet English Canadians continued to demand it.[3]

The *nationalistes* continued to contrast the government's request to wage a war for liberty with their fight for French-language education at home in Ontario. They gained a powerful ally on 9 January 1915 when Quebec Cardinal Louis-Nazaire Bégin published a letter that he had sent to Archbishop Paul Bruchési on the validity of Regulation 17 in December. The cardinal wrote that, "if, which God forbid, the trial ... be prolonged, it will be the noble duty of the French and Catholic province of Quebec to assist with all its influence and all its resources."[4] The Quebec legislature followed Bégin's lead and unanimously passed a resolution condemning the Ontario government's refusal to protect Franco-Ontarians' right to French-language education.[5] Bourassa's fellow *nationaliste* Armand Lavergne was more strenuous in his rejection, proclaiming in a letter to the Kingston *Standard* that "this country was born Bi-lingual and it will remain Bi-lingual, or it shall end ... We will have [the official language of this country], just as English, taught in our schools or there will be no schools at all."[6] Despite disagreement between the *nationalistes* and other French Canadians over the war effort, they were united in defending their linguistic rights against English Canadian discrimination. As historian Mason Wade once noted, a "passionate emotional reaction ... always developed [in Quebec] whenever one of the essentials of national survival [was] endangered."[7] That protective instinct sharpened during the year as the date for a ruling by the Supreme Court of Ontario on Regulation 17 approached in the fall.

The *nationalistes* had always been one of the leading defenders of French-language schooling in Ontario, and Bourassa did not hesitate to join the Catholic Church in continuing the years-long campaign for Ontario's

French minority. He viewed that instinct as inseparable from a nationalist opposition to the war. Both demanded that French Canadians assert themselves within a bicultural national union. He had the opportunity to explain this overlap on 14 January 1915 when he and his supporters celebrated the fifth anniversary of the founding of *Le Devoir* and gathered at the Monument-National in downtown Montreal for the occasion.

It was a festive occasion in stark contrast to the thwarted speech at the Russell Theatre a month earlier. The night began with J.-N. Cabana, president of the Friends of *Le Devoir*, G.N. Ducharme, president of the Board of Administration, and Armand Lavergne giving speeches to warm up the crowd for the main event. Eventually, Lavergne introduced Bourassa to the audience: "At first, we thought the race was doomed to die, and we had only one hope, that of seeing it die well. But times are changing. There is no longer any question of dying, for the race will live." "One man saved it," he continued before the crowd drowned out his words with cheers of "Bourassa!"[8] The devout who had gathered to hear him speak were absolutely convinced that he alone stood for French Canada. "My critics in English Canada want to hang me for my words," Bourassa said at one point during his speech, and a voice from the crowd replied "and we want to hang with you!"[9] The audience in Montreal that night adored him as he used the history of *Le Devoir* to defend his vision of Canada, its importance for Quebec, and the continued relevance of his arguments.

His anniversary speech touched on many of the criticisms directed at Bourassa over the past five months as he affirmed the value of his newspaper to public discourse in Canada. He believed that the issues confronting French Canadians in 1915 were much the same as those that he had debated since the founding of the newspaper despite the war and his critics. Bourassa linked the continuing struggle of Franco-Ontarians to his current positions, highlighting the necessity of shaping public opinion to improve their plight. He boasted to his audience that *Le Devoir* had swayed Quebec to the side of Franco-Ontarians.[10] It would no doubt continue to influence the national mood, even if in early 1915 Bourassa stood alone on the national stage deconstructing the war.

Although some doubted the purpose of the paper, Bourassa assured them that it continued its fundamental mission. It was a crucial organ of *nationaliste* beliefs about Canada and, perhaps taunting Abbé D'Amours, a Catholic journal but not a voice for the Catholic hierarchy.[11] This misconception had caused tension the year before, and the ultramontane Bourassa made sure to distinguish that *Le Devoir* was independent even though it upheld the authority and unity of the Catholic Church. He wanted to demonstrate that he could disagree with the episcopacy without ceasing to be Catholic and, importantly, that the church was not responsible for *Le Devoir* editorial decisions.[12] He promised that *Le Devoir* would continue to be non-partisan and try to force political parties to work for the "good of the nation instead of corrupting its spirit."[13]

Bourassa then reviewed the paper's previous campaigns, such as those against imperialism, in defence of French Canadians' religious and linguistic rights, and in support of Catholic unions and temperance. He ended with an appraisal of the greatest obstacle facing Canadians in 1915: unity between its French-speaking and English-speaking peoples. "The fundamental fact of our past, present, and future national situation," he pronounced from his pulpit, "is that we have no more the right to want to make Canada an exclusively French country than Anglo-Canadians have the right to make it an English country."[14] Thus, *nationalistes* should be opposed to the exclusion of French or English since both were integral to Canadian identity, and they must put Canadian interests before those of Britain, France, or any other country. *Le Devoir*, Bourassa proclaimed, would continue to search for "a common ideal, made of Canadian traditions, rooted in Canadian soil and having no other object than the moral and material greatness of the Canadian homeland."[15] He ended his speech with an impassioned plea for donations:

> In return for everything you can do for *Le Devoir* and its works, I make you only one promise, which is that as long as I live, it will not fail. Before it fails or betrays the mission I have outlined for it, even though it will be the end of all my ambitions and of all my hopes, I will kill it with my own hands![16]

In expressing the totality of the continuing mission of *Le Devoir*, Bourassa set out his own path for the coming year and proclaimed that old and new issues were the same. The war had not changed the political issues of the day; although dimmed they might have been in its long shadow, Bourassa was sure that *Le Devoir* had a part to play in the continuing struggle to unite Canada's peoples. Not to do so would mean the death of the country.

The next week Bourassa returned to sharp critiques of Robert Borden's wartime government and demanded that it represent Canada more strongly in the British Empire for the sake of the Canadian war effort. Or, more precisely, his vision of Canada. He did so against the backdrop of public ruminations about the Canadian role in a British war effort. When asked about the planned Imperial Conference for 1915, Ontario Liberal Party leader N.W. Rowell told journalists on 27 January that "to have representatives from the Empire meet and take counsel together" would "give to Europe a ... splendid manifestation of the unity of the Empire and of the determination of all parts to see this fight through."[17] Although the conference was cancelled for that year, many raised the idea of imperial reform in the coming months. Author and imperialist Castell Hopkins mused in Hamilton that February about the possibility of an Imperial Council that included the dominions, an idea that had a nucleus stretching back to the 1880s.[18] To Bourassa, these musings only confirmed that imperialists were abusing the war to achieve their own goal of fulfilling the dream of an inclusive empire that melded Canada to Britain forever. When Borden eventually met with the British cabinet during his trip to England in July, advocates of imperialism were understandably pleased, and the press was effusive in its praise of the important precedent.[19]

Bourassa took little stock in the posturing of the government. True Canadian autonomy was the future of the young dominion, not simply being granted the opportunity to meet the British cabinet hat in hand. Bourassa reminded his readers that in 1910 Borden had promised that, if Canada fought an imperial war, it would be accompanied by actual participation in imperial government with actual influence on its decisions. Yet he saw no evidence of it in 1915. Even as Minister of Justice Charles Doherty claimed that Canada's entry into the war was spontaneous and voluntary, meaning that Canada had exercised its right to choose whether or not to participate in the British conflict, Bourassa saw little proof of independence in its conduct of the war.[20] Borden wanted to secure imperial reform, but now that he had the opportunity to do so Bourassa saw little action on that front. If the governing Conservatives were honest in their ambitions, then now was the time to ensure Canadian input in the British cabinet and war effort. "The wine is poured, saviours of the Empire," Bourassa wrote, "you cannot let others drink it."[21] As Canadians waited for Borden, the British government led the war without any concern for Canadian interests.

Bourassa viewed Borden's motivations with suspicion. Even a small increase in Canadian involvement in empire affairs represented what Bourassa had argued against for the previous decade and a half. The cancellation of an Imperial Conference only confirmed that Britain had no desire to inform its colonial subjects about the war, even though Borden remained aware of cabinet decisions and was as involved as any Canadian prime minister had ever been. To Bourassa, it was a sign of delusion, and the imperial relationship was becoming only further imbalanced. He predicted that eventually Canada and the other dominions would realize the faulty premise of their involvement in the war, and the ensuing anti-imperialist reaction would pose a greater threat than "German barbarity."[22] Great Britain had always acted in its own global interests, and the war proved more than ever that it had long ago become "a global power rather than a European one."[23] Britain cared little for Canada, and Canada ought to return the favour. As supporters of the war listed the rewards of Canadian participation, Bourassa repeated his position of moderate Canadian participation without obligation, as he had advocated in 1914, and raised the spectre of Canada's "oppressed" Franco-Ontarians, who still faced the "assimilating Prussian tyranny of Ontario."[24] When his opponents talked of the war's potential for "reform" and "British liberties," he saw little more than hypocrisy and self-delusion.[25] To the *nationaliste*, the absence of participation in imperial affairs underlined the terrible cost of a war that risked Canadian lives and little to show for it.

The release of the Canadian budget further frustrated Bourassa, for it emphasized in real terms the price of the war for Canada. On 11 February, Minister of Finance William T. White revealed that Canadian debt had spiralled out of control since the beginning of the conflict. The country had spent $190 million against a revenue of only $130 million. White estimated that the war would cost Canada a further $100 million by the end of the fiscal year and that its debt would increase to $110 million.[26] "The 'saviours of the Empire' may well be the destroyers of their own country," Bourassa remarked, for it became all too evident that Canada could not in fact afford "the weight of glory."[27] As Canadians paid more taxes to save the British Empire, Bourassa wondered how long it would be until they realized the farce of a poorer nation supporting a richer one.[28] Bourassa saw little difference in Canadian policy despite the changed circumstances of the war. The costs of Canada's imperial obligations grew greater while the rewards dwindled – if they had existed at all.

The House of Commons at least should have been asking questions about Canada's growing commitments to the war. Yet Bourassa observed only uncritical acceptance in Parliament of the war policy. The "party truce" that Laurier had declared in August 1914 was still in effect, and the House of Commons passed legislation without serious comment from the opposition benches. The finance minister's budget focused parliamentary discussion on increased taxes and tariffs, which the Liberals opposed only half-heartedly. In 1910, the Liberals had campaigned against protectionist policies, yet Laurier now accepted them "due to the exigencies of the present situation."[29] Bourassa considered this policy of "all for Empire, and nothing for Canada," a foolish result of the opposition Liberals placing war patriotism above Canadian interests.[30] These taxes and tariffs weakened the Canadian economy and budget as Parliament operated firmly within a colonial mindset. The only worthwhile criticism in Laurier's speech on the budget, according to Bourassa, was demanding that tariffs vary based upon merchandise and the needs of the poor, echoing his own position.[31]

These concessions had grave consequences, Bourassa foretold, for "a people do not play war with impunity."[32] He agreed with his critics that war was not a time to make *quick* decisions on national matters, but that did not mean making unexamined ones or that they were free of consequences. Government policy had a long-term impact on the country. Justifying its passing unanimously in the House of Commons by virtue of politicians' loyalty and patriotic enthusiasm did not mean that it was good policy. All of the sacrifices that the country had made for the war effort and those that it had yet to make would be for nothing if Canada gave up on protecting its interests.[33] Instead, Bourassa demanded a Canadian government that carefully made decisions, balanced and informed by what was best for Canada, and carefully considered ideal courses of action. Parliament was a farce, he declared, a "patriotic theatre" performing for the nation at war.[34]

There was no problem with patriotism, Bourassa explained to his readers. It was a natural instinct tied to an attachment to a homeland, half egotism and half noble sentiment. Unfortunately, the patriotism of wartime was hollow. It was "atrophied by colonial servility, less strong, less active, than the patriotism of a free people, masters of their world."[35] True patriotism was not expressed in Canada during the war. Supporters of the war appealed to loyalty to encourage enlistment, not patriotism. Bourassa pointed to lower recruitment among native-born Canadians compared with British-born Canadians.[36] Clearly, Canadian patriotism demanded something different from British patriotism. Instead, "loyalism" was demanded of Canadians, "a feeling – and often a hypocritical profession of faith – that depends on external and distant circumstances."[37] Canadians loyal to Britain might have joined the army, but that did not mean that all patriotic Canadians shared their convictions. Any patriotic Canadian could find the conduct of the war unwise for the nation or raise questions unbecoming of someone loyal to Britain. Bourassa argued that he was performing his patriotic duty as he continued to raise questions "disloyal" to Britain.

No one else was publishing his type of questioning editorials, which extended to the broader international picture of the war. As Canadian soldiers established themselves on the front lines in Belgium, Bourassa offered his readers an analysis of foreign policy that went deeper than reporting the news. He shared his insights on events in long columns on the front page of *Le Devoir*, and they were far more detailed than the editorials of other daily newspapers.

On 3 March, Bourassa offered an examination of Russia's interest in Constantinople and its impact on the political and economic aspects of the war. He examined the statement in February 1915 that Russia would permanently occupy the Turkish capital and gain access to the Mediterranean from the Black Sea. Foreign Secretary Edward Grey supported this stance in the House of Commons on 25 February.[38] However, if the Russian declaration was true, then governments had misled the public about the nature of the war. "In any war, the general public sees only the dramatic and bloody side of it," Bourassa wrote, but "it is the force of economic resistance that will give the Allies final victory, more than all their feats of arms; it is the strongest political influence that will settle the conditions for peace and divert or precipitate the causes of future conflicts."[39] Whereas other newspapers looked to the Canadian soldiers recently sent to the trenches of the Western Front, Bourassa asked why Canadians risked their lives in Europe for Russian claims to territory 1,000 kilometres away.

Unknown to anyone in 1915, Britain and Russia signed a secret agreement formalizing Russia's annexation of the straits and Constantinople just weeks after Grey's comment.[40] At the time, Bourassa took Grey at his word. In the House of Commons, Grey responded to Russia's claim by saying "that is an aspiration with which we are in entire sympathy. The precise form in which it will be realised will no doubt be settled in the terms of peace."[41] Leaving such determinations to the terms of peace was a reasonable position, though again Bourassa asked what sort of world might emerge from an Allied victory and whether it would be to Canada's benefit. Allowing Russia to extend its empire so far south was as dangerous as Germany's expansion against which the Allies now fought. Quoting H.N. Brailsford, Bourassa reminded his readers that "our imperialists will be calling out for a strong Germany to balance a threatening Russia" by the end of the war if Russia controlled the Bosporus and Dardanelles straits.[42] He predicted that this "peace" would only lead to future war. The insatiable thirst of empires for conquest, domination, and wealth had forced the world into war, he warned, and only when they were extinguished would the world know peace.

As spring continued, Bourassa's dedication to exploring the intricacies of wartime diplomacy was unwelcome. Canadians finally confronted the brutal reality of the conflict that they had joined eight months earlier. They experienced their first major casualties when the Germans launched devastating gas attacks against Canadian soldiers at the Ypres salient in April 1915. Few Canadians were ready for the extent of the losses, suffering more than 6,000 casualties over a single week.[43] Less than a month later, German U-boats torpedoed the RMS *Lusitania* off the coast of Ireland as part of their campaign to restrict transatlantic shipping. The Germans alleged that the civilian liner was carrying weapons, but few people in the Allied countries believed them. Historian Ian Miller wrote in his study of Toronto during the Great War that the events of April and May 1915 changed the war from a "Great Adventure" to a "Great Crusade" imbued with a moral necessity to stop Germany.[44] This imperative, interpreted nearly a century after the fact, reflected Bourassa's greatest fears.

As others imbued these events with great significance, Bourassa believed that the sinking of the *Lusitania* was a shocking result of failed British policy once championed by imperialists, and he followed the ensuing American response to it closely while explaining it to his readers. The *Lusitania* tragedy mocked the supposed British dominance of the sea with its Dreadnought fleet so urgently required in 1909 and 1910, which Bourassa well remembered given his involvement in the Canadian debate. Despite its naval power, it now appeared that Britain could not actually protect shipping from German naval forces. Months before war broke out, Admiral Sir Percy Scott had warned of British vulnerability to submarines, but it was too late.[45] To Bourassa, bellicose patriotism had trumped common sense. If there were not enough destroyers to escort ships, then it was because the British had spent the last ten years building dreadnoughts.[46] He also worried that the incident would push one more nation into the worldwide conflict. The United States was still neutral in the war, and President Woodrow Wilson tried to keep the nation removed from European affairs. Wilson, Bourassa believed, was aware of the appalling consequences that would result from a hasty decision.⁴⁷ He hoped that Wilson would react reasonably and continue the stance that he had advocated so far.

The hope of Allied war supporters that the United States would enter the conflict because of the loss of Americans on the *Lusitania*, who had willingly travelled the seas under threat, was farfetched to the French Canadian journalist.⁴⁸ Bourassa kept his readers appraised of the unfolding tensions between the United States and Germany in the following weeks. On 13 May, American Secretary of State William Jennings Bryan warned Germany that the Americans would not hesitate to perform "[their] sacred duty of maintaining the rights of the United States and its citizens."⁴⁹ Bourassa agreed with the *Montreal Herald*, which termed the American position as "boiling neutrality," but he believed that the heat would dissipate.⁵⁰ Still, if the Germans did not temper their actions, then the United States would have no choice but to enter the war in defence of its interests. In that context, Bourassa wondered what effect Japan's entry into the war on the side of the Allies had on American opinion, for the Japanese had their own interests in the Pacific that might oppose American interests there.⁵¹ The French Canadian did not believe that American entry into the war hinged on the single moral issue of civilian deaths. Rather, he perceived the complex political and moral facets that had no easy resolution.

By 8 June 1915, Secretary of State Bryan had resigned his post in protest against President Wilson's asking him to send a more aggressive response to the German government. The implication that the United States could respond to any "infringement of [American] rights, intentional or incidental," was unsettling to Bryan, who believed that Wilson was effectively opening the door to an American declaration of war against Germany.⁵² Bryan believed in American neutrality, and he saw Wilson's warning as an ultimatum on the path to war. Bourassa agreed with the principled position of Bryan, for neither wanted to see the country enter the war, even on the side of the Allies. Neither believed that the United States could choose sides in the conflict so blithely. Neutrality, even in the face of losses, was the only way to uphold American interests. For Bourassa, "German brutality" and the "British morgue" comprised a poor set of options.⁵³ Although the United States would eventually join the war in 1917, again under the pressure of submarine warfare, Bryan's resignation in 1915 was an important reminder that the world was not completely subsumed in a binary between the Allies and the Central Powers.

Months later Bourassa returned to the correspondence between the United States and Germany that continued after Robert Lansing replaced Bryan as secretary of state. Germany protested that Britain had instructed its merchant vessels to seek protection behind neutral flags while increasing the arms of its shipping fleet. Germany argued that the attack on the *Lusitania* and other neutral ships had been for its own defence.[54] Bourassa analyzed the German note of 8 July, calling it "a singular blend of impudence, skilful dialectics and open sincerity."[55] It was honest at least. Instead, Bourassa believed that Britain was being disingenuous in its response. It was in Britain's interest to focus American attention on the deaths of civilians rather than on the German naval threat to British security and commercial shipping. The Americans could easily "protect their country from the horrors and crimes of war" by not using British ships to transport goods.[56] The Germans had promised on 7 June that they would no longer attack passenger liners,[57] a polite response that considered President Wilson's desire to avoid any future incidents such as that of the *Lusitania*. Contrary to the protests of the British press, the Americans were better off acceding to German demands and staying out of the war altogether. Of course, despite Bourassa's narrow view of the matter, the Americans, as John Coogan writes, were "a partner, and not always a silent partner, in the allied economic campaign to strangle Germany," and President Wilson was particularly concerned about the cotton industry in the Democrat-dominated South.[58] Although American neutrality was maintained that summer, reaction to the sinking of the *Lusitania* demonstrated to Bourassa that few rational voices prevailed on the international stage, and those that did, such as Bryan, were forced out by the harsh extremes of political brinkmanship. It was an increasingly familiar fate, for Bourassa faced similar isolation at home.

In May, he once again raised the torch in the struggle to protect Franco-Ontarians during the changing circumstances of the war. Bourassa delivered a speech to the Association catholique de la jeunesse canadienne at a benefit for the Franco-Ontarian campaign. He defended "the French language in Canada, its rights, its necessity, and its advantages."[59] He argued that protection of the French language was entirely legitimate as part of the legal and cultural history of British North America. He affirmed that "the Canadian Confederation was born of a fruitful alliance of the two races; it will only live by mutual respect for their rights." He rejected opponents' claim "that a bi-ethnic and bilingual people cannot form a homogeneous nation and that the minority must speak the language of the majority."[60] Bourassa reiterated the *nationalistes'* arguments since their formation a decade and a half earlier: the French language was an irrevocable facet of Canadian identity. The right to pass it on to the next generation was unalterable.

Although proponents of Regulation 17 claimed that linguistic unity was eclipsed by national unity during wartime, Bourassa reminded his audience that "it is only in French that we wage war."[61] The journalist evoked the rhetoric of war supporters to convince his listeners to donate to the cause. "The best British traditions and the very conservation of Canadian heritage" demanded a fair and intelligent solution. Surely, the Ontario schools merited as much support as the French Canadian war effort. "In a magnificent outpouring of generosity," Quebec had donated men and money to a British war, and Franco-Ontarians now deserved the same generosity. They fought for a cause as just and as sacred as the one in Europe, Bourassa declared, "[a] cause that has no other defect than to be ours and not to expect support from the foreign nations to whom we give our gold and blood."[62] His juxtaposition of the purpose of the war and the treatment of French Canadians underlined the contradiction of recruitment campaigns in the province. Why fight for Britain, France, or Belgium when they had not yet won the fight for Franco-Ontarians at home? At the end of the gathering, the audience unanimously passed a motion supporting French-language rights and "the precepts and practice of the cordial understanding that unites England and France on the battlefields of Europe."[63] Cultural unity at home had to be combined with national unity. If equality and liberty were worth dying for in the trenches of Europe, then surely they were worth defending in Canada as well.

That disconnect between the purpose of the war and the means by which that purpose could be achieved was increasingly worrisome. Where was British liberty in wartime Canada? A protest against conscription reinforced Bourassa's doubts about his position on the war. On 23 July, a group of about 1,000 anti-conscription protesters broke up a recruitment meeting at Montreal's Parc La Fontaine.[64] The Montreal *Gazette* declared in response that conscription was possible but would come at too great a cost for the nation and could never happen. The law, the *Gazette* explained, did not allow for conscription for foreign wars. Although a few voices were in favour of conscription in 1915,[65] the government reacted to the disturbance by categorically denying the possibility of conscription in Canada. One of its Quebec ministers, Postmaster General Thomas Chase-Casgrain, issued a statement on 28 July in reply to the incident: "You can state, in the most positive manner, that the question has never come up, directly or indirectly ... We are happy to see that in all parts of the country Canadian patriotism is manifested so eloquently ... I am pretty accurate in my political predictions, and I can say that there will be no Conscription."[66] The government assured the people that forced military service was not necessary to win the war.

Bourassa scoffed at the government's promise in Chase-Casgrain's words. He argued that only those who had already opposed the legal and moral obligation of Canada to fight for Great Britain had the right to argue against conscription. Was Canada not conscripted to fight for the British Empire time and again? Anything else was idealistic, if not delusional, since the road to conscription was paved with government policy that encouraged militarism in Canadian society.[67] Bourassa pointed to Prime Minister Borden's repeated expansions of the Canadian army throughout 1915. The greater the demands of the Canadian army, the greater the chance that conscription would be necessary.[68] Alone such policy was dangerous, but worse was that it lay in the hands of politicians who were not "Canadians before imperialists."[69] Bourassa believed that they would interpret or change the law in any way that they desired in order to fulfill their commitment to the war with little opposition. Outside Parliament, he declared, only *Le Devoir* had thoroughly contested the claim that Canadian liberty and security were threatened by Germany and stood opposed to policy that increased Canadian militarism. "We seemed to be preaching in the desert," he wrote.[70] Bourassa condemned the *Gazette*'s naivety in *hoping* that conscription would not happen as a matter of law. If conscription was enacted, then it would have to be opposed by those willing to defend their principles.

In August 1915, the war was a year old. Canadian soldiers had experienced long months of trench warfare and had fought brutal battles at places such as Ypres in April and Festubert in May. They were neither defeats nor victories. The war had reached a stalemate. Sanitized newspaper reports from the front arrived, and letters home often downplayed the terrible conditions of trench life.[71] In the public sphere, Canadians continued to offer stalwart support for the war, though they might have been less certain of Borden's stewardship of it. There were rumours of an election that year as reports of government corruption involving numerous war contracts appeared in newspapers.[72] Liberal papers such as the *Winnipeg Free Press* were particularly vocal in their denunciations, but even its editor, J.W. Dafoe, believed it best to extend the government's mandate until the war was over.⁷³ Some Liberals urged their party to put the government performance before a vote, but Laurier unequivocally stated that his party would not seek an election.⁷⁴ No one expected the war to conclude in 1915, and the warring nations prepared for a much longer conflict than they had foreseen a year earlier.

The Great War's first anniversary was lamented in the Vatican, where Pope Benedict XV grieved the war that marked his ascent to the papacy in 1914. For a year, he had tried to intervene where he could, including trying to circumvent war between Italy and Austria-Hungary, hosting representatives from neutral nations such as the Netherlands and United States hoping to organize peace conferences, and attempting to negotiate peace between Germany and Belgium.⁷⁵ On 28 July, exactly a year after Austria-Hungary declared war on Serbia, Benedict released an "apostolic exhortation" to the belligerent nations. The pope was saddened that his advice to end the conflict had gone unheeded. "May this cry," he hoped, "prevailing over the dreadful clash of arms, reach unto the peoples who are now at war."⁷⁶ His appeal was not couched solely in Christian morality. The pope reminded all involved of their "tremendous responsibility of peace and war." This echoed his letter to Cardinal Vannutelli in May after the sinking of the *Lusitania* and the introduction of gas warfare, when he noted that "the war continues to ensanguine Europe, and not even do men recoil from means of attack, on land and on sea, contrary to the laws of humanity and to international law."⁷⁷ The pope emphasized the value of international law and above all moderation and compromise as means of ending the terrible war that beset the people of the world.

Bourassa took heed of the pope's message as further proof that his path was the correct one. After first thanking the sovereign pontiff for having given humanity "this luminous and consoling word," he quoted the papal statement directly and thrice noted the sentence "why not from this moment weigh with serene mind the rights and lawful aspirations of [all] peoples?"⁷⁸ Bourassa called out to "the conquerors of Alsace and Transvaal, the tyrants of Belgium, Poland and Ireland, the persecutors of Schleswig, Ukraine, and French Ontario!"⁷⁹ He knew, however, that they would not listen to the pope, who alone had a practical plan to resolve the conflict – practical, at least, to Bourassa's ultramontane thinking. Pope Benedict XV asked that the nations at war work for peace rather than war, and Bourassa naturally placed the Roman ontiff in the position of neutral international arbitrator.

Bourassa was not surprised by the muted response to the pope in most quarters. In his mind, the worst transgressors against peace and moderation were the nations that had turned away from the papacy. The liberty and democracy that the belligerent nations claimed to protect had only led to the "weakening of any principle of authority, the laxity of the family bond, the negation of social duty, individual selfishness, class hatred, the unbridled worship of physical well-being, [and] the thirst for wealth – to paganism."[80] Bourassa looked to the world that ignored the pope's message and saw "a soulless humanity."[81] The passion in his words emphasized his serious reception of papal missives. For Bourassa, Pope Benedict XV was not simply another contributor to the array of opinions on the war. Here was the word of God given to his people. Often the most excessive and evocative of Bourassa's war editorials dealt with the Vatican, and even in 1915, long before the war intensified to more frightening levels, the pope's words moved the devout Bourassa to dismal depths. Seeing so many Catholics ignore Benedict's words was outrageous to him.

The journalist instead sought other voices that truly fought for the equality and liberty that he demanded, but he found few in Canada. He found them across the Atlantic, where British anti-war commentators earned his approval that summer. Bourassa published a letter that he had received from Lord Leonard Courtney, a former cabinet minister under Prime Minister William Gladstone who had campaigned with his wife against the Boer War fifteen years earlier. Courtney affirmed that he stood on common ground with Bourassa.[82] The British politician was also a member of the Union of Democratic Control (UDC), and Bourassa republished sections from its first pamphlet in a June editorial.[83] A group of British politicians and intellectuals had formed the UDC in August 1914 as a rejection of the British Liberal Party's decision to support the war. They criticized the British war effort and, like Bourassa, did not question the legitimacy of defending Belgium; rather, they offered a more nuanced perspective on the reason for and purpose of the war. They asked Britons what obligations Britain would have had if its foreign policy had been open to democratic approval instead of ministerial control.[84] Their first pamphlet outlined four points to inspire the "conditions of the peace": one, that no province be transferred without plebiscite; two, that Britain sign no treaty without parliamentary approval; three, that Britain should not form an alliance for the purpose of maintaining the balance of power, and instead a public international council should settle disputes; and four, that Britain propose a drastic reduction in armaments among all belligerent nations.[85] Bourassa had been impressed with the writing of UDC member Noel Brailsford a year earlier and continued to praise its program for peace and its active resistance against the British war effort.

It is little wonder that Bourassa found solidarity with the men and women of the UDC during the war years. He admired these "men of high value, ready to risk their popularity and chance of personal success, to break their party ties and associations of interests, to defend a legitimate freedom and support a principle or idea."[86] Their radical advocacy for peace and demand for "democratic control" struck a chord with the French Canadian nationalist. Bourassa also wanted Canadians to have control over their own foreign policy. Further, the UDC demands proved that British liberty allowed dissidents to express themselves. If it was indeed "not time to talk of such things," as his critics claimed, then why were prominent British intellectuals free to express similar thoughts? To Bourassa, the UDC seemed to be relatively well received in Britain, free of the criticisms and threats that he received in Canada. Although this was not in fact the case, especially after the UDC began expanding and holding public meetings in 1915, it never reached the same level of vitriol that Bourassa confronted in Canada.[87] Despite the glorious claims of Canadian supporters of the British Empire, Bourassa saw no evidence that "true British freedom" had made it across the Atlantic.[88]

The UDC argument against the war closely mirrored his own. In both Canada and Britain, supporters of the war claimed that it would not end until the destruction of Germany and the elimination of Prussian militarism. Both the UDC and Bourassa had declared the goal an impossibly idealistic view of continental Europe. Germany would never be destroyed unless the Allied nations – "the champions of superior civilization" – decided to kill every man, woman, and child in Germany. Even if they somehow accomplished that brutal task, militarism would still thrive among the Allied states. These contradictions seemed to be especially relevant to a Canadian audience. The refusal to acknowledge the impossibility of the purpose of the war was the crux of Bourassa's growing opposition. Until Canadians woke up to the "ignorance" and "invincible torpor" of colonialism, they would never truly understand the virtues of British civilization embodied by the UDC and to which the war supporters claimed loyalty.[89]

At least across the Atlantic, dissent could be expressed as writers asked important questions about their country's actions. An article by John

Keating also suggested changing attitudes in Britain toward the war. Keating, editor of the Jesuit periodical *Month,* attacked the rise of "British Bernhardi-ism" and warned of the Allies' failure to examine their own actions in the war.[90] Friedrich von Bernhardi was one of the most famous German authors in the years before 1914. A military historian and Prussian general, he advocated an aggressive, unrestrained foreign policy based upon war to achieve German dominance. His best-known book, *Germany and the Next War,* had been published in 1912, and "Bernhardi-ism" meant unrelenting militarism.[91] Alongside the works of Treitschke and Nietzsche, Bernhardi symbolized the alleged German barbarity that led many among the Allies to believe that Germany had planned the war.[92]

Keating was among them when he wrote that Britain must remember that war was never desirable. As the British people embraced total war against militarism, they could not fall victim to the same "Prussian ideals" that caused militarism.[93] Keating made the same distinction as Bourassa, that war for the sake of war was a faulty and hypocritical doctrine. If British values were lost in the process of defending them, then victory over Germany mattered little. Both Bourassa and Keating asserted that Britain hardly had a moral high ground on which to stand given its record of ignoring international law. It could not ignore its national conscience. Canadians were quick to ask what was wrong with Germany, but Bourassa asked what was wrong with England?[94]

In the late summer, he denounced the rallying call of the Allies, "the war on war," as he returned to the work of the Union of Democratic Control and a recent article by its founder, E.D. Morel.[95] By mid-1915, the group had solidified but faced increasingly oppressive and sometimes violent reactions to their anti-war movement.[96] They worked for the same goal as Pope Benedict XV: to eliminate war. Their war on war – truly against war, not the war proclaimed by the "men of profit and blood" – was a movement to abolish war as an international practice.[97] Bourassa repeated the four points that guided the UDC, emphasizing the third point, which asked for an international organization to settle international disputes. The French Canadian was particularly interested in Morel's references to Canada and the British dominions. Bourassa cited sections of Morel's work explaining that it was now the second time that the former colonies had contributed money, soldiers, and lives to policies that they had had no part in forming (the first being the Boer War of 1899–1901). Morel saw little chance that it would continue. If the British Empire was to be preserved, the British author wrote, then the dominions would no doubt be a part of the peace settlement.[98]

Both the British anti-war group and Bourassa desired an equitable peace and believed that it was possible in spite of the dominant influence of the war. Bourassa accepted the UDC view of the world, though the union couched it in modern terms that seemingly rejected the traditional leaning of the Catholic Church. Morel spoke of "great forces, some measurable, some intangible," drawing "civilised people closer to one another, to accentuate the mutuality of human needs ... The whole tendency of modern development emphasises the interdependence of civilised peoples."[99] Bourassa would have read much the same message in the pope's words: "The equilibrium of the world, and the prosperity and assured tranquillity of nations rest upon mutual benevolence and respect for the rights and dignity of others ... May they resolve from now henceforth to entrust the settlement of their differences, not to the sword's edge, but to reasons of equity and justice."[100] The progress that compelled the UDC vision of British foreign policy and European relations mirrored the worldly Catholic position espoused by Pope Benedict XV. Both desired an end to the "diabolical domination of the capitalists" who profited from a prolonged war – Morel as a left-wing radical, Bourassa as an ultramontane liberal and "utopian corporatist."[101] More than ever Bourassa personified the name given to him by his former mentor, Wilfrid Laurier: castor-rouge, denoting his fusion of conservative and liberal beliefs.[102] The UDC vision of the world inspired Bourassa, and he took heed of Morel's rallying call, "Organise, still Organise, again Organise!"[103] He promised once again that, though they were isolated, the *nationalistes* would do their best.

With that in mind, Bourassa continued his work exploring international affairs for his readers. After Russian defeats in the summer, Germany occupied and reformed the state of Poland in August, though it was ordered that a Hapsburg monarch would rule it at some point in the future.[104] Still, German Chancellor Theobald von Bethman-Hollweg used it as an opportunity to decry Russian behaviour in the region while maintaining that Germany was "a shield of peace, and of the freedom of great and small nations."[105] In reply, British Foreign Minister Sir Edward Grey restated Germany's guilt in invading Belgium, reiterating the Allied war aim of "freedom and safety" from Germany's desire "to control the destiny of all other nations."[106] Nearly a year after the beginning of the war, the belligerents' published war aims were vague, but their public pronouncements allowed commentators some insights into why these nations were involved in the terrible European war.

Bourassa had little time for their posturing. He saw no value in the claims that the belligerents were protecting nations other than themselves. Even Britain, which had declared war in the defence of Belgium, could not justly denounce Germany for controlling other nations. Britain, Bourassa noted, continued to demand naval supremacy across the globe and control of the seas and peoples of its empire.[107] He had once appreciated Grey's suavity in dealing with the July Crisis. A year later he believed the British claim of a just war to be a lie. Both sides were invested in winning the war for their own advantages. The belligerent peoples had been lied to, and Bourassa would believe the words of historian Michael Howard decades later: "The flower of British and French manhood had not flocked to the colours in 1914 to die for the balance of power."[108] Neither the British reply nor the German one spoke to the cause of peace as the pope and Morel had done a few weeks earlier.

Soon Bourassa returned to the issues of nationality at home as he prepared for the court ruling on the legality of Regulation 17. In September, he left for a tour of New England and presented lectures to Franco-Americans. They received him as a "champion of the race." The small North American francophone communities huddled in the American northeast greeted Bourassa with fanfare, decorating automobiles and proclaiming him the great defender of French minorities.[109] After this cheerful interlude, the Supreme Court of Ontario upheld Regulation 17 against the arguments of lawyer and Senator Napoléon-Antoine Belcourt in November.[110]

Belcourt was French Canadian, a former Liberal MP, and appointed to the Senate by Prime Minister Laurier in 1907. He was deeply aware of the division between French Canadians and English Canadians. As a young lawyer, he had established his office across the Ottawa River in Ontario at a time when no French-speaking lawyer practised there. Belcourt married an Irish Catholic woman and, after her death, a Protestant woman. He worked hard to raise his children to be as bilingual as he was.[111] Rising tensions over the issue of French-language schooling in Ontario led Belcourt to become more involved in advocating for Franco-Ontarians, and he had often discussed the need for unity between Canada's two founding peoples.[112] He was the first president of the Association canadienne-française d'éducation de l'Ontario, founded in 1910 after it became clear that Ontario had concerns about the quality of French-language education in the province. When Regulation 17 passed in 1912 to "solve" the "problem" by abolishing bilingual schools, Belcourt was one of the most prominent opponents of this heavy-handed solution.[113] He presented cases before the Appellate Court and Supreme Court of Ontario defending various actions aimed at delaying or overturning Regulation 17. The loss in November 1915 before the Supreme Court left him no choice but to appeal to Britain's Judicial Committee of the Privy Council – then the highest court in the land.[114] The fate of francophones in Ontario would have to wait until the following year, but the deferral of a final decision continued to spark French Canadian dissent among elites, as it had since 1912.

Surprisingly, only a single article detailed Bourassa's response to the ruling. In it, Bourassa reprinted section 133 of the British North America Act, which detailed the bilingual nature of Parliament and the Quebec legislature. To him, this proved that Canada recognized two official languages and thus the right to French education in every province as well as the binational nature of the Canadian federation.[115] He fully agreed with Belcourt's arguments. The *nationaliste* admired the ardent defence of Franco-Ontarians and claimed Belcourt as one of the group's own (despite his Liberal allegiance). Recent scholarship has placed Belcourt in a middle ground between Liberal and *nationaliste* views. Geneviève Richer argues that his fight against Regulation 17 was driven by his belief in "the longevity of French Canadians in Ontario and Canada, Catholicism and national unity."[116] They were similar, certainly, but the vision of the nation proposed by Belcourt was not the one proposed by Bourassa. Still, they remained friends until Belcourt's death in 1932.

The ruling and Bourassa's return home from his visit to the United States invigorated the author. That October he finished his first major publication on the war, *Que devons-nous à l'Angleterre?* (What Do We Owe England?) and prepared for its December release, which was a great success. Bourassa delivered speeches repeating its argument to crowds of Québécois, and at a dollar a book it sold quickly.[117] The work was the culmination of a year and a half of observation during the war and underlined the dangerous consequences of wartime imperialism.

The 420-page book was essentially a history tracing the origins of the "profound and radical" revolution that had transformed the constitution and government of the British Empire.[118] The title echoed numerous articles on the war from September 1914, as well as the celebrated slogan of Premier of Quebec Honoré Mercier more than two decades earlier:

"We owe nothing to England."[119] Using government documents and parliamentary excerpts, Bourassa argued that there was a "solemn contract" that defined Britain's relationship with Canada. Britain alone had the power and responsibility to defend its colonies against foreign powers, while the colonies were obliged only to defend themselves.[120] He cited several moments from 1854 to 1865 that had set this precedent. He began with a dispatch from Governor General Lord Elgin to Secretary of State for the Colonies Sir George Grey during the Crimean War in which Elgin stated that imperial authorities were tasked with protecting the colonies from hostilities "in which they had no share in provoking."[121] That policy was renewed through other treaties and agreements over the next decade and once more during the negotiations on Confederation. Only in the past few decades of Canadian political life, Bourassa argued, had that relationship radically diverged from the national traditions and principles of the past.[122]

In his view, expansion of the British Empire in the last quarter of the nineteenth century matched the emergence of the imperialist ideology that advocated reform of the traditional relationship. In this new empire, colonies helped Britain to maintain its newly enlarged territory while imperialism expressed a "moral obligation" to fight in its wars.[123] Thus, when Prime Minister Laurier stated in 1910 that, "when Britain is at war, Canada is at war,"[124] it revealed how the "imperialist revolution" had transformed a benevolent Britain overseeing an empire into one collective imperial unit. The Great War, Bourassa believed, had completed the revolutionary trend as Canadians eagerly offered sacrifice after sacrifice without compensation.

In the final pages of his analysis, he returned to the war itself and qualified the support that he had offered more than a year earlier. Bourassa reaffirmed that, though Canada had no moral or legal obligation to the British Empire to fight in the war, his statement on 8 September remained true: Canada was "linked to England and France by a thousand ethnic, social, intellectual and economic ties, Canada has a vital interest in the conservation of England and France, in maintaining their prestige, their power and their global action."[125] This time, however, he added an important caveat. He gave his support only if he believed that "the power and global action of France and England remain within their limits and do not, in turn, become a threat to world peace and equilibrium."[126] Of the two, Bourassa now believed that Britain was the most likely to cross that line. Everything that he had witnessed in Canada and Europe since the beginning of the war proved the danger of a British victory or at least its similarity to a German one. The "arrogant brutality of Canadian anglicisers" against French Canadian Catholics, particularly in Ontario, hinted at the dangerous extreme of a British apogee.[127] Still, the French Canadian did not yet fully reject Canadian participation in the war in his December publication. He only outlined the reason why he might do so.

Reaction among supporters of the war was understandably negative. The editor of *Le Canada*, Fernard Rinfret, called the book "unpatriotic and pro-German propaganda" and entirely rejected Bourassa's arguments. Canada, Rinfret argued, had entered the war voluntarily to defend the world, not its own borders.[128] Many other newspapers echoed Rinfret's denunciation. English Canadian papers scoffed at all of Bourassa's dissentious claims. Often their quotations of Bourassa seemed to be so ludicrous (and out of context) that one historian has suggested that they were deliberate attempts to provoke patriotic responses from readers.[129] The *Globe* wrote in a 23 December editorial that Bourassa was playing both the hero and the martyr, and his nationalism "repudiated all the vital claims of the Internationalism of the world ... It is not a principle, it is a pose."[130] Meanwhile, the Kingston *Standard* again called Bourassa a traitor, while others simply decried his "criminal" activities during wartime.[131] Most of his critics' initial reactions focused on his conclusions rather than on his evidence.

The publication of *What Do We Owe England* alarmed his fellow Canadians so much that Chief Censor E.J. Chambers, appointed in June 1915, was flooded with letters demanding that he silence Bourassa. Minister of Justice Charles Dougherty told Chambers that the government was hesitant to censor *Le Devoir* since the order-in-council that had formed the Censor Office was "intended to prohibit publication of facts in the nature of news or information concerning the movement and preparation of the forces, rather than criticism of the policy or administration of His Majesty's Government."[132] Bourassa would be allowed to continue publishing his work despite opposition, but the government was clearly wary of his role on the home front.

His book was undoubtedly historically minded but spoke to the present in which Bourassa wrote. For the ultramontane journalist, history had a divine character. Since God was the ultimate power, what had happened in the past must be the fulfillment of God's will. Sylvie Lacombe argues that Bourassa saw the study of history as paramount to a coherent understanding of present-day affairs. She writes that he believed that by studying history "men can unleash the providential mission that distinguishes their collective existence, and justifies it by its very fact."[133] When Bourassa referred to past events, he imbued them with divine purposes, giving them far more importance than simply reminding his readers that they had once occurred. History was how God's plan for humanity unfolded. Thus, those who ignored history ignored divine providence itself. As a result, Bourassa often offered historical knowledge without context since the fact that something had occurred was proof of its import. Two hundred pages of his book consisted of reprinted excerpts from his sources with select phrases bolded for the reader's attention. His analyses drew quotations from these documents but did not situate them within historical contexts. As a result, the history was focused entirely on explaining the present, not the past. The permanence of the past meant that the events of the present were more important: only in the present could humanity fulfill God's purpose in the future. God had willed historical events, but contemporary ones still allowed for the possibility of conforming to God's desires. This religious urgency lingered throughout Bourassa's work, helping to explain the tenaciousness of his appeals and incomplete historical presentations. Not until 1918 would one of his critics, Louis Georges Desjardins, respond to Bourassa's treatment of history in *What Do We Owe England?* Desjardins criticized Bourassa the historian, writing that no historian would read the sources that he provided and come to the same conclusions. Britain's military did not form with the purpose of world domination, nor had imperialism coalesced around the aim to suppress the colonies of the British Empire.[134] Yet Bourassa's goal was not the same as a historian's goal. Bourassa was an ultramontane Catholic and a journalist, not a historian, and he focused on changing the Canada of his present.

By New Year's Eve 1915, Bourassa was pessimistic. He reflected that "the sun rose in 1915 in a cloud of fire. It sets in a sea of blood."[135] He affirmed that only one voice in the world continued to rise above all of the others from the first turbulent year at war: Pope Benedict XV. To Bourassa, few had been as devoted to the cause of peace as the pope. The folly of the war was wholly apparent to the French Canadian since no side had presented a worthwhile reason for its continuation. Those who perceived the conflict in the same way were rare. Few had pierced "the veil of lies" that stymied the free expression and exchange of ideas.[136]

On the final day of 1915, Bourassa examined some of the advocates of peace in light of the war's terrible consequences. He reproduced the

Christmas message of the British socialist newspaper the *Labour Leader*, noting that it was the most similar to the message of the pope. It demanded that the people of Europe unite against the suffering of all common people. So did the nine-point "minimum program" of The Hague's Peace Conference of Neutral Nations in April 1915.[137] Bourassa noted their demands for annexed people to have the right freely to exercise their own languages, a right that he hoped to see given to the French-speaking "free subjects" of the British Empire in Ontario as well as to Alsatians, Flemings, Walloons, Poles, and Ukrainians. Like the *Labour Leader*, the neutral nations – a grouping of Protestant or non-religious nations (save Catholic Spain) that agreed with the position of the Vatican – were an unlikely source of support. Regardless of their source, Bourassa heralded them as the most reasonable opinions in an unreasonable time.

He welcomed them after what had been a bloody year. Although Europe had yet to witness the slaughter of the Somme or Verdun, the first major Canadian action at Ypres in Belgium had occurred that April. The Germans' use of poisonous gas had shocked Allied soldiers and the home front alike.[138] A committee headed by Viscount James Bryce released its report on "alleged German outrages" in May, publicizing German atrocities in Belgium on the front lines a few weeks after U-boats sank the RMS *Lusitania*.[139] Letters from the front lines were published in newspapers across Canada detailing supposed German crimes against POWs and civilians, as were stories on the execution of British nurse Edith Cavell for supposedly spying on German authorities and aiding Allied soldiers.[140]

By the end of a terrible year, Bourassa was convinced that the compromise he had envisioned at the outset of the war was nearly impossible. That realization led him to a far different conclusion than that of most Canadians. Bourassa knew that the war had become more than a political debate about Canada's imperial ties or the relationship between its French and English populations. His examinations of the words of the pope, the Union of Democratic Control, and others conveyed a much larger picture of the war that underlined how serious its impact could be in Canada. Ultimately, for Bourassa, the year had reaffirmed that if there was one certainty in wartime it was his faith. He believed that God did have a plan for the world that included such atrocities, but human failings twisted the path toward salvation. He strove to convince others to join him on the right path.

The path that God had laid out for the world seemed to be hazardous, but Bourassa believed that it was worth the cost if the voices that desired peace could overcome those that desired war. He did not hear many of them in Canada. A few weeks before his New Year message, the opposition Liberal Party affirmed that, as long as the war continued, the party would "give loyal support to all necessary war measures," though "exercising a vigilant supervision of the conduct of the Government in military and civil matters."[141] Bourassa could not accept such moderation and compromise. To him, the war "[marked] the collapse of the political system elevated by the false wisdom of men, by proud diplomacy, by the thirst for conquests and the pagan cult of gold and brute force."[142] The only feasible solution was destruction of those systems and re-establishment of the moral authority of the pope in world affairs. The pope was far better than the other forces shaping the world in December 1915, which Bourassa listed as German scientific militarism, English mercantile imperialism, the debilitating democracy of the French Revolution, savage mysticism, and the perfidy of pan-slavism.[143] He hoped that the pope's moral authority would continue to draw together those striving for peace. Bourassa found that he could no longer abide by the war supporters' incessant demands, and he found it more and more difficult to support the war in any form. In the coming year, the war would intensify for Canadians once more as the Battle of the Somme raged across the Western Front. Sadly, the war's savagery surpassed that of 1915, and Canadians began to wonder what price would be worth the cost of winning the war. Their answer would not satisfy the *nationaliste*.

4
The Soul of Canada

January–September 1916

IT WAS LESS THAN A MONTH after Bourassa asked in his provocative book what Canada owed England that he formally renounced any support for the war. At the sixth anniversary of the founding of *Le Devoir* on 12 January 1916, before an audience of devoted *nationalistes,* Bourassa delivered an impassioned speech clarifying his position on the war.[1] Once, he told them, he had tried to achieve reconciliation and reach a compromise by offering conditional support for the war. Rather than discuss the concerns of *nationalistes,* however, war supporters had denounced them. They had ignored Canada's legal and constitutional tradition and used the war as an opportunity to impose their vision of Canada on Canadians. Bourassa now promised his followers "a full and sincere confession" and a repudiation of the position that he had outlined in his "so badly treated" article of 8 September 1914.[2] It was time "to entrench in the solid positions of integral nationalism ... It was on this solid ground that we fought our first battles against British imperialism. It is on the same ground that we resist today's panic."[3] The *nationaliste* leader was no longer concerned with convincing Canadians that the war required compromise. The threat to Canada was not Germany, as his critics claimed, but the militaristic imperialism that he saw guiding Canada's war rhetoric. That winter he rallied against its insidious influence.

The complete rejection of imperialism and foreign conflicts marked Bourassa's return to his traditional *nationaliste* perspective, but by early 1916 the movement could not offer a unified perspective on the war. In November 1915, Minister of Militia Sam Hughes had asked Bourassa's lead disciple in the *nationaliste* movement, Armand Lavergne, to help form a new battalion; Lavergne had publicly refused, but then Hughes had extended the offer to Olivar Asselin, who had accepted it.[4] Lavergne, a lieutenant colonel in the militia, explained that army enlistment was faltering. He expected conscription within six months and could not in good conscience abandon his *nationaliste* principles or encourage any Canadian to join the war.[5] Lavergne stood loyally on side with Bourassa, whereas Asselin had grown distant from his de facto leader's position. He had strongly disagreed with Bourassa's acquiescence to Catholic Church support for the war in 1914, and his attacks on the church had not endeared him to Bourassa either.[6] Before joining the army with the rank of major and placed in charge of the 163rd Battalion, Asselin wrote to Lavergne explaining that his loyalty to France and a sense of adventure had led him to accept the offer from Hughes.[7] Bourassa felt betrayed: after Asselin joined the army in December 1915, his name was never to be mentioned in the offices of *Le Devoir* while its editor was present.[8]

Supporting Asselin was Jules Fournier, who had also rejected Bourassa in 1914. Although Fournier remained personally opposed to the war, he found no issue with Asselin's decision to enlist since Fournier had always supported the individual's right to fight in the conflict. Asselin's decision to defend France did not repudiate his *nationaliste* beliefs. His former leader, Bourassa, had not stayed as true to those principles, and Fournier found it outrageous that Bourassa treated Asselin so poorly after supporting the war in 1914.[9] After Bourassa formally rejected it in January 1916, Fournier prepared a response to the *nationaliste* leader in the summer of 1916 that remained unpublished during his lifetime. His wife eventually published the unfinished article, "The Bankruptcy of Nationalism," in 1922 as part of a collection of his writings, four years after he had died from influenza.[10]

Fournier did not accept that Bourassa could support the war while staying true to his nationalist principles. Instead, Fournier argued that in the first sixteen months of the war Bourassa had nominally accepted the principle of Canadian participation, but then he had changed his mind suddenly without prior notice in January 1916. Fournier examined Bourassa's articles from 1914 in detail and condemned the intensive culture of "only" that he found within them.[11] That is, Bourassa always qualified his reasons for supporting the war with other statements. Although he continually declared himself in support of Canadian participation, he also continually found reasons that it was unjust or illogical. "In other words," Fournier wrote, "the intervention, to hear it, seemed to [Bourassa] to be the indisputable 'duty of the hour,' – *only* he could not help but recognize, however, that this enterprise essentially lacked common sense, and that we had every reason in the world to abstain from it."[12] Fournier condemned

Bourassa's inconsistency in offering tacit approval of the war while detailing its problems, and Fournier believed, as the title of his article suggests, that Bourassa had failed the *nationaliste* movement.

Bourassa's return to "the strong positions of integral nationalism" of 12 January was equally problematic. Fournier saw his speech as intellectually dishonest given the reality of his position in 1914. According to him, Bourassa depicted his change in position as occurring after the publication of his 8 September article, so sometime in October 1914, despite never having publicly repudiated the war until January 1916. It also made it seem as if Bourassa had never opposed intervention, only its imperialist character, and that there were two distinct periods when he was for the war and then against it.[13] None of this was true, Fournier argued. Instead, Bourassa had vacillated between being for and against the war, never clearly explaining the contradictions of his position. What his inability to communicate meant to Fournier is unknown – the unfinished article ends there.

The severity of his refutation of Bourassa speaks to the drastic impact of the war on French Canadian *nationalistes*. It was a harsh dissection of Bourassa's failure as a *nationaliste* and leader of the movement. Fournier wrote that Bourassa's "imperative need to display his erudition," "his inability to act," and "his inexperience and disdain for men" explained his inability to achieve his goals after twenty years.[14] "Two things," Fournier concluded, "will always be missing from the nationalist leader's political action: a little human indulgence and human sympathy. He will have missed knowing men, and loving them."[15] Although Armand Lavergne and Omer Héroux stood by Bourassa, the departure of Asselin and Fournier was a grievous blow to the intellectual heart of the movement. By the end of the war, the *nationalistes* were a spent force, and while Quebec nationalists still thrived they did not do so under the leadership of those who had named themselves *nationalistes*.

Bourassa continued to serve as the popularly identified centre of opposition to the war, even as others denounced the validity of his changing views. A few days after the anniversary of *Le Devoir*, his new spirit of opposition emerged in earnest as he reflected on the first British conscription legislation in living memory in comparison to the latest developments in the efforts to fulfill Canadian army commitments.

Across the Atlantic, the British government introduced the "Bachelor Bill," compelling military service for unmarried men between the ages of eighteen and forty-one, amid fierce cabinet debate. British Prime Minister

Herbert Henry Asquith met resistance to the extent and effectiveness of the bill, and the final compromise did not resolve the dispute between advocates and adversaries of conscription. Sir John Simon, the only cabinet minister to resign over conscription, prophetically asked in Parliament on 5 January "does anyone really suppose that once the principle of compulsion has been conceded that you are going to stop here?"[16] Both Simon and the pro-conscriptionists believed that its passing was a partial measure since it included many exemptions, such as for Ireland, married men, and employment of national importance.[17] Britain would indeed require more men and revisit the acrimonious battle over conscription only six months later (and once more in April 1918).

Canada too was searching for more enlistments. The government had increased the size of the army to 150,000 men in July 1915, to 250,000 in late October, and to 500,000 in January 1916.[18] Recruitment turned toward "local" battalions in the last half of 1915, linked to communities and "respected men," spurring the offer from Hughes to Lavergne, with some success.[19] Still, the dramatic increase seemed to make conscription all but certain – at least to historians, as Chris Sharpe noted.[20] In his Speech from the Throne of 13 January, Borden reminded Canadians that 120,000 of them had already crossed the ocean and that the call for more enlistment had been met with "warm enthusiasm." The prime minister addressed the "unabated vigour and varying fortunes" of the war and heralded the "spirit of splendid loyalty and unfaltering devotion, [and] India and the Overseas Dominions have vied with each other in co-operating with the Mother Country."[21] Canada's contribution, justified as necessary to secure a definitive victory, continued to grow in scale.

Bourassa praised the moderation in British policy but saw none in Canadian policy. Canada gave much but received little in return for its service. He was tired of watching the poor political theatre play out in Ottawa compared with what he considered a vigorous debate and measured compromise in the British Isles. Why, Bourassa protested, could Canada not follow the example of Ireland? Delaying the "Home Rule" Bill for Irish autonomy until after the war allowed Irish nationalist politician John Redmond to ask that Irish volunteers only defend Ireland and free British soldiers to fight on the continent. His influence helped to secure Ireland's exemption from British conscription.[22] Bourassa noted that the autonomy of Ireland had given it valuable distance from the imperial war effort. If Ireland had such pressing concerns that it could reject the false principle of "imperial solidarity," then so could Canada.[23]

Bourassa disputed Borden's claim that the dominions and colonies were vying over who could contribute the most or that it was in their best interests to do so. Instead, Canada had sacrificed far more than other parts of the British Empire, and none of the sacrifice had resulted in the sort of allowances Ireland had received.

Meanwhile, the British offered reasoned policies such as the exemption of "employees of national importance" (e.g., munitions factory workers) from conscription. According to Bourassa, the British refusal to conscript from the munitions industry was a clear-headed policy meant to ensure the continued production of armaments for Britain and its allies. "It is hardly believable," he remarked, "that the British government will send more soldiers into the fire than it can properly arm – except the colonials, of course, those good beasts."[24] In the same editorial, Bourassa reminded his readers of Foreign Minister Edward Grey's reluctance to commit to a full blockade of Germany. Britain still allowed neutral goods to flow into Germany, and Bourassa used the British concession as further proof that the war was not about ending militarism but about preserving present and future economic prosperity for Britain and its empire.[25] Destroying the German economy would add little value to British interests after the war – though Britain abandoned protection of neutral shipping rights in February.[26] Bourassa had little time for the "pantomime of political puppets" in Parliament, which had deceived Canadians about the disastrous consequences of the war for too long.[27] Even if there was glory in serving as cannon fodder for the empire, Bourassa saw none in playing "the Orgons and Dandins of the imperial comedy."[28] Dandin and Orgon are references to the work of French playwright Molière, *George Dandin ou le mari confondu*, which follows the tribulations of its insipid, weak-willed, and gullible protagonist Dandin, while Orgon is the foolish adulating character of *Tartuffe* who is blind to imperfections. Bourassa was certain that before the end of the war Canada would know "hard and sterile bitterness" from its leaderless government.[29] The French Canadian's disdain for Parliament and its members grew as Bourassa urged Canadians to stop praising the heroic determination of Britons to sacrifice Canadians for liberty.

His outrage over the Speech from the Throne was quickly surpassed by the next item of parliamentary business in the new year, an extension of the Borden government's term past the five-year limit coming up in 1916. For Bourassa, the discussion on its justification was more damning than the motion itself. Laurier directly attacked the *nationalistes* in a long refutation of their position while justifying the extension. He addressed the motion with an avowal of the Liberal opposition's responsibility to "criticise fairly under all circumstances,"[30] a curious echo of Bourassa's own promise from September 1914, before blaming the *nationalistes* for any crack in national unity. The final decision to prolong Parliament and avoid a wartime election in 1916 passed on 8 February, with both Borden and Laurier offering eloquent approvals of the extension. "It is sought of us," Laurier declared, "not to do away with the control of the Canadian people over this Parliament, but simply to suspend for a short twelve months the verdict of the Canadian people upon Administration, upon its policy, and upon the general questions arising out of the war."[31] Bourassa deplored Laurier's justification that it was only a suspension and not a modification of the Constitution.

To Bourassa, Laurier's comments in January and February amounted to the "senile grudge of a fallen idol."[32] The truth, Bourassa rejoined, was that he and his *nationalistes* had offered to support the war on "the only place where hearts and minds could come together: as a reasonable and effective intervention, proportionate to the country's resources."[33] Although other members of Parliament spoke at length, Bourassa reserved special vitriol for Laurier, listing the many times when the Liberal leader had opposed militarism and imperial involvement as prime minister. If French Canadians were not eager to spill their blood for Britain, Bourassa concluded dryly, it was because of a generation that Laurier had raised and taught. The hypocrisy of the Liberal leader, who once ardently defended Canadian autonomy at least in part if not in full, riled his former follower. Much like Laurier's previous capitulations to "the demands of imperialism" during the Boer War and Naval Crisis, the latest surrender once more ignored "liberal doctrines, and respect for laws and individual freedoms."[34] Here was the crux of Bourassa's condemnation of his former leader. In his mind, Laurier's support for the imperialist war was not so much a rejection of Bourassa's *nationaliste* views as a rejection of liberalism. No true liberal, Bourassa believed, would compromise the country's or the individual's legal and constitutional rights for the sake of war.

Laurier's ability to compromise had always been a source of his political strength – and his weakness. Balancing the concerns of English Canadians and French Canadians while navigating the crises of the Boer War, the Alaskan boundary dispute, and French-language schooling had allowed Laurier to remain prime minister for fifteen years. Yet it was the cause of his downfall in 1911, when Bourassa accused him of being too British, while his Conservative opponents claimed that he was not British enough.[35]

His opponents did not understand historian Blair Neatby's point that, for Laurier, "compromise was a means to an end, not a principle."[36] He sought to achieve Canadian autonomy from Britain in steps, fearing the consequences of the sudden break that Bourassa's *nationalistes* advocated. Moderation led Laurier to support the war in August 1914. By 1916, the Liberal leader still believed that the wartime conditions required flexible liberal principles, especially if the Liberals wanted to win a wartime election while maintaining their control over Quebec.[37] At the same time, he became wary of Bourassa's increasingly belligerent provocations. Bourassa rejected Laurier's compromise as tantamount to betrayal, and Laurier saw in his former student a dangerous narrow-mindedness that focused on the *nationalistes'* ideological goals above all else. "Bourassa is playing with fire," Laurier warned Liberal Senator Raoul Dandurand in January 1915, and "if he thinks that he will be able to extinguish it he may have a rude awakening."[38] Liberal principles meant little if French and English animosity tore the dominion asunder. Laurier's liberalism, notwithstanding Bourassa's criticism, continued to lead his party down a middle path between the extremes of *nationaliste* and imperialist.

As a critic, Bourassa had little consideration for Laurier's concerns as leader of a national party and his role to shepherd its political fortunes. To Bourassa, extending the parliamentary term was proof that the pressures of wartime were drastically transforming Canadian governance for the worse. "In the past five years, we have moved further back on the path to national independence than we have in a century. Parliament's new approach is one more step backwards," he concluded.[39] For a castor-rouge such as Bourassa, any depreciation of law and rights in order to serve the war effort was a grievous mistake. How much further would Parliament go to win the war? "Canada will have to nationalize again, and save its life," Bourassa warned, "or imperialize itself permanently, and commit suicide."[40] The more the nation bound itself to a militarist imperial future, to imperial conflict, and to the needs of the British Empire over the needs of Canada, the weaker the nation would become. Bourassa believed that the laws that safeguarded society could not be casually amended for the sake of convenience. During wartime, when the threat of militarism was even greater, these laws were vital protection for society.

By 1916, both the war supporters and Bourassa were ensnared in the growing intensity of the war, and each side repeated its arguments ad nauseum as the gravity of the war drove each side to extremes. When Prime Minister of Australia William Hughes passed through Canada on his way to the "Mecca of the Empire," London, Bourassa mocked his empty speeches about the fight for freedom and liberty on European battlefields. Bourassa remarked that "this banal ritournelle takes on a taste of bitter irony" given that French Canadians were deprived of their rights in Ontario.[41] The ritournelle is a fast-paced dance from the seventeenth century set to repetitive musical phrases as its introductory musical theme reappears throughout the piece. So too were speeches urging support for the war peppered with repetitive phrases and rhetoric – though Bourassa himself was guilty of playing his own ritournelle. In each editorial, he returned to the themes of government mismanagement, unseeing devotion to the imperial cause, and long-term consequences of Canada's place in the conflict. Often he repeated descriptive phrases. There was little debate between the two sides as they disregarded their opponents' rallying cries as absurd repetitiveness and further deepened the divide between them in a game of political brinkmanship.

His own ritournelle returned to a familiar melody as Bourassa examined the topic of Canada, imperialism, and his national vision for a second major publication on the war. He held a series of six public lectures from 2 March to 6 April for the "Friends of *Le Devoir*." The series was published as *Hier, aujourd'hui, demain* (Yesterday, Today, Tomorrow), a nominal sequel to the book that he had published four months earlier. The lectures first appeared as *Le Devoir* editorials, but the most complete account of his writing was within the book itself. In six sections, Bourassa outlined new thoughts while playing on many of the same themes. He reviewed the history of Canada's colonial autonomy again, highlighting the role of French Canadians and their clergy throughout the process. Once more he condemned the appearance of an alleged "imperialist revolution" on Canadian shores. *Yesterday, Today, Tomorrow* explained to Canadians how the insidious force of the war, militarism, collided with the radical imperialist thought. Despite an ocean between them and the conflict, they were no safer than Europe from the impacts of the war. Yet he made sure to introduce the "solutions of tomorrow," which foresaw a reinvigorated Canada that asked itself whether it stood for peace or war. If it stood for peace, then it could survive the dark clouds under which the world lived.

Yesterday, Today, Tomorrow added to the argument that Bourassa had made in December, further depicting the war as a revolutionary – and imperialist – moment. This time he included in his history of Canadian autonomy a damning indictment of the Quebec Catholic hierarchy. After assessing historical examples of Canadian bishops who protected Canadian autonomy from the control of the British government, such as during the Revolutionary War, the War of 1812, and throughout the nineteenth century, Bourassa contrasted the bishops of yesterday with those of 1916. There was no "episcopal tradition," he wrote, that demanded support for the war or surrender of the right of Canada to be at peace when Britain was at war, directly attacking the claims of Abbé d'Amours in *L'Action sociale* (retitled *L'Action catholique* since 1915). The position of the Quebec bishops against historical tradition was further proof of how "Canada's participation in the current war, *as a British colony*, therefore constitutes a revolution, a profound, radical revolution in Canada's national charter." The bishops were complicit in the transformation and participated in the "work of revolutionaries."[42] Bourassa's encompassing view of the war's "revolution" now included the Quebec bishops alongside Borden's government. Canadian autonomy once might have been possible within a liberal imperial association for its North American dominion, he wrote, but wartime militarism had corrupted British and Canadian imperialists while drawing other societal groups to their cause. All collusion with imperialists now set the country on a dangerous course. Bourassa reminded his readers that "Britain wants to maintain its maritime supremacy, to keep the immense lands it has conquered over the past half century, and to tell the world: '*What we have, we hold.*'"[43] The empire that he portrayed existed not for the sake of its subjects but for the interests of Great Britain and its grip on the world.

This "imperialist revolution" was not inevitable. It was the culmination of more than a century of "good" and "bad" events. Bourassa readily acknowledged the positive benefit of British liberalism and its protection of individual freedom, but he contrasted it with a history of growing colonial domination that continued even after the independence of Canada in 1867. To him, French Canadian *nationalistes* were defending "these rights, traditions, freedoms, and duties" of British liberalism, and "it was at the school of England that we learned to respect, appreciate and love them: they cannot find it wrong or unfair that we jealously defend them."[44] The same British institutions and ideologies had been corrupted by the war. Bourassa worried that Canada at war had no place for the British liberal tenets that guided so many of its citizens (or, for that matter, his Catholic values). His greatest fear was that this militaristic and imperialist revolution would lead to a lasting transformation of Canadian society, one that had no space for the French Canadian people to survive.

Bourassa believed that an imperialist vision of Canada had been wedded to an increasingly militaristic Canadian society that undid the progress and balance of the past half century. In 1916, the subservience of all aspects of Canada's economic, political, and social structures to the needs of the military was both "antisocial and anti-national [and] ... the result pursued by the imperialist revolutionaries," and Bourassa warned that "it is rare that revolutions are not also directed against the social order and national patriotism."[45] The topics that he covered weekly in his editorials, such as the introduction of new taxation, the threat of conscription, and the efforts to quell public dissent, all pointed toward the growing influence of militarism. The militaristic project would not disappear after the war finished and would continue to deform social structures and national identity. The transformation of Canadian society would be permanent and far-reaching. The fear of these consequences – rooted in old concerns about imperialism and nationalism – was now the foundation of Bourassa's war resistance.

Bourassa offered three potential solutions to the problem of rampant militaristic imperialism. "Tomorrow's solutions" were independence, imperial association, and annexation.[46] Canadian independence from the British crown was his preferred solution – albeit one with its own share of familiar dangers. Bourassa feared the threat of war without British protection, but he reasoned that Canadian involvement in imperial wars was just as dangerous.[47] Independence, he mused, might also antagonize Canada's internal conflicts, such as the rivalry between French Canadians and English Canadians, between immigrants and Canadians, and between eastern Canada and western Canada. Yet imperialism surely did not prevent these internal fractures. If anything, its policy of anglicization deepened the separation between Canadians. The best solution to the "problem" of imperialism was independence. Although some believed that "it is something to be part of a great empire," Bourassa told his readers that "there is, for yourself and for others, for peace, freedom, progress and the good balance of the world, 'something' better than 'being part of a great empire': it is to be a nation, even a modest one."[48] However, he decided that independence was an unlikely outcome since only a minority of Canadians supported the idea, and it required far more stability than the country could offer. As he had written in 1901, "the first necessary condition for the independence of a people is to be assured of inner and outer peace."[49]

Instead, Bourassa wrote that it was far more likely that Canada would form some sort of imperial association, "the most logical [outcome] of the abnormal facts created by the imperialist revolution."⁵⁰ At least imperial representation would help to correct the excesses of the militant imperialism that currently reigned in Britain, Canada, and the other colonies. Since his opposition to the Boer War in 1899, Bourassa had long maintained that participation in imperial conflicts deserved Canadian representation in imperial governance, so his cautious endorsement in 1916 was understandable.⁵¹ Its most appealing aspect was the possibility of dissolving the empire eventually. Imperial association would be an invaluable "colonial reform school" that exposed "colonial" Canadians to the larger issues of modern global politics. Perhaps after ten, fifteen, or twenty years the governments and peoples of the colonies would be "prepared to play their role[s] as nations with infinitely more sobriety, wisdom and dignity than they are today."⁵² Although it preserved a connection to Britain and its foreign conflicts, imperial association at least held the promise of further separation. It was a solution that Bourassa could accept, though not one that he could embrace.

The third option was the least desirable result of Canada's national dilemma and not a real solution according to Bourassa. Annexation through a political union with the United States was the natural outcome "of the causes and facts accumulated by our extravagances, and especially by the supreme madness of our deviant participation in the current war."⁵³ Those who championed the British Empire and Canada's limitless participation in the European conflict led Canada down a road of false hope and economic ruin. When Britain emerged from the war weaker and unstable, Bourassa feared that Canadians would naturally turn from an imperial identity to an American one. Increased American immigration and economic integration would begin when the war ended regardless of historical and cultural connections to Europe. The devastated European states would not have the economic power that they once had. Bourassa warned that American supremacy would mean extinguishing an English Canadian identity and destroying the possibility of a Canada that fused French and English together. It was only French Canadians, Bourassa claimed, who could resist American influence with their strong linguistic and religious identity. Although the United States would treat French Canada far better than it was currently treated in Canada, the country as a whole would be weaker.⁵⁴ French Canadians would survive in a North American union, whereas Canada would not.

In the final section of the booklet, Bourassa examined the future of Canadian foreign relations after the war. Regardless of the outcome, he anticipated a shifting international landscape that required an independent Canadian foreign policy removed from its "childish and disastrous colonial mentality, be it English or French."[55] He believed that Canada would be more autonomous and choose its own allies. France and England naturally would still be Canada's greatest supporters, but the country could also form relationships with other European nations. In this new world, the United States and Canada could forge a North American partnership. Together they could defend North America, prosper through economic and political agreements, and keep Canada out of wars.[56]

As long as they had no interest in any sort of imperial relationship with their northern neighbour, the neutral Americans were the ideal partners for postwar Canada. The United States and Canada could resolve the problems that had caused a world war. "The appalling bankruptcy of the old system of alliances, the balance of brutal forces, secret diplomacy, and excessive armaments," had all been justified to "ensure world peace," Bourassa wrote, but in fact had only caused the present war to erupt.[57] The solutions were much the same as those in a Union of Democratic Control pamphlet: a new international system focused on disarmament, the neutrality of all maritime shipping, the publication of all international treaties, the suppression of secret treaties, and the nullification of any agreement made without the assent of a nation's representatives.[58] Ultimately, Bourassa chose the United States as the only nation committed to peace and capable of reforming the international system and a worthwhile future ally for Canada.

If Canada supported this postwar system under American guidance, and reaffirmed its right to neutrality in any war that did not menace its territory, then perhaps it could repair the damage caused by listening to the "apostles of hatred" who dominated wartime discourse. Bourassa envisioned a Canada that added its voice to the "concert of nations that [will decide] the fate of humanity in this war." That Canada would be "free to pursue an ideal of peace, justice, order and true freedom."[59] He rededicated himself to educating the people of Canada to bring about that future. The booklet ends on this optimistic tone for the future, neatly presenting why the journalist confronted the issues raised by the war in *Le Devoir*.

His condemnation of the revolutionary nature of Canada's war experience alongside his vision of the future marked a new depth of criticism. For the first time, Bourassa considered the long-term consequences of the war on Canada's place in the world. Imperialism combined with militarism in Canada led only to ruin. Bourassa confronted the spectre of total war in Canada, experiencing the same "intensity and scope of popular mobilization" that historian Roger Chickering found in Britain and Germany.[60] Terming this transformation a "revolution" was not an act that Bourassa took lightly. For the ultramontane Catholic and French Canadian, social order was intrinsically linked to a stable and modern society. Revolution was a violent process, even if it did not appear as physical violence, and by its nature it caused social turmoil. Previous certainties, such as a political balance between Liberals and Conservatives or Canada's distance from foreign conflicts, were no longer assured. The sudden reactionary change wrought by the war threw the future of Canada into question. Bourassa argued that Canadians already bore witness to small but significant revolutionary transformations induced by the war. If those changes became irreversible, then there was no way that Canada could truly emerge victorious.

Bourassa's potential solutions all pointed to the unsustainability of the war experience. Each connected the Canadian identity to something concrete, either itself, Britain, or the United States. Meanwhile, the "imperialist revolution" bound Canada to an ephemeral identity and the temporary cause of victory in a war that was not its own. Bourassa feared the long-term consequences of that binding. In his ideal world, the same principles and values from before the war would continue to guide Canada. The revolution nurtured new principles, such as unthinking service to the empire, glorification of soldiers, and suppression of dissent. If Britain won the war, Bourassa claimed, then the values that guided the nation during wartime would become permanent. Then the militarism of the imperialists would be the same as the Prussian iteration against which they now fought. The revolutionaries would continue to "use Canada's resources, in men and money, for the glory and benefit of England."[61] He feared that this Canada could not survive. French Canadians would not submit to the militarism and anglicization of this radical imperialism.[62] Canada would emerge from the war politically, economically, and spiritually weakened. Unless Canadians adopted one of his solutions, its national life was at risk.

Strangely, Bourassa's arguments were not that different in tone from those presented in the pages of English Canadian newspapers. There editorials and columns acknowledged the revolutionary impact of the war on the Canadian people. English Canadian papers hailed the war's "purging of materialism and selfishness" and the "virtuous nature of the fight and its salutary influence on Canada."[63] Whereas Bourassa viewed the war's militarism as a corrupting revolutionary influence, English Canada perceived the war as a crucible for positive change. German militarism was a dangerous threat, but it was not the same sort of militarism that appeared in Canada. As one anonymous writer in the *Montreal Star* noted in September 1916, "a patriot ... is one whose bosom swells with pride of his country ... while in a jingo the swelling appears in his head."[64] English Canadian public commentary justified the growing influence of militarism as necessary to defeat Germany, or at least as having potentially positive effects, but Bourassa made no distinction between them. To him, any ideology or circumstance that unevenly valued military endeavours and soldiers was detrimental to the health of Canada's liberal democracy.

Bourassa returned to the international situation in the spring of 1916 after his incisive Canadian analysis. After nearly two years of modern industrialized war, state leaders and diplomats had to envision the resolution of the war and the future that would come of it or risk losing sight of its purpose. On 4 March 1916, Pope Benedict XV wrote to Cardinal Pompilj, the general vicar of Rome, asking the faithful to pray for peace during Lent. The letter added to a wealth of public statements from Rome on the necessity of peace and asked that the belligerent nations declare their "aims and objects" for the war.[65] Bourassa reiterated that Benedict XV alone could outline the conditions "of a true peace, a just, Christian, and lasting peace."[66] Although Bourassa treated politicians with cynicism, he always welcomed words from the Vatican. He translated large parts of the pope's message from 4 March, and it is clear that they drove his own beliefs. One reproduction of the papal missive is telling:

> Throwing Ourself as it were among the belligerents, as a father might do between sons at strife, We have entreated them, in the name of that God Who is Himself Love Infinite, to renounce the purpose of mutual destruction, to declare clearly once for all, whether directly or indirectly, what are the aims and objects of each nation, bearing in mind, as far as is just and practicable, the several national aspirations, but accepting, where need is, for the sake of equal good in the general commonwealth of nations, whatever sacrifice of self-love or selfish interest may be demanded. That was, that is, the only way to calm this monstrous conflict according to the dictates of justice, and to reach a peace profitable not to one alone of the contending parties, but to all, and thus a peace equitable and lasting.[67]

Bourassa's feelings were evident. "What strength! What truth! What justice!" Bourassa wrote, "what deep knowledge of true human politics, founded on divine law!"[68] Benedict XV was a unique figure on the world stage. Bourassa saw in him the authority and influence to bring both sides to the negotiating table, and he gladly embraced the neutrality of the papal position. That neutrality could overcome the powerful allure of militarism that enveloped the warring nations of the world.

The possibility of extreme change wrought by wartime pressure became a reality on 24 April when posters around Dublin proclaimed a provisional government for the Irish Republic. "We declare the right of the people of Ireland to the ownership of Ireland," the posters said, "standing on that fundamental right and again asserting it in arms in the face of the world, we hereby proclaim the Irish Republic as a Sovereign Independent State." The republic claimed the allegiance of all Irish and guaranteed their "religious and civil liberty, equal rights and equal opportunities," and it "resolve[d] to pursue the happiness and prosperity of the whole nation and of all its parts."[69] With that high purpose, the Irish Republic fought for its national life, and the Easter Rising had begun.

The actual fighting of the uprising was short lived, but the British reaction was swift and brutal. The rebels took control of Dublin, though they failed to seize the city's key points. Officers and students at the Officer Training Corps defended Trinity College Dublin against the rebels, while other forces successfully held the centre of British rule in Ireland, Dublin Castle. Nor could the rebels take Dublin's train stations, so the British were able to funnel in troops and easily outnumbered the rebels within a few days. With machine guns and artillery, they slowly pinned down the rebels. Soon artillery shelled the Irish Republic headquarters at the General Post Office, and the total defeat of the rebellion soon followed. On 29 April, after realizing that further resistance would only waste civilian lives, the rebels surrendered to the British authorities, who arrested 3,430 men and 79 women. In May, those who had signed the proclamation announcing the short-lived republic were executed. Some of those whom the British arrested were freed, but 1,480 men were imprisoned for longer terms.[70]

Bourassa offered qualified sympathy to both sides of the nationalist movement in Ireland, empathizing with the politician John Redmond, who had worked within the parliamentary system, as well as understanding the motivation of those Irish Volunteers who had resorted to violence. Bourassa reminded his readers of suspended national aspirations throughout Europe and within Canada. Although he never condoned violence, Bourassa counselled that if French Canadians wanted to understand better what compelled the Irish to extreme action, they only had to reflect on their own history.[71] Redmond could easily be Louis-Hippolyte Lafontaine, the cautious political reformer of the 1830s and 1840s, whereas the Irish Volunteers would be the party of Bourassa's grandfather, Louis-Joseph Papineau, who had led the Lower Canadian rebellions of 1837–38 and wanted political and educational reform. Surely, he noted, the Irish were only standing up for the principles and rights of the Irish people.[72] Bourassa was fully aware of the limited rights of traitors who rose up against the government during wartime, but he rarely missed an opportunity to underline the implicit falsehoods of war rhetoric. The Irish were only seeking the same freedom for which the Allies fought in France and Belgium.

As the Irish rose up in rebellion, Canada's French minority continued their own struggle against perceived English Canadian persecution. Liberal Senator P.A. Choquette addressed an audience on 2 March warning of the impact of Regulation 17 on Quebec sentiments: "These young-blooded fellows may start an agitation to abolish the use of English in the Quebec schools, despite the calmer councils of older men like myself."[73] Meanwhile, Robert Sellar's denigrating work, *The Tragedy of Quebec,* continued to sell well, and Sellar updated the 1916 edition to address Regulation 17. "The issue," he wrote dismissively, "is simply whether this Canada of ours is to be British ... or whether it is to be a mongrel land, with two official languages and rules by a divided authority."[74] Both sides waited on the decision of the Judicial Committee of the Privy Council in London, but until then they were uncompromising in their stance against the other side.

On 9 May, the issue was put to debate before the House of Commons. Liberal MP Erneste Lapointe submitted a resolution asking that during "this time of universal sacrifice and anxiety, when all energies should be concentrated on winning of the War, ... it [be made] clear [to Ontario] that the privilege of the children of French parentage of being taught in their mother tongue be not interfered with."[75] Lapointe made his motion with the support of Laurier, who had become increasingly interested in the plight of Franco-Ontarians over the course of the war. He had offered pragmatic compromises to resolve the issue of French-language education during his tenure as prime minister, but he remained aloof from the Ontario situation until the First World War. On 18 April 1916, however, he wrote to Ontario Liberal leader Newton Rowell: "If the party cannot stand up to the principles [of provincial rights and defending minorities] advocated, maintained and fought for by Mowat and Blake, I can only repeat to you that it is more than time for me to step down and out."[76] His principled position aside, Laurier believed that the Lapointe motion would help him to maintain leadership in Quebec in light of the growing influence of Bourassa and the *nationalistes*. Only Laurier and the Liberals could preserve the fragile unity of the nation.[77] Lapointe's resolution did not (and could not) compel the Ontario government to action, but it officially stated the Liberal position and forced the federal legislature to debate the motion. Laurier threatened to resign if English Canadian Liberals who opposed the motion did not follow the party line. They voted in favour of it, but they resented "the bilingual episode" and would remember it a year later when Laurier again evoked the spectre of preserving national unity over the issue of conscription.[78]

Bourassa welcomed the Liberal motion but believed that it was too moderate. Debates in Parliament underlined how the ongoing dilemma weakened the Canadian war effort. Bourassa would have preferred going in the other direction. He noted two faults with Lapointe's resolution – "the lack of a practical sanction and the untimely coupling of the Ontario issue with Canada's participation in the war."[79] Bourassa himself had linked the Franco-Ontarian question to larger war issues repeatedly, but he argued that when Laurier did the same he should have raised the illegitimacy of fighting for British civilization without finding it at home. The journalist agreed that Regulation 17 negatively affected the war effort but not solely because it threatened national unity – it undermined the justification of the war itself. The government's refusal to intervene proved its disdain for French Canada. Bourassa juxtaposed the intent of the statement with the reality of the province:

> The motion of the Hon. member for Kamouraska [Erneste Lapointe] provided moral support, a public and solemn expression of sympathy from the nation's representatives to the French Canadians of Ontario, to the valiant mothers of families, to the heroic little schoolmasters who defend French civilization against the stupid and cunning hatred of the Toronto Huns ... The great struggle will continue until the final triumph.[80]

The debate solved little since all parties continued their wait for the decision of the Judicial Committee in London, entirely convinced that they were in the right.

In June, Bourassa highlighted two important obstacles that he had encountered during his growing and vocal opposition to the war effort. First, the press consistently muted the voices of those opposed to the war. For instance, the "proponents of total war" interpreted any suggestion of peace in their favour. If a German spoke of peace, then it meant that Germany was weakening. If an Englishman raised the subject of negotiations before Germany was defeated, then he was a traitor. Nuanced discussions of the war were unpopular because they involved questions whose answers defied the rhetoric of the war. Second, the rallying *patriotic* call to support the war was misleading and dangerous. It was not patriotism expressed by the war supporters but loyalism. They asked for absolute loyalty to the British crown and its endeavours. In truth, Bourassa explained, Canadian patriotism had often emerged in conflict with British loyalism. "It was by fighting against imperial authority and its supporters in Canada," he claimed, "that the two races of Canadians had gradually come closer together and began to bond by a common attachment to the Canadian homeland."[81] Patriotism had once unified the Canadian nation, but now loyalism divided its French and English peoples. By muting the voices of patriotic but dissenting Canadians like Bourassa, the country could not possibly hope to resolve the issues raised by the war.

In these turbulent times, after months of repeating his position and exploring its historical and contemporary relevance, Bourassa received a letter from a cousin whom he barely knew, Talbot Mercer Papineau. His cousin asked him to support the war, but he did so by dismissing everything that Bourassa had written about it and mirroring the very grievances that Bourassa had laid out against his critics in June. It was not a good start to a debate about the purpose of the war.

Perhaps they never could have rationally discussed the conflict. Papineau came from a world vastly different from that of Bourassa. The younger Papineau was born into privilege at his family's estate at Montebello. He spent his early years travelling between it and Philadelphia, where his mother belonged to a prominent American family. His father, the grandson of his famous forebear, was an alcoholic and estranged from his mother when Papineau was young, so his American mother raised him near Philadelphia.[82] Despite his English Presbyterian upbringing, he called the French and Catholic province of Quebec home. His family's social and economic status created few worries and many opportunities as he matured. The early years of his life reflected a curious mix of English Canadian, French Canadian, and American cultures. Although Papineau primarily referred to himself as a French Canadian, sometimes he was simply a Canadian – and once he noted that he was "three quarters American."[83] He moved easily between cultures and nationalities. Still, his paternal ancestry forever marked Papineau as a great-grandson of Louis-Joseph Papineau. Immediately identifiable with the prominent French Canadian name, he could not help but be intimately connected to his heritage.

Papineau was wealthy, well connected, and unsure of what to do with his life when Britain declared war in 1914. That August he found himself on the far side of the country, speaking to the Canadian Club in Vancouver on the subject of nationalism in Quebec.[84] He spoke with authority and publicly assured his listeners that "as many French Canadians as English Canadians [would] take up arms in defence of the Empire."[85] With that heartfelt hope, he rushed eastward to fulfill his words and volunteered for the newly formed Princess Patricia's Canadian Light Infantry. Joining as a lieutenant, Papineau hoped to be among the first Canadian soldiers to land in Europe to make a name for himself while furthering his career and public life.[86]

After surviving a year on the front lines and winning a Military Cross, in October 1915 Papineau met with Sir Max Aitken while visiting London. Although not their first encounter, they were impressed with one another, and the connection was a fruitful one. Aitken, the future Lord Beaverbrook, was an influential figure within British and Canadian political circles.[87] He had made millions before moving to England and obtaining a parliamentary seat and knighthood. After the war broke out, Robert Borden appointed him in May 1915 as the Canadian eyewitness to the war, effectively becoming Canada's official record officer.[88] In February 1916, Papineau was promoted to captain and became the aide-de-camp to the Canadian Corps commander, General Sir Edwin Alderson. In June 1916, Papineau joined Aitken's War Records Office as an official eyewitness. This put him in a unique position amassing information on the activities of the Canadian units and writing communiqués released to newspapers around the world. As a result, he travelled extensively across the front lines, visiting with generals and privates and collecting information on every branch of the service. His daily roving gave Papineau the chance to see the breadth of the Canadian experience of the First World War.[89]

In the months before that formative experience, his vision of Canada at war took shape as Papineau confronted the mounting casualties among the Canadians from his perspective on the front lines. In light of Quebec's estrangement from those who supported the war, he wanted to explain his actions to his fellow citizens and elicit their support. As well, he felt obligated to counter the influence of his cousin. To that end, Papineau drafted a letter to Bourassa in March 1916 arguing for greater French Canadian participation in the war effort. The letter is a glimpse not merely of Papineau's political beliefs but also of the life of a soldier on the front lines and a man torn between two cultures.

The great distance between Papineau and Canada elongated the process of finalizing the public letter. Papineau first wrote a draft in March and sent it to his friend and law partner Andrew McMaster in Montreal, requesting that he release it to the newspapers as well. McMaster, when he replied in late April, doubted the value of releasing the letter. He questioned Papineau's intent and noted that the young officer did not realize how much Canada had changed during the war.[90] On 15 July, McMaster sent a revised letter written in English to Bourassa. Not knowing that Bourassa was travelling and had not received it, McMaster assumed that he had no reply and released it to papers across Canada on 28 July. Within a week, the *London Times* published it, and Papineau's name became known throughout the dominion and the empire. Bourassa issued a reply on 2 August in *Le Devoir* to much less domestic and international publicity.

It had been a long and brutal summer for soldiers on the front lines in 1916. The Somme Offensive began on 1 July as hundreds of thousands of British soldiers surged across no man's land. Most failed to meet their objectives. A generation of Newfoundlanders had their worst day of the war when a regiment was devastated at Beaumont-Hamel. At Verdun, the Germans continued to bleed France white as the battle stretched on for months. In the midst of these offensives, Bourassa shared the international spotlight with his cousin. The sparring between them revealed the vast difference between their visions of Quebec and their conceptions of the war.

At best, Papineau's letter was a fervent plea for Canadian unity to the man who was at the heart of its discord, but according to Bourassa it was a misplaced *cri de coeur* that revealed the depth of Papineau's estrangement from the state of affairs in his province.[91] Despite the honest attempt to improve the situation, Bourassa saw an irrelevancy and distance in Papineau's arguments. Papineau was not describing the Quebec experience of the war that Bourassa had known; instead, he was speaking from the battlefields of Europe. He began with the faulty accusation that Bourassa had opposed the war from August 1914 onward. This was an inauspicious start to a letter meant to rouse an enemy to his side. Papineau then faltered again: "I shall not consider the grounds upon which you base your opposition to Canadian participation ... Rather I wish to begin by pointing out some reasons why on the contrary your whole-hearted support might have been expected." Papineau refused to meet his opponent head on, dismissing not only Bourassa's beliefs spanning fifteen years of careful reasoning but also the vast majority of his editorials published in the previous twenty-four months. It became evident that, though Papineau ostensibly wrote to Bourassa, he had not followed his cousin's evolving commentary closely. There is no mention of the pope, or of the British radicals in the Union of Democratic Control, or of numerous other inspirations and guiding forces that Bourassa publicly and repeatedly addressed.

What followed was a list of reasons why the *nationaliste* was wrong and why he had betrayed his compatriots and the civilized world. The argumentation was straightforward. Papineau contended that Canada became a belligerent the moment that Germany declared war on Great Britain, when Canada became "subject to invasion and conquest." It was not a war for Britain but a defensive act to protect its territory. He wrote that "proof may no doubt be made that one of the very purposes of Germany's aggression ... was the ambition to secure a part if not the whole of the English possessions in North America." This was a bold claim for 1916 but not entirely unlikely. The Americans had vigorously defended their Manifest Destiny in the Western hemisphere for almost a century, so the idea that Germany's military might could extend across the ocean was implausible.[92] Yet stories of German agitation in the United States led some to believe that an invasion from the south was possible. Several plots had been widely publicized, including a plan by a group of Germans in the United States to blow up the Welland Canal.[93]

It would be even worse, said Papineau, if the Allies won and Canada did not fight at all. He spoke directly to the self-respect of French Canadians, hoping to shame them into fighting: "What of the Soul of Canada?" How could a nation assured of its "national life" by the actions of English soldiers then refuse to make sacrifices for them in their time of need? That would be a nation without pride. If Bourassa "was truly a nationalist," then he would "recognise this moment as [Canada's] moment of travail and tribulation." A loyal Canadian would fight for his country in this moment of national birth. In Papineau's view, Bourassa's support should stem from this patriotic impulse to defend "Canadian territory and Canadian liberties."

Bourassa's reply repeated his familiar argument that the federal government, the press, and politicians of both parties "applied themselves systematically to obliterate the free character of Canada's intervention." Bourassa became opposed to the war when supporting it no longer became a matter of choice but a matter of "blackmail, intimidation and threats." Surely, the high ideals of British civilization were being eroded as foreign "aliens" were imprisoned, citizens harassed on the streets, and opponents of the war silenced. Censorship and oppression pervaded public life in Canada. Bourassa did not support the war, not because he was a traitor as Papineau implied, but because he was standing by the principles that he had repeatedly expressed before and during the conflict. Canada's involvement in British wars, Bourassa had predicted during the Boer War fifteen years earlier, resigned it to future participation in what Laurier had called the "vortex of European militarism."[94] Inevitably, Bourassa had stated, the Old World would dissolve into conflict, and that would lead to Canada's ruin. "All the nations of Europe are the victims of their own mistakes, of the complacent servility with which they submitted to the dominance of all Imperialists and traders in human flesh," Bourassa insisted in his response.

Papineau argued that a "spiritual union" existed between Great Britain and Canada, one that demanded national responsibility. These bonds "unite [Canadians] for [a] certain great purpose and ... have proved so powerful." To fight the war is "to preserve and perpetuate that invaluable *spirit* which alone makes our union possible." In addition to this connection between Britons and Canadians, Papineau stated, there existed the racial strength of French Canadians that superseded the century-and-a-half-old conquest. A race that survived – and even thrived – under British rule deserved defence. Concessions were inevitable, individuality sacrificed, all so that "the greatest opportunity ... to show unity of purpose" could be fulfilled. This would finally prove that French Canadians loved their country too. The low recruitment numbers in Quebec, Papineau believed, reflected Bourassa's negative influence. Bourassa had built his politics upon "strife and enmity" and brought "disfavour and dishonour upon [his] race" while the "honour of French Canada" and "the unity of [the] country" were at stake. At the least, French Canada's "bond of blood relationship between the Old France and the New [France]" demanded that French Canadians fight.

Bourassa scoffed at the younger man's claims. "His long and diffuse piece of eloquence," he replied, "proves that the excitement of warfare and the distance from home have obliterated in his mind the fundamental realities of his native country." Papineau's words, as grandiose as they might have sounded, reflected a view of Canada and Quebec from an ocean away. Bourassa argued that the recruitment of French Canadians, rather than being unusually low, was merely representative of the higher number of native-born Canadians among them.[95] Those who had lived on their land for centuries were less likely to leave it to fight a European war. English Canadians who volunteered were largely recent immigrants from the United Kingdom, Bourassa maintained, and thus retained more affinity with Scotland or England. He alleged that low recruitment in Quebec stemmed not from one man or even one movement but from "hereditary instincts, social and economic conditions and a national tradition of three centuries."[96] Papineau's inability to comprehend the Quebec that Bourassa knew and nurtured was evident. Papineau represented a French Canadian of a very different sort from his cousin. Not only had he joined the army, but he also defended it. He wrote in English to French Canada. Bourassa's hereditary instincts, social and economic conditions, and a national tradition might be vague categories, but surely Papineau did not fill them.

Papineau closed his letter ominously, and his final flourish revealed a stark difference between him and French Canadians at home. He became the soldier: the one who had seen artillery shells explode friend and enemy alike, the one who had edged his way across no man's land under machine gun fire, the one who fought simply because not to fight was to die. He wrote that "for those who grew fat with the wealth dishonourably gained by political graft and by dishonest business methods at our expense – we shall demand a heavy day of reckoning. We shall inflict upon them the punishment they deserve – not by ... violence ... but by the invincible power of our moral influence." With these threatening words, Papineau delivered his *coup de grâce:* beware the soldiers, for *they* were the "Soul of Canada," and when they returned they would control the country. The war had changed the young Canadian lawyer who had left for Europe in 1914. Its outcome held a deadly significance for him, as did the support of his fellow French Canadians in order to secure victory for the Allies and the soldiers on the front lines. The men in the trenches were going to fight for the Canada that they wanted, not the one envisioned by those living safely on the home front.

Papineau's dire warnings did not faze Bourassa, who saw little truth in them. His reply to Papineau ended with a similar retort: "Those [who have grown fat with the wealth dishonourably gained by war contracts] are not to be found in nationalist ranks: they are all recruited among the noisiest preachers of the holy War waged for 'civilization' against 'barbarity,' for the 'protection of small nations,' for the honour of England and the 'salvation' of France." Bourassa did not worship soldiers simply because of their service or courage. He did not see the soul of Canada within those who fought in a British war. Canada had its own interests and values that ought to be defended. Which people were taking advantage of the war – of the deaths of hundreds of thousands – to improve their own circumstances? Papineau believed them to be the *nationalistes* and Bourassa, using it for their own political machinations. Bourassa believed that imperialists were using it for profit and a means to impart their ideology to Canadians. These viewpoints were not mutually exclusive. Both were rooted in their own experiences of the war, and Bourassa's was supported by years of editorial comment.

The public nature of the letter and its utter failure to engage Bourassa's position on the war help to explain the *nationaliste*'s aggressive condemnation of it. If Papineau had written privately to his cousin to ask whether he "was truly a nationalist" and would "recognise this moment as [Canada's] moment of travail and tribulation," then perhaps Bourassa would have replied more calmly. Publication of his letter, while repeating the same argument that Canada had thrived within the British Empire, not in spite of it, forced Bourassa to respond harshly. In his eagerness to speak to all Canadians, Papineau dismissed all that Bourassa had done to elucidate his perspective on the conflict. "If Canada has become a nation respected and self-respecting," Papineau warned, "she owes it to her citizens who have fought and died in this distant land and not to those self-styled Nationalists who have remained at home." As one of those "self-styled" nationalists, Bourassa believed that he had every right to offer a dissenting view, especially since the federal government, the press, and politicians of both parties had "applied themselves systematically to obliterate the free character of Canada's intervention." Bourassa dismissed Papineau as for the "most part [an] American" who possessed only "the most *denationalised* instincts of his French origin." Papineau was removed from the reality of true Canadian nationalism with little insight to offer on his country's place in the conflict, let alone on Bourassa himself. The *nationaliste* journalist ignored Papineau as yet another sign of the imperialist revolution that threatened the nation.

Although both spoke of Canadian nationalism, they had entirely different understandings of it. Bourassa addressed the points that Papineau raised, such as the purpose of the war, the future of Canada after the conflict, and the role of supporters and dissenters. In some ways, their positions overlapped. Contrasting Papineau's letter with Bourassa's booklet *Yesterday, Today, Tomorrow* is revealing. Both men believed that the war was transformative: Papineau believed that it was creating a stronger Canadian national identity, whereas Bourassa believed that it was fundamentally weakening it in favour of an imperialist one. Both foresaw a new role for Canada after the war linked to the British Empire, though Bourassa preferred other possible outcomes. The key difference between their positions was that Papineau believed that the war was an integral part of Canadian progress toward a more autonomous nation. Bourassa had argued since 1899 that Canada could become its own nation, without British help, spearheaded by its own citizens. The Canada that he envisioned was as united in its national purpose as the Canada that Papineau foresaw, but the war was interrupting that process rather than initiating or intensifying it. At the beginning of the war, perhaps, the cousins would have had more common ground to discuss their ideas, but by the summer of 1916 the chasm between them was insurmountable. Papineau's appeal no longer even dealt with the same basic facts as Bourassa's view of the war. Two entirely different understandings of the war had developed. By the fall, Bourassa was more committed than ever to his ideas. If anything, Papineau had succeeded only in convincing his cousin that his oppositional voice was a necessity if Canada and its French-speaking people were to survive the conflict.

5
The Possibility of Peace

September 1916–Spring 1917

AFTER REJECTING THE IMPASSIONED plea of his cousin Talbot Papineau in August to support the war, Henri Bourassa spent the fall and winter of 1916 examining the possibility of peace. He worked in the shadow of the Somme Offensive, which had begun with a slaughter on 1 July 1916 and finished on an equally bloody note that autumn. In September, Canada's sole French Canadian combat unit, the 22nd Battalion, endured three days of German counterattacks as it successfully held the village of Courcelette.[1] Over the following weeks, Canadian soldiers took more German trench lines at high costs. The last months of autumn resulted in thousands of Canadian casualties. By the end of the Somme Offensive, 24,029 Canadians had been killed or wounded – nearly a quarter of the original strength of the Canadian Corps.[2] The failure of the Allies to achieve progress toward victory, and German successes against Romania and Russia, led the belligerent nations to discuss seriously, for the first time, the possibility of peace.[3]

From his outside perspective, peace seemed to be a distant possibility to the French Canadian in the summer of 1916. The list of those who sought a peaceful end to the conflict remained much the same as the one that Bourassa had outlined eight months prior, in December 1915.[4] The most prominent group was again the British Union of Democratic Control, which, Bourassa observed, every other Canadian press virtually ignored.[5] The UDC was concerned with more than a peaceful end to the war. It outlined the necessary policies that might avoid future conflicts. Its directions were straightforward: no annexations of independent states such as Belgium; reasonable attention given to "oppressed" nationalities such as the Poles, the Alsatians and Lorrainers, or the Slavs within the Austro-Hungarian Empire; international guarantees against war on land and sea; and the creation of an organization that could mediate international disputes.

All of this aligned with the position of Pope Benedict XV and affirmed the wisdom of both positions in Bourassa's eyes. The pope called for an "equitable peace" that avoided laying down the foundations of another war.[6] His position was especially frustrating to Bourassa given that the hierarchy of the Catholic Church in Quebec continued to stand behind the Canadian government. In August, Archbishop Bruchési reminded French Canadians that "there is no doubt as to which side the law and justice are on in this terrible war."[7] Bourassa denounced the faithful who prayed for peace while working for war, which to him was "pure hypocrisy or puerile inconsequence."[8] Even in Germany, where voices in favour of peace were persecuted (as the imprisonment of socialist Karl Liebknecht indicated), they still seemed to be freer than those in Canada. Bourassa noted that the archbishop of Treves could echo the pope's views and condemn the jingoistic press in the *Petrus-Blätter* but without the allegation of treason that the French Canadian faced in Canada. After two years of brutal warfare, Canadian voices calling for peace remained muted except for Bourassa and his supporters.

In September, British Secretary of State for the Colonies Andrew Bonar Law raised the issue of the future of the empire after the war, and Bourassa offered a series of articles communicating his personal response.[9] The series was titled "The Reorganization of the Empire," and he began by quoting Bonar Law's speech on 14 September to the West India Club in London:

> This War, so far as our Dominions are concerned, is being carried on under conditions which never existed in the world before. It required ... an arrangement to work by which one set of men should contribute lives and treasure and have no voice as to the way in which those lives and that treasure are expended. That cannot continue. There must be change.[10]

This seemed to send a clear message that, despite his critics, who always told Bourassa that "now was not the time to speak of such things," the future of Canadian imperial participation was open to debate. The year before, Britain had promised that the dominions would be consulted on the terms of peace.[11] Earlier in 1916, Prime Minister Robert Borden had been invited to the Paris Economic Conference of the Allies, and though he had declined to attend it since it was for "discussion only" it presaged greater dominion involvement in empire affairs.[12] To Bourassa, Bonar Law was taking it a step further and suggesting that the former colonies had the right to some form of independence. "We had no power to compel any one of them to contribute a single penny, or to send a single man," Bourassa quoted from Bonar Law's preface to Max Aitken's *Canada in Flanders*, and "after this war the relations between the great Dominions and the Mother Country can never be the same again."[13] What a contrast, Bourassa noted, from the position of British Prime Minister Herbert Asquith at the 1911 Imperial Conference, at which he had proclaimed "that [imperial] authority cannot be shared."[14] Bourassa decided to explore what the future might hold for Canada and the British Empire and eventually collected his series of commentaries as a booklet under the title *Le problème de l'empire*.[15]

Lionel Curtis was a prominent imperialist intellectual whose book represented the culmination of fifteen years of working toward closer imperial ties across the empire. He had begun his political journey in the midst of the Boer War, in which he was an army messenger. After the conflict, he served as Sir Alfred Milner's assistant imperial secretary in South Africa. Milner famously gathered a group of young imperialists known as "Milner's Kindergarten" who worked to unite the fractured South African colonies. Over the next decade, they helped to fashion a single state from the disparate groups, which came to fruition in 1910. Curtis believed that South Africa was a microcosm of the empire and that their methods could achieve a worldwide imperial union.[16] The resulting movement, the Round Table, was established in 1909, and its members were tasked with setting up local groups throughout the empire and establishing a periodical for the group, aptly titled the *Round Table*.[17] The Great War increased the popularity of the movement, but it was quickly evident that wartime circumstances were changing the relationship between Britain and its dominions faster than the Round Table had foreseen.

In 1915, Curtis published *The Problem of the Commonwealth* to spur debate about the future of the British Empire. He consciously advocated extreme views to provoke debate and analysis.[18] In it, he argued that the dominions had to take control of their defence and foreign policy through an Imperial Parliament – the final step of their journey toward self-government.[19] Much like Bourassa's work, it was rooted in historical research and opinionated pronouncements about the shape of the future empire. Some of the vision presented by Curtis was not well received even among imperialists, such as granting Britain the right to tax its dominion subjects, but it did incite debate.[20] Among its opponents was Bourassa, who nonetheless held a grudging respect for the clear and comprehensive arguments of Curtis.

Curtis was the sort of opponent whom Bourassa wished to see in Canada. His praise for *The Problem of the Commonwealth* was effusive: "It is the most lucid, complete, compact and also the most loyal and *practical* imperialist thesis I have ever read."[21] The first thirty-four pages of Bourassa's book broke down Curtis's thoughts on the future of the empire for his French-speaking readers with his own comments included. His thorough exposition of Curtis's work proved that the nationalist and imperialist agreed on the basic facts of Canada's relationship to the empire. Both writers acknowledged that the national status of Canada was a matter of law. For instance, Britain could not order Canada into a war without the consent of Canadian ministers. Self-government was an integral characteristic of British government, and thus Canada could declare its neutrality in the case of British wars. Nor could Britain demand more support than the colonies were willing to offer in wars that the colonies entered voluntarily. Both affirmed that the current war, in Bourassa's words, was "a radical revolution in the order established by the colonial constitutions." There were only two feasible options as a result of the new relationship: absolute independence or imperial association with the United Kingdom. They both feared the implications of the war's quicker timetable for these outcomes. Clearly, if they had to choose, Bourassa differed from Curtis on which choice was better, but ultimately they agreed with the "national status of the autonomous colonies" in fact and in law, as outlined by the statesmen of Britain and Canada who had shaped the Canadian Constitution.[22]

Bourassa explained that Canadian wartime imperialists had a significantly different perspective on Canada's imperial relationship from that of Curtis, and Bourassa could not align with their views as easily. Although both Curtis and Bourassa believed in the concrete principles of British constitutionalism and democracy that outlined the relationship between its people and their government, Canada's "new school of ultra-imperialist theologians" envisioned those principles in name only, not in practice.[23] Instead, Bourassa claimed, Canada's imperialists opposed democracy and parliamentarianism. The war had only exacerbated the problem because the British government made life and death decisions for Canadian soldiers while being answerable only to the British electorate, not the Canadian one. It was the oppression of one democracy by another, Bourassa declared. Canadians had no way to express disfavour of their foreign policy or the conduct of the war, an action essential to Canada's British-based political system. The "false, revolutionary, [and] anarchic" relationship between Canada and Britain during the war endorsed by the imperialists was unsustainable. Bourassa warned that, if the colonies did not proclaim their independence soon, they would adopt the same negative sentiments of the Americans for their former motherland.[24] According to the logic of the *nationaliste*, the imperialists ought to adopt the views of Curtis if they actually wanted to improve Canada's place in the British Empire. Bourassa, as he had in 1914, believed that Canada at least ought to fight as an equal in such a costly war.

At the crux of his opposition to wartime imperialism was this desire to see Canadians control the decisions that affected their nation. His criticism, especially in the midst of a war that Canada could not leave of its own free will, was concerned with the imperial political system, not the British values themselves. Britain was a champion of many of the democratic and liberal rights that Bourassa supported. However, he did not see those political values reflected in the system that governed the empire and its dominions. He saw the illusion of political freedom hiding Canada's ineffectual control over its own affairs. The freedom of Canada was really just "voluntary servitude," a state even worse than slavery imposed by force. *Nationalistes* demanded change. He wrote that "we preferred national independence, neutrality, and peace. But if it is necessary to wear the uniform of war and help England to police the world, we prefer that it be to responsible partners, rather than under the domestic livery, if it costs us more to *cooperate* than to *serve*."[25] Unlike Curtis, Bourassa no longer believed that the empire could transform itself into a just, equitable system of governance. If he had to live under its constraints, then Canada should be included as an equal partner, as Curtis argued, but that would require that the empire truly represent the liberal values that Bourassa had once admired. In its current form, he saw it only as an agent of conquest, moral domination, and stifling mercantilism rather than a force for peace, progress, order, and a place for the national aspirations of its dominions to prosper.[26] His great fear was that the war seemed to solidify the former system and discourage the growth of the latter. When, Bourassa wondered, will it have changed too much?

That autumn the question of Canadian bilingualism was finally resolved as both the papacy and the Judicial Committee of the Privy Council pronounced their judgments on the case of French-language education in Ontario. Napoléon Belcourt had presented his arguments before the

Judicial Committee in Britain in the summer. He had argued that there was a constitutional right to French-language education and that Regulation 17 caused serious harm to Franco-Ontarians' religious freedom. The Judicial Committee rejected his position and ruled in favour of the Ontario government. Although Regulation 17 was upheld in the October 1916 decision, the Judicial Committee did disallow the takeover of the Ottawa Separate School Board by the province, meaning that French-language education could continue in some form.[27] It was a meagre victory for French Canadians.

A worse moral defeat had occurred a few weeks earlier when Pope Benedict XV sent a letter to Quebec's Cardinal Louis-Nazaire Bégin requesting that French Canadian Catholics moderate their views and accept the decision of the Ontario government. The pope based his comments upon a report by Apostolic Delegate to Canada Archbishop Pellegrino Stagni, who had submitted a report to Vatican authorities that concisely reviewed the situation in Canada to date. He concluded that the bilingual schools question was "not essentially a religious matter" and specifically criticized the Quebec episcopate for interfering in the affairs of Ontario Catholics.[28] Intervention from Catholic clergy on both sides had fuelled the flames of the dispute, and Stagni concluded that "if priests kept themselves completely outside this and similar matters of race the occasions for disagreement among the laity would be much rarer."[29] This report shaped the papal letter, which ultimately asked all Catholics involved to end the conflict and seek compromise because the issue was not a religious one.[30] Bourassa offered no public reply to the papal decision, but he was disappointed. Privately, he admitted that on reading it he had felt "a painful feeling and even a feeling of irritation." He blamed the insidious influence of the imperialists on the Catholic episcopacy, which he believed influenced the pope's view of the Canadian circumstances. His opponents had won the day. The solution, Bourassa explained, was to keep trying to convince the pope of the justness of their cause.[31]

Instead of publicly deliberating on the papal decision, Bourassa looked to the United States for encouraging signs of the state of the world and the future possibility of peace. The re-election of Woodrow Wilson in November affirmed the importance of the Democrats' election slogan "He Kept Us Out of the War." Bourassa dismissed American concerns during the campaign about the electoral influence of "hyphenated Americans" such as German-Americans or Italian-Americans as ridiculous. One might better talk about the influence of hyphenated pro-Allies and pro-Germans, he wrote, welcoming Wilson's return to the White House.[32] Backed by popular support, the president was now in a position to nurture a peaceful resolution to the European war. Bourassa reasoned that, if Wilson "offered his mediation and support to war-torn peoples to help them regain the invaluable benefits that the American people, rightly, did not want to give up, the peace movement would soon become irresistible."[33] Bourassa hoped that Wilson could make some progress on the issue of peace since no one else seemed to be willing to do so. Bourassa was partially right. In December 1916, Wilson became actively involved in defining the terms of a peace treaty – but not before Germany made its own offer.

After two years of warfare, the belligerent nations seriously considered the possibility of peace for the first time in the winter of 1916. Both alliances faced difficult circumstances after the costly Somme Offensive and Battle of Verdun. Austria-Hungary tottered on the edge of collapse, and privately Lord Lansdowne challenged the British cabinet to consider peace.[34] European political leaders were at least willing to contemplate an end to the war to avoid more disastrous stalemates. Germany, as leader of the Central Powers, was the first to issue publicly a formal proposal to enter peace negotiations with the Allies in December, stating that it was spurred "by the desire to stem the flood of blood and to bring the horrors of war to an end."[35] Germany offered to discuss the terms of peace, though it did not go so far as to outline the terms that would satisfy it.

Bourassa approached the prospect of peace with typical self-confidence and intellect. Two days after the announcement, he commented on the timing of Germany's peace offer and the hidden motivation behind it in an article in *Le Devoir* titled "Germany's Approach: Hope for Peace – Probable Obstacles."[36] His careful deconstruction reminded his readers of the recent German victory in Romania and the acquisition of the oil fields there, which put the Germans in a stronger position than the beleaguered Allies. The peace proposal reflected not a new desire to end the war, he noted, but a new belief that a negotiated peace would be beneficial at that time. It made sense that Germany would offer peace when it had the most to gain from it. It was clear to Bourassa that Germany sought to appear "before world opinion as protagonists of peace and to blame their enemies for a total war."[37]

All of this could be a reason to reject the German proposal, but for Bourassa it represented a crucial opportunity. It was the possibility for an honourable and immediate peace. The Allies could take Germany at its word and consider the terms and, if they were not acceptable, reject them. In response, the Allies could offer their own terms, and the neutral countries and opinion of the world could form a reasonable middle ground between the two. Then an agreeable and equitable peace could be fashioned. Only through that process could the "rights of conscience, justice and reason" prevail against the "savage passions."[38] In short, Bourassa did not simply react to the German offer and accept it as a means to end Canada's involvement in a war that he did not support. He honestly examined the proposal and accepted it as a *possible* means to end the war. The German terms should be met openly at least, he argued, for any chance of peace was worth pursuing.

Bourassa's reaction stands as an honest intellectual inquiry about the German peace offer and the best response to it. Within the first few paragraphs of his article, Bourassa accepted and understood the offer as a means to end the war in Germany's favour. Rather than condemning its deceit, he accepted the offer as inevitable and proposed a course of action that allowed for progress. He realized, realistically, that each side would only offer peace to serve its own best interests. Accepting this truth was crucial in moving toward an end to the war.

The patriotic press of English Canada did not recognize this important fact. Consider the headline from the *Globe* on 13 December 1916: "Foe Peace Proposals Accompanied by Threats: Allies Will Continue to Fight for Human Liberty," or its editorial, which declared that accepting the peace was "tantamount to an admission of defeat by the Allied nations ... The Allies cannot sheathe the sword until their ends are accomplished."[39] This perspective reflected English Canadians' belief that the war had become a patriotic conflict requiring a "total Canadian war effort."[40] The majority of English Canadian newspapers emphasized that Canadian triumph would be found in commitment to the war and the justification for it. Although the Canadian press was not monolithic in its coverage, it still clashed greatly with Bourassa, who articulated a significantly different understanding of the war.

He continued his analysis by outlining what he saw as the most significant obstacles to peace. Bourassa named the "advocates of total war" as one of the greatest barriers, though they took different forms among the belligerent nations.[41] He commented briefly on the aristocratic Junkers in Germany and their dwindling influence. As aristocratic power weakened, he argued, German socialists gained prominence. The German peace offer, Bourassa incorrectly believed, was a consequence of the rising calls of German socialists for the end of the war.[42] His appraisal of the German situation spoke to the variety, and weakness, of his sources. Still, they led him to the reasonable belief that diminishing support for total war in Germany had opened a new window of opportunity for peace. Instead, Bourassa believed that the most serious obstacle to peace was Russia. As he had since 1914, when he first echoed the words of Noel Brailsford, he claimed that history would come to see this as a Russian war over Turkish succession, the final struggle between "Slavs and Teutons to scavenge the remains of the Ottoman corpse."[43] The driving force behind the prolongation of the conflict, in his view, was Russian determination to claim Constantinople and to achieve Balkan supremacy, which closely paralleled traditional papal fears regarding the creation of an "Orthodox St. Peter's" by the Orthodox Church.[44]

Bourassa's claims might seem to be exaggerated given what historians now know about the fate of Russia's imperial ambitions and the crumbling czarist regime of 1916–17, but explaining the war as a titanic struggle between German and Slavic peoples must be understood in the context of the previous decades of European history. Since the Russo-Turkish War of 1877–78, the Balkans had been the centre of conflict among Russia, Austria, the Ottomans, and the smaller Balkan nations. The First and Second Balkan Wars had been fought only a few years earlier, in 1912 and 1913. To a contemporary and informed observer of European affairs, such as Bourassa, solving the "Balkans problem" could be one of the final results of the bloodshed on European battlefields. The entire conflict had begun there, and Bourassa argued that it would end there: "If the war continues, if any chance of peace is missed, if millions of English, French, and Canadian soldiers continue to perish in the trenches or survive mutilated, it will be mainly because Russia has not yet achieved its supreme objective: the capture of Constantinople."[45] The seizure of Constantinople would finish the war in the eastern theatre and bring about a Russian victory, an outcome that Bourassa found problematic. Russia was by far the least democratic of the great powers (though its autocratic ruler would be gone a few months later), but it was also the linchpin of Allied victory, serving as a crucial second front against Germany in the east. Still, Bourassa mocked Britain and France for supporting an ally so obviously not interested in liberty, civilization, or progress. To him, the alliance with czarist Russia was impossible to reconcile with Allied claims of fighting for democracy against the German kaiser. As long as Russian success remained an important part of the objectives of the Allies, their war effort would be tainted, and peace would depend on victory in the East as much as the West. For Canadians, such a victory ought to have little value.

Most important, Bourassa noted for his readers, the inability of the belligerent nations to end the war would have a terrible cost for Canada, and that alone should convince them that any peace proposal was worthwhile. Fighting in Europe meant the deaths of tens of thousands of Canadians; ending the war would mean tens of thousands of lives saved. His simplest observation was perhaps the most valid. If the war was solely about saving lives, then it would be over within a day. Clearly, this was not the case. Bourassa wrote in his final line that "the bloody, mutilated, exhausted peoples will eventually listen."[46] His words were an ominous prediction that the obstacles to peace might be too great at the moment, and though peace might come in the future it would come with catastrophic consequences. He worried that Canadians, and all the people of the belligerent nations, would be too slow in recognizing that fact.

The article struck at the centre of the myth of the Allied war effort and at the hearts of many patriotic Canadians. Portraying the war as a political and economic manoeuvre was especially challenging to zealous patriots who claimed moral superiority over their enemies. If Britain fought for wealth and power, and not for civilization and liberty, then it was perhaps not worth the increasing cost. This view of the international system differed from that portrayed in the rest of the Canadian press. Drawing on earlier articles that he had written,[47] Bourassa depicted the war for a scrap of paper and Belgian security as a means to an end, a solution to the problem of rising German dominance that had threatened the British Empire for the past two decades. Belgium, Poland, Serbia, Romania, and Greece were all victims of "the ambition and [the] infamous calculations of their large neighbours, unscrupulous manipulators of the 'European balance.'"[48] The primary tenet of the international system that had maintained relative peace across the continent since the Vienna Congress of 1815 had been the preservation of this "balance of power." The corruption of that balance by the great powers in the twentieth century resulted in more than just the outbreak of the First World War. Bourassa implied that the system, which had once ensured the continuance of European peace, now ensured the continuance of war. The Germans were intent on influencing the small powers of Europe and seeing the scales tip in their favour, while the British and the French were determined to see the opposite. Neither of the great power alliances wanted to see the other benefit from the end of the war. Germany's proposal, a gauntlet thrown down when the balance was so tenuously in its favour, could not and would not be accepted.

Closely following the German peace proposal was a "peace note" released by President Wilson on 18 December 1916. His refusal to enter the war hinged on holding a belief that he could mediate peace between the belligerents as well as having a "manifest duty" to maintain a detachment from European affairs.[49] Wilson, who ran as the man who had "Kept America Out of the War," wanted nothing more than to end the conflict and avoid an increasingly inevitable American entry if it continued.[50] Pacifist organizations in the United States had been asking him to mediate since the beginning of the war, and after defeating Hughes in November 1916 he was finally ready to launch his initiative.[51] His peace note was not a peace proposal. It suggested that the powers involved in the conflict declare their war aims. Wilson proposed that this would allow neutral nations to understand better when and how the war would end.[52] Wilson made it clear that his note, arriving on the heels of the German offer, neither was a response to it nor connected to it in any way. It represented the call of a neutral nation to the warring ones: a call not for peace but for clarity.

Bourassa deconstructed Wilson's note in the same manner as he did the German proposal. In an article titled "Hopes for Peace" in the 27 December 1916 issue of *Le Devoir*, he discussed the significance of the note while echoing many similar themes from the previous weeks.[53] He outlined three important facets of Wilson's effort: "the intrinsic value of the President's note; the favourable reception it receives in peace-loving, neutral or belligerent circles, [and] the violent opposition it receives from demagogues, jingos, and profiteers of the massacre."[54] Each point reinforced Bourassa's personal appraisal of the situation. The president did not compromise his neutrality. Instead, he asked both the Allies and the Central Powers to present their goals for the war and let the world judge them impartially. Wilson was "the voice of the head of the greatest neutral nation" that had "the highest moral authority in the world."[55]

Bourassa argued that the best possibility for peace lay not with the belligerent nations but with neutral intermediaries, such as Switzerland, Holland, and the Scandinavian countries – those best positioned to understand the horrors of the war inflicted on their neighbours. He believed that this granted them the moral influence and opportunity to mediate the conflict. Bourassa assumed that Wilson's call for a statement of war aims meant the mobilization of these neutral powers and the prospect of ending the war. Bourassa had set out the logic behind the self-interest of governments and their reasons for wanting the war to continue. Now he argued that it was in the best interests of the neutral nations that it ended. It was up to them to represent the "general interest of humanity."[56] Bourassa split the political scene into its logical power blocs, separating the interests of the Allies, the Central Powers, and the rest of the world. While those at war sought an end through victory, the neutral powers alone sought an end through negotiation.

To Bourassa, the attack by ardent supporters of the war against those who wished for peace exposed their duplicity as they further abandoned the pretense of a just war. Still, his arguments spiralled close to the ridiculous as he accused the "vampires" of each nation of paying others to support it and terrorizing any who did not agree.[57] After first insisting that the American government gave a material advantage to the Allies in the name of democracy and liberty, "overseas vampires are now making it a crime for [Wilson] to want to end the conflict, a source of unprecedented profits for his own country."[58] Bourassa argued again that the war was about profit and that peace was unattainable as long as corporate and political interests suffered little but gained much. Peace offered justice and alone gave "to nations at war a chance to emerge honourably from [the] conflict before their total exhaustion."[59] With so much at stake, Bourassa wondered how the Allies could think of continuing to fight; even a major defeat was better than total annihilation. Quoting at length from the liberal Manchester *Guardian,* he stated that many Britons were against the war, but their opinion was "unfortunately not very well expressed," and when it was expressed "its interpreters are isolated, powerless, hunted down, and denounced as traitors."[60] As a result, the dominant view became the only view.

Bourassa's religiosity also infused his international political analysis with a moral attitude and supreme confidence.[61] His article on the peace invoked a common refrain in his work since 1914, the moral superiority of Pope Benedict XV. The war would not conclude until the aggressors accepted "the mandatory and necessary sacrifices of self-esteem and special interests," and the peace must not benefit only one of the parties but all of them. "More than ever," Bourassa continued, "[we] have a duty to pray for peace to be restored."[62] His assurance that he spoke of higher truths translated into a ferocious writing style and evocative images when discussing Benedict XV's comments on international affairs.

Yet, as throughout 1914–18, Bourassa's prose appeared to be out of touch with the reality of a nation at war. His deeply held beliefs left little room for compromise; just as with the "jingoists," his was a world of black and white. One either agreed with Bourassa or was his enemy. It is little wonder that English Canada vilified him. After all, he called out the most devoted war supporters as hatemongers with short-sighted minds who, if they could, would have God himself in their armies.[63] A grievous insult in the mind of the Catholic journalist. These were the men and women of Toronto, or Winnipeg, or Victoria. These were his fellow Canadians. His anger might have been justified to him, so fiercely did he hold his opinions, but Bourassa did not earn himself many friends with it. Neither side was willing to admit that the other could be correct within the worldview that it held. His analyses of these peace proposals, as insightful as they might have been, often suffered from the frustration that they revealed. For a man supposedly trying to encourage peace, his tone was decidedly belligerent.

In Quebec, fierce critics of Bourassa deplored his vision of French Canada and the war. That summer Abbé D'Amours had returned to pillory the *nationaliste* in the pages of *La Presse*, the largest French-language newspaper in the country. From July to September, D'Amours, publishing under the pseudonym of "Un Patriote," attacked the *nationaliste* leader and his views on the war, the Catholic Church, and Quebec. Eventually, the articles were collected in a booklet titled *Où allons-nous? (Where Are We Going?).*[64] The abbé rejected the premise of Bourassa's arguments that *nationalisme* was a positive force and that there was an unbreakable link between Canadian nationalism and the state. Bourassa had written time and again that the national interests of Canada demanded careful reflection on the war and, since January, had rejected it entirely in favour of eventual independence. For D'Amours, these arguments were inherently faulty and potentially dangerous.

He examined the "solutions" that Bourassa offered in his booklets from the previous year and believed that they were an unrealistic view of the world. Throughout the work, D'Amours attacked the idea that there was a problem that nationalism and autonomy had to solve. Bourassa's nationalism, which exaggerated the threat of imperialism, was the real problem.[65] D'Amours termed it "egotistical nationalism," a force that separated French Canadians from the Catholic Church by placing the nation above the church in Quebec society.[66] Nor did D'Amours accept Bourassa's belief that a pan-Canadian nationalism was capable of joining

French Canadians and English Canadians. Perhaps in a more homogeneous nation it might have been possible to fashion a worthwhile nationalism, he mused, but in Canada "nationality is still too unstable" and would lead to a disaster.[67] French and English had their differences that demanded separation and non-interference, not unification.

Like other French Canadian supporters of the war, D'Amours argued that the participation of French Canadians was ultimately beneficial for them. If they fought in Britain's war, they fulfilled an agreement that had kept them safe from American assimilation and had sheltered their North American existence for centuries. His argument hinged on his own understanding of patriotism and the duty that it entailed. D'Amours believed that it contradicted nationalism since it demanded that a people submit to their sovereign power, in this case Britain, since Canada was a British territory.[68] Canada had a patriotic duty to support the European war. Likewise, patriotic French Canadians ought to fulfill that obligation so that they might continue to enjoy the benefits of their association with Britain. D'Amours warned of Bourassa's radicalism and its potentially disastrous impact on French and English relations in Canada. If French Canadians wanted to continue benefiting from their partnership with English Canadians, then they ought to demonstrate their commitment to their shared ruler, the British crown, and reject Bourassa.

He paid little attention in the pages of *Le Devoir* to the renewed offensive by D'Amours. It was not until several months later, in December 1916, that Bourassa finally addressed the polemic against the *nationaliste* position, dismissing it in a short editorial just before Germany announced that it was seeking peace. He reminded readers that D'Amours did not represent the views of the Catholic Church – and it was a shame that some might have thought that he did. Otherwise, he was not too concerned. "It is not he who will sing our libera," he wrote, referring to a Catholic hymn sung at a funeral.[69] The *nationalistes* remained strong and confident that they had to oppose the war.

A harsher and more complete response came from L.O. Maillé, a *nationaliste* agitator, who published an answering booklet in January 1917. He condemned the imperialist arguments of D'Amours and the war that they supported. Imperialist actions during the war would long be remembered, Maillé wrote, and "this work of ruin and destruction will bring you eternal shame."[70] England and the Allies were not the paragons of civilization that D'Amours suggested. Look at Ireland, Maillé demanded. Instead of fighting a just war for the betterment of the nation – a war that could not even gather a sufficient number of volunteers – the imperialists went against everything that a free Canada (and a Christian church) represented.[71] The intensity of Maillé's response revealed the widening gap between supporters and dissenters of the war. As conscription loomed on the horizon, each side was honing the arguments that would convince fellow citizens of the necessity of its cause.

Still, conscription was months away. In early 1917, Bourassa remained focused on the Canadian and international war efforts. That January, as Germany restarted unrestricted submarine warfare and the United States swung toward the side of the Allies, Bourassa debated how Canada could contribute to a lasting peace. From 17 to 24 February, he wrote a series of articles to Prime Minister Robert Borden, who had left for London on 12 February to attend the Imperial War Cabinet.[72] In his Speech from the Throne, Borden had declared that the British War Cabinet would consider "urgent questions affecting the prosecution of the war, the possible conditions on which the Allied Nations could assent to its termination, and the problems which would then immediately arise."[73] While Borden was travelling (he arrived only on the 23rd), Bourassa thought it important to suggest how the prime minister should deal with these questions since the members of Parliament had forgone offering any critical perspective. Instead, Parliament had resorted to "the empty and stereotypical phrases that have been around for two and a half years."[74] Bourassa advised that Borden should remember all of those affected by the conditions of peace discussed among the empire's representatives, which included the belligerent nations, the nations of the British Empire, and the people of the world.

What followed echoed much of Bourassa's previous writings, though this time his tone was demure. If Canadians were fighting and dying in a war to free oppressed peoples, to make the world more peaceful, and to safeguard democracy while erasing militarism, then the peace forged by it should take a similar shape. Bourassa wrote that the Allies should avoid demanding territorial and monetary compensation from the Central Powers as terms of peace. Canada and most of the Allied nations had not yet taken any enemy soil, so demands that adjusted European borders should be raised cautiously. As well, the current war was bankrupting all of the participants – what money was there left to demand?[75] It was unlikely that Canada would receive any money, so Borden should not press for financial compensation from the peace. Demanding German colonies was an equally foolhardy endeavour. Again Bourassa highlighted the absence of any benefit for Canada. Annexed territory would belong to the British Empire, certainly not to any of its dominions. Besides, he added, German colonists would only represent yet another group of British subjects who would require assimilation. If Germany lost its colonies, he reasoned, then its emigrants would travel to foreign countries seeking better conditions. Would they come to Canada or the United States seeking better lives, as so many already had? That had not worked out in their favour. German Americans had demonstrated their influence on American affairs in the election when Wilson feared offending them, but in Canada "the concentration camps and the riots in Berlin-Kitchener testify that among these 'excellent Canadians,' the voice of blood is not extinguished."[76] If Borden truly wanted to see a lasting peace, then he would temper the "imperial ambition of Prussian junkerism" but not the "colonial expansion of the German people."[77] Only then would the peace be beneficial to Canada and avoid another conflict. Any end to the war, Bourassa implied, could not be simply a matter of compensating the damage done to the victorious coalition. It had to consider long-term and future international disputes.

The principle of free national expression, which demanded the defence of Belgium in August 1914, had to be defended in the aftermath of the war. There were two ways of envisioning European nationalism, counselled Bourassa. The first stemmed from the natural rights and history of a people. Each group could possess the "key elements" of nationalism: territory, government, laws, and social organization. They should also be given the right to independence.[78] The second, "the true principle of nationalities," according to Bourassa, was the application of God's eternal moral principle to international affairs: "Do not do unto others what you do not want done to you."[79] The pope had already outlined how to consider freedom and nationalities in international affairs. Bourassa quoted Pope Benedict XV's letter of 28 July 1915, on the first anniversary of the outbreak of the war, which clearly outlined the proper behaviour between nations: "Why not from this moment weigh with serene mind the rights and lawful aspirations of the peoples? ... The equilibrium of the world ... and the prosperity and assured tranquillity of nations rest upon mutual benevolence and respect for the rights and the dignity of others."[80] This affirmed that national aspirations were a worthwhile cause for Bourassa and Borden alike and reasserted the authority of Rome and the word of God to guide human affairs. Bourassa was quick to point out who ignored this wise council: the supporters of total war against Germany more interested in imposing their social ideas, their government, and their "superior civilization" on others. There was no guarantee that triumphant but transformed Anglo-French democracies, which Bourassa saw as a mixture of "egalitarianism and plutocratic mercantilism," would be better than Prussian militarism.[81] The only peace worth pursuing had to follow those true principles of national expression. That meant freedom not only for the peoples of the Central Powers, such as Belgium, Serbia, and Montenegro, but also for those of the Allies, such as Ireland, Poland, and Finland. And, implicitly, French Canada within the federation. The peace had to be all or nothing, Bourassa told Borden, or it would not be worth the lives sacrificed for it.

Bourassa then highlighted his fears about the future of the international system, using the familiar example of Russia's desire to control Constantinople to explain the war's prolongation. He repeated the claim to Borden in his next article, reminding the Canadian leader that the conflict meant to secure Russian control over the Dardanelles. "According to what principle of international law or morality," Bourassa asked, "must Canadians shed their blood and money to allow Russia to settle in Constantinople?"[82] None, he answered. A fairer plan would impose "absolute neutrality" on the Bosporus straits and grant control to Greece, which had a better historical basis for ownership than Russia. The impossibility of such a plan, Bourassa wrote, was evident. He quoted the seventeenth-century French poet Jean de La Fontaine to underscore his point: "that since time immemorial / The little ones have suffered from the nonsense of the grown-ups."[83] In a line, Bourassa revealed his concern about the impact of the war on the international system: the weak always suffered at the hands of the powerful.

The Allies had no moral high ground or at least could not claim that they were building a better world than the one wrought by German victory. Imperial ambitions would not disappear at the end of the war, and Russia was as likely to compete against Britain and France for control over the world as Germany had before 1914. Japan also had a precarious position in the alliance. Both Japan and Russia had interests in Asian expansion, and after the war, Bourassa believed, they would come into conflict again, as they had in 1905. Prime Minister Borden, if he truly represented Canadian interests, should inquire into the British position on the future of Asia and the Pacific.[84] If Canada was inexorably linked to British interests, then at least it deserved to be informed about those interests. Of course, Bourassa chided, such questions might be considered too close to the "utilitarian heresy" in which reason triumphed over passion – an approach that Canadian policy had studiously avoided.[85]

Borden's dominant argument raised to justify the Canadian war effort, and perhaps the most compelling, was to champion British democracy against Prussian militarism. Bourassa urged Borden to consider fully the validity of such justifications, translating a quotation from Sir Edward Grey. In a speech in October 1916, "Why Britain Is in the War," Grey stated that "we shall fight until we have established [for all states] ... free development under equal conditions, and each in accordance with its own genius."[86] Grey, along with many supporters of the war, repeatedly argued that they were fighting to preserve some sort of independent democratic character for the nations of Europe. Who was to say that democracy was so much better than any other political system? Democracy, Bourassa emphasized, had initiated invaluable economic and social reforms while stopping the inherent abuse of monarchies, but it had also "caused harm and abuse" of its own.[87] He also asked what sort of democracy should the victors impose on the defeated nations? Should it be the democracy of France? England? Italy? Or the democracy forming in Russia after the tsar devolved power to the Duma (parliament)? Besides, he added, democracy was subverted the moment that some of the Allied nations entered the war because their parliaments or people had not approved their foreign policies.[88] If they were fighting to preserve democracy and replace "autocratic" Europe, then they should take a closer look at their own understanding of it.

If Borden did manage to secure the peace that Bourassa envisaged, then it would be meaningless if another war broke out in the future. Again, he wrote, the goal for the Allies must be not only to end the current war but also to create an international system that would avoid future wars. Even if Europe liberated oppressed nations, resisted imperialist pressure, rejected the alliance system, and preserved the freedom of the seas, the continent could still take the road to war if militarism remained a viable ideology. Bourassa ridiculed the Roman axiom *si vis pacem para bellum* ("if you want peace, prepare for war"). Of all maxims, he wrote, none was "more misleading than this one, so contrary to reason, to simple common sense, to the reality of the facts." "War preparations lead to war," he continued and advised Borden that, "if we want to establish peace, we must work for peace."[89] It was the work of all nations of the world. Surely, not just Prussian militarism had caused the crises of Tunisia and Morocco, or wars in Afghanistan and the Sudan, or the conflict between Russia and Japan.

Militarism was not just about increasing the quantity of guns or dreadnoughts or soldiers. To Bourassa, the greatest threat of militarism was the *mindset* that led nations to believe that they required these larger and larger armies. Armies were necessary – if only to defend against other nations – but their continual expansion was not. According to Bourassa, the "warmongers" sought to focus exclusively on Prussian militarism, for if all militarism was rejected they would lose the source of their "odious profits."[90] The only way that Borden could truly establish a lasting peace was to advocate for the real solution to war: abolishing all forms of militarism.

Accordingly, Bourassa insisted that the peace must address the worldwide and pervasive threat of militarism. The journalist raised the arguments from an American publication, *The Basis for a Durable Peace*, written by future Nobel Laureate and President of Columbia University Nicholas Murray Butler (under the pseudonym "Cosmos").[91] Butler wrote that "one way in which Prussian militarism might emerge victorious ... [was] if the spirit and policies of Prussian militarism should conquer the mind of Great Britain or that of any other allied Power."[92] Bourassa returned to the argument that he had made almost a year prior in *Yesterday, Today, Tomorrow* highlighting the potential for Canada to be "conquered" as Butler feared. It seemed to Bourassa that soldiers had already become a separate caste of Canadian society and were treated differently by its citizens and its laws, a point that his cousin Talbot Papineau had emphasized the year before. Bourassa perceived this as a sure sign of the rising influence of militarism over the past two years of war. Prime Minister Borden should "promise to undo just about everything [that militarism has] done here" and denounce British "navalism" as another form of militarism if he truly sought an end to the German variation of it.[93] The victorious Allies ought to impose the same principles of peace, which demanded the fight against militarism, not just in a defeated Germany but also in Russia, France, Britain, or Canada.

In this somewhat cynical mood, Bourassa witnessed the progression toward the American entry into the war. The resumption of unrestricted submarine warfare in January 1917 made American intervention increasingly likely, while the publication of the Zimmermann telegram in the US press on 1 March shocked the American public. It took the name of German State Secretary for Foreign Affairs Arthur Zimmermann after Germany sent the telegram to the German ambassador in Mexico promising that, if Mexico allied with Germany, it would transfer American territory if the United States entered the war. Previous concerns about the nation's dignity and rights were abstract to the American republic – but Germany's promise of entire states to Mexico (a foreign power invaded by the Americans the year before) suddenly gave the Great War new relevance.[94] President Wilson's inauguration speech on 5 March spoke to his continued commitment to the "principles of a liberated mankind" that the United States stood for "whether in war or in peace." Wilson listed the positions that defined America's view of the world, including the equality of nations, that no peace could rest on an "armed balance of power," that government power derived from those that it governed, the freedom of the seas, and the limitation of armaments.[95] These positions echoed the views of the UDC, the pope, and Bourassa himself and would ostensibly form the basis of the American cause for war.

On 6 April 1917, the United States entered the war on the side of the Allied Powers. It was an extraordinary turn for a country that had been trying to act as mediator a mere four months earlier. Although Bourassa did not want to see the United States go to war, he argued that at least the country would fight the war on a solid moral foundation. Canada could claim no such justification for its role in the conflict. "It's so much easier and more profitable," Bourassa wrote of his own nation, "to follow blindly and howl with the wolves."[96] In his view, the Americans went to war for rational reasons. The Germans left them no other choice. Secretary of State Robert Lansing had pointed out the tenuous nature of the American position in December 1916 after Wilson's peace note. He announced that "the sending of this Note will indicate the possibility of our being forced into the War. That possibility ought to serve as a restraining and sobering force safe-guarding American rights."[97] The Americans were well aware of the probability of renewed German submarine attacks and had offered mediation alongside the ultimatum that, if mediation failed, the United States would go to war. In turn, the Germans had threatened American territory in their message to Mexico. It was a clear reason matched with a clear purpose. Canada, Bourassa lamented, did not share the same clarity in its war effort.

A month after the American declaration of war, Bourassa turned to the subject of the American intervention. He devoted ten editorials to explaining the American declaration. He had spent much time in the United States in the fall and winter of 1916–17. The health of his wife, Joséphine, was failing, and the Bourassas travelled south of the border in the hope that the better climate would help.[98] Direct exposure to American politics allowed Bourassa to follow it much more closely than he had back home in Montreal. During his travels, he read newspapers and discussed the state of the country with Americans. He paid more attention than he otherwise might have to the American election in the fall of 1916, to the peace offers of December, and to the subsequent slide from the United States as the "champion of peace" to "the herald of war." After months of watching the jingoistic press insult and dismiss Wilson the advocate of peace, Bourassa saw the same newspapers herald Wilson the declarer of war as one of the greatest statesman of the age. This shift in American policy deserved explanation. "In all countries," he clarified to his readers, "there are many motives for public opinion."[99] With that in mind, he began a dissection of the complex chronology behind the American republic's entry into the First World War. Like much of his work, it was incisive and informative, but it was also tinged with a tone of lament reflecting the long months that Bourassa had hoped to see the supporters of peace have their voices not only heard but also understood. Their failure and the American intervention seemed to extinguish the best hope for negotiating a peaceful end to the Great War.

From 7 to 19 May, Bourassa outlined his view of the "extraordinary evolution" of American sentiment and international policy. He described the difficulty for the United States in choosing one European coalition over another and painted a picture of the American sentiment on the conflict based upon his personal observations. In July and August 1914, the United States had been as close to Germany as it had been to the Allied nations. President Wilson had noted in his second inaugural address that "we are of the blood of all the nations that are at war."[100] American suspicion of Britain lingered, and autocratic Russia remained an unlikely partner. France, according to Bourassa, was in the middle. The Franco-Americans of New England and Louisiana supported it, but Catholics did not trust its republican anti-clerical state.[101] Neutrality was the natural result of preferring neither side in the conflict.

Bourassa presented a timeline of the American transition from neutrality to war, tracing how the tide of American public opinion turned against the Germans as the war intensified. The violation of Belgian neutrality and France's heroic defence endeared the Allies to the American people. The British blockade pushed Germany toward submarine warfare, which devastated shipping and emphasized German brutality to the public. At the same time, Bourassa claimed, newspaper barons such as J.P. Morgan organized press campaigns that pushed the American people further into the Allied camp.[102] After the sinking of the *Lusitania* in May 1915, American attitudes moved further against the Central Powers. When the champion of American neutrality, Secretary of State William Jennings Bryan, resigned a month later, war seemed to be a likely prospect. Only the German renunciation of unrestricted submarine warfare allayed the fears of Americans and helped to prevent their intervention that summer.[103] The next year the presidential election seemed to indicate the desire of the American people to avoid war since they re-elected Wilson.

At that moment, Bourassa claimed, the possibility of American intervention was uncertain, but a "group of Anglo-American financiers" required an American declaration of war and began actively influencing American policy. They had lent hundreds of millions of dollars to the entente powers that was in danger of defaulting. Only by lifting the embargo against the Allied nations and allowing the financiers to use foreign goods as guarantees could their dire situation be resolved. In November 1916, when the United States seemed to be firmly opposed to intervention, the financiers began a campaign in the newspapers that they controlled to appeal to American sentiment on the necessity of joining the war against Germany – all designed, Bourassa alleged, to preserve their fortunes and the British economy.[104] Wilson's appeal for the conditions of a peace treaty and his attempts to outline an American vision of "peace without victory" were part of the process of clarifying the terms and objectives of an American war effort. Wilson had honestly tried to avoid war, but Bourassa believed that he had no other option. "Rarely," he wrote, "has a head of state shown such a concern for his responsibilities, such a great foresight of the consequences of his actions."[105] The final push occurred in February 1917 when the Russian Revolution tempered the powers of the tsar and introduced democratic government, an important step for the fiercely republican Americans. Now the Allies could present a united front against the autocracies of the German, Austrian, and Ottoman Empires.[106]

Next Bourassa examined the motive and mode of American intervention in the war. Bourassa chose to look at the opinion of President Wilson alone rather than the diverse sentiments expressed by the American people. Bourassa admired much in Wilson's "peace program," but he was unsure about its translation into a "war program."[107] The journalist wondered if Wilson could still achieve "peace without victory." Wilson had distinguished his position as a peacetime observer by his ability to separate the required conditions and the desired conditions of peace. He had recognized the required conditions for a lasting peace, such as freedom of the seas and democratization of governments, while other national concerns, such as settling territorial disputes in Alsace-Lorraine, were simply desired conditions for it. His goals changed after the American intervention. Wilson was now constrained by the conditions of peace that he could expect his new allies and the Central Powers to accept and not those conditions that he hoped to see.[108] The president, Bourassa noted, wanted to address the underlying causes of the war rather than right specific wrongs for one side or the other. It remained to be seen if Wilson could achieve his goals while also fulfilling his new allies' war aims.

Regarding the mode of American intervention, Bourassa saw the war effort that he had demanded for Canada since the beginning of the war. He hoped that the Americans would learn harsh lessons from the previous two and a half years of Allied blunders. Already Congress had begun passing legislation to organize national resources better for the war effort, while Bourassa observed that his own country had bankrupted itself to help the "mother country."[109] American conscription was reasonable and restrained, befitting a nation that had to catch up. In Canada, Bourassa wrote, "it was the triumph of militarism in its most dangerous and dumbest form." In the United States, "it was the subjection of the military organization to the supreme interests of the nation."[110] He was unfair to Canada, which had entered the war at least as unprepared as the Americans in 1917 (if not more so). His ongoing critique of Canadian militarism had focused on legislation and measures intended to secure an adequate Canadian war effort under the pressures of time and manpower, just as the Americans were now undertaking. Yet Bourassa's preliminary comparison of two similar circumstances found Canada wanting. His own bias was clear.

One worrisome aspect of the American war effort was the speed with which it aligned itself with the Allied Powers. Bourassa noted that the American government and financial elite were firmly on side with Britain and France as soon as war was declared. Of the two, France might have been more popular, he wrote, but it was Britain that shaped the American war effort.[111] He warned Americans of the dangers of friendship with Britain. He quoted La Fontaine's translation of the Aesop fable "The Lion's Share." In it, the powerful lion is hunting with a fox, a jackal, and a wolf. They kill a stag and argue about how to split the spoils of their hunt, but the lion, as the most powerful, decides that all of it will be his. "This right," Bourassa quoted, "is the right of the strongest."[112] The United States ought to be careful of its new ally and its interests, which might conflict with its own. The cultural and economic ties between America and Britain were nothing new, but their partnership now shaped the future of the Allied war effort and the world. Their decisions affected everyone, including Canada – for better or for worse.

Finally, Bourassa theorized about the potential result of American intervention in the war. American soldiers could help to shorten or prolong the war depending on the evolving situation in Russia, the army strength and domestic situation of Germany, and the performance of the global economy. A German victory on the eastern front would prolong the war, whereas a defeat there would shorten it considerably. Otherwise, it might push Germany and Austria toward their own revolutions, in which case President Wilson might demand that these new democracies be recognized as new nations. Then Wilson would achieve his vaunted "peace without victory." Regardless of the outcome of the war, the global economic upheaval as nations' economies shifted to war production and accrued billions of dollars of debt and their subsequent shift back to peacetime might make any benefit of the American entry pointless. The war had impoverished the warring nations, and now the United States, the last unaffected bastion of the global economy, had joined their ranks.[113]

Despite his tepid affirmation of the American action, the clearest consequence of American entry to Bourassa was that yet another nation had fallen victim to militarism. It was probable that the American intervention would be beneficial, but war was a dangerous affair. Bourassa pointed to the Russian Revolution in February as demonstrative of how completely social order could dissolve under the pressures of wartime, and he warned that any nation at war could suffer the same fate. "Revolution," he wrote, "is everything; it is the whole social order threatened, it is the canker that devours Europe and the world."[114]

Bourassa was referencing the work of Donoso Cortés, a Spanish-born Catholic diplomat and philosopher who had written *Essays on Catholicism, Liberalism, and Socialism* in the shadow of the 1848 revolutions. Once a liberal, Cortés had renounced his views and published a long series of devotional tracts praising the Catholic Church. He became famous as an anti-liberal Catholic who posited that, when religion was subordinated to the political realm, society and governance inevitably slid toward revolution, atheism, and chaos.[115]

Cortés was a friend of another of Bourassa's intellectual inspirations, the ultramontane writer Louis Veuillot, so it is no surprise that Bourassa had read Cortés.[116] Historian Brian Fox summarizes Cortés's view of mid-nineteenth-century European politics and reveals why Bourassa would have found his writing compelling: "Authority was the moral voice of society and its amalgam of localized points of liberty embedded in various corporate institutions – the primary authority was the Catholic Church."[117] Cortés understood the world much like Bourassa did, though the French Canadian imagined that the fusion of British liberalism and Catholicism functioned so long as the Catholic Church could control the expression of that liberalism. Ultimately, the nineteenth-century thought of Cortés encapsulated Bourassa's own fears of revolution. Cortés counselled that "there [was] no revolution which [did] not involve for society a danger of death," and he warned that "to such a degree is it necessary that all things be in perfect order, that man, though turning everything into disorder, cannot conceive disorder; every revolution, when destroying ancient institutions, rejects them as absurd and injurious; and when substituting others of individual invention, says they constitute excellent order."[118] In his final analysis of the American intervention in the European war, Bourassa saw many of the same dangers that Cortés had discussed in the aftermath of 1848. Societies were not so easily made and remade to the vision of the beholder. Social authority depended on society's belief in it. If the United States wanted to remake the society of nations, then it would have to imbue that new system with the authority to prevent future wars. It was a dangerous gamble. For an ultramontane Catholic, any refashioning of social order was hazardous. Bourassa only hoped that the new international society be baptized in "the waters of eternal truth and unalterable justice [and] international agreements."[119] As he had argued through the winter of 1916–17, papal authority could provide the necessary bulwark for a new international system devoted to peace.

The change from the possibility of peace to the certainty of American intervention saw the French Canadian journalist adopt a bitter tone. In December 1916, when President Wilson released a peace note asking for clear statements of war aims so that, at the least, the world could see what *might* end the war, Bourassa praised the president as a voice of reason amid the cacophony of militarism and false patriotism. By the time of the American entry into the war, Bourassa tried to discuss it in a positive light, but it was clear that the war would not end until there was a clear victory or defeat. The fate of the world was sealed in a sense – the war would be fought to the end. With such hopes and fears in mind, Bourassa turned his critical eye away from the international stage and back toward Canada.

The government proposed legislation for conscription that May, and the coming months would throw him once more into fierce debates about the meaning of patriotism, nationalism, and Canada. Although the international situation seemed to be dismal, Bourassa hoped that he could avert the worst of its impact in his homeland.

6

The Wall of Deceit

Spring–July 1917

THERE HAD BEEN CALLS for conscription in Canada throughout the war, but they reached a fever pitch after Prime Minister Borden doubled the size of the Canadian army in January 1916 from 250,000 to 500,000 soldiers. Faced with faltering enlistment, a group of enterprising Canadians established the National Service League in April to bolster recruitment and pressed Borden to move toward conscription, though he refused since it would be unenforceable with the United States still neutral.[1] Borden and his ministers repeatedly stated that conscription would never come to pass in Canada.[2] By the end of 1916, however, the National Service League sent out cards to Canadians eligible for service asking them to register on a national list if conscription was ever declared.[3] The government hoped that this would encourage enlistment, and in December Borden refused to rule out conscripting new soldiers since privately he had doubts about sustaining the Canadian forces at their current strength with diminishing recruits.[4] By March 1917, the government proposed an alternative to conscription, and Minister of Militia Edward Kemp (who had replaced Sam Hughes in November 1916) launched a campaign to raise 50,000 men for home defence. These soldiers were stationed in Canada as a means of encouraging enlistment without the threat of seeing battle. The government hoped that these men could eventually be convinced to go overseas.[5]

Borden was not in Canada during the months before he introduced conscription. He had left to meet with British officials in February after an invitation in December 1916 to join the Imperial War Cabinet made up of the British War Cabinet and representatives of the dominions. Its goal was to allow the former colonies of the British Empire to discuss the conduct of the war with Britain, ostensibly as equals, and it fulfilled the long-held dream of Canadian imperialists to have an active voice in the affairs of the empire. David Lloyd George replaced Herbert Asquith as prime minister of Great Britain in early December 1916, and he and Lord Milner – the old imperialist from South Africa – had decided to call together the dominion prime ministers.[6] Borden used the Imperial War Cabinet meetings from March to May 1917 to raise the issue of dominion autonomy and, alongside South African General Jan Smuts, helped to write Resolution IX. The now famous resolution asked for an Imperial Conference after hostilities to recognize the dominions as fully "autonomous nations of an Imperial Commonwealth" that had "an adequate voice in foreign policy and in foreign relations." It guaranteed that Canada would gain its autonomy after the war, and Borden's biographer hails it as one of the prime minister's proudest accomplishments.[7] Borden returned home in May enthusiastic about Canada's contributions to the war and its new role within the British Empire.

With Borden away meeting Britain's highest officials and before the announcement of conscription, Bourassa anticipated its consequences for Canadians. He had warned of the perils of conscription throughout the war, and in March 1917 he considered whether national registration and home defence recruitment would lead to conscription. "Will we have conscription?" he asked in *Le Devoir* on 26 March. Bourassa believed that it did not matter. "Conscription ... is merely the extreme way ... to redeem the commitment made by the entire Parliament to devote all of Canada's resources to the 'salvation' of the Empire." Bourassa argued that, since Borden had not consulted the Canadian people before committing more men, for all intents and purposes, a "blood tax" was already levied on the Canadian people.[8] Canada had effectively "conscripted" its resources to fight a war for Britain from the beginning. By 1917, the enormity of the war effort extended to all elements of Canadian society, and conscription of manpower logically followed after committing every other national resource to the war. The House of Commons had supported Canada's contribution "without limits and without reservations," offering no resistance as Borden had expanded the army to some 500,000 soldiers. The attitude of MPs was epitomized for Bourassa in Arthur Meighen's proclamation in 1914 that Canada would bankrupt itself for the empire.[9] No one mentioned conscription over the winter of 1916–17, but it seemed as if the proposed options could not meet the obligations agreed to by Canada's leaders or fulfill the sacrifice that their rhetoric demanded.

Nor were political leaders alone in preparing the way for conscription, at least as far as Bourassa was concerned. The Quebec episcopate had directed the province's Catholics to support the war. For the first time in the country's history, Bourassa wrote once more, the Quebec bishops advised Canada to fight in a European war – but not for the defence of Canada. Their press organ, *L'Action catholique,* championed the war with extraordinary zeal, going so far as to argue that Canada had a legal and moral obligation to come to the aid of Britain.[10] The bishops tacitly accepted the imperialist justification for the war. It followed that, if the religious authorities accepted the necessity of fighting the war, they would also accept any measure that achieved victory. Bourassa rebuked the decision of the bishops and professed his shock that Canada had reached the point where conscription was possible by virtue of their complicity. If conscription came because no one opposed the ideas of militarism, then the silent were to blame.[11] Later it became clear that conscription was one step too far for the Quebec bishops, but Bourassa had no mercy in his condemnation of their actions before its enactment.

He also disagreed with the tepid position of the Liberal Party, against conscription but in favour of the war. Its vocal opposition to conscription could not be reconciled with a Canada that continued to fight. The Liberals had spent the past three years proving that "by Natural Law ... Canada has a moral and even legal obligation to fight for England, even against the will of its citizens," yet now they argued that "Canadians, individually, have the right to avoid this obligation."[12] Yes, under the auspices of a just war, Bourassa admitted, conscription was a legitimate policy, as long as the Canadian government had received the approval of Parliament. The state had every right to compel military service as much as it had asked for voluntary service. Thus, to rationally oppose conscription, only total opposition to the war itself would suffice – if the war was legitimate, then so was conscription. Bourassa believed, however, that the war was simply a vessel for corrupting and chaotic forces. "It is pure demagogy, it is revolt and anarchy," he wrote, and the Liberals had endorsed this total war effort, so conscription was the consequence. Here, as with his depiction of the Catholic Church in Quebec, Bourassa condemned their unthinking devotion without regard for consequence, though his opponents would have seriously disagreed with his characterization of their positions. Bourassa believed that the only way to combat conscription with logic and sincerity was to recognize that the *nation* of Canada had as much right as the individual to decide its level of participation. Only then could a real debate begin on the advantages and disadvantages of national and individual participation. Without admitting one or the other, critics of conscription were accepting the validity of "demagogues" and "politicians in search of popularity."[13]

That March Bourassa predicted that Canadians would see conscription introduced in the House of Commons in one form or another within three months.[14] The government could act to avoid conscription, but he saw little hope of such an effort. He offered an alternative policy; instead of enlarging the army, the government could use more manpower to continue making the vital war materials and supplies that fuelled the Allied forces. It would satisfy Canadian commitments as well as enrich the nation and its people, a goal that both imperialist and nationalist could support. Bourassa was pessimistic about the likelihood that Canada would adopt that approach. He was resigned to the eventual appearance of conscription on the home front, as there were too few voices of dissent to prevent it. "We will only get what we want and deserve," Bourassa acknowledged.[15] This was the total war against which he had spent dozens of front-page editorials detailing, disputing, and rejecting, but his view had too few voices to support it. Without organized and widespread resistance from the people or their governments, the war would continue to transform Canada and all of the belligerent nations.

Only a week after Bourassa's lament, Canadian soldiers engaged in battle on the slopes of Vimy Ridge from 9–12 April 1917. Their success justified for many Canadians all of the sacrifices that Bourassa decried. Although later the battle would take on heroic proportions for Canadians as the birthplace of the Canadian nation, when it occurred in early April 1917 it was just a much-needed and hard-fought victory.[16] As part of the greater Arras Offensive launched by the British Army, the Canadian success at Vimy Ridge was one victory during an operation filled with defeats. The rest of the Allied lines advanced slightly on the first day of the assault on 9 April but stalled after their initial success.[17] Only the Canadian soldiers significantly expanded their front lines and held on to their gains against heavy German counterattacks – but at the cost of more than 10,000 casualties. French newspapers heralded Canada's "Easter Gift to France," and King George V heartily congratulated his Canadian subjects.[18] Prime Minister Robert Borden visited the divisions preparing to launch the attack and the wounded afterward, calling it a "splendid victory."[19] Foreign Secretary Arthur Balfour arrived in Canada on his way to the United States and told Canadians on 21 April that their sacrifice at Ypres and Vimy demonstrated that "you have combined to the utmost of your powers, energy and mercy in your prosecution of the war."[20] This validation of the

Canadian war effort did little to convince Bourassa, whose criticisms had little relation to the definitions of success held by supporters of the war.

If the battle had any impact on Bourassa, he did not discuss it publicly in his column. Soon after the Canadian seizure of Vimy Ridge, though, his arguments warning of the war's militarizing effect on Canadian society turned again to foreboding predictions. "After the War, the Revolution" was the headline of a vitriolic editorial on 23 April. Bourassa repeated his views on the "revolutionary character" of the Canadian intervention. The two major parties colluded as "the instruments of British imperialism and British high finance."[21] He now alleged that Laurier had betrayed his followers and merely pretended to oppose imperialism during his decade and a half as prime minister. Further, the war had thus formalized a hegemonic political alliance between Liberals and Conservatives that had been ongoing since at least 1899, as the party truce in 1914 had demonstrated. Enticed by wealth and power, the journalist maintained, Canada's politicians had endorsed in all but name the imperialist revolution and its dire intent.[22] From his perspective, the victory at Vimy Ridge was little more than a step toward a future that he did not want.

Bourassa refused to let this "revolution" continue unimpeded. He denounced the great illusion of the imperialist revolutionaries and their mistaken belief that "they can blind common sense at will and always disguise the truth under the deception of hollow words and arguments alongside them."[23] Bourassa believed that he saw through their falsehoods. His critics' attack on his commentary revealed the terrible truth of Canada's new revolutionary society, in which the revolution was indistinguishable from the state itself. Thus, any attack on the revolutionary transformation was an attack on the state itself. Denunciations that Bourassa was a traitor only further proved that the state and the revolution were the same. He was criticizing changes not only in Canadian society, but in the state and nation of Canada itself. He saw in the nation at war the same turbulent pendulum of the French Revolution, with its excesses between autocracy and democracy, as an example of what lay ahead for Canada. The only way to avoid it, he pleaded once more, was to join his campaign against the extremes of the Canadian war effort and to reveal the truth of its consequences.

For Bourassa, the worst aspect of the war narrative was that it had seemingly convinced Canadians of its benefits without reflecting on its detriments. They simply accepted the necessity of a war economy, of conscription, and of winning the war at any cost. Bourassa argued that, in accepting these war policies, the people of the Allied nations threatened to overturn centuries of progress in Europe and North America. In the Canadian context, they endangered the partnership of French Canadians and English Canadians crafted at Confederation. These fears had formed the basis of his rejection of expansive and possessive British imperialism since the Boer War, but by 1917 he believed that the war had shifted the balance much further than at any other point in the young nation's history. It might soon be too late to reverse regressive imperialist and militarist ideologies. Bourassa foresaw a new Canada emerging, one defined by the brutal conditions of warfare, not by the compromise of Confederation.[24]

His distress was so great that he veered into the world of outrageous conspiracy theory. The Allies aided the Russian Revolution, Bourassa told his readers, because they were eager to bring the United States into the war and remove the troublesome autocracy.[25] He offered a new version of the causes of the war, rejecting earlier pronouncements that the war was to prevent Russian claims on Constantinople. Instead, all monarchies, including that of the Allies, were targets of a wave of militarized "democracy" that swept the world. "The protagonists of the revolution are the most ardent denunciators of any attempt at peace," he wrote, and "they count on the suffering and exasperation of the popular masses, irritated and bitter by total war, to make their projects prevail." All autocratic nations would eventually succumb to the pressures of wartime and revolutions that followed their inevitable collapse. Bourassa argued that "war democracy" was no better than imperialism; both sought the expansion of European empires, their wealth, and their power. The formation of an imperial republic had been the goal of imperialists for decades, Bourassa alleged, and the war overcame the opposition that once prevented it.[26] As with all conspiracies, a kernel of truth was present here. Imperialists had indeed hoped that the war could change Canada's relationship with Britain, though of course nowhere near the scale of the "revolution" that Bourassa claimed. He offered little evidence – other than the unbridled ferocity of his words – for these opinions presented as facts.

Bourassa outlined the danger of an imperial republic. The British Empire included hundreds of millions of people, stretching from Britain, to Canada, to Australia, to India, to South Africa. If bound together economically and politically, then these peoples would represent the most powerful military and far-reaching economy in the world. Two obstacles had previously stopped this imperial association: one being Canadian autonomy, the other being Britain's traditional monarchy.[27] The British, Bourassa warned, could overturn the British crown by the end of the war. The imperialists would not hesitate to dethrone the king if doing so was necessary "to ensure the triumph of the pluto-democratic army that they have built from mahouts" (Indian servants who rode elephants).[28] He provided British Prime Minister David Lloyd George's support for the new Russian government as proof that the monarchy was no longer sacrosanct. It benefited only the figures pushing for an imperial republic, the true benefactors of the war: the plutocrats, wealthy financiers who produced war armaments and bought political influence from politicians who needed votes. As in all revolutions, it would be the masses who were hurt the most and exploited for their labour and wealth. No one was safe since the war demonstrated that even the highest political and religious offices were not beyond becoming "the instruments and accomplices of the revolution."[29] Amid this horrific future, Bourassa turned forlornly to Pope Benedict XV as a beacon of hope. Only Rome understood the dire situation of the world. Bourassa continued to put his faith in Rome, believing that one day those who refused to endorse the war would be acknowledged as "farsighted patriots" who had remained loyal to the British king.[30] In the meantime, Rome's message of peace was a single light in the darkness.

His late-April series "After the War, the Revolution" was more scornful and alarmist than his previous writing. Bourassa was always evocative to the point of hyperbole and offered passionate arguments meant to stir opinions in his readers, but that spring he took his basic set of assumptions about the war and its impact and pushed it further than a rejection of the war. He outlined a global conspiracy, costing millions of lives and dollars, all to increase the wealth of an elite class. The imperialists were no longer political opponents but extremists who wanted to overturn the international system in favour of the British Empire. His tone became radical, more like that of the far left and the socialists than that of a moderate liberal nationalist, let alone an ultramontane Catholic. The American entry into the war and the Russian Revolution in February drove Bourassa to new heights of suspicion and extreme conclusions. His skepticism had reached a fanatical level, questioning even the basic diplomatic manoeuvres of the great powers as part of a larger and nefarious scheme.

Three days after his return from Europe, Prime Minister Borden announced in Parliament on 17 May that, despite earlier public denials, the government was enacting conscription legislation. It is unclear exactly what caused Borden to change his mind. J.L. Granatstein and J.M. Hitsman, in addition to detailing the failure of national registration and home defence to supplement recruitment, note a letter from Borden to Archbishop Bruchési in Montreal. Borden reflected on his recent European trip: "What I saw and learned ... made me realize how much more critical is the situation of the Allies and much more uncertain is the ultimate result of the great struggle."[31] John English emphasizes cabinet's agreement that conscription was necessary because of lower enlistment, despite the knowledge that it would "kill [the Conservative Party] politically ... for 25 years."[32] Other historians, such as Ramsay Cook and Robert Craig Brown, frame the decision to enact compulsory military service around Borden's recognition that a coalition government, between Liberals and Conservatives, was the best resource for uniting the national war effort. Conscription was introduced as a "radical change in enlistment policy [that had] a catalytic effect on domestic politics by forcing a coalition of those groups who genuinely placed winning the war above every other consideration."[33] One way or the other, conscription was a solution to a problem at a time when few others presented themselves. Regardless, whether faltering enlistments, increasing casualties in the face of renewed pressure for victory (Canadians suffered more than 10,000 casualties at Vimy Ridge), concerns about domestic unity, or a combination of them, Borden's decision to renege on his previous promises forever changed the Canadian nation.

Bourassa addressed the nation that May when he published a series of articles that he eventually released as a pamphlet, *La conscription,* in June. The pamphlet included his writing on conscription in *Le Devoir* from 28 May to 6 June as well as an appendix citing other *nationaliste* statements about conscription and quoting Borden's and Laurier's rejection of conscription from January 1916. Bourassa modified it slightly to consider the issue of a coalition government raised after he had written the articles.

Bourassa hoped that the pamphlet would continue to encourage resistance to conscription and "the sway of imperialism" that drove it.[34] Petitions and written refutations were "infinitely more effective than street demonstrations," he reminded readers as violent demonstrations broke out throughout Quebec to demand that conscription not be passed in the summer of 1917.[35] French Canadians could not afford to forget, he counselled, that they were "the defenders of order and constitution, the guardians of the national tradition and legitimate, popular freedoms." It would do no good to save Canada at the cost of social order. Opposition to conscription had to be "reasonable" and "reasoned."[36] Bourassa did his best to follow his own advice and laid out a rational rejection of the policy. Conscription, he wrote, was not merely unjust but also led Canada closer to bankruptcy as it further hurt the economy. Conscription was an inefficient policy that permanently damaged Canada, which had already contributed more than enough to the war effort. According to Bourassa's calculations, Canada's per capita contribution of men was at least equivalent to that of France and Britain. It was more when Bourassa compared the per capita cost to field each army since Canada paid its soldiers better daily wages.[37] As well, Canada had already spent more than a billion dollars on the war and took on debt at a rate that Bourassa believed made it nearly impossible to pay back.

He speculated that conscription of the remaining able-bodied men would cause more economic hardships. Agricultural production would drop as farmers left their fields, further harming the war effort. Britain did not need Canadian soldiers as much as it needed the bread, meat, and potatoes of Canada.[38] If food production dropped, then famine might cost even more lives. Bourassa stressed that industrial labour was as important as army labour. Munitions, agriculture, lumber, mines, and nearly every Canadian industry helped the Allied war effort in ways far more important than using Canada's soldiers to raise rifles. At least, he pointed out, industrial work was more effective than the cost of equipping and sending them to die on European battlefields.[39] Even if Canada conscripted men to serve in industry rather than the army, there was no proper way to assess the value of every individual to the war effort. The government should focus on the conscription of wealth through war taxes, he argued, but only if they were imposed in proportion to citizens' capacity to pay them. Anyone making a profit from the war deserved to pay a respectively higher tax, for anything else was "unjust, immoral, contrary to social order and economic balance."[40] There must be equal sacrifice of wealth before human life; otherwise, conscription would lead to social unrest and economic ruin.

Bourassa noted that some supporters of conscription argued that the continuing tension between English Canadians and French Canadians was a threat to national unity and that conscription would "fix" an imbalance. French Canadians, they alleged, contributed less to the war effort. Bourassa understandably dismissed such arguments, especially since he was one of the primary instigators of French Canadian apathy (or perhaps rationality, depending on one's perspective) toward the war. Instead, he offered examples of compromise and cooperation between French and English. There had always been a divergence of opinions, sentiments, and aspirations between them, but there should be no expectation that they always had to agree. If anything, their differing cultures and histories had led to inevitable disagreements; however, that difference was reconcilable. After all, he explained, the two peoples had agreed to a constitutional arrangement that satisfied both in forming Canada in 1867. Bourassa emphasized the compact between the "races" of Confederation and its role in shaping the Canadian nation. It outlined the relationship between French and English as well as the nature of the relationship between Canada and Britain. There was no obligation to defend British land, or to fight British wars, only to defend Canada when it was threatened. Since they were equal partners, the French Canadian minority did not share an obligation undertaken by the English Canadian majority.[41] When that compact was upheld, national unity flourished. When it was broken, fractures in unity appeared. Conscription, Bourassa wrote, broke the compact and further deepened the cracks in Canadian consensus.

Part of the problem derived from the lingering connection between English Canada and its former motherland. French Canadians had had only one *patrie* (Canada itself) since they had separated from France centuries ago, whereas English Canadians still clearly identified with their British forebears. Bourassa argued that French Canada's circumstances especially changed as British immigrants had shifted the character of English Canada over the past two decades. So, while French Canadians remained "exclusively Canadian," English Canadian interests divided between their *patrie* and *mère-patrie*.[42] National disunity and a lack of French Canadian support were not results of the differences between the two "races," Bourassa clarified, but derived from a systematic deception of Canadians. He wrote that two errors explained the lack of support for the war in French Canada. First, French Canadian leaders convinced their people to support Canadian entry into the First World War using appeals of loyalty to Britain and France. Those appeals were doomed to fail since they could not transform the French Canadian mentality or temperament, particularly since French Canada had opposed the doctrine of international obligations for more than a century.[43] French Canada could not sustain long-term interest in a British or European war that did not threaten their homes or their people. Second, English Canadians denounced French Canadians for not contributing enough to the war effort and not enrolling with the same enthusiasm. Bourassa warned that this action "[leads to] acrimonious explanations, bitter disappointments and above all very dangerous reactions."[44] Conscription was one more brick in "the wall of deceit that separates them."[45] The construction of this "wall of deceit" had begun long before 1917, but the previous three years of war alongside the acrimonious debate about bilingual schools had expanded it greatly.

According to Bourassa, Canadians across the country opposed conscription. A large portion of 2 million French Canadians certainly rejected it, but he noted growing opposition in English-speaking provinces. Bourassa shared conversations that he had had with English Canadians, who had told him that Canada had done more than enough for the war effort. Even if they were not vocal, their "silent vote" showed that they were opposed to conscription. Thus, he reasoned, foreign powers in Europe drove the political support for the policy, not the will of the Canadian people. This would become clear if Ottawa held a referendum on the issue.[46] Bourassa wrote that, if a majority of the electorate unreservedly accepted conscription, then French Canada might submit to it. A majority of French Canadians and English Canadians could send a clear democratic message. Yet, if all of Quebec rejected the proposal and a parliamentary majority from English-speaking provinces enacted forced military service, then it might result in violence or other extreme reactions. One way or another, a referendum would clearly distinguish the possibilities and the limitations of conscription.

Bourassa returned to his conclusions about foreign influence as he pondered what had caused Borden to renege on his promise not to impose conscription. He proffered three major events from 1917 that might have influenced him: submarine warfare, the Russian Revolution, and American intervention. Each changed the nature of the war for the prime minister, but Bourassa disagreed that it was enough to justify conscription. The threat of submarine warfare and blockade meant that Canada had to commit to more industrial and agricultural production. The revolution in Russia weakened the Allies but did not require Canada to contribute lives to their cause. After all, the American intervention promised thousands more troops and resources than Canada could ever provide, and thousands of their soldiers had already joined the Canadian forces.[47] Yet the American intervention and enactment of a conscription policy meant that, if Canada did not do the same, then "slackers" would have a refuge from the United States to avoid conscription. Bourassa proposed that the real reason Borden had abruptly introduced conscription in Canada was to be consistent with its American neighbour. The declaration of war by President Wilson and the Congress vote on conscription had forced Borden to accede to British demands for more troops. Conscription represented Borden's continued subservience to foreign powers.

In the final part of his analysis, Bourassa reflected on the proposal for a coalition government. Canada required an election before Borden formed a coalition government. Bourassa rejected the legitimacy of the sitting Parliament that had extended its term, in violation of the Constitution, to avoid an election in 1916. An election, with or without a coalition government, also could not be a substitute for a plebiscite on conscription. It was impossible to Bourassa to vote legitimately without a separate referendum.[48] What if a riding had no candidate who supported conscription or vice versa? How could a voter express his (women could not yet vote) democratic voice in favour of or against the proposition? A coalition government restricted the choice of the voter, he proclaimed, and subverted the basic tenets of democracy. Bourassa cautioned that, if Canadians could not cast their votes against conscription in an election (since both Liberal and Conservative candidates might be parts of the coalition in favour of it), then it was undemocratic. Further, taking away democratic rights was an open invitation to insurrection. Without a voice in deciding the future government, he warned, Canadians might resort to violent means to achieve their goals. Bourassa declared that "any coalition of parties, at this time, would be unnecessary, dangerous and immoral ... The current or future parliament must not vote for conscription ... [since] the opinion of the people can only be freely expressed through a plebiscite."[49] Anything else denied the people's right to express themselves.

Wilfrid Laurier had already fashioned his own position on conscription and believed that a referendum was the best compromise between wartime necessity and national unity, but he faced some dissent within his party. There was growing pressure for a coalition government throughout the early months of 1917 and demands that Laurier align himself with the government position. Newspapers and some Liberal politicians demanded a coalition even as Conservatives were suspicious of any question about their party's wartime leadership.[50] After the announcement of conscription, Borden approached Laurier on 25 May about joining a coalition government. Laurier gave no immediate answer and instead took stock of his support among Liberals and the reactions against conscription. Quebec Liberals would not support conscription, and Laurier returned to Borden on 6 June to reject his offer while advocating for a referendum on the issue of forced military service. The delay allowed Laurier to see which Liberals supported conscription, and in turn his referendum proposal forced pro-conscription Liberals to support conscription via plebiscite or to leave the party.[51]

Desire for a referendum and fear about the consequences of imposing conscription shifted Laurier closer to the position of Bourassa. Although Laurier was concerned about the legitimacy of Canadian democracy and its impact on national unity, like his former MP, he was afraid of the growing influence of Bourassa. Writing to Quebec Liberal Premier Lomer Gouin, Laurier explained that, "as to conscription, there can equally be no hesitation. After the agitation which has been carried on upon this subject, if we were to hesitate at this moment, we would hand over the province to the extremists; in place of promoting national unity, it would open up a breach, perhaps fatal."[52] By raising the Liberal banner in Quebec against the imposition of conscription, Laurier provided a way for French Canadians to funnel their dissatisfaction. He believed that he could guide the province on a more balanced path than Bourassa. The result was that, for the first time in nearly a decade and a half, Laurier and Bourassa stood in partial public agreement, and it is worth grouping them as a middle-class elite opposed to more radical protestations.[53]

On 11 June, Borden introduced the conscription bill in Parliament, noting that "it was my strong desire to bring about a union of all parties for the purpose of preventing any such disunion." The bill would not come into effect until after a general election so "that there might be a united effort to fulfill the great national purpose of winning this war ... [and] to throw the full power and effort of Canada into the scale of right, liberty, and justice."[54] Despite Laurier's refusal, Borden still hoped to form a coalition to lead the country, and he appealed to prominent English Canadian Liberals to join him. Throughout June and July, Parliament debated forced military service under the cloud of political division and conflicted loyalties. Former Laurier Cabinet Minister Clifford Sifton, who had left the Laurier government on bad terms a decade earlier, began organizing pro-conscription Liberals to join Borden's coalition government.[55]

Laurier responded with a demonstration of the leadership that had protected his place as Liberal leader for almost three decades. Even as Liberals left to join the pro-conscriptionists, he counselled a loyal English Canadian Liberal: "Do not, however, think hard of them, for I do not. They have behaved all through most honourably, and there is not and there will not be any loss of friendship between us. The pain is not less acute on their side than on mine, and I know only too well the difficulties which faced them."⁵⁶ Despite the divisive national debate about conscription, Laurier tried to preserve a moderate and understanding stance toward his former members. Bourassa, whose fear of conscription was different from Laurier's political concerns, showed no such restraint.

On the fiftieth anniversary of Confederation, Bourassa believed that the war had corrupted the dominion. The Canada that had been created half a century earlier seemed to be far from that which fought the Great War, when its leaders spent the day in the "exaltation of dedication to a foreign cause."⁵⁷ Whereas Prime Minister Borden spoke of how proud the Fathers of Confederation would be to see their country, Bourassa saw little reason to be proud of "a nation immersed in war whose causes, direction, and resolution are totally beyond the immediate control of its government."⁵⁸ It was time for the courage, Bourassa urged, to admit that for twenty years Canada had had no true moral or intellectual progress. Both its public morality and its private morality were debased, its patriotism false, its vision obscured, its sense of order diminished, and the nation and "spiritual matters" were buried under vulgar ambition and vanity.⁵⁹ The pressures of wartime had deformed the nation that had entered the war in 1914.

Bourassa painted a picture of an inchoate and aggressive English Canada against a calm and collected French Canada. He argued that, in much of the effusive praise for Confederation and fifty years of "accomplishments" in Canada, the true voice of French Canada was absent from the boastful claims of government leaders. "The French language," he reminded his readers, "is the language of truth, justice, courage, probity, [and] logic ... Do not invite it [to] pay homage [to the deceivers and fools]."⁶⁰ Bourassa reiterated the cultural divisions between Canadians over the issues of the war. He saw a divide between French and English that was greater than any previous debate within the Canadian federation.

In the battle over conscription, Bourassa was glad to have new allies – at least since the beginning of the war. Alongside Laurier and the Liberal Party, the Quebec bishops also denounced conscription. They had echoed the rallying call to support the war on the premise that there would be no conscription. Archbishop Bruchési felt betrayed by Ottawa's change in policy. He had supported voluntary enlistment, and Borden had promised him that there would never be conscription.⁶¹ The archbishop let the public know of his anger in *L'Action catholique,* in which he rallied journalists to defend the liberties of Catholics.⁶² Bruchési wrote privately to Bourassa admitting that "on conscription I think absolutely like you. And I don't think I lack logic because I accepted Canada's participation in the current war."⁶³ Bourassa replied that he was ready to work with the archbishop against the measure. The French-language press in Quebec almost unanimously opposed the measure, except for *La Patrie*, which attempted to explain the logic of Borden's position.⁶⁴ French Canadian opposition to conscription even extended to Borden's cabinet. Minister of State and Minister of Mines Esioff-Léon Patenaude resigned on 5 June, citing his inability to support conscription since "the proposed law threatens to destroy unity and to give rise throughout the country to deep internal divisions, of long duration, and even detrimental to the needs of the present moment."⁶⁵ As riots erupted in the streets of the province, and as its leaders publicly and privately expressed their deep misgivings, vocal resistance to the war definitively expanded beyond Bourassa's weekly editorials.

A few French-speaking Canadians did support conscription. The most prominent political voice in this vein was that of Conservative Member of Parliament Albert Sévigny. First elected in 1911 as part of Bourassa's "Conservative-*nationalistes*," he subsequently served as deputy speaker and speaker of the House. In 1917, Sévigny became the minister of inland revenue, and as the law at the time dictated he had to run in a by-election in January for the riding of Dorchester. The bitterly contested election was between Sévigny and a vocal opponent of the war under the Liberal banner, Lucien Cannon. Sévigny barely won the riding by 257 votes.⁶⁶ He was one of the few French Canadian Conservatives to campaign actively in favour of conscription alongside the former postmaster general, Lieutenant-Colonel Pierre Blondin. Sévigny accepted Borden's argument that conscription was necessary, and he was prepared, in the words of his biographer, to commit political suicide.⁶⁷ Admittedly, he had reservations about Borden's approach to the issue of conscription in Quebec. Borden's announcement of conscription without talking to Laurier or prominent Quebec politicians proved that the prime minister did not understand the French Canadian mentality.⁶⁸ Still, Sévigny stood by his leader and gave speeches in favour of conscription throughout 1917.

Another pro-conscription voice was that of Ferdinand Roy, a Quebec City lawyer who published a supportive pamphlet in July 1917. It was a moderate, reasoned response to the anti-conscription arguments titled *L'appel aux armes et la réponse canadienne-française* and a direct response to

Bourassa.[69] Roy agreed with many of Bourassa's arguments. He acknowledged the insidious influence of imperialism on French Canadian society and the failure of Canada's political leaders to stem it. However, Roy laid some of the blame for the state of affairs in 1917 at Bourassa's feet. Bourassa was wrong to speak of the war only as Britain's war and to disassociate French Canada from the conflict.[70] Roy questioned the willingness of French Canadians and their clergy to accept Bourassa's portrayal of the home front even as he accepted his right to make those arguments:

> Faith in a prophet who does not have the self-satisfaction and vanity to claim infallibility is not a blind faith, and reason demands that we carefully examine his thesis, which is not a dogma, and to judge whether its doctrine, however logical it may be, or captivating and dangerous it is to our racial hatred, is not based on error.[71]

Roy believed that French Canadians were indeed fighting for themselves, for their French heritage, and all that made them unique. By resorting to violence or resistance, French Canada only tarnished its reputation and left a poor legacy for its children. Would French Canada be content with the shame of refusing to fight and "never raising their heads, humiliating themselves?"[72] Roy argued that, though French Canadians might resist conscription, their duty and honour required them to enlist and fight regardless of the outcome. If they did not, they risked indictment in the court of public opinion and domination by the English Canadian majority that controlled Parliament.[73] Any other reaction to the imposition of conscription led to ruin.

Like Bourassa, Roy asked for a reasonable debate on the issues of the war. He saw in the French Canadian reaction to conscription an unquestioning acceptance of Bourassa's views, in whole or in part. He warned of the dangerous path on which his countrymen trod, asking "do we really want our lines of defence, instead of being in Flanders, to be entrenched in our province?" "We must," he continued, "through actions, through a manifest change in attitude, emerge from the whirlwind of incoherence into which we have been pushed, take root on the solid ground that is there, and no longer let ourselves go, lost, undecided and inert, adrift."[74] Roy discussed anti-militarism, the bastion of Bourassa's own position against the war, but apparently misunderstood his arguments. Roy believed that any anti-militarist sentiments comprised pacifism and that pacifists refused to fight for the defence of Canada.[75] Bourassa was concerned more with the pervasiveness of militarism than with a moral judgment of war itself.

Roy's foray into public commentary is a fascinating glimpse of the mind of a French Canadian opposed to the increasingly dominant narrative fashioned by Bourassa and his supporters. Much of Roy's tone mirrors that of Bourassa. Both believed in the validity of critical thought, in the problem of mass acceptance of a single set of beliefs, and in the dangerous outcome of violent resistance to conscription. Ultimately, Roy concluded, French Canada must join the fight on the assumption that, for Canada to function in the future, there must be respect between its French and English peoples. Quebec ought to fight for its own honour and salvation as much as for Britain or France. The contrast between the two is apparent. Bourassa also highlighted a divide between Canada's peoples in his book on conscription, and he argued that cooperation between Canada's founding peoples was possible only if each side respected the other as an equal. Yet, in his view, English Canada had to respect that French Canada had no stake in the European war, contrary to Roy's interpretation that French Canada had to respect the absolute investment of English Canada in the war. Both wanted to avoid violence, French Canadian subservience, and the rule of incoherent thought, but they offered different means to do so.

It is difficult to gauge the impact of Roy's work, though it was likely minimal. Bourassa never referred to it in his public commentary, and Castell Hopkins of the *Canadian Annual Review* bemoaned its meagre reception compared with anti-conscription writing.[76] Historian Serge Durflinger suggests that even Bourassa was increasingly out of step with the zeitgeist of the Québécois rejection of conscription that summer; however, since the radical speeches in the streets echoed Bourassa's arguments, more work examining their relationship remains to be done.[77] It is fair to conclude that French Canadian attitudes did not change in the way that Roy demanded, nor was there ever widespread support for conscription among French Canadians. In that respect, we can assume that Roy's ideas had minimal impact, and anti-conscription sentiment only grew in the final year of the war. Still, Roy stands as a clear voice proposing an acceptance of conscription not based upon English Canadian or imperialist rhetoric. He did not demand that his fellow French Canadians accept the legitimacy of an English Canadian war effort; rather, he argued that both English Canada and Bourassa had misrepresented the war. Consequently, French Canadians could attach their own meaning to the war. Roy's work was not an ideological polemic as much as an argumentative essay.

Without reference to Roy, Bourassa rejected the premise of his arguments when he succinctly summarized why Canadians opposed conscription in mid-July for the *New York Evening Post*. Americans saw the situation in Quebec as a curious phenomenon, and the New York paper asked Bourassa to submit a piece on conscription, followed by similar articles from Édouard Montpetit, a professor of political economy at Laval University, and Paul-Émile Lamarche, the only loyal Conservative-*nationaliste* MP who had resigned over the issue of bilingual schools in 1916.[78]

Canada's French-speaking peoples, Bourassa wrote, could never accommodate conscription. He listed the reasons why Canada should not adopt conscription: the country had already contributed an impressive amount to the war; any further contribution risked weakening Canada's agricultural production and industry; the country could not shoulder any greater economic cost; conscription threatened Canada's political independence; and finally it would create disunion and strife for the country and the continent.[79] Conscription, Bourassa maintained, was not in Canada's national interest but continued to serve the imperial interests of the British Empire and its European war. If Canada had an international obligation, then it was to strive for a peaceful resolution to the conflict and to preserve the international system, not to witness its systematic degradation. Conscription, he warned, could create "a second Mexico north of the 45th and 49th parallels," a relevant if somewhat exaggerated warning for American readers.[80] Bourassa saw no value in the cooperation for which Roy advocated since conscription meant domination, oppression, and violent reaction.

As the Military Service Bill worked its way through Parliament that July, Bourassa followed the debates closely. In his view, none of Canada's parliamentarians raised the question of how conscription would affect national interests or Canadian citizens. Bourassa's narrow vision of national interest likely did not include interests raised by the House of Commons debate. For instance, there was a long discussion on the specific phrasing of how exemptions would be granted on the basis of "national interest." Solicitor General Arthur Meighen explained that MPs were basing it on the British legislation stating that national interest should be "construed broadly. It covered not only services which minister directly to the prosecution of the war, but also services which were essential to the country at the present time."[81] Liberals pressed the government on its somewhat ambiguous definition of national interest and its fair application. MPs mentioned national unity often. Both sides of the House of Commons raised the spectre of national unity in light of conscription many times during the final month of the debate. Laurier argued that the government's introduction of conscription had committed the "greatest possible injury" to coalition government and national unity. "There is something more important even than the [coalition government] which [Borden] has sought," he told the House, and "that is to maintain the unity of the nation, and the unity of the nation is seriously compromised today."[82] Similarly, Meighen concluded the debate on the third reading of the Military Service Act with an impassioned rejection of Laurier's appeal:

> We either have national aims, a national will and a sense of national honour, or we have not ... Let the right hon. leader of the Opposition say now whether the time has not come for him to take his place beside those who sustain the national will and the national honour of Canada ... Then there will not be found the disunion which he predicts this afternoon; nor will there be encountered a disunion infinitely worse than that which he describes – a disunion between the nation at home and its defenders overseas.[83]

It is unclear whether Bourassa had followed the debates, and perhaps he did not closely follow the long discussion of national interests, but he certainly rejected Parliament's understanding of them. Meighen's words were distant from anything that Bourassa would have believed, and even Laurier and other Liberals couched the issue in careful phrases that the *nationaliste* found wanting. "The minister's policy," he declared in late July, "directly threatens national security and the freedom of citizens."[84] Where were the defenders of the Canadian nation? Bourassa saw only the lamentation of wartime policies as a cause of disunity rather than the war itself. He sarcastically noted that Canada might as well be Senegal fighting for France for all the influence that it had on the war effort. By not going before the electorate, Canada was now sending its citizens to fight and die for a foreign power without acknowledging their dissent. To him, the lacklustre debate on conscription pointed to the continued failure of Canadian democracy and the triumph of militarism.

For the French Canadian journalist, the government had unavoidably changed the nature of the coming election by its meagre debate on the bill in Parliament. Bourassa compared the process unfavourably with the vote on conscription in Britain, where MPs had examined its impact on

Britain's domestic and international situation, or in Australia, where there was sufficient opposition to keep it from passing. Since the Canadian Parliament had not consulted the Canadian people directly, Bourassa also drew comparisons to the situations in Ireland and Russia, where the involuntary nature of a war effort had contributed to revolution.[85] He termed the passage of conscription as "electoral conscription."[86] By hinging the upcoming election on the issue of conscription, Borden had turned it into a campaign on the value of Canada's contribution to the war. The election would be contested over conscription, Bourassa predicted, not over the ability of either party to lead the country during wartime.[87]

In late July 1917, the House of Commons was finishing its debate on conscription legislation. It was the epitome of Bourassa's fears about the war. The journalist saw little of value in Canadian politicians' long debate: even the words of Liberal leader Laurier, who opposed it, seemed to be empty. His final words before the Military Service Act passed on 24 July 1917 called for moderation:

> I oppose this Bill because it has in it the seeds of discord and disunion; because it is an obstacle and a bar to that union of heart and soul without which it is impossible to hope that this Confederation will attain the aims and ends that were had in view when Confederation was effected. Sir, all my life I have fought coercion; all my life I have promoted union; and the inspiration that led me to that course shall be my guide at all times so long as there is a breath left in my body.[88]

When it did pass 119 to 55, the vote split between French-speaking and English-speaking MPs. Only five French speakers voted for the bill: two cabinet ministers, one MP from Saskatchewan, one from New Brunswick, and the former speaker of the House Albert Sevigny.[89] Laurier had made his stand alongside the other French Canadians against the imposition of conscription by an English Canadian majority. For the first time in many years, Laurier and Bourassa shared a position, though for different reasons. Laurier believed that conscription was unpopular among Canadians and was concerned about the future political fortunes of his party, whereas Bourassa rejected any military service in a war fought for the British Empire and not Canada. Both believed that passing of the bill had divided Canada for the worse.

Protesters held anti-conscription meetings across the province in late July and August, and some became violent riots. The atmosphere in Quebec was tense. Early in the morning of 9 August, an explosion rocked the Montreal suburb of Cartierville. The summer residence of the newly minted Baron Atholstan, Hugh Graham, had been dynamited. Graham was the owner of Montreal's largest English-language newspaper, the *Star*, and an outspoken and prominent advocate of imperialism, the Canadian war effort, and conscription. In May 1917, he received a peerage for his "extraordinary initiative and zeal in promoting and supporting measures for safeguarding Imperial interests."[90] After an investigation, authorities discovered that masked men had stolen dynamite from a local quarry. Eventually, the police arrested a group of men, all of whom were associated with anti-conscription agitation.[91] Their trial revealed their motivation – in the words of conservative English Canadian Castell Hopkins – as "partly fanaticism evoked by superheated politics, partly the real criminality of desperate characters."[92] Bourassa, no friend of Graham or his newspaper, was appalled.

In an article on 11 August, he condemned the culprits and denounced violent reaction to conscription. Violence only weakened the legitimacy of the opponents of conscription. Those who used conscription as a pretense for extremism were no better than those who sought to impose conscription on Quebec. The only successful way to oppose this "tyrannical measure," Bourassa advised, was to have all opponents meet on common ground. Violent action excluded anyone who believed in law and order.[93] He scolded the most virulent leaders of the meetings, noting that conscription was not solely a measure aimed at French Canadians. There were two enemies of French Canada, those who "have systematically applied themselves to plug the eyes and ears of the people," while preaching "abject servility and outrageous loyalty," and those who sought to avoid the consequence of the first group's faulty doctrine by "riot, murder and depredation."[94] Servility led to revolt, but only by opposing the first could they denounce the second. The symptoms should not be confused with the disease.

Bourassa concluded with a discussion about the value of passive resistance. Was the law terrible enough to justify defying it? Many laws were odious or unpopular, but that alone did not mean that they ought to be disobeyed. "For my part," he told his readers, "I will never take the responsibility of advising passive resistance to the conscription law: and those who do not have these scruples have a strict duty to consider all the consequences of it."[95] Conscripts were soldiers, and if they disobeyed their orders they could face the death penalty. The only legitimate resistance to militarism and military service was rejection of the amoral means to achieve their goals: violence. French Canadians, Bourassa proclaimed, would not be complicit with the agents who sought to deceive them or the demagogues who sought to incite them.[96]

The long debate on conscription revealed to Bourassa how pervasive militarism had become in Canada. It affected even those opposed to it, for violence begat violence. Throughout the months-long public deliberation, Bourassa remained convinced that it would have greater repercussions beyond forced military service. The disturbances that followed passing of the conscription bill and the explosion at Lord Atholstan's house in August underlined the dangerous game that Canada's government was playing. Bourassa believed that such outbursts were an inevitable result of subverting democratic rights.[97] For years, he had described the transformation of Canadian society because of the war, and in the summer of 1917 it seemed as if his worst fears had come to pass. He suspected that things would get worse before they got better. A federal election was scheduled before the year was out, and seemingly the war still had no end in sight. His warning in August that physical violence was not the answer was worthwhile but ignored his own role in it. Although Bourassa never asked for popular manifestations of resistance on the street, neither were his words conciliatory. He had spent years writing about the Boches of Ontario and their discriminatory policies and the incapability of war supporters to consider anything less than total support. The final year of the war revealed how dangerous the situation had become alongside the growing disunity of the Canadian nation.

7
Silenced

August 1917–April 1918

AFTER THE VIOLENT RESPONSE to the passing of conscription in late July and August 1917, Henri Bourassa turned his gaze beyond Canada's borders to the international stage. He looked to the chief advocate for a peaceful resolution to the ruinous conflict: Pope Benedict XV. The failed peace negotiations of 1916 and the American entry into the war compelled the pope to release his most strongly worded peace note to date. He wrote to the belligerent peoples and their leaders on the third anniversary of the outbreak of war, promising

> to maintain an absolute impartiality towards all belligerents, ... to endeavor continually to do the utmost good to all without distinction of persons, nationality or religion, [and] to contribute to hasten the end of this calamity by trying to bring the peoples and their leaders to more moderate resolutions in the discussion of means that will secure a "just and lasting peace."[1]

The pope outlined a clear international position as the head of the Catholic Church that did not favour any side since there were Catholics among both the Allied Powers and the Central Powers. It was the sort of diplomatic balancing act that he was well experienced at performing.

Pope Benedict XV was born Giacomo Giambattista Della Chiesa and replaced Pope Pius X, who died on 24 August 1914 – apocryphally from a broken heart over the outbreak of a general European war. Della Chiesa had been a cardinal for only six months before he became pope, though he had had a long career of diplomatic posts within the Vatican. He worked closely with Cardinal Mariano Rampolla, Pope Leo XIII's (1878–1903) secretary of state, and performed admirably. Contemporaries heralded him as the "new Consalvi," referring to the worldly cardinal who had positioned the papacy after the Vienna Congress of 1815 as a neutral power, restored the Papal States, and preserved its international relevance.² Despite the commendable credentials of Della Chiesa, his election to the papacy came as a surprise to contemporary observers. Few people outside Rome had heard of him, but, as his biographer writes, of all the papal candidates in the 1914 conclave, Della Chiesa was the most *papabile*. He fulfilled the description of the "ideal" pope who possessed "superior intelligence, holiness of life, and Christian charity."³

Benedict XV immediately set out to resolve the terrible conflict that split his flock – or at least to mediate its horrific consequences as much as he could. From September 1914 on, the Vatican commented on and engaged with each of the belligerent powers in its efforts to stop the war. Although the pope ultimately failed, his long years of diplomatic intervention earned him the name Pope of Peace. Often unjustly characterized by contemporaries as having done nothing during the Great War besides meddle in diplomatic affairs, recent historians have demonstrated the immense commitment that Benedict XV made to ending the war and aiding its victims.⁴ Both the Allied Powers and the Central Powers were suspicious of his actions during the war. The Treaty of London that brought Italy into the war specifically forbade any papal presence at future peace negotiations. Some members of the Roman Curia hoped for a Central Powers victory precisely because it could resolve the "Rome Question" and perhaps restore the Papal States, only annexed sixty years earlier in 1860.⁵ Although some members of the Curia might have been sympathetic to the German and Austrian war effort,⁶ Pope Benedict XV was committed to his policy of strict neutrality. His papal notes throughout the conflict sought to bring about an end to the war without favouring one side over the other. The most famous was that of 1 August 1917, declaring the pontificate's impartiality and commitment to ending the conflict.

Bourassa found Pope Benedict XV's argument that the war would end only when just and fair arbitration took precedence over the force of arms compelling. The French Canadian agreed with the underlying philosophy that participation in or support for the war was a sin for Catholics (or believers in any moral code). For years, he had attempted to persuade his countrymen of the validity of the pope's words, confronting those who claimed moral superiority without the papacy's moral authority. Accordingly, Bourassa unconditionally affirmed the pope's message and impartiality – largely because of his religious beliefs but also because the pope called for peace for the sake of peace without caring who won or lost the war. Whether the war ended in victory or defeat for either side, the cost of thousands of lives every day affronted Bourassa.

In his editorial reply to the pope's note on 18 August, Bourassa responded to the accusation that the pope was a German sympathizer. The claim stemmed from detractors in Canada and Great Britain who attacked Benedict XV after he appealed for peace early in the war. Again, after this latest proposal, the "vampire press" painted the pope as a "docile and hypocritical instrument of the Kaiser."[7] Bourassa reiterated in detail the pope's plan and denied what he described as falsehoods in other newspapers. Outlining each point, he defended the spiritual leader against those who tried to make his ideas seem both "too absolute and too favourable to Germany" and "too vague and insufficient."[8] Bourassa remained optimistic that a true peace was possible by paying heed to the reasoned and moral voice of the pope. He hoped that the pope's words could convince others to reject "the hideous vampires who gorge themselves with the blood of the nations," and the people of the world could then force their leaders to action.[9]

Bourassa's position on the war has been termed "Christian pacifism,"[10] but a more proper description might be "Catholic neutrality." Bourassa was a devout Catholic, and his faith played an integral role in shaping his wartime views. But he was an ultramontane, which influenced him in different ways than other wartime Catholics. His ultramontane belief in the supremacy of the pope over civil authorities or national church hierarchies created a definitive understanding of the war through that lens. Although Bourassa might not have been absolutely certain of the pope's judgment in temporal affairs, he was certain that the pope was the least fallible voice in the world.[11] Bourassa's thoughts on the war were undoubtedly Catholic in nature; however, they significantly diverged from the positions taken by other Catholics in the belligerent nations, including Canada. For instance, English-speaking Catholics used the war as a tool to emphasize further the differences from French Canadian Catholics, seeking to balance their loyalty to Britain and maintaining sympathy with their fellow Catholics.[12]

Just as important to understanding Bourassa's position is the concept of neutrality. Bourassa did not espouse a "pacifist" view (moral opposition to any violence). He contested the justification for and consequences of the First World War itself. This departed slightly from Pope Benedict XV's official position of "absolute impartiality," which denoted a subtle but often misunderstood difference from neutrality. "Absolute impartiality was more than simply a tightened concept of neutrality," Charles Gallagher clarifies, since "absolute impartiality distinctly forbade public moral determinations by non-belligerent states."[13] The Holy See refused to draw moral judgments on warring states, with Benedict XV trying to position the Vatican as both politically and morally neutral in the conflict.

Bourassa's sententious writing did not follow this dictate closely. Rather, the journalist argued for a peaceful resolution to the European war while denouncing those who refused to consider peace as a viable option. He effectively situated himself as "neutral" within an older context of neutrality. During the nineteenth century, neutrality was a key element in maintaining the balance of power in Europe and restraining larger nations' aggressive tendencies. M.M. Abbenhuis observes that this was a "legitimate foreign policy option," and a nation's intent not to fight in a war was just as valid as a nation's intent to do so.[14] Thus, Bourassa did not oppose the war for the sake of opposing it. He expressed, through a religious lens, his belief that moderation, restraint, and limited (not total) war were the only ways to ensure European stability and maintain the virtues of civilization for which both sides claimed to fight.

Bourassa's neutrality was not a passive abdication of war for religious reasons, as the term "Christian pacifist" might suggest. It was a resolute stance against the excessive incarnation of war, rooted in Benedict XV's wartime policy of impartial moderation. Above all, the French Canadian Catholic commentator trusted the righteousness of the pope to guide humanity. It was in this frame of mind that Bourassa returned to the political events developing in Ottawa.

Throughout August 1917, Prime Minister Robert Borden's efforts to forge a coalition of Liberals and Conservatives continued without the support of Sir Wilfrid Laurier. Borden believed that he could entice a group of pro-conscription Liberals to join the government and break away from Laurier's party. Borden pursued prominent Liberals from across the country, such as Premier of Alberta Albert Sifton (brother of Laurier's former Cabinet Minister Clifford Sifton), Saskatchewan MP James Calder, progressive Manitoban Liberal Thomas Crerar, Ontario Liberal leader Newton Rowell, and New Brunswick MP Frank Carvell. Conscriptionist Liberals tried to move the party away from Laurier's influence without success.[15] At a Liberal meeting on 7 August, much of the rank and file enthusiastically supported Laurier, whose decision to support a referendum left the Liberals who wanted conscription with no place in the party. Consequently, the pro-conscription Liberals reluctantly agreed to enter a coalition with the Conservatives as part of the new Unionist Party. Believing that the Laurier Liberals faced annihilation in the coming election, the Liberal-Unionists saw themselves as preserving the Liberal Party outside Quebec and ensuring its future longevity.[16]

Bourassa approved of Laurier's refusal to support forced military service and even his policy of a referendum, recognizing that Laurier was in a complicated and difficult situation. Bourassa believed that the Liberal leader was trying to avoid conscription in any form but could not outright declare his change in position and thus supported a referendum. Bourassa told his readers that Laurier was personally and sincerely opposed to conscription, but the circumstances of the war and the chains that Laurier himself had forged now entrapped the Liberal leader. Liberal complicity during the Boer War and subsequent imperial ventures – including the past three years of the current war – had plunged Canada into its current position. Now Laurier was trying to correct his party's past mistakes. "Mr. Laurier," Bourassa declared, "owes it to himself, he owes it to his faithful supporters, he owes it to his compatriots, he owes it to the whole country, to get out of the wilderness and place himself on solid ground to fight the election battle openly."[17] A Liberal election victory was dependent on not alienating the party from the pro-conscription vote. Bourassa believed that Laurier offered support for conscription as a means of ensuring electoral success for the Liberal Party. During the debate on the legislation, Bourassa had been lukewarm toward Laurier's efforts to oppose the bill, but now he accepted that a Liberal victory was the only way to correct the wayward direction of the country.

The election preoccupied Canada's political leaders in the fall of 1917 while Canadian soldiers fought costly engagements in the mud of Passchendaele. Prime Minister Borden, fearing an election loss even with some Liberals on his side, passed two crucial pieces of election legislation in August and September: the Military Voters Act and the War Time Elections Act. The Military Voters Act gave the vote to all soldiers, and those who did not name a constituency were able to cast a "floating vote" assigned to any constituency that the government wanted. In mid-September, the War Time Elections Act gave the vote to the wives, widows, mothers, and sisters of soldiers and simultaneously disenfranchised "enemy alien" citizens naturalized after 1902 unless they had relatives serving in the armed forces. Borden's legislation aimed to ensure a victory for his coalition government regardless of lingering disputes about conscription.[18] Two Liberal victories in the provincial elections of Alberta and

Saskatchewan earlier that year were allegedly attributable to the "foreign vote," and the Conservatives were wary of its influence.[19]

The Liberals stood firmly against the bill and spoke out vehemently against it in the House of Commons. They did not accept the government's claims that the legislation would reveal "the real views of the Canadian people," insisting that it was intended only to bolster the government's electoral results.[20] J.H. Sinclair, the Liberal MP for Guysborough in Nova Scotia, said on 10 September, "Let me suggest to the Secretary of State that he change the name, and call it 'The War-Times Prussian Junker Act.'" "The idea behind this measure is military autocracy," he continued, reminding his fellow parliamentarians that "we, on this side of the House, I am proud to say, stand for democracy."[21] The Liberals condemned the establishment of what they saw effectively as a separate social caste for the military, calling it the founding of a Prussian Junker aristocracy and "oligarchic Kaiserism."[22] None accepted that selectively expanding the electoral franchise was bettering Canadian democracy.

Bourassa understood the government's intention as well, baptizing its new law the "Mad-Time Elections Act."[23] He also perceived the legislation as the creation of "a privileged military caste" in which women related to soldiers earned suffrage solely because of their relation to "*heroes.*" Even giving women the vote seemed to be an extraordinary act to the Catholic journalist, adding yet another revolutionary facet to his critique of the war.[24] Equally unsettling was the government's disenfranchisement of foreign-born Canadians. To Bourassa, disavowing Canadians already acknowledged as citizens was outrageous. "Such is the trust," he wrote, "that the saviours of the 'small nationalities' give to their protégés."[25] They were already British subjects, they had paid their taxes, they had set down roots and become Canadians, yet now they were to live as pariahs in their new home. In the conclusion to his thoughts on the Wartime Elections Act, Bourassa ranked it even worse than conscription. He told his readers that, "by its inspiration, its motives, its immediate consequences, and its far-reaching scope, this legislation is infinitely more criminal and dangerous than the conscription law. It oozes out of its pores iniquity, lies, deceit, and cowardly despotism."[26] At least, Bourassa concluded, the Liberals opposed the motion. For the first time in several years, he readily admitted that the opposition was doing its job to resist unjust government action.

The debates about conscription and Borden's election legislation finally rehabilitated Laurier in Bourassa's eyes. "On behalf of all true and sincere nationalists," Bourassa wrote that summer, "I accept the remedy proposed by Mr. Laurier."[27] Robert Rumilly recounts the story of their first meeting after several years in the fall of 1917. Louis-Athanase David, a Quebec Liberal MLA, wrote to both Bourassa and Laurier telling them that they wished to see one another. Bourassa travelled to Ottawa to see his former chief, and Laurier opened his arms, saying, "What's happening to me today, you predicted it to me eleven years ago ... Now I know where to find real friends."[28] The two had reconciled their differences to work together against a common foe.

When Borden formally announced the formation of the Union government on 12 October and presented its program and cabinet on the 18th,[29] Bourassa affirmed that Laurier and his partisans needed "the foresight and energy to understand the situation." The only hope for the future of Laurier and his Liberal Party was to understand the depth of Canada's "complacency toward false gods."[30] Real and honest Canadians were tired of the government's lies, Bourassa predicted, and were waiting for a party to lead them. Laurier's Liberals had become that party.

In late October, just days before Borden called the election for 17 December, Bourassa outlined the international situation enmeshing Canada. He attached none of the high meaning to the cause of victory repeated in newspapers, posters, and speeches across the country. He saw little proof that the war was anything more than for the profit of "financiers."[31] He drew new inspiration on the topic from an article by American writer Frederic C. Howe entitled "Financial Imperialism."[32]

Howe was the president of the League for Small and Subject Nationalities, a New York–based organization that aimed to ensure that all of the nationalities of the world had representation on the international stage as well as at the peace conference that one day would decide the terms of the end of the war.[33] Like Bourassa, Howe agreed with the work of British radicals such as Noel Brailsford and J.A. Hobson and pointed to financial imperialism as one of the leading causes of modern war.[34] Howe considered imperialism, or "dollar diplomacy" in an American context, as the fusion of financial development with foreign policy. It was an action of finance rather than trade and included "(1) the lending of money, often to weak or dependent countries or to rulers of doubtful legitimacy; (2) the building of railroads, canals, and the public utility enterprises; and (3) the development of mines, plantations, and other resources."[35] Howe explored the history of these practices in recent memory, touching on the British and French intervention in Egypt and the Moroccan Crisis of 1911, while connecting each international incident to financial investment from great powers. He considered these investments to be dishonest or exploitive, benefiting the wealthy and powerful nations of the world at the expense of poor or less developed peoples. Thus, the global economic conflict between great powers was a cause of the current war, Howe argued, and only democratic freedom and economic peace could correct these "monopolistic conditions" and avoid future conflicts.[36]

Finance was the arbiter of international politics, Bourassa declared, and he repeated Howe's narrative of events and his argument. Britain would emerge from the war as a financier and creditor regardless of Germany's victory or defeat. The only desire of the "English plutocracy" was to entrap every nation of the world in its financial clutches. Just as these plutocrats had ensnared France and Russia, so too had "the demon of gold seized the leaders of American society."[37] Amazingly, in contrast to his previous writing that spring, Bourassa alleged that Britain had been one of the firmest opponents of the American entry before the collapse of Russia in 1917 because the United States had little value to British plutocrats. The end of the war might see democracy in Germany, but it would come after British (and now American) financiers had total economic control.[38] Behind all of the justifications for the war, he wrote, "everywhere stands the hideous spectre of mercantile greed, the horrible and insatiable demon of gold."[39] If that was the war for which Canadians died and campaigned, then Bourassa saw no hope of redemption for "the perpetrators of the revolution."[40]

In his final article on the subject, Bourassa investigated the "deteriorating moral character" of the Canadian nation in light of the upcoming election. On 31 October, the day that Borden announced the election, Bourassa wondered what future lay with the "Ministry of National Treason."[41] Canada had everything to lose and nothing to gain. The nation ruined itself for the profit of Great Britain today and for that of the United States tomorrow. There was little chance of economic recovery after the war, so Canada would look to the United States, but "the only nation that can get us back on our feet is, at the same time, our only creditor."[42] Ottawa now took orders from London and New York, claimed Bourassa. How else to explain the alliance between the "ultra-jingos of Toronto" and "the former and modern annexationists of the West and Nova Scotia" (the pro-conscription Liberals)?[43] He believed that the newly formed Unionist Party had committed national treason since it had sold out Canada to foreign powers, which made the choice between Borden and

Laurier clear. Laurier was "honest, honourable, and notoriously superior," Bourassa wrote. Despite his writing from earlier in 1917, he now declared that Laurier, "at least, has never been sold." Borden was "following the foreigner's watchword," so Laurier had to rally all those of "sincere conviction to defend what remains of our national heritage."[44] Canada under Union government was on a dangerous path, and only a Laurier victory could prevent further degradation.

Despite his impassioned pleas, Bourassa held little hope for a Liberal victory, but he remained optimistic about the future of the party. The war had corrupted and broken the spirit of the party as some of its members had left to join the Unionist Party. Neither the Liberal nor the Conservative Party, he wrote, would ever be the same party that it had been before the Great War. "The names may remain," he foresaw, "but the groups will no longer be the same, not the same men nor the same spirit."[45] Instead, Canada's political parties would emerge as new entities. "The parties – like the people themselves," Bourassa wrote, "will remake themselves in the norm of new currents, of the ideas of tomorrow, according to the antagonism of the principles that reflect the harsh reality of the things born of war and the post-war."[46] He hoped that Laurier could help one day to repair the damage that had been done. The Liberal leader had the solemn responsibility of making the "supreme effort to restore the Canadian nation's consciousness of itself, of its real duties, of its positive rights to snatch it from the false gods of imperialism, to stop it in its race to commit suicide, to close its gaping wounds and to prepare a new vitality for it."[47]

During the election campaign, Bourassa maintained a pessimistic tone in his editorials. For years, he had extolled in the pages of his newspaper how and why the war should end, yet in the final months 1917 he had less confidence in the immediacy of that change. Instead, he hoped that one day Canada could become the country that he envisioned, for it was obvious that that would not happen under Union government.

The federal election campaign of November and December 1917, as historian Michael Bliss described, was "the most bitter in Canadian history, viciously fought on both sides. Virtually everyone's loyalty and morality were called into question."[48] Although the Unionists and the Liberals had comprehensive electoral platforms, the election was ultimately about the future conduct of the war effort. The Unionist platform promised conscription and civil service reforms such as abolishing patronage and providing oversight of government purchasing.[49] The Laurier Liberals vowed to reduce wartime taxes and tariffs, to provide better for soldiers' families, and to eliminate the corruption that had plagued Borden's government.[50] These platforms were superfluous. The campaign would be fought between two positions. The Unionists would impose a unified war effort through conscription, whereas the Liberals would hold a referendum for the sake of a unified war effort. The Unionists had to focus on conscription and the war given that pro-conscription Liberals did not trust the Conservative-led coalition, while some Conservatives did not accept the Liberal presence in the new party. The war and conscription were the only issues on which they could all agree. Laurier, however, embraced conscription as an electoral issue. He returned to familiar territory by defending traditional liberal values of individual freedom and resistance to oppression.[51] Each side argued that only it could successfully navigate the turbulent waters of wartime unity by virtue of its position on conscription.

In an election campaign focused on the war, there was little room for compromise or moderation. As Unionist and former Liberal Newton Rowell remarked on 21 November, "what is the alternative to this Union Government? ... If you think of quitting the War, you have an alternative, but if you are in favour of ... a victorious conclusion [to the war], then I say in all sincerity you have no alternative to Union Government."[52] Both Unionists and Liberals presented voters with a stark choice: choose us or face ruin. In Quebec, the decision was clear.[53] Few there wanted conscription, and fewer trusted Union government, which had a definitively anti-Catholic and anti–French Canadian tone.[54] Unionist candidates in the province faced unruly mobs, interrupted speeches, few press organs that would express their views, and even death threats.[55]

The election helped to cement Bourassa's position as one of the most-well-known leaders of the Quebec resistance to the war in both English-speaking and French-speaking Canada, with varying degrees of animosity to and praise for it. His words evoked nothing less than a life-or-death struggle against the blight of imperialism and English Canadian domination.[56] "The Unionist program," he told French Canadians, "is the antithesis of everything we love, everything we believe, and everything we want. It is the synthesis of everything we hate, of everything we have spoken about – men, ideas and tendencies – in both parties."[57] *Nationalistes,* he advised, should vote for Laurier. It was in their best interest to support one party over the other rather than abstain or vote for independent candidates.[58] The chance of a Unionist winning a Quebec seat was too dangerous to risk. Bourassa's appeals and Laurier's careful positioning of the Liberal Party as nominally against conscription virtually assured a Liberal victory in the province. As one historian noted, Québécois would have voted for a telephone pole as long as it was not in favour of conscription.[59]

Bourassa was arguably at the height of his fame and notoriety, at least if the frequency of his appearance in English and French newspapers was any indication, but the united Canada that he had one hoped for was little more than a dream in the final months of 1917. English Canadian Unionists painted French Canadians as "shirkers" who did not want to do their duty or, worse, as traitors to Canada and the British Empire. These Unionists did their best to associate Bourassa with Laurier as much as possible to tarnish the reputation of the Liberal leader. They called Bourassa the "King of Quebec" and suggested that a Laurier victory meant that Bourassa would rule Canada.[60] Unionist propaganda pamphlets, such as *Plain Facts for English-Speaking Electors,* linked Bourassa and Laurier together while quoting from *Le Devoir* and other French Canadian newspapers as proof that French-speaking Canadians sought the dissolution of Confederation and took orders from the pope in Rome.[61] Laurier did his best to disassociate his party from the *nationalistes,* at least outside the borders of Quebec, emphasizing that he was not against the war effort, only against the government's conduct of the war.[62] Despite his efforts, many English Canadian papers condemned the Liberal leader, some more virulently than others. The Toronto *News* called Laurier "a demagogue, a charlatan and a mountebank," while in Montreal an English-speaking Canadian wrote that "if Laurier were to win he would win leading the cockroaches of the kitchen of Canada to victory."[63] Both sides used vitriol and hyperbole to convince voters that only their leaders could bring the nation to victory.

In the last two months of 1917, Bourassa wrote only one article that did not discuss the election. It examined a new public advocate for peace in Britain, Lord Lansdowne. Almost a year after the German peace proposal and President Wilson's note, Henry Petty-Fitzmaurice, 5th Marquess of Lansdowne, released a letter to the press in late November. Lansdowne, the former governor general of Canada as well as the former leader of the Conservative Party in the House of Lords, had an illustrious career in the service of Britain.[64] The "Lansdowne letter" was an edited version of a memorandum originally circulated to the British cabinet after Prime Minister Herbert Asquith asked for the views of cabinet members on potential peace terms in early November 1916.[65] Although its context was the aftermath of the Somme campaign, not the fall of 1917, Lansdowne specifically chose to respect cabinet tradition and never disclosed to the public that the upper echelons of the British government had already discussed it in 1916. In it, he called for a negotiated peace that preserved Germany as a great power while ensuring economic trade and European stability. He eventually published it in the London *Daily Telegraph* on 29 November 1917 to "set out aims that are moderate and will appeal to moderate minds in all countries."[66]

A long history of diplomatic and government service had convinced Lansdowne of the power of diplomacy to resolve disputes and secure a peaceful solution to European and imperial conflicts.[67] With that in mind, he urged a negotiated end to the war. For Lansdowne, no victory would be worth the cost of the continuation of the war, which simply shed more blood while threatening the stability of Europe and Britain. He argued that "we are not going to lose this war, but its prolongation will spell ruin for the civilized world and an infinite addition to the load of human suffering."[68] Lansdowne feared that the necessary reparations for such a brutal war would make lasting peace impossible since, as dreadful as the Great War was, he was sure that "the next war [would] be even more dreadful than this [one]."[69] The belligerents had to balance reparations with their impacts on the defeated peoples, Lansdowne wrote, and that might mean asking for little or nothing at all. Ending the war and preventing future ones ought to be the sole war aim of the Allies.[70]

Few British commentators agreed with Lansdowne during wartime. When he published his letter in the *Daily Telegraph*, his plea for peace was widely denounced in the British Parliament and British newspapers, though press reaction among the Allied Powers varied from ignoring it to praising it.[71] Although those who deliberated over peace negotiations received the note as well,[72] others in Britain denounced Lansdowne as a "defeatist."[73] The Union of Democratic Control, meanwhile, praised Lansdowne's vision, and one of its members, British pacifist Bertrand Russell, noted optimistically that the "letter represents the first beginnings of a return to a sanity."[74] Still, the letter ultimately did not have the impact that Lansdowne had hoped. The venerable politician later published two more letters in the press analyzing Allied diplomacy as the end of the war drew closer.[75] Their publication occurred in much better circumstances for the Allies than the first letter, and the reaction to them improved considerably as a result.

Bourassa's comments on Lansdowne were brief but significant.[76] Whereas Lansdowne was more concerned about ending the war in a way still beneficial to Great Britain, Bourassa saw the proposal as another initiative to stop the war before it caused any further harm. The first part of his article reminded his readers of such and linked it to thoughts that the pope had already expressed. The letter was merely "the translation, into political and human language, of the various manifestations of the thought of the Supreme Pontiff."[77] It mirrored the papal peace, which aimed at stopping the terrible slaughter of the war as soon as possible; it was not a political or an economic analysis of the disastrous cost of the war for England. In this case, Bourassa's Catholic values clouded his reaction to Lansdowne's words. He saw what he wanted to see in the aristocrat's writing. He compared it to Wilson's grand claim of a peace that would "make the world safe for democracy." Lansdowne proposed a peace that was not "only the only just and lasting peace [but] ... also the only possible peace."[78] To Bourassa, the president's willingness to participate in the butchery in France had corrupted the American vision of peace, and he welcomed new allies who understood the senselessness of the war. Instead, Bourassa heralded Lansdowne as a true supporter of peace because he called for the cessation of hostilities by both sides without regard for political or military considerations.

A quick end to the war was the best possible solution for humanity, and Bourassa approved of Lansdowne's five points to encourage peace negotiations.[79] The journalist agreed that reassuring Germany that defeat did not mean destruction, politically or economically, would make the Germans more amenable to negotiations. Nonetheless, Bourassa noted the irony of the belligerents' positions. The situation in late 1917 was a reversal from that of the previous year, and he asked whether the "exploiters of human flesh will win ... the round this year in Germany, as they did last year, in allied countries."[80] The greatest impediment was not, he suggested, that one side feared a peace without victory; both the Allied Powers and the Central Powers feared a peace with defeat. Just as the Allies had rejected losing the war through peace terms in 1916, so too Germany now refused to consider a peace that amounted to an Allied victory. Bourassa repeated Lansdowne's belief that the great powers fought for security foremost, and a longer war meant a greater chance of revolution and disorder. He warned that to ignore the cause of peace, which echoed "in the souls of millions of human beings," would lead to a war against any state that denied it and lead to universal civil war.[81] Ultimately, Bourassa wanted to put an end to the tragic loss of hundreds of thousands of lives before more people died.

In a final appeal to his readers two days before the 17 December election, Bourassa lamented the sorry state of Canadian democracy and urged them to vote against Union government. He longed to see the former *nationalistes* who had run for the Conservatives in 1911 finally punished for their treason. "We need to clean up the political stage from their presence and contortions," Bourassa wrote.[82] At least the election would allow Quebec to flush out its "disloyal" representatives, even if the process was a poor example of democratic government. "One of the worst and most absurd inconsistencies of the electoral system," he explained, was that "it is impossible to support both the best candidate and the best policy."[83] He told voters that the electoral contest had become a plebiscite whereby Canadians could either vote for conscription or vote against it. It was not a fair contest between policies and leaders. Bourassa advised Canadians to vote for the Laurier Liberals, who offered the best alternative to the Unionists.

When election day arrived, the Union government won a resounding victory in English Canada. Of the 264-seat Parliament, the Unionists took 152 seats, and the Liberals took 82 seats. Sixty-two of the sixty-five seats in Quebec went to the Liberals, who garnered 73 percent of the popular vote. The Unionists swept the English-speaking parts of the country. The Liberals fared better in the Maritimes, winning ten of twenty-one seats, but in Ontario they won only eight of eighty-two seats. Borden, worried that the Liberals might benefit from rural objections to conscription, had promised farmers an exemption from forced military service – an action that helped the Unionists to achieve such an overwhelming victory in English Canada. A single French Canadian Unionist candidate was successful, Conservative incumbent Dr. John Léo Chabot for Ottawa.[84] In the words of one Liberal candidate, "the 1917 election was essentially a one-party election, one party only in Quebec and one party only in other provinces."[85] The country divided between French and English, Unionist and Liberal, conscripted and voluntary service.

After the result, Bourassa denounced the great danger of a Union government that ignored Canada's racial divide and further threatened Canadian national unity. He reversed his previous position that the election had effectively been a plebiscite on conscription as the depth of his bitterness seriously swayed his work. He now proclaimed that the election was not just about conscription and did not signify general acceptance of a war without limits. The promised exemption of farmers had led many of them to vote for Union government, Bourassa argued, and thus a true referendum on conscription would have seen their votes go to the Liberals.[86] He disagreed with those who argued that the election demonstrated "the isolation of Quebec." The truth, he explained, was that "various groups and provinces of the country voted against unionism because of their direct resistance to imperialist training."[87] True Canadians had voted against conscription, Bourassa insisted. He pointed to the support for it in the west since they were newer and less traditional provinces with populations that had only "recently" arrived in the country. The Prairies "have lost the notion of national stability."[88] Ultimately, the country's disunity was not the fault of French Canada. Instead, the Unionist victory demonstrated that the rest of Canada was isolated from those who preserved its true character, such as the French Canadians.

Bourassa explained that Union government would have the opposite result implied by its name. Unionists had denigrated French Canadians over the course of the election campaign, and they had divided the country. Therefore, Bourassa wrote, French Canada was not isolated from the rest of Canada of its own accord. French Canadians had been the targets of anti-Catholic and anti-French rhetoric. "The so-called 'national union,'" Bourassa argued, "disunited the Canadian nation and planted a new seed of disintegration in the already cracked soil of the British Empire."[89] Although Canada had dealt with racial and religious division before, he clarified that wartime had allowed the Unionists to weld English Canadian patriotism to the interests of a foreign power, Britain. Unlike previous conflicts between French Canadians and English Canadians, he explained, nobody could oppose the war without becoming a traitor to the Canadian nation. Supporting the war meant supporting Canada, and in turn supporting Canada meant supporting Britain. The three were indivisible in the minds of English Canadian war supporters, and to reject one was to reject them all. Bourassa predicted that after the war Liberals and Conservatives would cleanly divide along racial and regional lines, French versus English and east versus west. The Canadian federation, he mourned, was broken.[90]

Even if French Canadians were present and influential in the Union government, Bourassa asserted, it could not repair the damage that the election had caused. He no longer believed that French-speaking Canadians were in an equal partnership with English-speaking Canadians. Those French Canadians in government were mere puppets of English Canadian politicians. Their role consisted of "breaking the energies of their compatriots to numb their vigilance, to make them grant humiliating concessions always under the easy pretext of reconciling the majority, and to keep their influence in the cabinet and to obtain for the province of Quebec its share of the remains."[91] The supposed isolation of French Canada was not the result of its turning its back on English Canada; rather, English Canada had turned its back on French Canada, reneging on the promise of equality and compromise implicit when it had pushed through conscription. The will of the majority had triumphed over the will of the minority. For Bourassa, the solution to the problem of French Canada's place in the Canadian democracy was clear: "At minimum, the Quebec delegation to federal parliament has no reason to bind itself to any government or party until it has obtained the conditions of association that are absolutely honourable for themselves, advantageous without being excessive for French-Canadian nationality, and beneficial to the entire Canadian nation."[92] Quebec's MPs had to represent French Canadian interests in the House of Commons since they could no longer trust the federal parties that drew support from English Canadian voters.

In December 1917, Bourassa was effectively arguing that the Liberal Party had to become a French Canadian party. In his mind, only a balance between French and English interests could guide Canada properly, and now he seemed to endorse the racial division that he had once strenuously rejected. The war had undermined his dream of a united Canada. If the English-speaking majority was not willing to listen to the French-speaking minority, then it was up to French Canadians to compel action, and the Liberal Party was the only vessel that they had available.

In the first month of 1918, Bourassa published his final book of the war, *Le pape: Arbitre de la paix* (The Pope: Arbiter of Peace). It collected his articles concerning Pope Benedict XV's attempts to produce a peaceful end to the European conflict and reflected on the papal influence on other peace initiatives. Although largely comprised of articles written over the previous four years, it marked Bourassa's final effort to discuss the possibility of peace, the international context of the war, and his last reflection on the pope. The final chapters were editorials from January 1918 addressing the latest international developments in the war.

The first examined the effort by British Prime Minister David Lloyd George to present British war aims. At a speech on 5 January, Lloyd George responded to the Lansdowne letter as well as the terms of the Treaty of Brest-Litovsk that ended the war between Russia and the Central Powers. The prime minister outlined conditions that could end the war based upon national self-determination and the establishment of an international organization to settle disputes after the war.[93] Historians have disagreed whether Lloyd George was attempting to moderate British war aims to make peace viable, responding to the demands of British radicals while bolstering morale, or affirming the results of Brest-Litovsk as a formula for future peace deals.[94] To an outside observer such as Bourassa, it was a welcome statement that perhaps presaged further peace initiatives. At least, he maintained, it aligned more closely with papal views on the matter.

Bourassa perceived Lloyd George's speech as an extraordinary evolution of the British position on peace. Reading between the lines, he wrote, Lloyd George's speech, the Lansdowne Letter, and the pope formed "a remarkable and substantive agreement."[95] Lansdowne, Bourassa agreed, had been correct in predicting terrible consequences by prolonging the war, and Lloyd George was attempting to avert them. Still, many details of the speech did not impress Bourassa. Lloyd George's affirmation that France and Italy would recover territory from the Central Powers drew criticism from Bourassa because he anticipated that it would only lengthen the war and entail additional sacrifice. He added his familiar refrain that nationalities deserved autonomy among all states, not just those that formed the Central Powers. Yet, despite its inconsistencies and shortcomings, Bourassa wrote, the speech was "the most formal one made so far, on the side of the Allies, for a peace that 'does not benefit only one of the parties, but all' – only the 'just and lasting' peace called by the pope."[96]

If Bourassa was mildly impressed by Lloyd George's speech, he was wildly enthusiastic about President Woodrow Wilson's "Program for World Peace" presented to the American Congress on 8 January. Wilson outlined his famous Fourteen Points to guide any possible peace settlement, proclaiming that "it is the principle of justice to all peoples and nationalities, and their right to live on equal terms of liberty and safety with one another, whether they be strong or weak."[97] His speech set out the points that would guide the Treaty of Versailles a year later and drastically transform the international system. Bourassa supported Wilson's confirmation of national self-determination and enthusiastically endorsed his peace program.[98] Its Fourteen Points spoke to a new vision of the international system that resolved grave problems that had led to the outbreak of the First World War nearly four years earlier. Bourassa was caught in the "Wilsonian moment,"[99] in which it seemed possible that the war would bring about substantial reform to the international system and yield a new liberal international order that emphasized self-government and democracy.

In a two-part series, Bourassa compared and contrasted Wilson and Lloyd George, focusing on Wilson's call to "free oppressed nationalities."[100] Both aligned with Pope Benedict XV's position by supporting a negotiated peace and rejecting the idea of annexation through conquest.[101] All of these commentators claimed to reject the subjugation of one nationality by another. Bourassa was glad that the statesmen had finally learned the lesson of history that conquest only led to further conflict.[102] Wilson's vision was far grander than that of the British prime minister since he "provided his suggestions within a framework of general application," allowing them to apply more broadly to the entire international system.[103] Bourassa believed that the president was extending a hand to Germany and acted in good faith toward the Central Powers. "[Wilson is inviting Germany] to join his program of global renewal," Bourassa wrote, "without sacrificing anything of its greatness, its aspirations, its very regime, provided that it renounces any idea of domination and is content with an 'equal place among the nations of the world.'"[104] He saw in Wilson's words an international system based not upon fear and antagonism but upon goodwill and justice, thus fulfilling the Catholic vision of international order espoused by Pope Benedict XV.

Bourassa concluded the book with an article titled "Triumph and Justification of the Pope" that discerned the growing influence of the papacy on international affairs. The world needed the pope "more than ever," he professed. He argued that the papal position must have inspired both Lloyd George and Wilson, whether they admitted it or not. One way or another, "they are forced to borrow more from the peace program of the Supreme Pontiff."[105] Bourassa reviewed Benedict XV's various peace notes during the war and highlighted how the pope had proposed a just and equitable peace that recognized national self-determination in an effort to forge a lasting and peaceful resolution to the war. "All of it was true, strong, just and infinitely more practical," he concluded, "than all the advice of hatred, the efforts of brute force and the debauchery of diplomatic trickery!"[106] Benedict XV's careful vision and impartial attitude had convinced the belligerent nations of the validity of his position over time. His enlightened analysis had shepherded the war's participants toward the possibility of peace, and the Catholic leader deserved credit for helping to avoid further catastrophe. Only the pope, Bourassa wrote, could finish the work that he had started and finally guide the world safely toward an unbiased peace: "Whether peace is made tomorrow or whether nations, stubbornly determined to lose themselves, continue their work of suicide and devastation, it is neither German peace, nor French peace, nor English peace, nor American peace, nor imperialist peace, nor democratic peace that will put an end to the massacre: it will be Christian peace, or social revolution."[107]

The ultramontane Bourassa relied heavily on papal discourse as a crucial component of his judgments. Although he engaged with Canadians who gauged the political purpose of the war through concepts of imperialism and democracy, Bourassa saw it entirely as a moral and religious issue. Whether Ontario Protestants,[108] or French Canadian Catholics of Quebec,[109] religious Canadians had to reconcile the atrocities of the war with their religious convictions. Bourassa did so by unquestioningly accepting the pope's position. Bourassa did not so much find the position of the Vatican in agreement with his own; rather, he allowed the Vatican to define his own position. In the introduction to *Le pape*, he noted that "I disavow all that could, in my deductions and judgments, bring the slightest alteration to the thought of the august Pontiff."[110] Bourassa was not in his usual role of impassioned advocate but a humble interpreter. Although he often cited other texts or writers to complement his arguments, he treated the words of the pope as sacred. Pope Benedict XV was the inspiration for his ideas, a voice of moderation, and the spiritual and intellectual leader who steered his religious beliefs. None could compare to the righteousness of the pope. Throughout the war, Bourassa contrasted other – sometimes faltering – voices with that of the papacy. The pope's consistency only further solidified his legitimacy in Bourassa's eyes.

A few English Canadian Catholic commentators shared Bourassa's views. For example, Toronto Archbishop Neil McNeil's twenty-four-page pamphlet in February 1918 titled *The Pope and the War* sold over 5,000 copies and refuted accusations against the pope, telling readers that "the Catholic Church is the only international power remaining unbroken by the conflict of nations and empires."[111] For most anglophone Catholics, however, the years-long battle over language education in Ontario had created so much tension between English speakers and French speakers that they vilified Bourassa as equally as Protestants did.[112] The hierarchy of the French Canadian Catholic Church had originally committed to the war effort, but only with the imposition of conscription did it align with the pope's position. The decision of the hierarchy to support the war was a source of strain for French Canadian Catholics since many parish priests sided with Bourassa's wider view of the war.[113] Bourassa was not unique among Canadian Catholics for contesting conscription or advocating the papal position, but he alone publicly rejected the war based upon a combination of Catholic devotion and critical inquiry.

In the final weeks of January, Bourassa examined the failure of Lloyd George's and Wilson's tentative but positive remarks on peace to establish negotiations. A two-part article, "Toward Peace," questioned the reluctance of the Central Powers to agree to peace. Bourassa delved into Germany's war aims and outlined what the country still hoped to achieve from the war. He concluded that German Chancellor Georg von Hertling agreed with President Wilson and Prime Minister Lloyd George on almost every point of Europe's territorial readjustment except one: Alsace-Lorraine, where "the harm done to France [should be] repaired, [but] the Germans had no response but silence."[114] This single issue blocked peace negotiations, and it was the biggest challenge that the two sides had to overcome. Until Germany was willing to negotiate, the war would continue.

That meant that Canada and the Allies might soon face more difficult circumstances at home than on the battlefield. The terms of peace aside, two threats endangered the world of 1918: famine and revolution. Bourassa warned that, if the forces of a starving, ravaged people met "the monstrous belly and the overflowing purse" of the plutocracy before the ruined nations of the world could regain normalcy, then "woe to the heads of state, woe to the rich, woe to the peoples, woe to the world!"[115] The terrible consequences of the war were deeper than a simple moral transgression. Continuing to fight the war to achieve security and power was at best idealistic and, at worst, suicidal. By 1918, the war stretched the morale and cohesion of all the nations involved. The spectre of the Russian Civil War loomed, and the belligerent countries risked devastation that might prevent them from fighting any war.

After the December federal election, the chance to end the war became a profoundly ethical issue for Bourassa. He focused on international issues in the first months of 1918. Despite his moral indignation that the war continued, and over the actions of those who sustained it, Bourassa did not allow himself to forget the real political implications of war and peace on the international stage. It was not about attacking English Canadians or British imperialism or about championing his province's rights. His visceral reaction was rooted in his analysis of events, his Catholic faith, and his confidence in Pope Benedict XV. It was more than a matter of political importance. Although his liberal nationalism shaped his political beliefs and the ideas that he expressed, the devout French Canadian seemed to be ethically obliged to question why the war could not be ended.

To evade such questions, as politicians did time and again, was morally dishonest.

In the weeks before Easter 1918, Bourassa devoted much of his writing in *Le Devoir* to disseminating information revealed by Russia's new Bolshevik government. On 22 November 1917, the Bolsheviks had published the texts of all treaties signed by the Allies and the former Czarist government. The UDC had wasted no time in publishing the treaties as a pamphlet, noting that "our statesmen have given the world a steady flow of assurance that we have entered and sustained the war for unselfish aims, that we coveted no territory, and that we were not fighting for conquests or annexations," and it had urged its readers to "critically examine the following treaties as a commentary on these wise intentions."[116] The publication had helped to spur President Wilson and Prime Minister Lloyd George to offer a more moderate peace program that January,[117] and Bourassa welcomed the release of treaties that seemingly justified all of his claims about the war. He was determined to break the press silence on them and detailed their contents over four weeks from 21 February to 18 March. "May this forced confession at least be followed," Bourassa hoped, "by sincere repentance and firm salutary words among all peoples and in the souls of all rulers!"[118] His examination repeated many of his arguments concerning the war, President Wilson, and the position of the pope as he detailed exactly where and how the secret treaties affirmed his views.

The dire impact of the war on Canada was clear in the midst of the 1918 German spring offensive when German armies pushed to the Marne River, within 100 kilometres of Paris. In late March and early April, the government enforced conscription against a sometimes unwilling populace. Riots broke out in Quebec City after the imprisonment of two men on 28 March for not providing their exemption papers. The police eventually released them, but a crowd of about 2,000 gathered and stormed the police station. The next evening a crowd of 8,000 civilians looted the offices of two pro-conscription newspapers, the *Quebec Chronicle* and *L'Événement,* and they burned down the offices of the Military Service Act registrar. These large mobs completely overwhelmed municipal police forces, and the local armoury dispatched 300 soldiers before the crowd dispersed. On 30 March, Prime Minister Borden declared that the federal government was now taking charge of peace and order in Quebec City. Ottawa immediately deployed a force of 780 soldiers and supplemented it by 1,000 soldiers from Ontario to reinforce the Quebec garrison.[119] Rioting continued through to 1 April as clashes broke out each night between rioters and soldiers. Over the Easter weekend, official reports stated, the unrest injured four civilians, wounded an unknown number, and injured sixty-two soldiers.[120] At its peak, the government feared revolution and widespread disorder across Quebec. It reacted quickly to stem further riots and deployed thousands of soldiers to Quebec City and Montreal. Bourassa, disgusted with the outbreak of violence and facing stricter censorship laws, wrote a single editorial in response on 5 April declaring that "public order must be maintained."[121] He was clearly dismayed with what the war had wrought.

Over the Easter weekend, Bourassa published several editorials condemning female suffrage, which went to print while he was observing the religious holiday. As Quebec City rioted, he questioned whether giving women the vote truly improved democracy. He presented a series of philosophical, political, and practical arguments against female suffrage. The "social contract" included women in the family, not as voters, he argued.[122] On 30 March, he dismissed supporters of women's suffrage as "superficial and short minds, unable to grasp the relationships of cause and effect, carefree and opportunistic, always ready to reconcile good and evil, false and true."[123] It was the last analysis that Bourassa offered Canadians before accepting the imposition of censorship later that month.

His glib words of 30 March, though directed against suffrage supporters, could have described his feelings about the violent demonstrators who roamed the streets that night. Bourassa repeated his counsel of August 1917 that it was "neither legitimate nor *practical* to fight" conscription with violence.[124] No matter how justified the rioters might have been in opposing conscription, he wrote, the primary duty of the state was to maintain public order. The government might enact legislation that was unfair or foolish, but it still played a vital role in protecting its citizens. Even citizens who faced unjust laws "shall not have the right to impede it by violence, to the detriment of public order." "General social principles," Bourassa continued, "take precedence over any particular grievance."[125] He feared armed insurrection against the government, an outcome that violated his belief in order and justice and promised far worse than anything that Borden's government had enacted. Bourassa's categorical condemnation of the riots did not leave any room for rejoinders to his arguments.

The riots were a confirmation of what English Canada had implied – or explicitly condemned – throughout the war: the French Canadian character was not suited for war. Whether that character was a result of nationalist propaganda or some intrinsic racial element, English Canada had lingering suspicions about French Canada's failure to support the war.[126] As English Canadians suspected, Bourassa was influential in shaping French Canada's views on the war throughout the election and in the months up to April 1918, but it is worth considering that he helped to moderate the crowds. Historian Béatrice Richard has argued that his role in the conscription crisis and its aftermath should be read as part of a larger "resistance against *both* conscription and revolution."[127] Compared with the leaders of the crowds roaming the streets, he called for sensible and restrained action.

For months, the *nationaliste* journalist had faced the threat of censorship. Throughout the election campaign that fall and into the winter of 1917–18, citizens wrote to the chief press censor's office asking it to silence Bourassa. During the tense months, leading up to the December election, Chief Press Censor E.J. Chambers refused to censor *Le Devoir* for fear that political opponents would see it as "an act of political warfare."[128] Chambers kept in contact with Georges Pelletier, one of the editors of *Le Devoir*, who agreed to temper Bourassa's writing in the months leading up to April 1918.[129] According to this correspondence, Bourassa had changed the tone and content of his articles to make them more amenable to the censor in the fall of 1917. Nonetheless, after the election, Chambers tried in February 1918 to stop the publication of *Le Devoir* for the duration of the war after Bourassa published his articles on the possibility of peace. The government rejected this suggestion.[130]

Two weeks after the Quebec City riots, Prime Minister Borden passed an order-in-council that prohibited the press from publishing, or an individual from publicly expressing, "any adverse statement, report, or opinion concerning the action of the allied nations in the prosecution of the war."[131] Two days later Bourassa explained to his readers that the government, "which bears full responsibility for the measures of war," believed that "the time has come to prohibit any expression of opinion that it judged inappropriate or likely to foster differences of opinion on the object or conduct of war." "It remains for us," he concluded, "to submit to the decision of the authorities and to leave it to the future to determine whether it is in the best interests of the country."[132]

Bourassa wrote nothing for *Le Devoir* until October except for a single article in May, and he waited for the end of the war in uncharacteristic silence. The illness of his wife, Josephine, worsened, and Bourassa became depressed.[133] He welcomed the new apostolic delegate, Archbishop Pietro di Maria, to Canada in October during such troubled times.[134] When Borden left for Versailles in early November to "take part in preliminary discussions respecting the terms of peace," Bourassa lightly questioned his wisdom in abandoning Parliament.[135] When word reached the journalist of the declaration of the armistice on 11 November, he feared the revolution growing in Germany and a return of "brutal force" in deciding worldly affairs. Bourassa declared that it was time for prayer:

> Let us thank God for silencing the murderous voice of the cannons, that is, the voice of pride, hatred, brutal and blind force. Let us ask him to make the voice of humility, repentance, reason enlightened by faith, true social charity, and speak louder than ever. Let us ask him to enlighten the conscience of the peoples and the minds of leaders.[136]

His prayer marking the end of the war reflected on the world that Bourassa had not seen for four terrible years. Now that the conflict was finally over, he prayed that humanity might emerge wiser from it so that people could "restore order to the chaos of moral and worldly ruins caused by the mad passions of men."[137] And Canadians would have to rebuild their fractured nation – but Bourassa would play little part in that rebuilding.

Conclusion

THE END OF THE FIRST WORLD WAR in November 1918 brought welcomed tranquility for most of its weary participants. The conflict had torn out the heart of the Old World and laid its crass inhumanity bare for all to see. Few could claim Europe to be the enlightened continent that held the future of human civilization. The belligerent nations that emerged from the conflict began the long road to recovery and struggled to make sense of the experience, free from the dark cloud of war. For the French Canadian nationalist Henri Bourassa, the armistice changed little. Months earlier the war had vanquished his vision of a bicultural and bilingual Canada unifying its English-speaking and French-speaking peoples. He no longer saw the future for the Canada that he had struggled to create over two decades as a politician, writer, journalist, and critic. Canada's war had unleashed forces far worse than the imperialism that Bourassa had rallied against before 1914: the mismanagement of parliamentary government, rampant militarism, social unrest bordering on revolution, and growing secularism.

Worse, his beloved wife and mother of their eight children, Joséphine Papineau, died after a long illness on 26 January 1919. Sir Wilfrid Laurier wrote his final letter to Bourassa mourning the passing of Joséphine. Bourassa replied, and Laurier received the letter two days before he too died on 17 February. Their passing, the one who had inspired Bourassa's heart and the other his mind, was a devastating blow to the fifty year old.[1] His *joie de vivre* was gone. Bourassa completed the process of withdrawing from the active role that he had played in Canadian politics for more than twenty years. The man who had been the beating heart of a Canadian nationalist movement, whose evocative and passionate writing was republished in newspapers across the dominion, whose words could entertain an ebullient audience for hours, was diminished. The war had taken away his hope for a better Canada, and cruel fate had taken away the love of his life as well as his former mentor-turned-nemesis within weeks of each other.

The day after Laurier died, Bourassa wrote a straightforward and respectful editorial appealing to all Christians to pray for Laurier. It would be difficult, he lamented, to convey the man's greatness properly:

> In the life of a head of state and party, the conscientious historian has a duty to search for multiple factors for his influence and public action, to distinguish between acts voluntarily committed and those that have been suffered or simply accepted. Always difficult, this task is particularly difficult in a country and at a time when there is hardly any opinion free of party passions. It is almost impossible while the contemporaries of an eminently sympathetic and charming man, whose strength and influence were based more on the affection of hearts than on the reasoned convictions of intelligence, live.[2]

Bourassa's effusive praise is a stark contrast to his depiction of "Laurier the Traitor" for much of the previous two decades. Clearly, Bourassa had forgiven Laurier for his mistakes, and his words are a useful warning to historians: Laurier so dominated his era that he overwhelmed it. Few could separate the political career that had intertwined with his life for nearly fifty years. Historians could say much the same about the grieving Bourassa. Like those of Laurier, his life and his legacy were so broad and far-reaching that to this day it remains difficult for historians to capture them entirely.

The comparison between Bourassa and Laurier was compelling to their contemporaries, as it is to their historians, and it reveals the difficulty in understanding Bourassa's wartime life. Politically, both men were French Canadian liberals, Canadian nationalists (though in different ways), and deeply involved in the politics of their time. In character, both were passionate, evocative speakers, capable of inspiring others to follow them, though Laurier was always willing to compromise to achieve his long-term goals. Bourassa could never accept capitulation on his positions. They took different paths throughout their careers even though it once seemed that Bourassa would follow in Laurier's footsteps. Their trajectories were often closer to each other than they would have admitted. Bourassa had spent the past decades opposing Laurier, but their rapprochement in 1917–18 revealed how much they had in common. In 1935, Bourassa was again an MP; when asked by Conservative MP I.D. MacDougall why he had betrayed Laurier, Bourassa reflected on his long relationship with his former leader:

> If my friend knew something more about the political history of the country, he would know that I fought Laurier when he was at the height of his popularity. When the Tory party was denouncing him from the Atlantic to the Pacific as the instrument of Catholicism and French domination, I stood by him. When he was the idol of Quebec, I stood almost alone against him in defence of the principle for which I have fought all my life. But when he was betrayed by his Liberal friends, when he was downtrodden during the war, I came to him and freely tendered him a helping hand, not to carry but to go through the elections of 1917 ... He knows now that although I fought him because of differences in principle, I loved him all my life; and he knew it then. The day I passed in his house in 1917, when he was betrayed by men whom he had covered with honours and favours – I never received anything from him and never asked – that day he pressed me on his bosom and said to me: "Bourassa, what has happened to me today you predicted eleven years ago. I know now where my true friends are to be found."[3]

It is difficult to ascertain whether the reconciliation was as complete as Bourassa outlined here. Had Laurier truly forgiven his wayward protégé? Each had offered harsh criticisms of the other before and during the war, up to the moment when their reunion occurred and in the last months of 1917. It is difficult to consider them friends or even on parallel tracks in 1916. Still, Bourassa's continuing reverence, which had survived those turbulent times, spoke to the depth of his respect for Laurier despite their disagreements. The contradiction of his love and his hate for Laurier is one of many inconsistencies embedded in Bourassa's political life, so difficult to untangle from his personal life.

I have endeavoured to portray Bourassa during the First World War through the beliefs that he embraced and the ideas that he espoused, and I hope that I have portrayed their contradictions clearly even if it is not possible to explain them fully. His beliefs and ideas were rooted in his religion as a devout Catholic and in his politics as an ardent liberal. Although historians have often explored his influence as a critic of Canadian politics, they have devoted considerably fewer pages to examining the depth of his opposing religious and political beliefs, how those contradictions flared during the maelstrom of the First World War, and consequently how those beliefs shaped the ideas of one of Canada's most forceful war resisters from 1914 to 1918. It is unfair, as some scholars have done, to judge Bourassa based upon his influence on Canadian and Quebec nationalism alone. There were scant venues for lengthy Canadian treatises on international affairs during the war years, and those that did exist remain sadly understudied.[4]

In fact, Bourassa's Catholic and liberal beliefs shaped his interpretations of international events. At home and abroad, Bourassa saw the state abusing its power and deceiving its people as militarism warped the societies at war. He also perceived the failure of the international system to avoid the war or to work meaningfully toward a peaceful resolution. Citing perspectives from Britain and the United States, Bourassa believed that the failure of the international system itself had caused the war to erupt and allowed it to continue. The Great War proved to him that, though the balance between the great powers of Europe had once brought stability and progress, it now promised only destruction as it collapsed. Their insatiable imperialism, unrelenting greed, and lust for power had corrupted the world. Bourassa agreed with Britain's Union of Democratic Control, which hoped for a new system of international arbitration rooted in democratic and liberal ideas. As a liberal and a Catholic, he had a moral obligation to warn Canadians about the dangers that he saw around them. He urged Canada and the people of the world to support peace proposals from the belligerent nations, concurred with the actions of President Woodrow Wilson, and praised the careful diplomacy of Pope Benedict XV. Bourassa deserves recognition as a unique voice in the transnational resistance to the war – though he was faint on its periphery.

It is understandably difficult to categorize Bourassa within that mostly left-wing reaction to the war. He was paradoxically a French Canadian Catholic and a liberal Canadian nationalist, and given some of his beliefs one might assume that he was an anachronistic Catholic caricature of the nineteenth century, not a contemporary and supporter of Noel Brailsford and the Union of Democratic Control. As a French Canadian, Bourassa saw his language, culture, and religion as inseparable parts of a whole. French was the language and Catholicism the faith of French Canadians that had guided them over three centuries of inhabiting North America. Bourassa was more devout than others in that respect. The ultramontane Catholic accepted that the Catholic Church had to be the guiding force in society. In Quebec and in the world, Catholicism was a force for social order and progress. The pope, as God's representative on Earth, delivered the holy wisdom of God to humanity. Although Bourassa sometimes disagreed with the Quebec bishops' interpretation of the papal position, he never questioned the sanctity of their place within the province's social hierarchy. Nor did he question papal dictates, even when they opposed his own position.

Despite his devotion to Catholic authority, Bourassa tempered his religiosity with a deep admiration for British liberalism. This was not so inconsistent as to be entirely irreconcilable – both demanded respect for social order and the rule of law, and both sought to better society, one by defending individual rights, the other through Catholic duty. Liberal nationalism defended the right of the French Canadian Catholic community to exist within a largely English and Protestant dominion. In turn, his Canadian nationalism was inherently bicultural and bilingual, and it included both its French-speaking people and its English-speaking people. Bourassa's Canadian identity accepted the two as equally important to its formation. As proven by Confederation in 1867, only the union of the two created something uniquely "Canadian." His beliefs overlapped seemingly without contradiction – though not without a hierarchy,[5] which the war gradually laid bare.

As the war continued, Bourassa was less confident that the world could avoid the moral deterioration and chaos antithetical to his Catholic faith and liberal ideals. Only the holy words from Rome, which proposed a system based upon trust, goodwill, and the word of God, could provide the order that liberalism demanded despite its antithesis to liberalism. Bourassa did not necessarily imagine a Catholic world, simply one that realized the truth and virtue of the pontiff's message. He increasingly found solace in his unshakable faith as war supporters in Canada ignored his political beliefs. Faced with a deficient political culture at home and a crumbling international order abroad, Bourassa turned to Pope Benedict XV as the sole moral power capable of surpassing human interests and defending the common good of all people. Such was the threat of militarism overtaking the values of the world's liberal democracies.

A hierarchy of beliefs was as clear to war supporters as it was to Bourassa. From his perspective, his critics' relentless attacks against his position and their accusations that he was unpatriotic or treasonous proved the pervasive nature of the militarism behind the Canadian war effort and the failing health of Canadian liberal democracy. The most ardent war supporters did not distinguish between the Canadian state and the war effort, so according to this logic Bourassa's dissent was an attack on the nation itself. The expansion of state powers during wartime to organize the Canadian economy and industry, and eventually the individual through conscription, revealed the totality of the conflict, reflected through literature and other popular manifestations.[6] Any sacrifice that they made in liberty was not as important as the victory that they sought. While other Canadians accepted these measures as necessary, Bourassa rejected them as manifestations of the same Prussian militarism that the war meant to overturn in Germany.

The difference between these hierarchies reflects historians' own disagreement over the causes of the war. Bourassa might have been correct in lamenting the structural causes of the war innate to, or accepted by, the international system of late-nineteenth-century and early-twentieth-century Europe. Yet his belief that imperialism and militarism caused the war and sustained it allowed little room for individual agency. The war could have been solely a result of decision makers' actions at the heads of nations and armies. In that case, as other Canadians believed, the war could have been understood as a legitimately defensive action against a German aggressor.[7] Each necessarily created a different understanding of the purpose of the war in Canada and a divergent hierarchy of what was more important. For Bourassa, this difference caused a reaction unlike that of his contemporaries. His frustration over his inability to influence other Canadians comes into better focus if we understand that his view of the war linked it to militarism, imperialism, and other *impersonal* causes. His arguments and his rhetoric were out of touch with Canadians who not only did not agree with what was most important about the war but also did not even conceive of the war in the same way.

In this respect, Bourassa aligned with international liberal dissenters who pointed to systemic causes rather than individual causes. Consider the words of Bertrand Russell, perhaps the most famous British radical to oppose the war. Like Bourassa, Russell gradually believed that the war was not a conflict between nations but a great struggle between militarism and anti-militarism.[8] As a member of the Union of Democratic Control imprisoned for his views during the war, he offered many of the same points as Bourassa in his wartime writing. "One of the most surprising things in this war," Russell noted in 1916, "is the universal appeal to atavistic moral notions which, in times of peace, civilised men would have repudiated with contempt."[9] He echoed Bourassa's fear that the rampant militarism of the war would wreak greater havoc than could be repaired after its end:

> The fear of defeat and the longing for victory have made men oblivious of the common task of Europe and of the work which Europe had been performing for mankind at large. In all that has made the nations of the West important to the world, they run the risk of being involved in a common disaster, so great and so terrible that it will outweigh, to the historian in the future, all the penalties of military defeat and all the glories of military victory ... [If] the war lasts much longer ... it is to be expected that a blind fury of destruction will drive us on and on until the good and evil of the old world have perished together in universal ruin. For this reason, [it is important to realize that] all that is detestable in the enemy is the result of war, is brought out by war, in a greater or lesser degree, on our side as well as on the other, and will cease with the conclusion of peace but not before.[10]

Neither Bourassa nor Russell saw a difference between a militarized democracy and the autocratic militarism of Germany. Democracy was weakened in both, and the result was the same. The Allied Powers and the Central Powers had lost the authority to claim the moral high ground after total war demanded greater sacrifices and state controls that placed democratic values beneath state demands for victory.

Bourassa's hierarchy of belief became increasingly clear after the war. As Russell and other dissidents turned to socialism and internationalism as a solution to militarism, Bourassa turned to Rome.[11] He saw a world overtaken by individualism and secularism, and as individuals turned away from God the Catholic social order threatened to dissolve. Réal Bélanger notes that after the war Bourassa "the ideologist and moralist would prevail over the politician and journalist, but not completely replace them."[12] In 1922, he had a semi-private audience with Pope Pius XI and received his blessing.[13] Four years later Bourassa returned to Rome to have an hour-long private audience with Pius XI. This time the pope warned his follower about the dangers of devotion to nationalism and praised Bourassa's position against Quebec nationalism. "At the present time, the main obstacle to the Papacy's and the Church's action in the world," Pius XI shared with Bourassa, "is the predominance of racial passions in all countries, it is the substitution of nationalism for Catholicism." Bourassa left the meeting profoundly affected, and he disavowed his former actions and partially withdrew from public life.[14] Although he continued to write articles on some international and constitutional issues, Bourassa gradually and voluntarily abandoned his role as the leader of the nationalist movement.

With renewed vigour, he opposed the rising Quebec nationalist movement of L'action française during the 1920s, inspired by Pope Pius XI's condemnation of extreme nationalism. Consequently, he rejected the movement's separatist aspirations. "The preservation of the faith," Bourassa advised a new generation of French Canadian nationalists, "is more important than the preservation of any language, than the victory of any human cause."[15] His denunciation weakened their movement, but as a result of his criticism Quebec nationalist Abbé Lionel Groulx supplanted Bourassa as the leader of a nationalist movement.[16] By the late 1920s, Bourassa was clearly out of step with the emergent faction in Quebec, which no longer advocated the Canadian nationalism that he and the *nationalistes* had supported but a Quebec nationalism.[17] Groulx himself devoted many pages to describing the decline of Bourassa after the war. Groulx claimed that Bourassa suffered from a hereditary "moral disease" marked by extreme religiosity and that his faded significance was a result of his degradation. Groulx described Bourassa in the 1930s in his memoirs, published in 1971:

> Between him and his countrymen, a wall of loneliness rose. He was walking in a half-forgotten world. Had his illness taken something from his prestigious faculties? He seemed to be fine. In the Ottawa Parliament, after a few dazzling appearances, the speaker, who once invariably emphasized the galleries, ended up speaking almost in a vacuum. At *Le Devoir*, where he only rarely writes, he no longer signs many articles with the master's signature. Never again did he find his vein or his triumphs of the great days. It's not sunset yet; [but] it's already dusk.[18]

Groulx, however, did have reason to diminish Bourassa's place in history compared with his own since he sought to replace Bourassa as the Quebec nationalist patron. Groulx's repudiation, whether true or not, underlined the generational shift between the Canadian nationalism of Bourassa, which had developed under the benign political reign of Laurier in peacetime, and that of Groulx and other Québécois who had matured during the dark days of the First World War.

Their development spoke to their experiences. Bourassa had emerged from one political culture, one that he had entered with Laurier in 1896, and gone into another, one that had seen the conscription crisis of 1917 and the dire consequence of industrial war. The younger generation could not help but be affected, nor could Bourassa hope to emerge unscathed. He still believed in Catholicism, liberalism, and nationalism, but the hierarchy that he applied to them was clearer as the ideas that he chose to express changed considerably. He was no longer an ardent liberal nationalist, preferring to side unequivocally with the view from Rome.

It is less clear how much his opponents during the war understood this transformation, as Groulx demonstrated, or even the basis of his support for and rejection of the war, especially as viewed by the shattered nationalist movement. Jules Fournier's unpublished article from 1916 stands as a solid critique of Bourassa's position from within the *nationaliste* movement. Why Fournier never published the article is unknown, but it highlights the impact of the war on the *nationalistes* and the shift away from Bourassa's brand of liberal and Canadian nationalism. Historian Hélène Pelletier-Baillargeon considers the article a reflection of Fournier's dissatisfaction with Bourassa's role in the formation and continuation of the *nationaliste* movement itself,[19] but it is equally a substantial criticism of Bourassa during the war. Fournier could not endorse any acceptance of the war effort, as Bourassa did from August 1914 to January 1916, and he perceived a contradiction in Bourassa's support for Canadian participation while critiquing its character so completely. Bourassa's ambiguity toward the war might also have been due partly to the position of the Catholic Church and his anxiety about any apparent contradiction with it.[20] Even without understanding his difficulty in contravening the position of the church, Fournier is unfair to Bourassa. Although Bourassa offered careful approval of the war, he promised his readers on 2 September 1914 that he would "research conscientiously, in all loyalty," the issues of the war that others ignored.[21]

This promise shaped Bourassa's critiques in the following months, which Fournier held up as proof of an untenable and hypocritical position. If we accept it as an honest attempt to satisfy his loyalty to both the church and the *nationalistes*, then it is understandable that Bourassa supported the war, but not unquestioningly, and he continued to follow the spirit if not the letter of the *nationaliste* movement. He was one of the few nationalist voices raising questions about the nature and extent of the Canadian war effort to a national audience, resisting the war narrative that took hold throughout the rest of the country. Speaking to a national audience about national ideas was the hope of the *nationaliste* movement first envisioned in 1903.

Equally, Bourassa's support for the war was not as great a leap as Fournier believed, but it is only by understanding the nationalists who succeeded Bourassa within Quebec that this distinction becomes clearer. Those nationalists were not federalists who perceived the whole of Canada as united through the pact of Confederation. Instead, they saw Quebec as a unique entity that had agreed to enter Confederation, an agreement that had failed because English Canadian views were inherently opposed to French Canadian views.[22] In contrast, Bourassa's bicultural and bilingual nationalism could consider and endorse the position of English Canada, even if it was not one that the French Canadian wanted. At the war's outset, he understood that many Canadians did support the war and that they ought to have a clear discussion on its implications for the nation. Bourassa expected, or perhaps desired, that English Canada would recognize and accept French Canadian differences on the issues of the war. It was English Canada's ongoing failure to acknowledge French Canadian views on the war that eventually helped to convince Bourassa to withdraw his support for it. The national compact between the two peoples had been broken, but it would not be by Bourassa. Later the imposition of conscription underlined just how broken Confederation had become, but unlike Fournier Bourassa never assumed that that division had to occur.

English Canadian intransigence during the war, particularly over the issue of conscription and the 1917 election, made the nationalist vision of Bourassa seem increasingly untenable and necessarily changed the beliefs that he had spent two decades cultivating and explained his turn toward his faith after the conflict. "All that I asked [of the imperialists]," Bourassa wrote to J.S. Ewart in 1918, "was to take no advantage of the wave of blind enthusiasm to compromise the issue of interimperial relations. Far from responding to that offer of truce ... [they] did their best to becloud the real issues of the war, to foster the blind hatred of everything German." Instead, Bourassa was convinced of his "duty to denounce [the imperialist revolution] and open the eyes of the people on the true object of the war policy."[23] Of course, after four acrimonious years of warfare, hindsight coloured his perspective of the beginning of the war. Still, his complaint to Ewart reveals how Bourassa wished that the war had unfolded. In his perfect world, a Canada not overtaken by the imperialist revolution could have offered its support to the European conflict and united rather than divided its two peoples through the war effort. English Canada had used the war to pursue its own ideological goals, something that Bourassa in his support for an "imperialist war" in August 1914 had outright rejected. Although his support was tepid and critical, he offered it nonetheless.

For some of his fellow *nationalistes,* these distinctions were esoteric. Fournier and Asselin could not understand the contradiction in Bourassa's early position (though Asselin supported the war as well). They believed that British imperialism ought to be opposed for the sake of Canadian nationalism. Olivar Asselin was still committed to their movement but saw no problem in joining the Canadian army in late 1915 to defend France against German aggression (but not on behalf of a British or imperial effort, at least in his mind). Asselin fought at the Battle of Vimy Ridge and experienced first-hand the terrible brutality of trench warfare. Writing to a friend in May 1917, he explained that his conscience had demanded that he enlist, for "there have been too many people who have enlisted others without going to the fire themselves." He did not regret his decision, but he discovered that war was "a dirty thing."[24] Asselin did not wholeheartedly accept the imperialist vision of the war – for instance, he and many other French Canadian soldiers opposed conscription.[25] Instead, he fashioned a *nationaliste* position in favour of the war distinct from that of Bourassa, and, as Fournier noted, at least it was consistent.[26]

Outside the wartime fragmentation of the *nationaliste* movement, the perception of Bourassa's position assumed a strangely impersonal tone. Most of his critics did not comprehend the basis of and motivations behind his views on the war. Like his *nationaliste* colleagues, they could not reconcile his different beliefs. Some did, such as Ferdinand Roy, whose *L'appel aux armes et la réponse canadienne-française* rationally rejected Bourassa's perspective on conscription as a path that would inevitably be detrimental to French Canadians' place within Confederation.[27] Most commentators simply rejected any position that did not endorse their views or, in the case of politicians, viewed Bourassa purely through a political lens.

Political perspectives on Bourassa raise an unstated dilemma in contemporary and historical treatments of him in the First World War. He was not a politician at the time, but this did not stop politicians such as Wilfrid Laurier and Robert Borden from fearing his impact on the fortunes of the parties that they led. Laurier wrote that he could not leave Quebec to the extremists, epitomized in his warning to Senator Raoul Dandurand in January 1915 that "Bourassa is playing with fire and if he thinks that he will be able to extinguish it he may have a rude awakening."[28] Laurier was convinced that the wartime commentary of Bourassa was part of a campaign to manoeuvre himself against Laurier's leadership of the province, as he had done since 1899. Borden was also cynical about Bourassa's dissent. In 1915, as officials and the public demanded that Bourassa be censored, Borden remarked in his diary that "Bourassa would like nothing better. I would not be so foolish."[29] Both federal party leaders portrayed him as a sort of political mastermind or manipulator willing to become a martyr on the altar of oppressed nationalism.

Although it is certain that Bourassa was a political agent, the cynicism embedded in Laurier's and Borden's views speaks to a larger problem when considering Bourassa's wartime commentary. Neither leader considered that Bourassa wrote because he sought honestly to express his beliefs about the war and to dissect the issues of the national war effort in which Canada had engaged. They believed that he was like them, playing a political game for political victory. Bourassa, however, had no party that he wanted to see in power. He was a political writer, not a politician, and he had none of the concerns and responsibilities of those in the House of Commons. He was a journalist in 1914 and remained so throughout the war. Clearly, Bourassa had political goals in mind when he published his articles, but to ascribe solely political motivations to his writing is a disservice to the public discourse that he offered. His shifting hierarchy of belief was also far more sustainable as a commentator first and political agent second, for he could freely contradict himself in the name of discourse but not in the name of ideology.

Bourassa believed that political issues ought to be debated publicly rather than accepted without question on a politician's word. His promise of 2 September 1914 openly established this obligation to his readers. When his contemporaries limited their responses to Bourassa to a political lens, they failed to appreciate that his arguments about the war hinged on his devotion as a public commentator in the truest sense of that title. His examination of international events revealed that Canada was deeply involved in global affairs in a way outside the political framework of the day. Canadians could use his writing to consider global events from a Canadian perspective. Bourassa devoted weeks of editorials to American politics, international diplomacy, and other distant happenings that affected Canada even if they did not appear to affect Canadians directly. His readers were exposed to events of the war in greater detail than appeared in other newspapers, just as they were confronted with a Canadian perspective on them. Although he reiterated the political concerns of Canadians within an international context, constrained as they were by a British imperial world system, he was not limited by that context. Bourassa was proof that Canadians, while enmeshed in a British world, strove to be free from it. His writing was certainly coloured by his beliefs, and sometimes weakened by them, but without question he presented global affairs through a uniquely Canadian lens not constrained by Canada's borders, both national and imperial.

Bourassa's opposition cemented his role in Canadian history, and afterward his dissent shaped the divergent popular memory of the war in both French and English Canada. His competing beliefs once again shaped views of Bourassa and served opposing roles in the two memories of the war that developed in its aftermath. English Canadians championed the enduring purpose of the war for English Canada within Victorian ideals, and French Canadians remembered the defeats in 1917 over conscription and the election victory of the Unionist Party as well as the Easter Riots.[30] The two early seminal works on Bourassa reveal his influence on the fashioning of that public memory, Elizabeth Armstrong's *The Crisis of Quebec, 1914–1918* and Robert Rumilly's *Henri Bourassa: La vie publique d'un grand Canadien*. Armstrong wrote in the 1930s and Rumilly during Bourassa's final years, though his book was published after Bourassa's death in 1952. These works and subsequent ones reveal the difficulty of categorizing any individual by the simplified needs of public memory, especially within the complexity of Canada at war.

Armstrong's work on Quebec was the first to consider Bourassa through a historian's lens. Armstrong approached him as a case study for a larger examination of Quebec nationalism during the First World War. To Armstrong, Bourassa became a political figure driven by his "dreams of French Canada as a proselytizing force which shall eventually bring the American continent back to the arms of Rome and to the glories of French civilization."[31] In her account, Bourassa was inhibited by his nationalism and Catholicism and unable to look beyond the borders of Canada or North America to understand the greater purpose of the war. Consequently, Armstrong considered Bourassa's defining characteristics through questions related to his Canadian nationalism rather than a detailed examination of the wartime dissenter.

Armstrong's portrayal of Bourassa shows how he would be remembered among English Canadians. In the immediate aftermath of the war, men such as Castell Hopkins, author of the *Canadian Annual Review*, preferred to minimize the influence of Bourassa in contrast to other "true" French Canadians.[32] As Jonathan Vance notes, English Canadians preferred to evoke men such as Talbot Papineau, or 22nd Battalion Victoria Cross recipients Joseph Kaeble and Jean Brilliant, to demonstrate Quebec's service during the war.[33] The war could then serve as an example of Canadian unity – at least an English Canadian vision of that unity. English Canadians and some French Canadians were convinced by the new national identity forged during the war, expressed by the "spirit of the trenches."[34] The soldier experience shaped English Canadian nationalism and memory of the war in the interwar period, and French Canadian opponents of the war such as Bourassa were dismissed, in Armstrong's words, as "passive nationalists" who would never fulfill their national desires.[35] Bourassa's Canadian nationalism was not equal to the vigorous English Canadian nationalism that had proven its worth on the battlefields.

Rumilly's biography of Bourassa, written in French for a Quebec audience, offered a completely different picture of his actions that reflected Quebec's memory of the war. Rumilly opened his history by remarking that Bourassa "summoned atavisms that must be called contradictory."[36] This reflected a common theme throughout the work, that Bourassa epitomized the best of French Canada. The traits that had propelled him to enter politics and defend French Canada were inherent to French Canadians themselves. Rumilly described Bourassa in 1918, writing that, though he could have split away with a new Quebec party, "his atavisms ... inspired a higher conception."[37] "Atavism," that one ought to be directed by ancient and ancestral traits, is referenced often in Rumilly's work. It is not derogatory but integral to its presentation of Bourassa as a uniquely French Canadian figure, impelled by his racial history as much as his personal beliefs.[38] Rumilly used the term to divide Bourassa's career between his opposition to imperialism and his devotion to Catholicism, noting that "the atavism of Papineau and the atavism of Bourassa are competing for the most important role in the first half of the twentieth century in Canada."[39] Just as Louis-Joseph Papineau's ancestral force had led Bourassa to become a "great Canadian," so too Rumilly mobilized Bourassa's ancestral force to inspire French Canadians to continue defending nationalism – though a far different version than the one that Bourassa had defined forty years earlier. Equally, it exposed his role in shaping Rumilly's history of the province, for the historian was also shaped by an atavism stemming from Bourassa himself.[40] This explanation of Bourassa's historical significance is a telling juxtaposition of English Canadian memory of the war.

Rumilly's appeal to ingrained French Canadian traits likely reflected his close relationship with Abbé Lionel Groulx, who defended inherently atavistic conceptions of the French Canadian "race" in North America and integrated them into his vision of Quebec nationalism.[41] Rumilly echoed Groulx's beliefs about French Canadians. The Bourassa whom he described was not an individual struggling to express his ideas about Canada and the war but a symbol of Quebec's struggle within Confederation. The final pages of the book render Bourassa's life in almost spiritual terms as Rumilly reminded Québécois that "Bourassa, the great Bourassa we just lost, continues to protect us."[42] Rumilly evoked the defensive inward-looking nationalism that defined Quebec in the decades after the First World War.[43] Bourassa's successors, be it Groulx or others, remembered the war as an integral part of their racial (or national as the years wore on) struggle to achieve autonomy in North America. In contrast to the English Canadian experience, their memory of the war became a testament not to a new identity that had emerged but to the one that they had almost lost in 1917.

Despite the flaws of Armstrong's and Rumilly's works, their constructions of Bourassa's meaning provide insight into the context of their times and the place of the First World War in Canadian history. Still, both authors misunderstood Bourassa's role in the war as limited to domestic issues, so consequently they emphasized his fierce nationalism, his place as a French Canadian and a Catholic, but minimized his international perspective that, despite its local Canadian lens, presented the world to his readers in a way unlike any of his Canadian contemporaries.

When academic Canadian historians returned to the First World War and Bourassa in the 1960s after Armstrong and Rumilly, these misconceptions lingered as English Canadians and French Canadians dealt with a new generation of answers to the "French Canadian question." Battles over bilingualism, Quebec nationalism, and Canadian identity marked the Canada of the 1960s and kept Bourassa's ideas and legacy at the forefront of political consciousness. Scholars rarely examined his wartime career explicitly, most focusing on his prewar career. Claude Ryan, editor of *Le Devoir*, offered a useful snapshot of Bourassa's historical significance on the centenary of his birth in 1968. He noted that Bourassa's redemption in English Canada as the prophet of an independent nation strengthened the peaceful coexistence of its two founding peoples.[44] To solve the "question," the Liberal government of Prime Minister Lester Pearson had proposed a bilingual and bicultural Canada. French Canadians were no longer an intransigent minority unwelcome under the umbrella of the ambiguous British Canadian identity forged after the First World War. The new Canada influenced historians and the public alike as they searched for new foundational myths.[45] Bourassa, whose support for a bilingual and bicultural Canada was a solution to a much different Canadian problem, was easily subsumed in the new story that Canadians sought to tell about themselves.

As Canadians rethought what it meant to be Canadian, Québécois also reimagined their province and their perspective on Bourassa. The province faced serious societal conflict in the aftermath of the transformative Quiet Revolution that modernized Quebec. A new historical consciousness was developing as historians debated the legacy of New France and Confederation for the Quebec of the twentieth century.[46] Most writers skipped over Bourassa's career as a subject of direct historical study, but they reflected on many of the same themes of nationalism, clericalism, and survival. Ryan's article reminded his readers that Québécois were praising Bourassa on the anniversary of his birth as a unifying figure and the grandfather of a new Quebec nationalism even as English Canadians were commending his bilingualism and biculturalism.[47] Bourassa was enshrined as a fundamental figure for a new generation of both English Canadian and Quebec nationalists, though it was a distorted view of him inherently framed by the context of Canada in the 1960s. Historians such as Ramsay Cook portrayed Bourassa as a sort of modern Canadian nationalist. Cook and Robert Craig Brown used their contribution to the Canadian Centenary Series to emphasize that the crux of Bourassa's position had been that Canada was more Canadian than British.[48] Cook, who wrote extensively about the French Canadian question, portrayed Bourassa's role in Quebec as a visionary of a unified Canada, though he questioned the dubious influence of his nationalism and religion.[49]

Recent scholarship on the First World War is not as bound as it once was to the commemorative narrative of the war that emerged in its aftermath, but Bourassa remains a stilted figure within the literature. In English Canada, historians have moved away from exploring political and intellectual figures during the war or reflecting on the questions about national unity that Bourassa raised, though their lens has widened considerably since the 1960s.⁵⁰ Meanwhile, Quebec historians have not studied the First World War in detail, largely as a repudiation of its continuing resonance for English Canadian scholars as a national moment for English Canadian identity.⁵¹ As different as the memories of Bourassa are in Quebec and English Canada, both cast him in their nationalist theatres. He is the opponent of the war that unified Canadians at Vimy Ridge in English Canada and the dissenter who failed to prevent conscription but ultimately nurtured the beginning of Quebec nationalism in French Canada.

Historians have given Bourassa an influential role in Canadian history, but actually gauging his influence is difficult. Countless French Canadians and English Canadians read his articles or heard his speeches. During the Second World War, the venerable journalist directly influenced Quebec nationalists who organized his return to the public spotlight with lectures on the issue of conscription. The Bloc populaire, a Quebec nationalist party, attempted to create a group of Quebec MPs who stood for Quebec's interests just as Bourassa had attempted in 1911 and had demanded in 1917. The party brought together a disparate group of old and new nationalists, some of whom were more loyal to his vision and younger ones who wanted to move away from his religious nationalism. The party dissolved after the Second World War, failing to unify the old and new strains of French Canadian nationalism.⁵² There are also examples of Bourassa's influence on English Canadian nationalists, such as George Grant, who privately cheered Bourassa's criticism of Prime Minister William Lyon Mackenzie King for aligning so closely with the United States during the Second World War.⁵³ Perhaps a better testament to Bourassa's lasting impact is the Quebec term *bourassisme*, used to describe the ideas and beliefs of his generation of French Canadian nationalists.⁵⁴ The diffusion of his ideas contributes to the difficulty in categorizing Bourassa by historians and contemporaries alike.

Henri Bourassa helped to shape twentieth-century French and English Canada, but he remains a product of the previous century. His ultramontane Catholicism mixed with his Gladstonian British liberalism was an outcome of European thought a generation out of date by 1914 and certainly by 1918. He conceived of a Canada with united "races" of French and English, a distinctly different conception of the nation from that envisioned by other Canadians during the war and even from the cultural unity envisioned by some Canadians in the 1960s. His belief in the implicit promise of equality between French and English at Confederation shaped his nationalism, but Bourassa had to accept the untenable nature of such a balance by 1918. By the end of the war, Canada had changed too much and become too divided to create the sort of compromise that he demanded. Although his ideas might have evolved over the course of the war, his core beliefs remained unchanged.

The war revealed the hierarchy that Bourassa applied to his complex web of beliefs as a liberal nationalist and ultramontane Catholic. He aligned himself with radicals such as those in the Union of Democratic Control, but he made sure to couch the reception of their ideas in the words of Pope Benedict XV. Bourassa critiqued the imposition of conscription as anti-democratic and illiberal, yet he envisioned a religious Quebec society attached to the Catholic Church, not the state. He demanded that the Canadian state recognize the rights of its linguistic and religious Franco-Ontarian minority for the sake of national unity, but he refused to moderate his comments that caused much disunity. Time and again, Bourassa criticized the imperialist vision of the war that did not align with his beliefs about Canada and its place in the world. Achieving the national cohesion that he envisioned was more important than building one that rejected his views.

The great difficulty for historians in dissecting Bourassa's positions, particularly during the First World War, is accepting their contradictory nature but not subsuming Bourassa within the powerful memory of the war itself. Despite the memory of the war shaping modern Quebec nationalism and English Canadian nationalism, reading these movements too closely back into the past is historical hindsight. His ideas were antecedents to Québécois and Canadian ideas, as Armstrong and Rumilly suggested, but not necessarily precedents. Despite his acceptance by modern English Canadian and French Canadian nationalists, Bourassa was an anti-modern figure who did not fit the role imposed on him. He understood Canadian nationalism as a union of "races," far different from its cultural conception in the latter half of the twentieth century. He would have disagreed with modern Québécois nationalism and its demands for protected privileges from the English majority. Bourassa preferred an equal contest between French Canadians and English Canadians in which both could express their views. He wanted not special status but equal status.[55] The great tragedy of the war was not necessarily the persecution of French Canadians, but it demonstrated the power imbalance between French and English in the country. Even minute details, such as the fact that the renowned newspaper journalist refused to own a radio or listen to one, reveal a man firmly entrenched in the Canada of pre-1914.[56]

Bourassa's passion and fiery rhetoric inspired enemies and allies alike. French Canadians and English Canadians considered Bourassa the leader of the resistance to the war – a claim demonstrated by how often critics and allies portrayed him as taking a primary role in it. Only 15,000 subscribers read his writing in *Le Devoir* during the war years, but it was his name that English Canadians would have heard during the 1917 election as the spectre of disloyalty. Whether one agreed or disagreed with him, Bourassa provoked a reaction. He knew how to incite a response among Canadians. His particular combination of political and religious views could only have appeared in French Canada, and it is easy to overlook those views in a Canadian context. Nonetheless, there is a uniqueness to his war experience compared with that of other international dissenters. Where else could a Catholic liberal nationalist oppose so strenuously the war and not only avoid imprisonment but even directly influence elections and political events? Bourassa was a prominent dissenter at home and given great latitude by authorities to promote his views because of the context of his life and times.

In speeches to Parliament in 1935, on the cusp of retirement from political life, Bourassa reflected on his actions during the war, with perhaps a small amount of indignant innocence:

> If I go out of public life with one feeling, with one conviction, it is this: a deep regret for many bitter words that I have used in my life, deep and sincere repentance for all my violences of language; but I hope they will be forgiven me by God and man because not once in my life have I attacked anybody unjustly, from my point of view at least, and without believing it was my duty to do so.[57]

False claims of absolution aside, Bourassa still held close the sense of duty that had compelled him to public commentary, to dispute government actions, and to examine international events critically. He was not afraid to anger his opponents, but sometimes he was too eager to reveal their falsehoods. Even as Bourassa sought the truth at all costs, he did not necessarily recognize it every time. The First World War intensified his duty, turning his editorials into fervent searches for the true meanings and consequences of the war. He did not shy away from one fundamental truth: the world at war was terrifying. Events once debated calmly were suddenly a matter of life and death. Old political issues took on new meaning and rancour. For Bourassa, an intense man by nature, the war years pushed him to new heights of analytical insight and new depths of conspiratorial allegation. Yet, as other Canadians failed to confront the issues and debates that should have taken place during such a serious time, he refused to ignore them. Bourassa's war, fought through words on the page, was no less important to the journalist than the one fought by Canadian soldiers on the battlefields of Europe. In his view, the only way for Canada to emerge stronger from the war, regardless of victory or defeat, was if Canadians could honestly and openly discuss the international and domestic challenges that confronted their nation.

Bourassa looked out to the world first and foremost as a Canadian, though today we have different definitions of that identity. All of his beliefs were contained in a Canadian context. His views were not intrinsically correct, or unbiased, or even justified, but they represented the views of an individual Canadian concerned about a global event. Few Canadians have left records of their views like that of Bourassa, let alone offered them publicly throughout war years. Thus, he stands as one of the most prominent Canadian intellectuals to have considered the global and local contexts of Canada at war. At the same time, Bourassa deserves recognition outside Quebec and Canada. In this book, I have addressed his ideas as they were presented so that they might stand on their own – not simply as part of a domestic debate in Canada about its identity and the war but also as part of an international reaction against the Great War. Bourassa rejected the war for a wide variety of reasons, but he concluded, like so many commentators across the belligerent nations, that peace and international reform required solutions to ensure that such a war never erupted again. Around the world, Bourassa and others like him were part of a movement spurred on by the war and their solemn belief that they, regardless of the consequences, had a duty to dissent. That duty helped to shape interwar politics and the League of Nations as well as the politics of their countries. The legacy of their efforts and the ideas that they espoused profoundly affected the world that emerged after 1918, even if they did not succeed in their goals during the war years. Likewise, Bourassa won or lost his war not on the battlefield but in its lasting impact on Canadian history. Although he failed as a dissenter during the war itself, his influence on his country and his province proved the success of his wartime career. Although the splash might mark the speed or size of the stone where it lands, the ripples mark the whole pond. Henri Bourassa, much like the thrown stone, ought not to be judged by his splash but by its rippling consequences to this day.

Notes

Introduction

1 Charles F. Brooks, "The 'Old-Fashioned' Winter of 1917–18," *Geographical Review* 5, 5 (1918): 405–14. December was one of the coldest on record, and temperatures across the country dropped between ten and thirty degrees lower than normal. Canada, Bureau of Statistics, *Canada Yearbook 1918* (Ottawa: Bureau of Statistics, 1918), 163.
2 Canada, *House of Commons Debates,* 12th Parliament, 7th Session (17 July 1917), 3487 (Wilfrid Laurier).
3 Béatrice Richard, "Le Québec face à la conscription (1917–1918): Essai d'analyse sociale d'un refus," in *Le Québec dans la Grande Guerre: Engagements, refus, héritages,* ed. Charles-Philippe Courtois and Laurent Veyssière (Québec : Septentrion, 2015), 124.
4 Henri Bourassa, "Le 'Devoir' et les partis actuels," *Le Devoir,* 8 November 1917, 1:

> Le programme unioniste, c'est l'antithèse de tout ce que nous aimons, de tout ce que nous croyons, de tout ce que nous voulons. C'est la synthèse de tout ce que nous détestons – hommes, idées et tendances – dans les deux partis ... Adversaires résolus du ministère de coalition, de toute sa politique et de tout son personnel, nous acceptons le programme de M. Laurier dans la mesure où il se rapproche de nos principes et de nos idées; nous le repoussons partout où il concorde virtuellement avec celui du ministère.

5 Ibid.
6 Henri Bourassa, "Avant le combat," *Le Devoir,* 10 January 1910, 1; "notre ambition se borne à chercher à faire de notre mieux ce que nous prêchons: le devoir de chaque jour."
7 For more on the decision behind the name of *Le Devoir,* see Réal Bélanger, *Henri Bourassa: Le fascinant destin d'un homme libre (1868–1914)* (Québec: Presses de l'Université Laval, 2013), 280–81.
8 Any error in translation is my own and, since I have no experience in translation, I apologize for it. I have added the original French for quotations that are more complex.
9 A bibliographical overview of Bourassa's career and work was published in 1966 with the help of his daughter; see André Bergevin, Cameron Nish, and Anne Bourassa, eds., *Henri Bourassa: Biographie, index des écrits, index de la correspondance publique 1895–1924* (Montréal: Éditions de l'Action Nationale, 1966).
10 Elizabeth Armstrong, *The Crisis of Quebec, 1914–1918* (Toronto: McClelland and Stewart, 1937). Many writers did discuss the Canadian war experience during and immediately after the war and included sections on Quebec and Bourassa, such as J. Castell Hopkins, *Canadian Annual Review War Series: 1914–1918* (Toronto: Canadian Annual Review,

1918), publications from the Canadian War Records Office, memoirs, and journalistic accounts.
11 Armstrong, *Crisis of Quebec*, 96.
12 Ibid., 143.
13 This point is raised by historian Joseph Levitt in the Carleton Library Edition of Armstrong's work, Elizabeth Armstrong, *The Crisis of Quebec, 1914–1918* (Montreal: McGill-Queen's University Press, 1974), viii.
14 Armstrong, *Crisis of Quebec* (1937), 53.
15 Although this term and its implications are present throughout the work, see Levitt, "Introduction," in Armstrong, *The Crisis of Quebec* (1974), v–xviii, for a succinct overview.
16 Armstrong, *The Crisis of Quebec* (1937), 180.
17 He appears in multiple volumes of Robert Rumilly, *Histoire de la province de Québec*, 41 vols. (Montréal: Valiquette, 1940–68); Robert Rumilly, *Henri Bourassa: La vie publique d'un grand Canadien* (Montréal: Éditions Chantecler, 1953). Before Rumilly's work, a brief analysis of Bourassa's nationalism appeared in 1951; see Marine Leland, "Quelques observations sur le nationalisme de Henri Bourassa," *Report of the Annual Meeting/Rapports annuels de la Société historique du Canada* 30, 1 (1951): 60–63.
18 Rumilly, *Henri Bourassa*, 577; "Bourassa développe une pensée équilibrée dans un monde affolé. Il reste seul de sang-froid dans le déchaînement des passions."
19 For an excellent overview of Rumilly that treats him with the attention that he deserves, see Jean-François Nadeau, *Robert Rumilly, l'homme de Duplessis* (Montréal: Lux Éditeur, 2009).
20 Rumilly, *Henri Bourassa*, 791; "Je connais de jeunes Canadiens français qui, lorsque la situation nationale leur paraît décourageante, se réconfortent en pensant: 'Il y a eu Bourassa! ...' Ainsi Bourassa, le grand Bourassa que nous venons de perdre, continue de nous protéger."
21 Anne Bourassa and Patrick Allen, "Le Bourassa de Rumilly: Deux appréciations," in *La pensée de Henri Bourassa*, ed. F.A. Angers (Montréal: L'Action Nationale, 1954), 198.
22 For example, see Martin P. O'Connell, "Ideas of Henri Bourassa," *Canadian Journal of Economics and Political Science* 19 (1953): 361–76; Martin P. O'Connell, "Henri Bourassa and Canadian Nationalism" (PhD diss., University of Toronto, 1954); F.A. Angers, ed., *La pensée de Henri Bourassa* (Montréal: Éditions de l'Action Nationale, 1954; this is a published version of an issue of *L'action nationale* that appeared in January 1954); André Laurendeau, "Henri Bourassa," in *Our Living Tradition*, ed. R.L. McDougall (Toronto: University of Toronto Press, 1962), 140–58; James I.W. Corcoran, "Henri Bourassa et la guerre sud-africaine (suite)," *Revue d'histoire de l'Amérique française* 19, 1 (1965): 84–105; and V.C. Smith, "Moral Crusader: Henri Bourassa and the Empire, 1900–1916," *Queen's Quarterly* 76, 4 (1969): 635–47. An important non-academic contribution is Casey Murrow, *Henri Bourassa and French-Canadian Nationalism: Opposition to Empire* (Montreal: Harvest House, 1968). There are numerous theses that touch on Bourassa, including Warren Alexander Clubb, "Henri Bourassa and the First World War" (MA thesis, University of Saskatchewan, 1974); and Charles Michael MacMillan, "Majorities and Minorities: Henri Bourassa and Language Rights in Canada" (PhD diss., University of Minnesota, 1979).
23 Joseph Levitt, *Henri Bourassa and the Golden Calf: The Social Program of the Nationalists of Quebec (1900–1914)* (Ottawa: Éditions de l'Université d'Ottawa, 1972); Joseph Levitt, "La perspective nationaliste d'Henri Bourassa, 1896–1914," *Revue d'histoire de l'Amérique française* 22, 4 (1969): 567–82. It is worth reading Richard Jones's reply to Levitt's article; Richard Jones, "'La perspective nationaliste d'Henri Bourassa, 1896–1914':

Commentaire," *Revue d'histoire de l'Amérique française* 22, 4 (1969): 582–86. See also Joseph Levitt, *Henri Bourassa on Imperialism and Bi-culturalism, 1900–1918* (Toronto: Copp Clark, 1970); and Joseph Levitt, *Henri Bourassa – Catholic Critic* (Ottawa: Canadian Historical Association, 1976). Levitt's chapter "Henri Bourassa: The Catholic Social Order and Canada's Mission," in *Idéologies au Canada français 1900–1929*, ed. Fernand Dumont, Jean Hamelin, Fernand Harvey, and Jean-Paul Montminy (Québec: Presses de l'Université Laval, 1974), 192–222, ably demonstrates how easily the war can remain absent from otherwise comprehensive works, notably on 217. Jean Drolet's succeeding chapter, "Henri Bourassa: Une analyse de sa pensée," in *Idéologies au Canada français*, ed. Dumont et al., 223–50, is similarly revealing.

24 Robert Craig Brown and Ramsay Cook, *Canada 1896–1921: A Nation Transformed* (Toronto: McClelland and Stewart, 1974), 274 and throughout; Michael Oliver, *The Passionate Debate: The Social and Political Ideas of Quebec Nationalism, 1920–1945* (Montreal: Véhicule Press, 1991), also includes an excellent discussion of Bourassa's role, though again purely within the realm of Quebec-Canada politics. Oliver's book was originally written in 1956 but published only in 1991, so it has an older view of Bourassa not informed by the French-English tension of the 1960s, but it still reflects on them with some hindsight.

25 Ramsay Cook, *Canada and the French-Canadian Question* (Toronto: Macmillan, 1966); Ramsay Cook, *Provincial Autonomy, Minority Rights and the Compact Theory, 1867–1921* (Ottawa: Queen's Printer, 1969); Ramsay Cook, *The Maple Leaf Forever: Essays on Nationalism and Politics in Canada* (Toronto: Macmillan, 1971); Ramsay Cook, *Canada, Quebec, and the Uses of Nationalism* (Toronto: McClelland and Stewart, 1986). Some of his most famous articles on Quebec appear in Ramsay Cook, *Watching Quebec: Selected Essays* (Montreal and Kingston: McGill-Queen's University Press, 2005). For a more complete bibliography of Cook's books and articles, see Michael D. Behiels and Marcel Martel, eds., *Nation, Ideas, Identities: Essays in Honour of Ramsay Cook* (Don Mills, ON: Oxford University Press, 2000), 233–37.

26 Susan Mann, *The Dream of a Nation: A Social and Intellectual History of Quebec* (Toronto: Gage, 1983); Susan Mann Trofimenkoff, *Action française: French Canadian Nationalism in the Twenties* (Toronto: University of Toronto Press, 1975); Susan Mann Robertson, "Variations on a Nationalist Theme: Henri Bourassa and Abbé Groulx in the 1920's," *Historical Papers* 1, 5 (1970): 109–19.

27 Mann, *The Dream of a Nation, 184–200;* Susan Mann Trofimenkoff, "Henri Bourassa et la question des femmes," in *Les femmes dans la société québécoise: Aspects historiques*, ed. Marie Lavigne and Yolande Pinard (Montréal: Boréal Express, 1977), 109–24; Susan Mann Trofimenkoff, "Henri Bourassa and 'The Woman Question,'" *Journal of Canadian Studies* 10 (1975): 3–11. See also Susan Mann Trofimenkoff, "Nationalism, Feminism, and Canadian Intellectual History," *Canadian Literature* 83 (1979): 7–20.

28 René Durocher, "Henri Bourassa, les évêques et la guerre de 1914–1918," *Canadian Historical Association Historical Papers* 6 (1971): 248–75; see also René Durocher, "Un journaliste catholique au XXe siècle: Henri Bourassa," in *Le laïc dans l'Église canadienne-française de 1830 à nos jours*, ed. Pierre Hurtubise et al. (Montréal: Fides, 1972), 185–213.

29 Jean-Philippe Warren, "L'opposition d'Henri Bourassa à l'effort de guerre canadien: Un pacifisme aux accents romains," in *Le Québec dans la Grande Guerre: Engagements, refus, héritages*, ed. Charles-Philippe Courtois and Laurent Veyssière (Québec: Septentrion, 2015), 110–28.

30 Réal Bélanger, "Bourassa, Henri," in *Dictionary of Canadian Biography*, vol. 18 (Toronto: University of Toronto; Laval: Université Laval, 2003–), http://www.biographi.ca/en/bio/bourassa_henri_18E.html. Bélanger's article has many additional titles dealing with Bourassa than those listed here, particularly French-language sources.

31 Bélanger, *Henri Bourassa*. Bélanger also addresses Bourassa's ideas in Réal Bélanger, "L'élite politique canadienne-française et l'Empire britannique: Trois reflets représentatifs des perceptions canadiennes-françaises," in *Imperial Canada 1867–1914: A Selection of Papers Given at the University of Edinburgh's Centre of Canadian Studies Conference, May 1995*, ed. Colin Coates (Edinburgh: University of Edinburgh, Centre of Canadian Studies, 1997), 122–40.

32 Sylvie Lacombe, *La rencontre de deux peuples élus: Comparaison des ambitions nationale et impériale au Canada entre 1896 et 1920* (Québec: Presses de l'Université Laval, 2002), 10. As a Quebec academic, Lacombe is unique in that she also discusses English Canadian imperialists through a nationalist lens, rather than simply a colonialist one, a thesis that Carl Berger presented three decades previously in *The Sense of Power: Studies in the Ideas of Canadian Imperialism, 1867–1914* (Toronto: University of Toronto Press, 1970), 259. Ramsay Cook makes this point in his review of *La rencontre de deux peuples élus*, by Sylvie Lacombe, in *Revue d'histoire de l'Amérique française* 56, 4 (2003): 557–60.

33 Lacombe, *La rencontre de deux peuples élus*, 19–26, 37–124. For her discussion of Bourassa and the First World War, including his reaction to American neutrality and subsequent entry into the war, see 107–24. Her conclusion to the section of the book on Bourassa (122–24) is both concise and informative. Lacombe has also published "Un prophète ultramontain: Henri Bourassa (1868–1952)," in *Les visages de la foi: Figures marquantes du catholicisme québécois*, ed. Gilles Routhier and Jean-Philippe Warren (Québec: Fides, 2003), 133–45.

34 Sylvie Lacombe, "Entre l'autorité pontificale et la liberté nationale: L'anti-impérialisme britannique d'Henri Bourassa," in *Le Devoir: Un journal indépendant (1910–1995)*, ed. Robert Comeau and Luc Desrochers (Québec: Presses de l'Université du Québec, 1996), 273–81. She refers to his points of radicalization on 273n3.

35 Yvan Lamonde, *Histoire sociale des idées au Québec*, vol. 2, *1896–1929* (Québec: Fides, 2004), 37–47, addresses Quebec during the war, but Bourassa is present throughout.

36 The most comprehensive work on *Le Devoir* is Comeau and Desrochers, *Le Devoir*. A collection of Bourassa's articles was published with some comments by its editor; see Pierre Anctil, ed., *Fais ce que dois: 60 éditoriaux pour comprendre* Le Devoir *sous Henri Bourassa (1910–1932)* (Québec: Éditions du Septentrion, 2010). A popular history of Bourassa was written by a journalist, Mario Cardinal, *Pourquoi j'ai fondé* Le Devoir*: Henri Bourassa et son temps* (Montréal: Libre Expression, 2010).

37 Many general French-language studies exist, such as Paul-André Linteau, René Durocher, and Jean-Claude Robert, *Histoire du Québec contemporain*, vol. 1, *De la Confédération à la crise (1867–1929)* (Montréal: Boréal Express, 1989). Other works on the war cannot avoid Bourassa's influence, such as the chapters in Charles-Philippe Courtois and Laurent Veyssière, eds., *Le Québec dans la Grande Guerre: Engagements, refus, héritages* (Québec: Septentrion, 2015).

38 A point I first had the pleasure of hearing from Réal Bélanger, "Henri Bourassa and the First World War," paper presented at 1914–1918: The Making of the Modern World, Bill Graham Centre, University of Toronto, 30 July 2014.

39 John Lukacs, *The Future of History* (New Haven, CT: Yale University Press, 2011), 123.

40 Michael Gauvreau, "Beyond the Search for Intellectuals: On the Paucity of Paradigms in the Writing of Canadian Intellectual History," in *Thinkers and Dreamers: Historical*

Essays in Honour of Carl Berger, ed. Gerald Friesen and Doug Owram (Toronto: University of Toronto Press, 2011), 55.

41 The *Journal of the History of Ideas* 73, 4 (2012): 583–665, had a section reviewing Bevir's work. Bevir fits between foundational and poststructural positions on the history of thought; however, as Daniel O'Neill points out in his article in that section, Bevir clearly distinguishes himself from the Cambridge School associated with Quentin Skinner and J.G.A. Pollock. See Daniel I. O'Neill, "Revisiting the Middle Way: *The Logic of the History of Ideas* after More than a Decade," *Journal of the History of Ideas* 73, 4 (2012): 584, 589–91. Bevir believed in "a radical historicism, according to which human life consists solely of a flux of activity without any basis in a formal structure or teleological movement": Mark Bevir, "Post-Analytic Historicism," *Journal of the History of Ideas* 73, 4 (2012): 657–58.

42 Bevir balances synchronic belief, in which a single belief exists in one moment as part of a wider web against the background of inherited traditions, with diachronic belief, the examination of multiple beliefs that change over time. He uses the term "dilemma" to describe situations that challenge beliefs when individuals must exercise their agency in transforming or maintaining them. In examining the origins of a web of beliefs and the dilemmas that individuals encounter, historians can trace how and why those beliefs change over time. See Mark Bevir, *The Logic of the History of Ideas* (Cambridge, UK: Cambridge University Press, 1999), 49–191.

43 In addition to the articles in the *Journal of the History of Ideas*, see the articles in a special issue of *Intellectual History Review* titled *Post-Analytic Hermeneutics: Themes from Mark Bevir's Philosophy of History* 21, 1 (2011): 1–119.

44 Bevir, *The Logic of the History of Ideas*, 150.

45 Vivienne Brown has criticized Bevir's approach and emphasized that historians must search for unintended and deeper meanings in textual sources. See Vivienne Brown, "On Some Problems with Weak Intentionalism for Intellectual History," *History and Theory* 41 (2002): 198–208. Bevir positions himself as a weak intentionalist in that authors' intentions can be ascertained through an examination of their "web of beliefs" via works/texts, and the meanings of their statements change for each individual, be it author or reader. Brown rejects an examination of the author since fundamentally "there is no 'object' of which the historian can seek to give an adequate account other than the work/text itself," for only texts exist as part of the historical record, not authors themselves.

46 Jonathan Floyd, "Why the History of Ideas Needs More than Just Ideas," *Intellectual History Review* 21, 1 (2011): 42. Floyd advises Bevir to place himself between the "material and the ideational," just as he has positioned himself between empiricism and postmodernism and determinism and autonomy.

47 In this sense, I am rejecting specific methodological or theoretical approaches to history other than general ones of studying "beliefs" (intellectual history) and an individual (historical biography) to reconstruct a facet of past experience as much as the sources allow against the backdrop of social and political contexts (also known as contextual reconstruction). Thus, I use Bevir's philosophy of history partly to inform this decision as well as to justify it; see Bevir, "Post-Analytic Historicism," 658, 665. A.P. Martinich's critique of Bevir's approach is also useful for a historian, explaining that Bevir "is not right in concluding that this flux cannot be categorized by words or ideas that human beings construct." A.P. Martinich, "A Moderate Logic of the History of Ideas," *Journal of the History of Ideas* 73, 4 (2012): 619, 624.

48 Sardica emphasizes "the purposes and value it allows as an instrument of knowledge" that supports a "'conventional' and reconstructionist approach to historical biography."

José Miguel Sardica, "The Content and Form of 'Conventional' Historical Biography," *Rethinking History: The Journal of Theory and Practice* 17, 3 (2013): 383–84.
49 Historical biography, Sardica notes, "represents a worthy academic work aimed at the greater public, a resurrection of one individual life and also a gateway to a larger understanding of one given frame of time and space with its prevailing social, cultural, moral, political, institutional and economic realities." Ibid., 393.
50 Ibid., 396.
51 For a recent discussion and overview of international relations literature on how Canadians viewed themselves in the world during this period, see Graeme Thompson, "Reframing Canada's Great War: Liberalism, Sovereignty, and the British Empire c 1860s–1919," *International Journal* 73, 1 (2018): 85–110. Thompson erroneously identifies Bourassa as part of a liberal elite enmeshed in a British nation in North America; in fact, his writing in *Le Devoir* during the war makes it abundantly clear that he wanted no part of that institution.

Chapter 1: Fais ce que dois!

1 Réal Bélanger, *Henri Bourassa: Le fascinant destin d'un homme libre (1868–1914)* (Québec: Presses de l'Université Laval, 2013), 16.
2 From his *mémoire* speeches in 1943, in which Bourassa recounted his life to audiences in Quebec, as quoted in ibid., 4; "C'est là ... dans la bibliothèque de mon oncle et dans la lecture de *L'Univers*, que j'ai puisé pour toujours mes notions sur le rôle de l'Église dans la société, sur les relations qui doivent exister entre l'Église et les chefs civils."
3 Sylvie Lacombe, "French Canada: The Rise and Decline of a 'Church-Nation,'" *Québec Studies* 48 (2009–10): 138.
4 Sylvie Lacombe, *La rencontre de deux peuples élus: Comparaison des ambitions nationale et impériale au Canada entre 1896 et 1920* (Québec: Presses de l'Université Laval, 2002), 10.
5 Lacombe, "French Canada," 145–46.
6 Louis François Laflèche, *Quelques considérations sur les rapports de la société civile avec la religion et la famille* (Montréal: n.p., 1866), 47. See also Nive Voisine, "Laflèche, Louis-François," in *Dictionary of Canadian Biography,* vol. 12 (Toronto: University of Toronto; Laval: Université Laval, 2003–), http://www.biographi.ca/en/bio/lafleche_louis_francois_12E.html.
7 For more on Catholic history in Quebec, see Jean Hamelin and Nicole Gagnon, *Histoire du Catholicisme québécois: Le XXe siècle,* vol. 1, *1898–1940* (Montréal: Boréal Express, 1985).
8 Nancy Christie and Michael Gauvreau, "Modalities of Social Authority: Suggesting an Interface for Religious and Social History," *Histoire sociale/Social History* 36, 71 (2003): 15.
9 Bélanger, *Henri Bourassa,* 13–14.
10 For outdated literature on Riel, see George F.G. Stanley, *Louis Riel* (Toronto: Ryerson Press, 1963), and Thomas Flanagan, *Louis "David" Riel: Prophet of the New World* (Toronto: University of Toronto Press, 1979). More recently, Riel has been re-envisioned as a Métis Father of Confederation and a sort of prototypical modern Canadian; see Jennifer Reid, *Louis Riel and the Creation of Modern Canada: Mythic Discourse and the Postcolonial State* (Albuquerque: University of New Mexico Press, 2008). Adam Gaudry has critically addressed both John Ralston Saul's and Jennifer Reid's treatment of Riel as a Métis Canadian in "The Métis-ization of Canada: The Process of Claiming Louis Riel, Métissage, and the Métis People as Canada's Mythical Origin," *Aboriginal Policy Studies* 2,

2 (2013): 64–87. Geoff Read and Todd Webb have examined the international reaction to Riel and drawn fascinating comparisons to the Sudanese religious zealot the Mahdi; see Geoff Read and Todd Webb, "'The Catholic Mahdi of the North West': Louis Riel and the Metis Resistance in Transatlantic and Imperial Context," *Canadian Historical Review* 93, 2 (2012): 171–95.

11 A.I. Silver, *The French-Canadian Idea of Confederation, 1864–1900*, 2nd ed. (Toronto: University of Toronto Press, 1997), 156–59.
12 Oscar Douglas Skelton, *Life and Letters of Sir Wilfrid Laurier*, vol. I (London: Oxford University Press, 1922), 314.
13 Bélanger, *Henri Bourassa*, 44.
14 Robert Craig Brown and Ramsay Cook, *Canada, 1896–1921: A Nation Transformed* (Toronto: McClelland and Stewart, 1974), 13–16.
15 Pope Leo XIII, *Encyclical* Affari vos *by Pope Leo XIII on the Manitoba School Question December 8, 1897*, as reproduced in Claude Bélanger, "Documents in Quebec History," http://faculty.marianopolis.edu/c.belanger/quebechistory/docs/manitoba/1897-5.htm.
16 Henri Bourassa, *Les écoles du Nord-Ouest, discours prononcé le 17 avril 1905 dans la grand salle du Monument National, à Montréal* (Montreal: Nationaliste, 1905), 10–11; "Puisse l'histoire du Manitoba et de ses déceptions, des abus de pouvoir, des faiblesses et des fourberies qu'elle a consignés dans nos annales, servir de leçon à l'heure actuelle!"
17 Bélanger, *Henri Bourassa*, 56–57. For more on the Alaska boundary dispute, see Allan Smith, "Alaska Boundary Dispute," in *Oxford Companion to Canadian History*, ed. Gerald Hallowell (Don Mills, ON: Oxford University Press, 2004), 30–31; on Bourassa's role in it, see Norman Penlington, *The Alaska Boundary Dispute: A Critical Reappraisal* (Toronto: McGraw-Hill Ryerson, 1972), 106–7.
18 Henri Bourassa, "Speech of Henri Bourassa M.P. on the Alaskan Boundary Commission Ottawa, Friday, October 23, 1903," CIHM 9-91168, University of Alberta Libraries. The dispute was eventually resolved in 1903 in the Americans' favour with British consent.
19 Carman Miller, *Painting the Map Red: Canada and the South African War, 1899–1902* (Montreal and Kingston: McGill-Queen's University Press, 1993), 16–17.
20 Carman Miller, "Framing Canada's Great War: A Case for Including the Boer War," *Journal of Transatlantic Studies* 6, 1 (2008): 16–17. See also Miller, *Painting the Map Red*, 154–55.
21 Henri Bourassa, *Grande-Bretagne et Canada: Questions actuelles* (Montréal: Imprimerie du Pionnier, 1901), 32; "M. Chamberlain a voulu la guerre d'Afrique pour arracher des colonies, à l'heure où l'ivresse de l'orgueil et des passions sauvages fait taire la raison, ce premier tribut du sang qu'elles lui avaient refusé jusque-là."
22 James I.W. Corcoran, "Henri Bourassa et la guerre sud-africain (suite)," *Revue d'histoire de l'Amérique française* 19, 1 (1965): 84.
23 E.H.H. Green, "The Political Economy of Empire, 1880–1914," in *The Oxford History of the British Empire*, vol. III, *The Nineteenth Century*, ed. Andrew Porter (Oxford: Oxford University Press, 1999), 347. Brown and Cook, *Canada 1896–1921*, 31, call this "new imperialism."
24 Duncan Bell, *The Idea of Greater Britain: Empire and the Future of World Order, 1860–1900* (Princeton, NJ: Princeton University Press, 2007), 263.
25 Green, "The Political Economy of Empire," 347–48.
26 Ibid., 352.
27 Ibid., 361–62.

28 This point is raised in Peter T. Marsh, "Chamberlain, Joseph (1836–1914)," in *Oxford Dictionary of National Biography Online* (Oxford: Oxford University Press, 2003), http://www.oxforddnb.com/view/article/32350.
29 Green, "The Political Economy of Empire," 366; emphasis added.
30 Carl Berger, *The Sense of Power: Studies in the Ideas of Canadian Imperialism, 1867–1914* (Toronto: University of Toronto Press, 1970), 250.
31 Richard Jebb, *Studies in Colonial Nationalism* (London: Edward Arnold, 1905), 2.
32 Benedict Anderson argues that nations are modern constructs, "imagined" by a community through media and common history. Benedict Anderson, *Imagined Communities: Reflections on the Origin and Spread of Nationalism* (New York: Verso, 1991), 41.
33 Berger, *The Sense of Power*, 49–77.
34 Simon J. Potter, "Richard Jebb, John S. Ewart, and the Round Table, 1898–1926," *English Historical Review* 122, 495 (2007): 107.
35 Douglas Cole, "The Problem of 'Nationalism' and 'Imperialism' in British Settlement Colonies," *Journal of British Studies* 10, 2 (1971): 179. Cole's scale is also useful in understanding the rise of English Canadian nationalism after the war that did not reject British culture but certainly embraced Canadian autonomy. For more on Berger's arguments on imperialism, see Simon J. Potter, "The Imperial Significance of the Canadian-American Reciprocity Proposals of 1911," *Historical Journal* 47, 1 (2004): 81–100; Douglas L. Cole, "Canada's 'Nationalistic' Imperialists," *Journal of Canadian Studies* 5, 3 (1970): 44–49; and Terry Cook, "George R. Parkin and the Concept of Britannic Idealism," *Journal of Canadian Studies* 10, 3 (1975): 15–31.
36 Bélanger, *Henri Bourassa*, 79; "Il veut former une opinion publique éclairée en transmettant aux Canadiens une compréhension plus nette des relations du Canada avec l'Empire et de la nature des rapports entre la majorité canadienne-anglaise protestante et la minorité canadienne-française catholique du pays."
37 Joseph Levitt, *Henri Bourassa and the Golden Calf: The Social Program of the Nationalists of Quebec (1900–1914)* (Ottawa: Éditions de l'Université d'Ottawa, 1969), 2. Brown and Cook, *Canada 1896–1921*, 136, describe them as middle-class professional elites. For concise biographies of two of these *nationalistes*, see Hélène Pelletier-Baillargeon, "Asselin, Olivar," in *Dictionary of Canadian Biography*, vol. 16 (Toronto: University of Toronto; Laval: Université Laval, 2003–), http://www.biographi.ca/en/bio/asselin_olivar_16E.html; and Laurent Mailhot, "Fournier, Jules," in *Dictionary of Canadian Biography*, vol. 14 (Toronto: University of Toronto; Laval: Université Laval, 2003–), http://www.biographi.ca/en/bio/fournier_jules_14E.html. *Dictionary of Canadian Biography* entries for Héroux and Lavergne have yet to be completed.
38 These periodicals were the inspiration for Bourassa's own paper, *Le Devoir*, founded in 1910. See Hélène Pelletier-Baillargeon, "*Les Débats* et *Le Nationaliste*, de bien curieux ancêtres pour *Le Devoir*," in *Le Devoir: Un journal indépendant (1910–1995)*, ed. Robert Comeau and Luc Desrochers (Québec: Presses de l'Université du Québec, 1996), 191–97.
39 For a collection of commentary on Canadian nationalism and imperialism, see Carl Berger, ed., *Imperialism and Nationalism, 1884–1914: A Conflict in Canadian Thought* (Toronto: Copp Clark, 1969).
40 This point can sometimes be obscured throughout the book since Canadian and French Canadian nationalism sometimes overlap. I also use "*nationaliste*" throughout the book as a general term to describe Bourassa and his supporters, not to be confused with a broader application of "nationalist" that would include English Canadians such as Ottawa lawyer J.S. Ewart. The *nationaliste* movement was complex, formed by different

people and opinions and led by the men mentioned above at this time. For the sake of simplicity, I conflate Bourassa's and the larger movement's ideas, for they are similar in attitude if not in detail.

41 Levitt, *Henri Bourassa and the Golden Calf*, 17, quoting Robert Rumilly, *Histoire de la province de Québec*, vol. 9 (Montréal: Valiquette, n.d.), 223.

42 Michèle Brassard and Jean Hamelin, "Joseph-Israël Tarte," in *Dictionary of Canadian Biography*, vol. 13 (Toronto: University of Toronto; Laval: Université Laval, 2003–), http://www.biographi.ca/en/bio/tarte_joseph_israel_13E.html.

43 Bélanger, *Henri Bourassa*, 27.

44 Réal Bélanger, "Le nationalisme ultramontain: Le cas de Jules-Paul Tardivel," in *Les ultramontains canadiens-français: Études d'histoire religieuse présentées en hommage au professeur Philippe Sylvain*, ed. Nive Voisine and Jean Hamelin (Montréal: Éditions du Boréal, 1985), 303.

45 Mathieu Girard, "La pensée politique de Jules-Paul Tardivel," *Revue d'histoire de l'Amérique française* 21, 3 (1967): 398. "Être séparatiste c'est pour Tardivel être catholique, c'est poser un acte de foi."

46 Pierre Savard, "Tardivel, Jules-Paul," in *Dictionary of Canadian Biography*, vol. 13 (Toronto: University of Toronto; Laval: Université Laval, 2003–), http://www.biographi.ca/en/bio/tardivel_jules_paul_13E.html.

47 Bélanger, *Henri Bourassa*, 79–86.

48 His views were also less compelling after Laurier was elected as Canada's first French Canadian prime minister, for it no longer seemed to be so urgent to have more coherent French Canadian political organization. See Brown and Cook, *Canada 1896–1921*, 136–37.

49 An excellent overview of social (or political) Catholicism in Europe is John W. Boyer, "Catholics, Christians, and the Challenges of Democracy: The Heritage of the Nineteenth Century," in *Political Catholicism in Europe 1918–1945*, vol. 1, ed. Wolfram Kaiser and Helmut Wohnot (London: Routledge, 2004), 6–37.

50 Reverend Harry C. Koenig, ed., *Principles for Peace: Selections from Papal Documents Leo XIII to Pius XII* (Washington, DC: National Catholic Welfare Conference, 1943), 53.

51 As cited and explored in Yvan Lamonde, *Histoire sociale des idées au Québec*, vol. 1, *1760–1896* (Québec: Fides, 2000), 367–79. Huguette Lapointe-Roy has argued that even Bishop Ignace Bourget, the ultramontane at the centre of much religious controversy in the 1870s, demonstrated a willingness to pursue elements of social Catholicism, at least through charitable work. Huguette Lapointe-Roy, "L'engagement social de Mgr Ignace Bourget," *Sessions d'étude – Société canadienne d'histoire de l'Église catholique* 51 (1984): 39–52.

52 Jean-Marie Fecteau, "La dynamique sociale du catholicisme québécois au XIXe siècle: Éléments pour une réflexion sur les frontières et les conditions historiques de possibilité du 'social,'" *Histoire sociale/Social History* 35, 70 (2002): 515.

53 Levitt makes this point in *Henri Bourassa and the Golden Calf* on 95 and throughout. Lamonde in *Histoire sociale des idées au Québec* reflects on Catholicism's changing relationship as urban populations grew and its public role changed and specifically addresses the *Rerum Novarum* on 481–82.

54 Levitt, *Henri Bourassa and the Golden Calf*, 93–115.

55 Alain Lacombe, "Bouchette, Robert-Errol," in *Dictionary of Canadian Biography*, vol. 14 (Toronto: University of Toronto; Laval: Université Laval, 2003–), http://www.biographi.ca/en/bio/bouchette_robert_errol_14E.html; see also Alain Lacombe, *Errol Bouchette, 1862–1912: Un intellectuel* (Québec: Fides, 1997), 72–74, 125, for his reputation in

English and French Canada as well as the *nationaliste* endorsement of him from Jules Fournier. Interestingly, Bouchette was a continentalist, not a nationalist of any sort, but one who understood that French Canada and the United States were irreconcilably different. See Damien-Claude Bélanger, *Prejudice and Pride: Canadian Intellectuals Confront the United States, 1891–1945* (Toronto: University of Toronto Press, 2011), 134–35.

56 Levitt, *Henri Bourassa and the Golden Calf*, 42–43.
57 Quoted in Réal Bélanger, "Bourassa, Henri," in *Dictionary of Canadian Biography*, vol. 18 (Toronto: University of Toronto; Laval: Université Laval, 2003–), http://www.biographi.ca/fr/bio/bourassa_henri_18F.html; "La patrie, pour nous, c'est le Canada tout entier, c'est-à-dire une fédération de races distinctes et de provinces autonomes. La nation ..., c'est la nation canadienne, composée des Canadiens-français et des Canadiens-anglais."
58 *Program of the Nationalist League – 1903*, as reprinted in Levitt, *Henri Bourassa and the Golden Calf*, 148–49; "la plus large mesure d'autonomie compatible avec le maintien du lien fédéral."
59 Bourassa, *Grande-Bretagne et Canada*, 40; "La première condition nécessaire à l'indépendance d'un peuple, c'est d'être assuré de la paix intérieure et extérieure."
60 Levitt, *Henri Bourassa and the Golden Calf*, 33–34.
61 Yvan Lamonde, *Histoire sociale des idées au Québec*, vol. 2, *1896–1929* (Québec: Fides, 2004), 27–28; "De même que M. Bourassa se méfie de ceux qui songent à fonder un grand empire britannique, ainsi nous sommes constamment en garde contre ceux qui travaillent à créer un grand tout canadien."
62 Ibid., 194–95, 226.
63 Olivar Asselin, *A Quebec View of Canadian Nationalism* (Montreal: n.p., 1909), 61.
64 Ronald J. Pestritto and William J. Atto, *American Progressivism: A Reader* (Lanham, MD: Lexington Books, 2008), 8–9.
65 Levitt, *Henri Bourassa and the Golden Calf*, 143–44.
66 Bélanger draws explicit comparisons between Bourassa and Laurier, for both adhered to the same brand of liberalism (though, as Lamonde noted, Bourassa's was a nationalist derivation of it), and describes their liberalism as the "exaltation of individual freedom in accordance with the Constitution and the law," the "defence of free and representative government, of the sovereignty of the people, of property and of the reforms carried out to ensure progress, happiness and prosperity," and the "the necessity of tolerance, justice, respect for the equality of individuals before the law and democracy," Bélanger, *Henri Bourassa*, 44; he is quoting his own book, *Wilfrid Laurier: Quand la politique devient passion* (Québec: Presses de l'Université Laval, 2007).
67 Bourassa's speech from 1900 is often quoted:

> Je suis un disciple de Burke, de Fox, de Bright, de Gladstone et des autres "Little Englanders," qui ont fait l'Angleterre et ses possessions ce qu'elles sont aujourd'hui; et je ne déserterai pas les rangs de leurs disciples fidèles, parce qu'il plairait à M. Chamberlain et à d'autres radicaux renégats, dévorés du délire de l'ambition, de traiter ces grands hommes d'insensés.

> Canada, *Débats de la Chambre des communes*, 8th Parliament, 5th Session, (13 March 1900), vol. 1, 1819 (Henri Bourassa). I first saw it in Lacombe, *La rencontre de deux peuples élus*, 64, who in turn cites Corcoran, "Henri Bourassa et la guerre sud-africaine (suite)." It is found in many other works on Bourassa, however, and examined at length by Bélanger as a response to the Boer War and the Laurier government's repudiation of

liberal beliefs by not letting Parliament decide the Canadian war effort. Bélanger, *Henri Bourassa*, 74–76.

68 Douglass North writes that institutions are the laws, frameworks, and procedures that constitute the "rules of the game," whereas organizations (and individuals) that operate within those institutions are the "players of the game." Douglass C. North, *Institutions, Institutional Change and Economic Performance* (Cambridge, UK: Cambridge University Press, 1990), 3–6. In this sense, Bourassa accepted "the rules" of British liberalism but rejected "the players." He wanted to play in another league, Canadian in name and spirit.

69 James Kennedy, *Liberal Nationalisms: Empire, State, and Civil Society in Scotland and Quebec* (Montreal and Kingston: McGill-Queen's University Press, 2013), 219–22.

70 Henri Bourassa, *Les Canadiens-français et l'Empire britannique* (Québec: Imprimerie S.A. Demers, 1903), 40; "Les Canadiens-français du peuple n'ont d'autre patrie que le Canada. Ils sont prêts à lui rendre tout ce qu'ils lui doivent; mais n'estimant rien devoir à l'Angleterre ni à aucun autre pays, ils n'en attendent rien."

71 Robert Rumilly, *Henri Bourassa: La vie publique d'un grand Canadien* (Montréal: Éditions de l'Homme, 1953), 274.

72 Levitt, *Henri Bourassa and the Golden Calf*, 35.

73 *McKim's Directory of Canadian Publications* lists *Le Devoir* as having 18,894 subscribers in 1915, a number that dropped to an estimated 14,000 by 1917. See *McKim's Directory of Canadian Publications* (Montreal: A. McKim, 1915, 1917). The directory estimated that Montreal, where *Le Devoir* was published, had a population of 600,000. It is estimated that the city was 25.8 percent English and 63.5 percent French in 1915. See Paul André Linteau, *Montréal* (Montréal: Boréal, 1992), 40, 160, 314.

74 Bélanger, *Henri Bourassa*, 536–37.

75 Patrice Dutil and David Mackenzie, *Canada 1911: The Decisive Election that Shaped the Country* (Toronto: Dundurn, 2011), 39–43.

76 Ibid., 47–52; Phillips Payson O'Brien, "The Titan Refreshed: Imperial Overstretch and the British Navy before the First World War," *Past and Present* 172, 1 (2001), 160–63. O'Brien paints the Canadians as intransigent and unwilling to spend money on the navy, whereas Brown and Cook, *Canada 1896–1921*, 169, portray British authorities as acceding to Canadian demands.

77 Canada, *House of Commons Debates*, 11th Parliament, 2nd Session (12 January 1910), vol. 1, 1735 (Wilfrid Laurier). Laurier later expanded his statement on 3 February:

> I was simply stating a principle of international law. It is a principle of international law that when a nation is at war all her possessions are liable to attack. If England is at war she can be attacked in Canada ... in short, anywhere that the British Fleet floats ... I do not say that we shall always be attacked; neither do I say that we would take part in all the wars of England. That is a matter ... which the Canadian Parliament will have to pronounce and will have to decide in its own best judgment.

Canada, *House of Commons Debates*, 11th Parliament, 2nd Session (3 February 1910), vol. 2, 2964–65 (Wilfrid Laurier). Despite this explanation, his original words were remembered as his position on the issue.

78 Brown and Cook, *Canada 1896–1921*, 169–71.

79 See Bourassa's articles "M. Laurier à Toronto," "Sur le bord de l'abîme," and "Laurier et Chamberlain," in *Le Devoir*, 11, 13, and 17 January 1910.

80 Bélanger, *Henri Bourassa*, 309. For an overview of the gradual decision to form an alliance with Monk, see 302–9.

81 Brown and Cook, *Canada 1896–1921*, 172; Bélanger, *Henri Bourassa*, 331–32.
82 Dutil and Mackenzie, *Canada 1911*, 81–87.
83 Ibid., 131–63.
84 Ibid., 252, 278–79.
85 For example, Henri Bourassa, "La vrai terrain de la lutte," *Le Devoir*, 2 August 1911, 1.
86 The extent to which Borden ignored Quebec would not be fully realized until 1913 when the Conservatives introduced their own Naval Aid Bill, though it was defeated in the Liberal-dominated Senate. Dutil and Mackenzie, *Canada 1911*, 294, conclude that the Conservatives could easily afford to reject Quebec demands given the seats that they had gained outside the province. They had enough seats in English Canada that, even if Quebec MPs voted against the government, they would still survive the vote. Bourassa realized this after no *nationaliste* MP was appointed to cabinet in November 1911; for his perspective, see Bélanger, *Henri Bourassa*, 378–81. Another useful work is Réal Bélanger, *Paul-Émile Lamarche: Le pays avant le parti (1904–1918)* (Québec: Presses de l'Université Laval, 1984), which explores Lamarche's career as a conservative-*nationaliste* MP.
87 Marilyn Barber, "The Ontario Schools Issue: Sources of Conflict," in *Minorities, Schools, and Politics*, ed. Ramsay Cook, Craig Brown, and Carl Berger (Toronto: University of Toronto Press, 1969), 74. The chapter is similar to her earlier article, Marilyn Barber, "The Ontario Bilingual Schools Issue: Sources of Conflict," *Canadian Historical Review* 43, 3 (1966): 227–48.
88 Many other works examine the bilingual school crises of Canada. For Ontario specifically, see also Margaret Prang, "Clerics, Politicians, and the Bilingual Schools Issue in Ontario, 1910–1917," *Canadian Historical Review* 41, 4 (1960): 281–307; Chad Gaffield, *Language, Schooling, and Cultural Conflict: The Origins of the French-Language Controversy in Ontario* (Montreal and Kingston: McGill-Queen's University Press, 1987); Gaétan Gervais, "Le Règlement XVII (1912–1927)," *Revue du Nouvel-Ontario 18* (1996): 123–92; and Jack D. Cécillon, *Prayers, Petitions, and Protests: The Catholic Church and the Ontario Schools Crisis in the Windsor Border Region, 1910–1928* (Montreal and Kingston: McGill-Queen's University Press, 2013).
89 Robert Sellar, *The Tragedy of Quebec* (Toronto: n.p., 1916), 282–84, as quoted in Brown and Cook, *Canada 1896–1921*, 255n13.
90 At that time at least; see Silver, *The French-Canadian Idea of Confederation*, 219–21.
91 Paul Rich, *Race and Empire in British Politics* (Cambridge, UK: Cambridge University Press, 1986), 7.
92 David Milobar, "Quebec Reform, the British Constitution, and the Atlantic Empire: 1774–1775," *Parliamentary History* 14 (1995): 70–71.
93 John George Lambton, Earl of Durham, *Report on the Affairs of British North America*, ed. Sir C.P. Lucas (Oxford: Clarendon Press, 1912), 16.
94 Ibid., 294.
95 François-Xavier Garneau, *Histoire du Canada*, vol. 1 (Québec: Imprimerie de N. Aubin, 1845), 28. Ramsay Cook notes that Garneau was critical of the Catholic Church in his first volume but expunged these criticisms in later volumes. Ramsay Cook, *The Maple Leaf Forever: Essays on Nationalism and Politics in Canada* (Toronto: Macmillan, 1971), 118–19.
96 Abbé J.-P.-A. Ferland took a more positive perspective on the Catholic Church in Quebec, while Thomas Chapais was generally accepting of the positive influence of British institutions on the province; see Cook, *The Maple Leaf Forever*, 120–22.
97 Phillip Buckner, "Reinventing the British World," *The Round Table: The Commonwealth Journal of International Affairs* 92, 368 (2003): 81.

98 André Siegfried, *The Race Question in Canada* (London: Eveleigh Nash, 1907), 2.
99 Ibid., 142.
100 Guy Laperrière, "Le congrès eucharistique de Montréal en 1910: Une affirmation du catholicisme montréalais," *Études d'histoire religieuse* 77 (2011): 21–39.
101 Henri Bourassa, *Religion, langue, nationalité: Discours prononcé à la séance de cloture du XXIe Congrès eucharistique, à Montréal, le 10 septembre 1910* (Montréal: Imprimerie du Devoir, 1910), 3–4.
102 Henri Bourassa, *French and English Frictions and Misunderstandings* (Montreal: Imprimerie du Devoir, 1914), 22. The pamphlet was also published as a series of articles in *Le Devoir* on 11, 12, 13, and 14 March 1914.
103 For more information on Bourassa's hometown during wartime, see Terry Copp's recent online publication *Montreal at War,* https://montrealatwar.com/; at the time of this writing, a print book is forthcoming from McGill-Queen's University Press. Other works remain comprehensive explorations of Montreal's development in the years leading up to the war, such as Paul André Linteau, *The Promoters' City: Building the Industrial Town of Maisonneuve 1883–1918* (Toronto: Lorimer, 1985), or Isabelle Gournay and France Vanlaethem, eds., *Montreal Metropolis, 1880–1930* (Toronto: Stoddart and the Canadian Centre for Architecture, 1998).

Chapter 2: The Duty of Canada at the Present Hour

1 A number of prominent Canadians were in the Old World that summer. Conservative Party whip Colonel John Stanfield, Quebec's provincial parliamentarian Joseph-Napoléon Francoeur, Chief Justice of the Supreme Court Sir Charles Fitzpatrick, and many others were caught in Europe as war approached. Most were in England or France and escaped easily through the Allied nations. See Réal Bélanger, *Henri Bourassa: Le fascinant destin d'un homme libre (1868–1914)* (Québec: Presses de l'Université Laval, 2013), 514, and Robert Rumilly, *Henri Bourassa: La vie publique d'un grand Canadien* (Montréal: Éditions Chantecler, 1953), 504.
2 For more about Wetterlé, see Émile Wetterlé, *Behind the Scenes in the Reichstag: Sixteen Years of Parliamentary Life in Germany* (New York: George H. Doran, 1918).
3 Ibid., 21–23. Bourassa discovered that others, such as Chanoine Collin of another dissident newspaper, the *Lorrain,* also fled to safety. See Henri Bourassa, "En France et en Alsace au début de la guerre," *Le Devoir,* 22 August 1914, 1. Bourassa falsely reported that Alexis Samain, former president of the *Souvenir Lorrain,* was shot in Metz on 3 August. This was later discovered to be a fabrication meant to inspire opposition to Germany. See Jeanyves Guérin, Jean-Kely Paulhan, and Jean-Pierre Rioux, *Jean Guéhenno, guerres, et paix* (Paris: Presses Universitaires Septentrion, 2009), 21–22.
4 Rumilly, *Henri Bourassa,* 503; see also André Bergevin, Cameron Nish, and Anne Bourassa, *Henri Bourassa: Biographie, index des écrit, index de la correspondance, 1895–1924* (Montréal: Les Éditions de l'Action Nationale, 1966), xlvii.
5 Bourassa, "En France et en Alsace"; "presque l'air d'une ville religieuse"; "Royalistes, impérialistes, républicains, socialistes, tous ne paraissent avoir qu'un cœur." For a more detailed account of his trip home, see Bélanger, *Henri Bourassa,* 528–30.
6 Bourassa, "Le Congrès eucharistique et la guerre," *Le Devoir,* 27 August 1914, 1; "ceux qui ont vécus ces heures-là en France peuvent dire qu'ils ont vu l'âme de la nation française."
7 Ibid.; "La guerre n'est pas l'enfer ... C'est le pire des châtiments sur la terre; c'est aussi la plus salutaire des expiations."

8 Best epitomized in Paul Maroney, "'The Great Adventure': The Context and Ideology of Recruiting in Ontario, 1914–17," *Canadian Historical Review* 77, 1 (1996): 62–98. Most historical studies focus on newspapers and urban centres and, armed with that evidence, suggest that there was a common thread of support for the war. See Jeffrey A. Keshen, *Propaganda and Censorship during Canada's Great War* (Edmonton: University of Alberta Press, 1996), and Robert S. Prince, "The Mythology of War: How the Canadian Daily Newspaper Depicted the Great War" (PhD diss., University of Toronto, 1998). One excellent example of the ubiquity of war support in an urban centre such as Toronto is Ian Miller, *Our Glory and Our Grief: Torontonians and the Great War* (Toronto: University of Toronto Press, 2002), 15. It is less clear without a more comprehensive study how much war enthusiasm extended into rural and less heavily populated areas or what regional differences existed, though suggesting reactions similar to those in urban areas are Desmond Morton, *Fight or Pay: Soldiers' Families in the Great War* (Vancouver: UBC Press, 2004); James M. Pitsula, *For All We Have and Are: Regina and the Experience of the Great War* (Winnipeg: University of Manitoba Press, 2008); Jim Blanchard, *Winnipeg's Great War: A City Comes of Age* (Winnipeg: University of Manitoba Press, 2010); and notable for its focus on a rural community, Jonathan Vance, *Township at War* (Waterloo, ON: Wilfrid Laurier University Press, 2018). Other work questions the evenness of war support across the country in 1914, and throughout the war years, such as Robert Rutherdale, *Hometown Horizons: Local Responses to Canada's Great War* (Vancouver: UBC Press, 2005), and Brock Millman, *Polarity, Patriotism, and Dissent in Great War Canada, 1914–1919* (Toronto: University of Toronto Press, 2016).
9 Henri Bourassa, "Le partage des responsabilités," *Le Devoir,* 29 August 1914, 1.
10 Bourassa was repeating demands also made by Omer Héroux; see Omer Héroux, "Autour de la guerre," *Le Devoir,* 6 August 1914, 1.
11 Bourassa, "Le partage des responsabilités"; "cet acte d'élémentaire justice et de politique intelligente fera plus pour assurer l'unité de l'Empire et de la nation canadienne que tous les dons de farine ou d'argent."
12 Excerpts from his speech to Parliament on 19 August 1914, as quoted in Robert Borden, *Robert Laird Borden: His Memoirs* (Toronto: Macmillan, 1938), 461.
13 J. Castell Hopkins, *Canadian Annual Review War Series 1914* (Toronto: Canadian Annual Review, 1918), 160–61. See also Robert Craig Brown, "Sir Robert Borden and Canada's War Aims," in *War Aims and Strategic Policy in the Great War 1914–1918,* ed. Barry Hunt and Adrian Preston (London: Croom Helm, 1977), 55–66.
14 R. Matthew Bray, "'Fighting as an Ally': The English-Canadian Patriotic Response to the Great War," *Canadian Historical Review* 61, 2 (1980): 142–43.
15 This continued throughout the war. See Prince, "The Mythology of War," 249–52. The defence of Belgium was an important issue, and both Borden and Laurier contributed statements to *King Albert's Book,* named after the Belgian king and sold to raise funds for Belgians. See Daily Telegraph, *King Albert's Book* (London: Houder and Sloughton, 1914), 24 (Borden's statement) and 52 (Laurier's statement).
16 Hopkins, *Canadian Annual Review War Series 1914,* 132–42.
17 Sylvie Lacombe argued this in *La rencontre de deux peuples élus: Comparaison des ambitions nationale et impériale au Canada entre 1896 et 1920* (Québec: Presses de l'Université Laval, 2002), 26–31 and throughout.
18 Hopkins, *Canadian Annual Review War Series 1914,* 514.
19 A.F. Duguid, *Official History of the Canadian Forces in the Great War, 1914–1919, from the Outbreak of the War to the Formation of the Canadian Corps, August 1914–September 1915,* vol. 2 (Ottawa: Department of National Defence General Staff, 1938), 344–45.

20 Hopkins, *Canadian Annual Review War Series 1914*, 193–94. Recently, Jean Martin has argued that French Canadian recruitment nationwide was double what was previously thought, from 20,000–30,000 to roughly 60,000, which places it on par with the enlistment of native-born English-speaking Canadians. Jean Martin, "La participation des francophones dans le Corps expéditionnaire canadien (1914–1919): Il faut réviser à la hausse," *Canadian Historical Review* 96, 3 (2015): 405–23. Importantly, contemporaneous accounts all placed enlistment in French Canada as lower than that in English Canada.

21 "Notre devoir," *L'Action sociale*, 11 September 1914, 1. D'Amours repeatedly wrote of Canada's "national duty," a direct reference to an article by Bourassa on 8 September entitled "Le devoir national"; "nous avons le devoir de donner à l'Angleterre ce qu'elle a droit de nous réclamer en toute équité et toute justice, pour le maintien et la défense de l'Empire dont nous faisons partie comme colonie britannique." For more on Catholic responses, see Rumilly, *Henri Bourassa*, 508–9, and Elizabeth Armstrong, *The Crisis of Quebec, 1914–1918* (Toronto: McClelland and Stewart, 1937), 61–62.

22 "Lettre pastorale de NN. SS les Archevêques et Evêques des provinces ecclésiastiques de Québec, de Montréal, et d'Ottawa sur les devoirs des catholiques dans la guerre actuelle," 23 September 1914, 4; "Il fera tourner cette guerre au profit de la justice et du droit ... Ce sera l'honneur et la gloire du Canada ... d'avoir concouru, par ses pieuses supplications, à restaurer la paix dans le monde, et à soulager, par ses généreuses contributions, les maux dont aura souffert l'humanité."

23 Hopkins, *Canadian Annual Review War Series 1914*, 288.

24 René Durocher, "Henri Bourassa, les évêques et la guerre de 1914–1918," *Canadian Historical Association Historical Papers* 6, 1 (1971): 252–53.

25 This later became the basis of Jules Fournier's criticism of Bourassa's leadership of the *nationaliste* movement; see Chapter 4 of this book.

26 Henri Bourassa to Bishop Georges Gauthier, 6 May 1916, as quoted in Durocher, "Henri Bourassa," 253; "j'osais encore croire que les évêques parleraient en évêques *nationaux*: je voulais me tenir aussi près que possible de leur attitude probable."

27 Durocher, "Henri Bourassa," 272.

28 Henri Bourassa, "Après la guerre, la famine," *Le Devoir*, 2 September 1914, 1.

29 Colin Newbury, "Milner, Alfred, Viscount Milner (1854–1925)," in *Oxford Dictionary of National Biography Online*, https://doi.org/10.1093/ref:odnb/35037.

30 Bourassa, "Après la guerre"; "s'il est nécessaire pour l'Angleterre, engagée directement dans le conflit européen, de tripler ses effectifs agricoles au risque de n'envoyer sur les champs de bataille qu'une armée à peine supérieure en nombre aux vaillantes phalanges belges."

31 Ibid.:

> Dans mon humble sphère d'action je me propose de rechercher consciencieusement, en toute loyauté, et de dire en toute franchise tous ce qu'il me semblerait urgent de prévoir et de faire, si l'on veut éviter au Canada et, par répercussion, à l'Empire, des désastres dont beaucoup de gens parlent dans l'obscurité, mais sur lesquels très peu semblent avoir le courage d'appeler l'attention des gouvernants et la coopération de toutes les bonnes volontés.
>
> Dans cette recherche et dans les conclusions qu'elle m'inspirera, je suis fermement résolu à ne pas me départir du ton que les circonstances devraient imposer à tous. Aucune provocation, aucune injure, aucune calomnie, aucune goujaterie

ne m'entraîneront au dehors de cette voie. Je ne rechercherai pas même les motifs des attaques brutales ou grotesques dont je pourrai être l'objet.

Les spectacles grandioses et touchants dont j'ai été témoin en Europe m'ont mis à même de faire la comparaison entre le patriotisme désintéressé, le dévouement vrai à la chose publique et l'exploitation sordide des choses les plus sacrées.

32 Henri Bourassa, "Le devoir national," *Le Devoir*, 8 September 1914, 1; "la nation anglo-française, liée à l'Angleterre et à la France par mille attaches ... a un intérêt vital au maintien de la France et de l'Angleterre"; "l'absence à peu près complète du sentiment des responsabilités réelles du Canada comme nation – responsabilités extérieures et plus encore responsabilités intérieures."

33 In the early days of the July Crisis, elements within the British government argued against intervention. By early August, almost all members of cabinet who had opposed participation had changed their positions after the German invasion of Belgium. On 4 August, British opinion supported intervention and cheered news of British entry into the war. After news of the British retreat from Mons on 25 August and newspapers published accounts of the German atrocities in occupied Belgium, particularly after the burning of Louvain on 29 August, British enlistment surged alongside support for the war. The war transformed from a necessary intervention to preserve France and the balance of power to a crusade to defend Britain from the morally corrupt German militarism now threatening the world. See Adrian Gregory, *The Last Great War: British Society and the First World War* (Cambridge, UK: Cambridge University Press, 2008), 9–39.

34 Henri Bourassa, "Une page d'histoire – IV: L'Angleterre et l'Allemagne," *Le Devoir*, 12 September 1914, 1. For the entire series, see *Le Devoir*, 9–14 September 1914. The White Papers were first published publicly on 5 August 1914 when they were presented to the British House of Commons "to inform Parliament as to the events which had brought about the war and the part taken in them by the British Government." See G.P. Gooch, D. Litt, and Harold Temperley, *British Official Documents on the Origins of the War, 1898–1914* (London: His Majesty's Office, 1926), vi. Other governments had already published similar collections of the official documents concerning their entry into the war, such as the French Yellow Book and the German White Book.

35 Henri Bourassa, "Une page d'histoire – V: La neutralité de la Belgique et du Luxembourg," *Le Devoir*, 14 September 1914, 1.

36 Ibid.; "fidèle à la grande tradition britannique, il a été avant et par-dessus tout l'homme de son pays"; "Il me paraît que le Canada ne saurait mieux démontrer son 'loyalisme' qu'en s'inspirant des exemples de la grande nation à qui il a emprunté ses institutions politiques."

37 Henri Bourassa, "Vrai loyalisme," *Le Devoir*, 19 November 1914, 1.

38 Mason Wade, *The French Canadians 1760–1945* (Toronto: Macmillan, 1956), 648–49, 652–53.

39 "Campagne odieuse d'un saltimbanque," *La Patrie*, 11 September 1914, 4.

40 These articles are reviewed in Wade, *French Canadians,* 652–53, and Rumilly, *Henri Bourassa,* 507–11.

41 "Notre devoir envers l'Angleterre," *L'Action sociale*, 14 September 1914, 1.

42 Jean Brisson [Roger Valois], "Les articles de M. Bourassa," *Le Pays*, 19 September 1914, 1. *Le Pays* remained critical of Bourassa and his views.

43 Thomas Chase-Casgrain, "Le rôle du Canada français," *La Patrie*, 14 September 1914, 4; reprinted in *Winnipeg Free Press*, 19 September 1914, 9.

44 Ibid.
45 The *Globe* mentioned the debate about Canada's entry into the war in a 24 September editorial; the *Toronto Star* did as well after C.H. Cahan wrote a letter to the editor on 19 September.
46 Rumilly, *Henri Bourassa*, 508–11; *Standard* [Kingston], 29 September 1914, 1.
47 "Bas le masque!," *La Patrie*, 31 August 1914, 4. Another editorial critical of Bourassa was published on 3 September 1914, 4; "Qu'il nous dise maintenant ce que nous devons penser du programme politique qu'il a formulé, et que le premier coup de canon allemand a réduit en poussière."
48 "The Real Bourassa," *Montreal Daily Mail*, 2 September 1914, 4.
49 "Churchill's Declaration," *Winnipeg Free Press*, 26 September 1914, 13. The discussion begins earlier in editorials from 21 and 22 September 1914.
50 Henri Bourassa examines this issue in "British Fair Play," *Le Devoir*, 26 September 1914, 1; again in "Vrai loyalisme"; and once more in a series of letters to the Winnipeg *Tribune*, "Une lettre de M. Bourassa a la *Tribune*, de Winnipeg," *Le Devoir*, 25 November 1914, 1.
51 Henri Bourassa, "Les foudres de Canadian Club," *Le Devoir*, 25 September 1914, 1.
52 Hopkins, *Canadian Annual Review War Series 1914*, 289.
53 These letters were published in *Le Devoir* as well: "Deux lettres de M. Cahan," *Le Devoir*, 16 Septemeber 1914, 1.
54 Bourassa to Cahan, 15 September 1914, Library and Archives Canada (hereafter LAC), Henri Bourassa Fonds, MG27-IIE1, reel M721.
55 Yvan Lamonde, *Histoire sociale des idées au Québec*, vol. 2, *1896–1929* (Québec: Fides, 2004), 40–41; Durocher, "Henri Bourassa," 252.
56 Le Kronzprinz [Olivar Asselin], "Simple briques," *L'Action*, 19 September 1914, 1.
57 Olivar Asselin, *Les évêques et la propagande de l'Action catholique* (Montréal: n.p., 1915).
58 Hélène Pelletier-Baillargeon, *Olivar Asselin et son temps: Le militant* (Québec: Fides, 1996), 644–52. See also Wade, *The French Canadians*, 677.
59 Jules Fournier, "Des Anglais et de quelques autres choses," *L'Action*, 31 October 1914, 1. Bourassa had addressed this point, though not to Fournier's satisfaction, in Henri Bourassa, "Deux témoins: Un vivant et un mort," *Le Devoir*, 18 September 1914, 1. In the summer of 1916, Fournier encapsulated his scorn for Bourassa's actions in 1914 in an unpublished article; see Chapter 4 of this volume. For brief mentions of Fournier's position, see also Rumilly, *Henri Bourassa*, 516–17.
60 Lamonde, *Histoire sociale des idées au Québec*, vol. 2, *1896–1929*, 133.
61 F.M. Leventhal, *The Last Dissenter: H.N. Brailsford and His World* (Oxford: Clarendon Press, 1985), 303.
62 Carnegie Endowment, *Report of the International Commission to Inquire into the Causes and Conduct of the Balkan Wars* (Washington, DC: Carnegie Foundation, 1914).
63 H.N. Brailsford, *The War of Steel and Gold: A Study of Armed Peace*, 10th ed. (London: G. Bell and Sons, 1918), 29–30.
64 A.J.P. Taylor notes that in editions published after the start of the war, Brailsford emphasized that colonial and economic forces had led Europe toward a general war. For instance, the following phrase was added: "War could never have come about save for these sordid colonial and economic issues ... The stake lies outside Europe, though the war is fought on its soil." See A.J.P. Taylor, *The Trouble-Makers: Dissent over Foreign Policy 1792–1939* (Bloomington: Indiana University Press, 1958), 123.
65 Ibid.

66 H.N. Brailsford, "The Empire of the East," *Contemporary Review* 116 (1914): 334–45. His article was also republished as a Union of Democratic Control pamphlet. H.N. Brailsford, *Origins of the Great War,* Union of Democratic Control Pamphlet 4 (London: Union of Democratic Control, 1914). Bourassa eventually republished the article as well. Henri Bourassa, *The Foreign Policy of Great Britain* (Montreal: Imprimerie du Devoir, 1915), 37–47.

67 Henri Bourassa, "L'orientation de la politique anglaise," *Le Devoir,* 28 October 1914, 1. Interestingly, Durocher cites a letter from Bourassa to Bishop Gauthier from 6 November 1914 that a reliable source had told Bourassa that "l'une des dernières paroles prononcées par Pie X avant sa mort, c'est que 'la Russie est la grande coupable.'" Durocher, "Henri Bourassa," 256. It is likely that this affected Bourassa's acceptance of Brailsford's arguments. Equally, the papacy irrationally feared Russian control of Constantinople and setting up an "Orthodox St. Peter's." See John F. Pollard, *The Unknown Pope: Benedict XV (1914–1922), and the Pursuit of Peace* (London: Geoffrey Chapman, 1999), 90–91.

68 Henri Bourassa, "Les responsabilités de la Russie," *Le Devoir,* 29 October 1914, 1.

69 H.N. Brailsford, "The Empire of the East," *Contemporary Review* 106 (1914): 344.

70 Bourassa, "Le partage des responsabilités."

71 J.S. Ewart, *The Kingdom Papers* (Ottawa: n.p., 1912). This was a series of papers eventually published together, though more were added throughout the war past its initial 1912 publication date. After the war, Ewart published *The Independence Papers,* which updated his previous arguments and demanded Canadian independence.

72 Douglas Cole, "John S. Ewart and Canadian Nationalism," *Historical Papers* 1, 4 (1969): 71–73.

73 Ewart, *The Kingdom Papers,* vol. 1, 55.

74 Frank H. Underhill, "The Political Ideas of John S. Ewart," *Report of the Annual Meeting of the Canadian Historical Association* 12, 1 (1933): 32.

75 J.S. Ewart to Sir Gilbert Parker, 18 August 1914, as quoted in Peter Price, "Fashioning a Constitutional Narrative: John S. Ewart and the Development of a 'Canadian Constitution,'" *Canadian Historical Review* 93, 3 (2012): 379.

76 J.S. Ewart, "Predisposing and Precipitating Causes of the War," *Ottawa Citizen,* 24 October 1914, 6.

77 Henri Bourassa, "M. Ewart et la guerre: Les causes 'prédisposantes' et les causes 'précipantes,'" *Le Devoir,* 6 November 1914, 1. Bourassa's article erroneously lists Ewart's article as appearing on 26 October.

78 Ewart to Bourassa, 1 December 1916, LAC, Henri Bourassa Fonds, MG27-IIE1, reel M721.

79 Rumilly, *Henri Bourassa,* 519–20.

80 Louis-Gérard Alberti, "Russell Theatre," in *Canadian Encyclopedia Online,* http://www.thecanadianencyclopedia.com/articles/emc/russell-theatre; Edward Bernard Kinsella, *Modern Theatre Construction* (New York: Chalmers, 1917), 23; Don B. Wilmeth and Christopher Bigsby, eds., *The Cambridge History of American Theatre,* vol. II, *1870–1945* (Cambridge, UK: Cambridge University Press, 1999), 489–91.

81 Henri Bourassa, *The Duty of Canada at the Present Hour* (Montreal: Le Devoir, 1915), 6. This booklet printed the speech that Bourassa was supposed to give that night and included the two pamphlets printed rousing action against his presence, one from a talk on 22 November, the other for his talk on 16 December.

82 The description of the event is drawn from Rumilly, *Henri Bourassa,* 521–22.

83 Bourassa, *The Duty of Canada,* 4.

84 Ibid.

Chapter 3: What Do We Owe England?

1. As mentioned in the previous chapter, Jean Martin recently suggested that low French Canadian enlistment numbers were based solely upon French Canadians in Quebec with French names. Using numbers drawn from cross-Canada recruitment and including French speakers with English names, Martin argued that Canadian-born numbers approached equality between French and English. Jean Martin, "La participation des francophones dans le Corps expéditionnaire canadien (1914–1919): Il faut réviser à la hausse," *Canadian Historical Review* 96, 3 (2015): 405–23.
2. J. Castell Hopkins, *Canadian Annual Review War Series 1915* (Toronto: Canadian Annual Review, 1918), 288. Hopkins also underlines the disproportionate share of British-born Canadians within English Canadian recruitment, noting that the numbers as of February 1916 broke down to 30 percent native born, 62 percent British born, and 8 percent "other" (219). The veracity of these numbers is questionable, but they were accepted at the time.
3. Terry Copp has recently questioned whether or not Regulation 17 was as influential on French Canadian support for the war as previously believed. Terry Copp, *Montreal at War: Chapter IV – Mobilizing*, https://montrealatwar.com/2017/07/12/mobilizing/. He argued that newspapers were largely concerned with normal day-to-day events rather than the political fortunes of neighbouring Franco-Ontarians, and he pointed out that faltering enlistment in Montreal, at least, was unsurprising given that "full employment in a city where sports, entertainment, alcohol and sensual pleasures were readily available did little to encourage enlistment or focus attention on a distant and seemingly endless conflict."
4. Quoted in Hopkins, *Canadian Annual Review War Series 1915*, 564.
5. Margaret Prang, "Clerics, Politicians, and the Bilingual Schools Issue in Ontario, 1910–1917," *Canadian Historical Review* 41, 4 (1960): 294.
6. Hopkins, *Canadian Annual Review War Series 1915*, 299.
7. Mason Wade, *The French-Canadian Outlook* (Toronto: McClelland and Stewart, 1963), 53.
8. *Le 5e anniversaire du "Devoir"* (Montréal: Le Devoir, 1915), 15; Robert Rumilly, *Henri Bourassa: La vie publique d'un grand Canadien* (Montréal: Éditions Chantecler, 1953), 526; "Au début, nous pensions la race condamnée à mourir, et nous n'avions plus qu'un espoir, celui de la voir mourir proprement. Mais les temps sont changés. Il n'est plus question de mourir, car la race vivra. Un homme l'a sauvée."
9. *Le 5e anniversaire du "Devoir,"* 41.
10. Ibid., 72–73. In late February, he published more on both the clergy and the parties to reinforce further the position of the newspaper. Henri Bourassa, "Le 'Devoir' et le clergé," *Le Devoir*, 20 February 1915, 1; Henri Bourassa, "Le 'Devoir' et les partis," *Le Devoir*, 22 February 1915, 1.
11. *Le 5e Anniversaire du "Devoir,"* 70.
12. René Durocher, "Henri Bourassa, les évêques et la guerre de 1914–1918," *Canadian Historical Association Historical Papers* 6 (1971): 256.
13. *Le 5e Anniversaire du "Devoir,"* 72.
14. Ibid., 59; "Ce fait primordial de notre situation nationale passée, présente et future: nous n'avons pas plus le droit de vouloir faire du Canada un pays exclusivement français que les Anglo-Canadiens n'ont le droit d'en faire un pays anglais."
15. Ibid., 68; "idéal commun, fait des traditions canadiennes, enraciné dans le sol canadien et n'ayant d'autre object que la grandeur morale et matérielle de la patrie canadienne."

16 Ibid., 75; "En retour de tout ce que vous pourrez faire pour le *Devoir* et ses oeuvres, je ne vous fais qu'une promesse, c'est que, moi vivant, il ne décherra pas. Avant qu'il ne défaille ou trahisse la mission que je lui ai tracée, dussé-je y voir la fin de toutes mes ambitions, de toutes mes espérances, je le tuerai de ma main!"
17 Hopkins, *Canadian Annual Review War Series 1915*, 168.
18 Others followed suit throughout the year. Ibid., 168–69.
19 Ibid., 179.
20 Henri Bourassa, "M. Doherty et le probleme imperial," *Le Devoir*, 18 January 1915, 1.
21 Henri Bourassa, "Le vin est tiré, il faut le boire," *Le Devoir*, 26 January 1915, 1; "Le vin est tiré, messieurs les sauveurs d'Empire, vous ne le ferez pas boire qu'aux autres."
22 Henri Bourassa, "La Conference imperiale," *Le Devoir*, 8 February 1915, 1. He returned to the subject with much the same to say in April. Henri Bourassa, "Abjection coloniale," *Le Devoir*, 23 April 1915, 1.
23 Henri Bourassa, "Une critique intelligente," *Le Devoir*, 9 February 1915, 1.
24 Ibid.
25 Critics wrote to him either privately or in the pages of *Le Devoir* to refute his arguments. In "Une critique intelligente," Bourassa responded to Maurice Hodent's criticism of his position on the outbreak of the war. Hodent was the secretary of the *Canadienne*, and *Le Devoir* had been publishing letters from him expanding his position against its editor.
26 Canada, *House of Commons Debates*, 12th Parliament, 5th Session, vol. 1 (11 February 1915), 80–82 (William Thomas White).
27 Henri Bourassa, "Le poids de la gloire: Le budget de la guerre," *Le Devoir*, 13 February 1915, 1; "Les 'sauveurs de l'Empire' pourraient bien être les destructeurs de leur propre pays."
28 Henri Bourassa, "Le 'Titan fatigué': La 'pauvre' Angleterre," *Le Devoir*, 17 February 1915, 1. Bourassa examined the cost of the war and war taxes in articles on 13, 15, and 16 February as well. He advocated more taxes on revenues and increased manpower at home for the production of goods and resources that could contribute to the war effort.
29 Hopkins, *Canadian Annual Review War Series 1915*, 201.
30 Henri Bourassa, "Tout pour l'empire, rien pour le Canada," *Le Devoir*, 18 March 1915, 1.
31 Henri Bourassa, "La tactique liberal: Sa faiblesse et ses inconséquences," *Le Devoir*, 19 March 1915, 1. Laurier agreed with the position that Bourassa had set out on 16 February, though it was unlikely a purposeful alignment.
32 Ibid.
33 Henri Bourassa, "Les conséquences de la guerre: Réaction nationaliste," *Le Devoir*, 20 March 1915, 1. Bourassa did not address any positive economic consequences of the war. For a recent study of how much the war positively or negatively affected the Canadian economy, see Douglas McCalla, "The Economic Impact of the Great War," in *Canada and the First World War: Essays in Honour of Robert Craig Brown*, ed. David Mackenzie (Toronto: University of Toronto Press, 2005), 138–53.
34 Bourassa, "Les conséquences de la guerre."
35 Henri Bourassa, "Les révélations d'Ottawa," *Le Devoir*, 25 March 1915, 1; "atrophié par le servilisme colonial, moins fort, moins agissant, que la patriotisme d'un peuple libre, maître de son action mondiale."
36 I have discussed the accuracy of enlistment numbers above in Jean Martin's work; see note 1 above (Chapter 3).

37 Bourassa, "Les révélations d'Ottawa"; "Le loyalisme est une conviction ou un sentiment – et souvent une hypocrite profession de foi – qui [dépend] de circonstances extérieures et lointaines."
38 United Kingdom, *House of Commons Debates* (25 February 1915), Hansard vol. 70, col. 364 (Edward Grey). Canadian newspapers reported on Grey's statement in late February as well.
39 Henri Bourassa, "La Russie a Constantinople," *Le Devoir*, 3 March 1915, 1; "Dans toute guerre, le gros public n'aperçoit que l'aspect dramatique et sanglant"; "C'est la force de résistance économique qui donnera la victoire finale aux Alliés, plus que tous leurs faits d'armes; c'est l'influence politique la plus forte qui règlera les conditions de la paix et détournera ou activera les causes de conflits futurs."
40 The revolutionary Russian government revealed this "secret treaty" and others after the czar was deposed. See F. Seymour Cocks, *The Secret Treaties and Understandings* (London: Union of Democratic Control, 1918).
41 United Kingdom, *House of Commons Debates* (25 February 1915), Hansard vol. 70, col. 364 (Edward Grey).
42 Bourassa, "La Russie a Constantinople." Bourassa is quoting from Brailsford's article titled "The Empire of the East" published in the *Contemporary Review*. He examined the article on 28 October. Henri Bourassa, "L'orientation de la politique anglaise," *Le Devoir*, 28 October 1914. He also reproduced Brailsford's article in his pamphlet *The Foreign Policy of Great Britain* (Montreal: Imprimerie du Devoir, 1915).
43 Tim Cook, *At the Sharp End: Canadians Fighting the Great War, 1914–1916* (Ottawa: Viking Canada, 2007), 165; see 109–70 for Cook's account of the battle.
44 Ian Miller, *Our Glory and Our Grief: Torontonians and the Great War* (Toronto: University of Toronto Press, 2002), 15–66.
45 Percy Scott, *Fifty Years in the Royal Navy* (London: George H. Doran, 1919), 274–80. First Sea Lord John Fisher had also been a vocal proponent of submarines as part of a "flotilla defence;" but it was opposed by some within the British navy, notably Admiral Lord Charles Beresford. See Nicholas A. Lambert, "Admiral Sir John Fisher and the Concept of Flotilla Defence, 1904–1909," *Journal of Military History* 59, 4 (1995): 639–60.
46 Henri Bourassa, "Le désastre du 'Lusitania' et l'attitude de Président Wilson," *Le Devoir*, 12 May 1915, 1.
47 Ibid.
48 See, for instance, the reaction in Toronto in Miller, *Our Glory and Our Grief*, 44–46.
49 United States Department of State, *Papers Relating to the Foreign Relations of the United States, 1915: Supplement, the World War* (Washington, DC: US Government Printing Office, 1915), 393–96, part of the University of Wisconsin Digital Collections, http://uwdc.library.wisc.edu/collections/FRUS.
50 Henri Bourassa, "La protestation du gouvernement americain," *Le Devoir*, 15 May 1915, 1.
51 Ibid.
52 United States Department of State, *Papers Relating to the Foreign Relations of the United States*, 396. Bryan's letter of resignation, Wilson's response to it, as well as further clarifications from Bryan are printed in "The Resignation of Mr. Bryan as Secretary of State," *American Journal of International Law* 9, 3 (1915): 659–66.
53 Henri Bourassa, "La démission de M. Bryan: La crise politique en Angleterre," *Le Devoir*, 10 June 1915, 1.
54 United States Department of State, *Papers Relating to the Foreign Relations of the United States*, 463–66.

55 Henri Bourassa, "La note allemande," *Le Devoir,* 14 July 1915, 1; "un singulier mélange d'impudence, d'habile dialectique et de franche sincérité."
56 Ibid.
57 United States Department of State, *Papers Relating to the Foreign Relations of the United States,* 435–36.
58 John W. Coogan, *The End of Neutrality: The United States, Britain, and Maritime Rights, 1899–1915* (Ithaca, NY: Cornell University Press, 1981), 193, 179–81, 249–51.
59 Henri Bourassa, *La langue française au Canada: Ses droits, sa nécessité, ses avantages. Discours prononcé au Monument National, le 19 mai 1915, sous les auspices du Comité régional de Montréal de l'A.C.J.C.* (Montréal: Imprimerie du Devoir, 1915). Rumilly, *Henri Bourassa,* 531, writes that Bourassa spoke for two hours.
60 Bourassa, *La langue française au Canada,* 36, 35; "la Confédération canadienne est née d'une pensée d'alliance féconde des deux races; elle ne vivra que par le respect réciproque de leurs droits"; "Si l'on va jusqu'à prétendre qu'un peuple bi-ethnique et bilingue ne peut former une nation homogène et que la minorité doit parler la langue de la majorité, on se heurte aux démentis les plus éclatants de l'histoire."
61 Ibid., 6; "Ce n'est qu'au français qu'on fait la guerre."
62 Ibid., 51–52; "Dans un magnifique élan de générosité, la province de Québec a versé son argent à pleine[s] mains pour venir en aide aux Anglais ... Ferons-nous moins pour nos propres nationaux? Ils soutiennent une cause aussi juste et aussi sacrée, cause qui n'a d'autre défaut que d'être la nôtre et de ne pouvoir attendre d'appui des nations étrangères à qui nous prodiguons notre or et notre sang."
63 Rumilly, *Henri Bourassa,* 533; "les préceptes et la pratique de l'entente cordiale qui unit l'Angleterre et la France sur les champs de bataille de l'Europe."
64 Hopkins, *Canadian Annual Review War Series 1915,* 296.
65 Ibid., 223–24.
66 Ibid., 258.
67 Henri Bourassa, "La conscription," *Le Devoir,* 26 July 1915, 1.
68 By June, the Canadian army had expanded to 100,000, and recruitment became difficult, as one recruiter noted: "The first 100,000 came easily. We found that other men were not coming." Quoted in J.L. Granatstein and J.M. Hitsman, *Broken Promises: A History of Conscription in Canada* (Toronto: Oxford University Press, 1977), 34–35. For information on recruitment in 1915, see Hopkins, *Canadian Annual Review War Series 1915,* 216–18. Again, despite some scholarly claims that support for the war was widespread, as early as 1915 enlistment was becoming difficult for the Canadian army.
69 Bourassa, "La conscription."
70 Ibid.
71 Jeffrey A. Keshen, *Propaganda and Censorship during Canada's Great War* (Edmonton: University of Alberta Press, 1996), 79, 143, 165, and throughout. The Chief Press Censor Office was established in June 1915 (66), a fact that Bourassa lamented, but it seemed to have little impact on his work early in the war. Henri Bourassa, "La censure," *Le Devoir,* 28 July 1915, 1. In 1915, the press censor declined to ban *Le Devoir,* though according to Keshen it did temper its "propaganda" (76–77, 94). Cook cites many letters home that were more blunt, but he also acknowledges the influence of censorship on filtering what Canadians learned about their soldiers. Cook, *At the Sharp End,* 76, 390. For an excellent overview of some of these letters and memoirs, see Maarten Gerritsen, "Corps Identity: The Letters, Diaries, and Memoirs of Canada's Great War Soldiers" (PhD diss., Memorial University of Newfoundland, 2008).
72 Hopkins, *Canadian Annual Review War Series 1915,* 283–86.

73 Ramsay Cook, "Dafoe, Laurier, and the Formation of Union Government," in *Conscription 1917*, ed. Carl Berger (Toronto: University of Toronto Press, 1969), 18.
74 Hopkins, *Canadian Annual Review War Series 1915*, 274–75. See also Oscar Douglas Skelton, *Life and Letters of Sir Wilfrid Laurier*, vol. II (London: Oxford University Press, 1922), 445–47; eventually, Skelton notes (453–55), Laurier would make the same decision about 1916.
75 John F. Pollard, *The Unknown Pope: Benedict XV (1914–1922), and the Pursuit of Peace* (London: Geoffrey Chapman, 1999), 117–19.
76 Pope Benedict XV, "Exhortation Allorchè Fummo to the Belligerent Peoples and to Their Leaders," in *Principles for Peace: Selections from Papal Documents Leo XIII to Pius XII*, ed. Reverend Harry C. Koenig (Washington, DC: National Catholic Welfare Conference, 1943), 180. Originally written in Italian.
77 "Letter era nostro proposito to Cardinal S. Vannutelli," in ibid., 170. Originally written in Italian.
78 Henri Bourassa, "L'appel du pape," *Le Devoir*, 3 August 1915, 1; Benedict XV, "Exhortation Allorchè Fummo," 181.
79 Bourassa, "L'appel du pape."
80 Ibid.; "affaiblissement de tout principe d'autorité, à la laxité du lien familial, à la négation du devoir social, à l'égoïsme individuel, à la haine des classes, au culte effréné du bien-être physique, à la soif des richesses – au paganisme."
81 Ibid.
82 "L'opinion d'un véritable anglais," *Le Devoir*, 12 June 1915, 2.
83 Henri Bourassa, "La saine opinion anglaise," *Le Devoir*, 12 June 1915, 1.
84 Marvin Swartz, *The Union of Democratic Control in British Politics during the First World War* (Oxford: Clarendon Press, 1971), 33.
85 The text of this pamphlet, *The Morrow of War*, can be found in Randolph Silliman Bourne, *Towards an Enduring Peace: A Symposium of Peace Proposals and Programs* (New York: American Association for International Conciliation, 1916), 86–107.
86 Bourassa, "La saine opinion anglaise"; "hommes de haute valeur, prêts à risquer leur popularité et leurs chances de succès personnel, à rompre leurs attaches de parti et leurs associations d'intérêts, pour défendre une liberté légitime et soutenir un principe ou une idée."
87 Swartz, *The Union of Democratic Control*, 105–29. A more direct and negative response to the UDC was from G.G. Coulton, *The Main Illusions of Pacifism: A Criticism of Mr. Norman Angell and of the Union of Democratic Control* (Cambridge, UK: Bowes and Bowes, 1916), first published as a pamphlet by the *Times Literary Supplement* in June 1915; see Swartz, *The Union of Democratic Control*, 110.
88 Bourassa, "La saine opinion anglaise."
89 Ibid.
90 John Keating, "British Bernhardi-ism," *Month*, February 1915, 166–79. Bourassa mistakenly identified the author as R.P. Keating.
91 Friedrich von Bernhardi, *Germany and the Next War*, trans. Allen H. Powles (New York: Longmans, Green, 1914).
92 Gregory Moore, "The Super-Hun and the Super-State: Allied Propaganda and German Philosophy during the First World War," *German Life and Letters* 54, 4 (2001): 310–30.
93 Keating, "British Bernhardi-ism," 166.
94 Henri Bourassa, "La guerre à la guerre," *Le Devoir*, 7 August 1915, 1.
95 E.D. Morel, "Union of Democratic Control," *Contemporary Review*, July 1915, reprinted in E.D. Morel, *Truth and War* (London: National Labour Press, 1918), 169–82.

96 They were preparing to campaign against conscription in 1915 and were worried about severe government reprisals. In some cities, such as Glasgow, UDC members faced violence, but it was mostly censorship as some newspapers voluntarily refused to publish their materials. Brock Millman, *Managing Domestic Dissent in First World War Britain* (London: Routledge, 2000), 49–58.
97 Henri Bourassa, "Le guerre à la guerre II: Nationalisme et imperialisme," *Le Devoir*, 10 August 1915, 1.
98 Morel, *Truth and War*, 180.
99 Ibid., 175.
100 Bourassa, "Le guerre à la guerre II." Bourassa translated the passage into French; the English version is found in Benedict XV, "Exhortation Allorchè Fummo," 181–82.
101 Joseph Levitt, *Henri Bourassa and the Golden Calf: The Social Program of the Nationalists of Quebec* (Ottawa: Les Éditions de l'Université d'Ottawa, 1969), 129–45.
102 Castor was the sign of ultramontanes, and rouge was the colour of liberals, so Bourassa combined Quebec's brand of conservative Catholicism and Britain's Gladstonian liberal politics. He was anointed with the name early in his career, six months after being elected in 1896 and still an MP with Laurier's Liberals. See Réal Bélanger, *Henri Bourassa: Le fascinant destin d'un homme libre (1868–1914)* (Québec: Presses de l'Université Laval, 2013), 44n2.
103 Morel, *Truth and War*, 177.
104 David Stevenson, "The First World War and European Integration," *International History Review* 34, 4 (2012): 846–47.
105 William Mulligan, *The Great War for Peace* (New Haven, CT: Yale University Press, 2014), 116. Hollweg's speech is printed in Theobald von Bethmann-Hollweg, *Sechs Kriegsreden des Reichkanzlers* (Berlin: Verlag Reimar Hobbing, 1916), 39–61.
106 Grey of Fallodon, *Edward Grey, Sir Edward Grey's Reply to Dr. von Bethmann-Hollweg: Being a Letter Addressed to the British Press on the 25th August, 1915, Together with a Statement Issued by the Foreign Office on the 1st September, 1915, etc.* (London: T. Fisher Unwin, 1915), 9–11.
107 Henri Bourassa, "Sir Edward Grey: Le programme de l'Angleterre," *Le Devoir*, 27 August 1915, 1; Henri Bourassa, "La réponse de l'Allemagne à Sir Edward Grey," *Le Devoir*, 1 September 1915, 1.
108 Michael Eliot Howard, *Studies in War and Peace* (New York: Viking Adult, 1971), 105.
109 Rumilly, *Henri Bourassa*, 539.
110 Gaétan Gervais, "Le Règlement XVII (1912–1927)," *Revue du Nouvel-Ontario* 18 (1996): 160.
111 Patrice A. Dutil, "Against Isolationism: Napoléon Belcourt, French Canada, and 'La grande guerre,'" in *Canada and the First World War: Essays in Honour of Robert Craig Brown*, ed. David Mackenzie (Toronto: University of Toronto Press, 2005), 99–102.
112 For instance, see Napoléon Antoine Belcourt, *Le français dans l'Ontario* (Montréal: n.p., 1912), or Napoléon Antoine Belcourt, *L'unité nationale au Canada* (Ottawa: A. Bureau, 1908).
113 Dutil, "Against Isolationism," 104–5.
114 Belcourt lost two major cases in 1915, the appeal of *Mackell v Trustees* in the Appellate Court of Ontario, where he represented the Ottawa Separate School Board. The board had been shut down in 1914 since it had been unable to pay its French teachers. Its closure actually allowed Ottawa to fund the board independently of Ontario's Ministry of Education under a City of Ottawa bylaw, thus continuing French-language education. Robert Mackell, who was suing the trustees for not following provincial law, asked for an injunction against its closure so that the Ottawa bylaw could not be used. The

Appellate Court sided with Mackell in July 1915. Belcourt's primary case against the legality of Regulation 17 was rejected by the Supreme Court in November 1915. See Dutil, "Against Isolationism," 106–11.
115 Henri Bourassa, "L'Article 133 et l'enseignement du français," *Le Devoir*, 15 December 1915, 1.
116 Geneviève Richer, "'L'apôtre infatigable de l'irrédentisme français': La lutte de Napoléon-Antoine Belcourt en faveur de la langue française en Ontario durant les années 1910 et 1920," *Francophonies d'Amérique* 31 (2011): 90; "l'ancienneté des Canadiens français en Ontario et au Canada, le catholicisme et l'unité nationale."
117 Rumilly, *Henri Bourassa*, 542.
118 Henri Bourassa, *Que devons-nous à l'Angleterre? La défense nationale, la révolution impérialiste, le tribut à l'Empire* (Montréal: Imprimerie du Devoir, 1915), v.
119 Gilles Gallichan, *Honoré Mercier: La politique et la culture* (Sillery, QC: Les Éditions du Septentrion, 1994), 70–71.
120 Bourassa, *Que devons-nous à l'Angleterre?*, 83.
121 Bourassa reproduces the correspondence in ibid., 277–78.
122 Ibid., 91.
123 Ibid., 96–97.
124 Canada, *House of Commons Debates*, 11th Parliament, 2nd Session (12 January 1910), vol. 1, 1735 (Wilfrid Laurier). See note 77 in Chapter 1 for more context on this statement.
125 Henri Bourassa, "Le devoir national," *Le Devoir*, 8 September 1914, 1; "lié à l'Angleterre et à la France par mille attaches ethniques, sociales, intellectuelles, économiques, le Canada a un intérêt vital à la conservation de l'Angleterre et de la France, au maintien de leur prestige, de leur puissance, de leur action mondiale."
126 Bourassa, *Que devons-nous à l'Angleterre?*, 253; "la puissance et l'action mondiale de la France et de l'Angleterre restent contenues dans de justes bornes et ne deviennent pas, à leur tour, une menace pour la paix et l'équilibre du monde." Durocher draws attention to this addition in "Henri Bourassa," 259–60.
127 Bourassa, *Que devons-nous à l'Angleterre?*, 253; "L'arrogante brutalité des anglicisateurs canadiens."
128 As quoted in Rumilly, *Henri Bourassa*, 543. One enterprising baker reacted to Bourassa's writing by placing ads in *Le Devoir* asking "Que devez-vous à votre estomac?" Quoted in Robert S. Prince, "The Mythology of War: How the Canadian Daily Newspaper Depicted the Great War" (PhD diss., University of Toronto, 1998), 101n57.
129 Prince, "The Mythology of War," 125.
130 "Bourassa: No Martyr, No Hero," *Globe* [Toronto], 23 December 1915, 4.
131 See Jean Noël Cossette, "La censure fédérale et les principaux journaux canadiens-français du Québec, 1915–1918" (MA thesis, University of Ottawa, 1971), 28.
132 This is a quotation from Minister of Justice Charles J. Dougherty, E.J. Boag to T.C. Casgrain, 29 October 1915, as quoted in ibid., 32. For newspapers that responded to Bourassa's book in December 1915, letters to the chief censor, and debate on the possibility of censuring Bourassa in 1915, see ibid., 27–37.
133 Sylvie Lacombe, *La rencontre de deux peuples élus: Comparaison des ambitions nationale et impériale au Canada entre 1896 et 1920* (Québec: Presses de l'Université Laval, 2002), 63; "les hommes peuvent dégager la mission providentielle qui singularise leur existence collective, et la justifie par le fait même."
134 Louis Georges Desjardins, *England, Canada, and the Great War* (Quebec: Chronicle Print, 1918), 140–42. Desjardins's work examines and rejects much of Bourassa's writings during the war.

135 Henri Bourassa, "Le pape et la guerre," *Le Devoir,* 31 December 1915, 1; "le soleil de 1915 s'est levé dans un nuage de feu. Il se couche dans une mer de sang."
136 Ibid.
137 Ibid.
138 Despite popular claims, gas shells had first been used as early as October 1914. See Tim Cook, *No Place to Run: The Canadian Corps and Gas Warfare in the First World War* (Vancouver: UBC Press, 1999), 17.
139 Viscount James Bryce, *Report of the Committee on Alleged German Outrages Appointed by His Britannic Majesty's Government* (New York: Macmillan, 1915).
140 Hopkins, *Canadian Annual Review War Series 1915,* 61–64. Hopkins includes some mention of German crimes on the Russian front as well.
141 Ibid., 278.
142 Bourassa, "Le pape et la guerre"; "[a marqué] l'effondrement du système politique élevé par la fausse sagesse des hommes, par la diplomatie orgueilleuse, par la soif des conquêtes et le culte païen de l'or et de la force brutale."
143 Ibid.

Chapter 4: The Soul of Canada

1 Henri Bourassa, Le Devoir *et la guerre: Le conflit des races. Discours prononcé au banquet des amis du* DEVOIR, *le 12 janvier 1916* (Montreal: Imprimerie du Devoir, 1916). Bourassa delivered the speech without notes, and the booklet cited is a reproduction based upon his recollection of its content.
2 Ibid., 16, 18.
3 Ibid., 22, 40; "il ne nous restait qu'un devoir: nous retrancher dans les solides positions du nationalisme intégral"; "C'est sur ce terrain solide que nous avons livré nos premiers combats contre l'impérialisme britannique. C'est sur le même terrain que nous résistons à l'affolement du jour."
4 J. Castell Hopkins, *Canadian Annual Review War Series 1915* (Toronto: Canadian Annual Review, 1918), 194, 294.
5 Lavergne explained his reasons to Asselin, reprinted in Olivar Asselin, *Pourquoi je m'enrôle: Discours prononcé au Monument National à Montréal (21 janvier 1916)* (Montréal: n.p. 1916), 9–10.
6 René Durocher, "Henri Bourassa, les évêques, et la guerre de 1914–1918," *Canadian Historical Association Historical Papers* 6 (1971): 260. For an example of his attacks, see Olivar Asselin, *'L'Action catholique,' les évêques et la guerre* (Ottawa: n.p., 1915).
7 Asselin, *Pourquoi je m'enrôle,* 10–12. For a more detailed account of Asselin's decision, see Hélène Pelletier-Baillargeon, *Olivar Asselin et son temps: Le militant* (Québec: Fides, 1996), 680–705.
8 Pelletier-Baillargeon, *Olivar Asselin et son temps,* 689.
9 Jules Fournier, "À propos de cet enrôlement. Qui manque de logique? Asselin ou *Le Devoir,*" *L'Action,* 4 December 1915, 1.
10 Jules Fournier, "La faillite (?) du nationalisme," in *Mon encrier,* ed. Thérèse Fournier (Montréal: Fides, 1965 [first published 1922]), 267–316. The title, "La faillite (?) du nationalisme," hearkens to an article that Asselin had penned under a pseudonym. See Le Kronzprinz [Olivar Asselin], "Simple briques," *L'Action,* 19 September 1914, 1.
11 Fournier, *Mon encrier,* 300–1.
12 Ibid., 308; "Autrement dit, l'intervention, à l'entendre, lui paraissait bien l'indiscutable 'devoir de l'heure,' – seulement il ne pouvait s'empêcher de reconnaître, par contre,

que cette entreprise au fond n'avait pas le sens commun, et que nous avions toutes les raisons du monde de nous en abstenir."
13 Ibid., 313–15.
14 Ibid., 271–72; "impérieux besoin d'étaler son érudition"; "son inaptitude foncière à l'action"; "son inexpérience et son dédain des hommes."
15 Ibid., 273–74; "Deux choses ... auront toujours manqué au chef nationaliste dans son action politique: un peu d'indulgence humaine et d'humaine sympathie. Il lui aura manqué de connaître les hommes, et de les aimer."
16 As quoted in R.J.Q. Adams and P. Poirier, *The Conscription Controversy in Great Britain 1900–1918* (Columbus: Ohio State University Press, 1987), 143.
17 Ibid., 140–41.
18 C.P. Stacey, *Canada and the Age of Conflict: A History of Canadian External Policies Volume I: 1867–1921* (Toronto: Macmillan, 1981), 177–91. For the text of Borden's January announcement, see Hopkins, *Canadian Annual Review War Series 1915*, 185–86. The reasons for his sudden announcement in January are unclear. It caught his cabinet off guard, and his biographer does not offer any detailed explanation. See Robert Craig Brown, *Robert Laird Borden: A Biography*, vol. II, *1914–1937* (Toronto: Macmillan, 1980), 60–61, for a short reference to it. Borden's diary offers similarly little detail. His entry is brief and uninteresting: "White Hughes and Reid came and I propounded to them proposal that force should be increased on 1st January to 500,000. They agreed." Robert Laird Borden, Diary, 30 December 1916, LAC, Borden Papers, M02611. Stacey wonders whether Borden intended to impress the British with the size of the Canadian commitment in return for more control over war policy. Stacey, *Canada and the Age of Conflict*, 191–92.
19 G.W.L. Nicholson, *Canadian Expeditionary Force, 1914–1919: Official History of the Canadian Army in the First World War* (Ottawa: Queen's Printer and Controller of Stationery, 1962), 213–14; Tim Cook, *At the Sharp End: Canadians Fighting the Great War, 1914–1916* (Ottawa: Viking Canada, 2007), 304.
20 Chris Sharpe, "Enlistment in the Canadian Expeditionary Force 1914–1918," *Canadian Military History* 24, 1 (2015): 21–22.
21 Canada, *House of Commons Debates*, 12th Parliament, 6th Session (13 January 1916), vol. 4 (Robert Borden).
22 The debate about conscription in England and its impact on Ireland echoed some of the themes in Canada, for instance that of an ethnic minority searching for exemptions in the conflict, but Canadian *nationalistes* did not have the political dynamism of Redmond's Irish nationalist rump in the House of Commons. See W.E. Vaughan, ed., *A New History of Ireland*, vol. VI, *Ireland under the Union, II: 1870–1921* (Oxford: Oxford University Press, 2010), 208–9, 234–38. The resurgence of Irish republicans after exemptions for the Irish were cancelled (though never implemented) in 1918 reflects the drastic impact of conscription on Quebec.
23 Henri Bourassa, "Solidarité impériale," *Le Devoir*, 15 January 1916, 1.
24 Henri Bourassa, "La conscription en Angleterre – Le rôle de la flotte," *Le Devoir*, 26 January 1916, 1; "Il n'est guère croyable que le gouvernement britannique enverra au feu plus de soldats qu'il n'en peut convenablement armer – sauf les coloniaux, évidemment, ces bonnes bêtes."
25 Ibid.
26 Eric W. Osborne, *Britain's Economic Blockade of Germany, 1914–1919* (New York: Routledge, 2004), 115–20.
27 Bourassa, "Solidarité impériale."

28 Bourassa, "La conscription en Angleterre." In his opinion, it was an apt comparison.
29 Henri Bourassa, "La tragi-comédie d'Ottawa," *Le Devoir*, 19 January 1916, 1.
30 Canada, *House of Commons Debates*, 12th Parliament, 6th Session (17 January 1916), vol. 1, 622 (Wilfrid Laurier).
31 Ibid., 635. For Borden's and Laurier's speeches, see 622–36.
32 Bourassa, "La Tragi-Comédie d'Ottawa."
33 Ibid.; "seul terrain où l'union des cœurs et des esprits pouvait s'opérer: celui d'une intervention raisonnable et efficace, proportionnée aux ressources du pays."
34 Henri Bourassa, "La prolongation du Parlement: Capitulation de M. Laurier," *Le Devoir*, 10 February 1916, 1.
35 Patrice Dutil and David Mackenzie, *Canada 1911: The Decisive Election that Shaped the Country* (Toronto: Dundurn, 2011), 288–89. "Being too British" and "not [being] British enough" come from a letter from Wilfrid Laurier to Lotus Botha, 1 December 1916. See Oscar Douglas Skelton, *Life and Letters of Sir Wilfrid Laurier*, vol. II (London: Oxford University Press, 1922), 466.
36 H. Blair Neatby, *Laurier and a Liberal Quebec* (Toronto: McClelland and Stewart, 1961), 212.
37 This point is made by J.W. Dafoe, *Laurier: A Study in Canadian Politics* (Toronto: Thomas Allen, 1922), 147–63, and more recently by Réal Bélanger, *Wilfrid Laurier: Quand la politique devient passion* (Québec: Presses de l'Université Laval, 2007), 384.
38 Skelton, *Life and Letters of Sir Wilfrid Laurier*, vol. II, 467.
39 Bourassa, "La prolongation du Parlement"; "Depuis cinq ans, nous avons plus rétrogradé dans la voie de l'indépendance nationale que nous n'avions avancé en un siècle. La nouvelle démarche du parlement est un pas de plus dans cette marche en arrière."
40 Bourassa, "La tragi-comédie d'Ottawa"; "Le Canada devra se nationaliser de nouveau, et réchapper sa vie, ou s'impérialiser à demeure, et se suicider."
41 Henri Bourassa, "M. Hughes, premier-ministre d'Australie," *Le Devoir*, 23 February 1916, 1.
42 Henri Bourassa, *Hier, aujourd'hui, demain* (Montréal: Imprimerie du Devoir, 1916), 39–40; "La participation du Canada à la guerre actuelle, *comme colonie britannique*, constitue donc une révolution, une révolution profonde, radicale, dans la charte nationale du Canada." Durocher, "Henri Bourassa," 261–63, also reviews these points and explains the reaction of Quebec bishops and priests to his writing.
43 Bourassa, *Hier, aujourd'hui, demain*, 55; "la Grande-Bretagne veut maintenir sa suprématie maritime, garder pour elle toute seule les immenses contrées qu'elle a conquises depuis un demi-siècle, et dire au monde entier: '*What we have, we hold.*'"
44 Ibid., 65; "Ces droits, ces traditions, ces libertés, ces devoirs, c'est à l'école de l'Angleterre que nous avons appris à les respecter, à les apprécier, à les aimer: elle ne peut trouver mauvais ni déloyal que nous les défendions jalousement."
45 Ibid., 107; "antisocial et antinational ... le résultat que poursuivent les révolutionnaires imperialists"; "Il est rare que les révolutions ne soient pas dirigées également contre l'ordre social et le patriotisme national."
46 Ibid., 119.
47 Ibid., 124–26.
48 Ibid., 133; "'C'est quelque chose de faire partie d'un grand empire' ... il y a, pour soi et pour les autres, pour la paix, la liberté, le progrès et le bon équilibre du monde, 'quelque chose' de mieux que de 'faire partie d'un grand empire': c'est d'être une nation, même modeste."

49 Henri Bourassa, *Grande-Bretagne et Canada: Questions actuelles* (Montréal: Imprimerie du Pionnier, 1901), 40; "La première condition nécessaire à l'indépendance d'un peuple, c'est d'être assuré de la paix intérieure et extérieure."
50 Bourassa, *Hier, aujourd'hui, demain,* 134.
51 Bourassa, ibid., 138–39, notes his letter to Laurier published in *La Patrie* on 20 October 1899.
52 Ibid., 142–43.
53 Ibid., 144; "elle est tout-à-fait dans la logique des causes et des faits accumulés par nos extravagances, et surtout par la suprême folie de notre participation dévergondée à la guerre actuelle."
54 Ibid., 144–50.
55 Ibid., 154.
56 Ibid., 157–68.
57 Ibid., 172; "Ce que la guerre actuelle démontre, au contraire, c'est l'effroyable banqueroute du vieux système des alliances, de l'équilibre des forces brutales, de la diplomatie secrète et des armements à outrance – toutes mesures nécessaires ... pour 'assurer la paix du monde.'"
58 Ibid., 172–76.
59 Ibid., 177–78.
60 Roger Chickering, "World War I and the Theory of Total War: Reflections on the British and German Cases, 1914–1915," in *Great War, Total War: Combat and Mobilization on the Western Front, 1914–1918,* ed. Roger Chickering and Stig Forster (Cambridge, UK: Cambridge University Press, 2000), 35.
61 Bourassa, *Hier, aujourd'hui, demain,* 110.
62 Ibid., 116–17.
63 Robert S. Prince, "The Mythology of War: How the Canadian Daily Newspaper Depicted the Great War" (PhD diss., University of Toronto, 1998), 147, 150.
64 From *Montreal Star,* 20 September 1916, 10, as cited in ibid., 186*n*42. Prince also explores the lingering doubt about militarism's growth in Canada and argues that the English Canadian press responded by emphasizing a nostalgic view of "traditional warfare" in contrast to the industrialized slaughter of the First World War. The press often talked about the use of cavalry, swords, and other "unmodern" ways of war while avoiding explicit discussion of modern military technology (see 361–69). Alexandre Dubé has recently explored the representation of total war to Canadians through propaganda in posters. Alexandre Dubé, "Construire la guerre totale par l'image au Canada (1914–1918): Acceptation différenciée d'un discours de guerre 'totalisé'" (MA thesis, Université de Montréal, 2017).
65 Pope Benedict XV, "Letter Al Tremendo Conflitto to Cardinal Pompilj, Vicar of Rome," in *Principles for Peace Selections from Papal Documents Leo XIII to Pius XII,* ed. Reverend Harry C. Koenig (Washington, DC: National Catholic Welfare Conference, 1943), 201. It was originally written in Italian.
66 Henri Bourassa, "Le pape seul veut la paix," *Le Devoir,* 13 April 1916, 1.
67 Pope Benedict XV, "Letter Al Tremendo Conflitto," 201.
68 Bourassa, "Le pape seul veut la paix."
69 For a copy of the poster, see the *Sinn Fein Rebellion Handbook* (Dublin: Irish Times, 1917), xvii.
70 There are many excellent works on the failed Easter Rising in 1916, but some of the recent histories used here are Michael Foy and Brian Barton, *The Easter Rising* (Sutton, UK: Stroud, 1999), and Fearghal McGarry, *The Rising: Ireland, Easter 1916* (Oxford: Oxford University Press, 2010).

71 Henri Bourassa, "La vengeance de l'Angleterre," *Le Devoir,* 10 May 1916, 1.
72 Ibid.
73 J. Castell Hopkins, *Canadian Annual Review War Series 1916* (Toronto: Canadian Annual Review, 1918), 393–94.
74 Robert Sellar, *The Tragedy of Quebec* (Toronto: n.p., 1916), 327–28, as quoted in Ramsay Cook and Robert Craig Brown, *Canada 1896–1921: A Nation Transformed* (Toronto: McClelland and Stewart, 1974), 259n37.
75 Canada, *House of Commons Debates,* 12th Parliament, 6th Session (9 May 1916), vol. 4, 3618 (Erneste Lapointe).
76 Skelton, Life and Letters of Sir Wilfrid Laurier, vol. II, 476.
77 Bélanger, *Wilfrid Laurier,* 387–89. J.W. Dafoe makes a similar point: "Laurier was out to demonstrate that he was the true champion of Quebec's views and interests, because he could rally to her cause the support of a great national party." J.W. Dafoe, *Laurier: A Study in Canadian Politics* (Toronto: Thomas Allen, 1922), 158.
78 Dafoe, *Laurier,* 158–63.
79 Henri Bourassa, "Le Parlement et l'iniquité ontarienne," *Le Devoir,* 16 May 1916, 1; "l'absence de sanction pratique et l'intempestif accouplement de la question ontarienne à la participation du Canada à la guerre."
80 Henri Bourassa, "Le Parlement et l'iniquité ontarienne II," *Le Devoir,* 17 May 1916, 1; "La motion du député de Kamouraska [Erneste Lapointe] apportait un appui moral, un témoignage public et solennel de sympathie des représentants de la nation aux Canadiens-français de l'Ontario aux vaillantes mères de famille, aux héroïques petites maîtresses d'école qui défendent la civilisation française contre la haine stupide et cauteleuse des 'Huns' de Toronto ... La grande lutte continuera jusqu'au triomphe finale."
81 Henri Bourassa, "L'enseignment du patriotisme," *Le Devoir,* 12 June 1916, 1; "C'est en luttant contre l'autorité impériale et ses tenants au Canada," he claimed, "que les Canadiens des deux races s'étaient rapprochés peu à peu et avaient commencé à se lier par un commun attachement à la patrie canadienne."
82 Sandra Gwyn, *Tapestry of War: A Private View of Canadians in the Great War* (Toronto: HarperCollins, 1992), 92–94.
83 Talbot Mercer Papineau to Beatrice Fox, 24 June 1915, LAC, Talbot Mercer Papineau Fonds (hereafter TMP Fonds), MG30 E52. His mother and grandmother were American. At the time, he was corresponding with his love interest, an American named Beatrice Fox, so perhaps he was emphasizing his American heritage to his own advantage.
84 Gwyn, *Tapestry of War,* 98.
85 Desmond Morton and J.L. Granatstein, *Marching to Armageddon: Canadians and the Great War, 1914–1919* (Toronto: Lester and Orpen Dennys, 1989), 6. See also J. Castell Hopkins, *Canadian Annual Review War Series 1914* (Toronto: Canadian Annual Review, 1918), 707, for another brief excerpt from his speech.
86 The Princess Patricias were formed in Ottawa and funded by Andrew Hamilton Gault with his own money in response to the pitiful size of the Canadian regular forces when the war began. They were the first Canadian unit on the front lines. Although primarily the officers had experience in the militia or the British forces, some with little or no experience, such as Papineau, were accepted to form the junior officer ranks. See Jeffery Williams, *First in the Field: Gault of the Patricias* (St. Catharines, ON: Vanwell Publishing, 1995), 64. For a history of the Princess Pats, see David Jay Bercuson, *The Patricias: The Proud History of a Fighting Regiment* (Toronto: Stoddart, 2001).

87 A few of the many biographies of Lord Beaverbrook are A.J.P. Tayler, *Beaverbrook* (New York: Simon and Schuster, 1972); Anne Chisolm and Michael Davie, *Beaverbrook: A Life* (London: Hutchinson, 1992); and, regarding his financial dealings before the war, G.P. Marchildon, *Profits and Politics: Beaverbrook and the Gilded Age of Canadian Finance* (Toronto: University of Toronto Press, 1996).

88 Aitken's account of Ypres was published on 1 May 1915. His own newspapers and political connections helped the publication spread, and it emphasized the heroism and worthy sacrifice of Canadian soldiers. See Tim Cook, "Documenting War and Forging Reputations: Sir Max Aitken and the Canadian War Records Office in the First World War," *War in History* 3, 10 (2003): 265–95.

89 Papineau described his position in a letter to Fox in October 1916: "You must understand that I am not a mere newspaper correspondent. Nothing makes me angrier. I write many official staff documents as well. For instance yesterday I made a complete tour of our whole battle front – interviewed almost all the Battalion commanders – personally examined the enemy lines and finally wrote a long report which the General favourably commented upon today." Papineau to Fox, 9 October 1916, TMP Fonds.

90 McMaster painted a very different picture from the one Bourassa presented in the pages of *Le Devoir*. "You speak of an imperial war," McMaster wrote to Papineau, "that is not the keynote of all the appeals made for patriotic purposes here – very often it is the Canadian note that is sounded & that the war is a war for civilization and liberty." McMaster to Papineau, 14 April 1916, TMP Fonds.

91 An English version of Bourassa's letter is cited here; see "Captain Papineau's Letter to M. Henri Bourassa (editor of *Le Devoir*)," TMP Fonds. Bourassa published it in French as "Reponse de M. Bourassa à la lettre du Capitaine Talbot Papineau," *Le Devoir*, 5 August 1916, 1. The following quotations are from Papineau's letter and Bourassa's reply cited here.

92 In Canada, there were those who illogically feared a German attack on its eastern coast (see the alarming warnings of Harry W. Anderson, "If Canada Were Invaded," *Maclean's*, 1 October 1914, 5), whereas the main worry for American diplomats was an extension of German hegemony to South America or the necessary militarization of the United States as a result of a German victory. For the most part, though, while the United States was nominally neutral, it was clearly tied culturally to Britain and its allies. It would have defended North America vigorously, and there was little real fear of a German invasion.

93 Hopkins, *Canadian Annual Review War Series 1916*, 225–27; see also Brandon Dimmel, "Sabotage, Security, and Border-Crossing Culture: The Detroit River during the First World War, 1914–1918," *Histoire sociale/Social History* 47, 94 (2014): 401–19.

94 Bourassa quoted Laurier in his letter, referencing his comment regarding his resistance during Imperial Conferences to British demands for a closer relationship between Great Britain and Canada.

95 These reasons for lower French Canadian enlistment were widely accepted at the time; see Hopkins, *Canadian Annual Review War Series 1915*, 216–18. As noted, recent scholarship has suggested that there were as many as 60,000 French Canadians in the armed forces; see Jean Martin, "La participation des francophones dans le Corps expéditionnaire canadien (1914–1919): Il faut réviser à la hausse," *Canadian Historical Review* 96, 3 (2015): 405–23. At the time, these numbers were not known. For example, in May 1916, Brigadier General James Mason told the Senate that the army consisted of 85,000 English Canadian–born, 12,000 French Canadian–born, and 180,000 British-born

soldiers, plus 18,000 foreign-born soldiers; see Hopkins, *Canadian Annual Review War Series 1916,* 349–50.

96 Bourassa's point might have been true, though most English Canadian newspapers perceived the influence of Bourassa as the primary cause of French Canadian apathy toward the war and enlistment; see Hopkins, *Canadian Annual Review War Series 1916,* 309, 566–67, 571.

Chapter 5: The Possibility of Peace

1 Geoff Keelan, "'Il a bien merité de la Patrie': The 22nd Battalion and the Memory of Courcelette," *Canadian Military History* 19, 3 (2010): 28–40. For a more in-depth study of the 22nd Battalion, see Jean-Pierre Gagnon, *Le 22e Bataillon (canadien-français), 1914–1919: Étude socio-militaire* (Québec: Presses de l'Université Laval, 1986).
2 Bill Rawling, *Surviving Trench Warfare: Technology and the Canadian Corps, 1914–1918* (Toronto: University of Toronto Press, 1992), 81.
3 Although Bourassa did not know it, British and French officials expected a German peace offer by October. See W.B. Fest, "British War Aims and German Peace Feelers during the First World War (December 1916–November 1918)," *Historical Journal* 15, 2 (1972): 286.
4 Henri Bourassa, "Le pape et la guerre," *Le Devoir,* 31 December 1915, 1.
5 Henri Bourassa, "L'effort pour la paix," *Le Devoir,* 12 August 1916, 1. For instance, there were only seven references to the UDC in the *Globe* and the *Star* for the entire war.
6 "Letter Al Tremendo Conflitto to Cardinal Pompili, Vicar of Rome," in *Principles for Peace: Selections from Papal Documents Leo XIII to Pius XII,* ed. Reverend Harry C. Koenig (Washington, DC: National Catholic Welfare Conference, 1943), 201.
7 Quoted in René Durocher, "Henri Bourassa, les évêques, et la guerre de 1914–1918," *Canadian Historical Association Historical Papers* 6 (1971): 264.
8 Bourassa, "L'effort pour la paix." In particular, he might have been thinking of Abbé d'Amours, who continued publishing throughout the war.
9 Henri Bourassa, "La réorganisation de l'empire," *Le Devoir,* 16 September 1916, 1.
10 The English version is found in J. Castell Hopkins, *The Canadian Annual Review War Series 1916* (Toronto: Canadian Annual Review, 1918), 180.
11 For the comments of then Secretary of State for the Colonies Lewis Harcourt in the British House of Commons, see Robert MacGregor Dawson, *The Development of Dominion Status, 1900–1936,* 2nd ed. (Hamden, CT: Archo Books, 1965), 174; see also J. Castell Hopkins, *The Canadian Annual Review War Series 1915* (Toronto: Canadian Annual Review, 1918), 168, for Canadian reception of the speech.
12 Minister of Trade and Commerce Sir George Foster attended instead. See Suzann Buckley, "Attempts at Imperial Economic Co-operation, 1912–18: Sir Robert Borden's Role," *Canadian Historical Review* 55, 3 (1974): 296–97.
13 Max Aitken, *Canada in Flanders: The Official Story of the Canadian Expeditionary Force,* vol. I (London: Hodder and Stoughton, 1916), vii–viii.
14 Quoted in Lionel Curtis, *The Problem of the Commonwealth* (London: Macmillan, 1915), 101.
15 Henri Bourassa, *Le problème de l'empire: Indépendance ou association impériale? Étude critique du livre de M. Lionel Curtis:* The Problem of the Commonwealth (Montréal: Éditions du Devoir, 1916).
16 Deborah Lavin, "Lionel Curtis and the Idea of the Commonwealth," in *Oxford and the Idea of the Commonwealth: Essays Presented to Sir Edgar Williams,* ed. Frederick Madden and D.K. Fieldhouse (London: Croom Helm, 1982), 99.

17 John Kendle, *The Round Table Movement and Imperial Union* (Toronto: University of Toronto Press, 1975), 64–71.
18 Ibid., 186.
19 Curtis believed that an Imperial Parliament was the only solution that could preserve the ability of British citizens to be involved in the democratic governance of their own country while granting the influence and rights owed to the dominions. Ibid., 135.
20 Curtis travelled to Canada, Australia, and New Zealand discussing and defending the book to gauge the reaction to it. Ibid., 185–205.
21 Bourassa, *Le problème de l'empire*, 6; "c'est l'exposé de la thèse impérialiste le plus lucide, le plus complet, le plus tassé et aussi le plus loyal et le plus *pratique* que j'aie encore lu."
22 Ibid., 35–36.
23 Ibid., 37–38. Worse yet, Bourassa added in a footnote, was the "bad faith" of clergy who attacked him for drawing attention to the danger of putting religion in the service of British imperialists. He named Abbé D'Amours, editor of the Catholic newspaper *L'Action sociale*, who continued to condemn Bourassa during the war (see below). We are with the pope, Bourassa chided, and "we will continue to say that the duty of Catholics is to want peace and not war."
24 Ibid., 39.
25 Ibid., 42; "nous préfèrerions l'indépendance nationale, la neutralité et la paix. Mais s'il faut porter l'uniforme de guerre et aider l'Angleterre à faire la police du monde, nous préférons que ce soit à titre d'associés responsables, plutôt que sous la livrée domestique, dût-il nous en coûter plus pour *coopérer* que pour *servir*."
26 Ibid., 43.
27 Patrice A. Dutil, "Against Isolationism: Napoléon Belcourt, French Canada, and 'la Grande guerre,'" in *Canada and the First World War: Essays in Honour of Robert Craig Brown*, ed. David Mackenzie (Toronto: University of Toronto Press, 2005), 113–14.
28 John E. Zucchi, ed., *The View from Rome: Archbishop Stagni's 1915 Reports on the Ontario Bilingual Schools Question* (Montreal and Kingston: McGill-Queen's University Press, 2002), 33. Zucchi's introduction gives a concise and worthwhile review of the bilingual schools question.
29 Ibid., 55.
30 Ibid., 109–14.
31 Henri Bourassa to F. Hébert, 18 December 1916, quoted in Durocher, "Henri Bourassa," 265.
32 Henri Bourassa, "L'élection de M. Wilson," *Le Devoir*, 15 November 1916, 1.
33 Ibid.; "offrait aux peuples ravagés par la guerre sa médiation et son appui afin de les aider à rentrer en possession des bienfaits inappréciables dont le peuple américain, avec raison, n'a pas voulu se départir, le mouvement en faveur de la paix ne tarderait pas à devenir irrésistible."
34 Fest, "British War Aims," 288–89. On Lansdowne, see Chapter 7 of this volume.
35 "Proposals for Peace Negotiations Made by Germany," in *Official Statements of War Aims and Peace Proposals, December 1916 to November 1918*, ed. James Brown Scott (Washington, DC: Carnegie Endowment for International Peace, Division of International Law, 1921), 3.
36 Henri Bourassa, "La démarche de l'Allemagne: Espoirs de paix – obstacles probables," *Le Devoir*, 14 December 1916, 1.
37 Ibid.
38 Ibid.

39 *Globe* [Toronto], 13 December 1916, 1, 6.
40 R. Matthew Bray, "'Fighting as an Ally': The English-Canadian Patriotic Response to the Great War," *Canadian Historical Review* 51, 2 (1980): 154. See also Robert Matthew Bray, "The Canadian Patriotic Response to the Great War" (PhD diss., Laurentian University, 1977).
41 Bourassa, "La démarche de l'Allemagne."
42 Historical work demonstrates that Bourassa's claim here is false. As the Junkers lost their influence, it was army officers such as Generals Erich Ludendorff and Paul von Hindenburg who gained it, not the socialist members of the Reichstag. For an excellent overview of the state of German politics throughout the war, see Roger Chickering, *Imperial Germany and the Great War, 1914–1918* (Cambridge, UK: Cambridge University Press, 1998). Nor were socialists the root of German calls for peace – it was the state of Austria-Hungary that led the Germans to offer peace terms. See Fest, "British War Aims," 289.
43 Bourassa, "La démarche de l'Allemagne."
44 John F. Pollard, *The Unknown Pope: Benedict XV (1914–1922), and the Pursuit of Peace* (London: Geoffrey Chapman, 1999), 90–91.
45 Bourassa, "La démarche de l'Allemagne"; "Si la guerre se prolonge, si toute chance de paix est écartée, si des millions d'Anglais, de Français, de Canadiens continuent à périr dans les tranchées ou survivent mutilés, ce sera principalement parce que la Russie n'a pas encore atteint son objectif suprême: la prise de Constantinople."
46 Ibid.
47 For Bourassa's review of the roles of Belgium and Britain at the beginning of the war, see his articles in *Le Devoir* from 28 August to 14 September 1914.
48 Bourassa, "La démarche de l'Allemagne"; "l'ambition et [les] infâmes calculs de leurs grands voisins, manipulateurs sans scrupules de 'l'équilibre européen.'"
49 "Manifest duty" is how Wilson termed it in his annual message to Congress of 7 December 1915. See Edgar E. Robinson, *The Foreign Policy of Woodrow Wilson, 1913–1917* (New York: Macmillan, 1917), 294.
50 Wilson also hoped to prevent former Secretary of State William Jennings Bryan from beginning an American peace movement. See Nicholas Ferns, "Loyal Advisor? Colonel Edward House's Confidential Trips to Europe, 1913–1917," *Diplomacy and Statecraft* 24, 3 (2013): 377–78.
51 David S. Patterson, "Woodrow Wilson and the Mediation Movement, 1914–17," *Historian* 33, 4 (1971): 551. For information on the petition given to Wilson in November asking that he demand the war aims of the belligerent nations, see Hopkins, *Canadian Annual Review War Series 1916*, 228.
52 Scott, *Official Statements*, 13–15.
53 Henri Bourassa, "Espoirs de paix," *Le Devoir*, 27 December 1916, 1.
54 Ibid.; "la valeur intrinsèque de la note du président; l'accueil favorable qu'elle reçoit dans les milieux favorables à la paix, neutres ou belligérants [et] l'opposition violente que lui suscitent les démagogues, les jingos, et les profiteurs du massacre."
55 Ibid.
56 Ibid.
57 Having barely avoided an attack by a mob of war supporters in Ottawa in December 1914, Bourassa knew that patriots were willing to go to extreme lengths to condemn dissenters. Although an extreme situation, it characterized the severe backlash that Bourassa experienced because of his critical opinions.
58 Ibid.; "les vampires d'outre-mer lui font maintenant un crime de vouloir mettre fin au conflit, source de profits inouïs pour son propre pays."

59 Ibid.
60 Ibid. This differed from his 1915 writing on the UDC, which claimed that it was unpersecuted in Britain.
61 As Durocher notes in "Henri Bourassa," 272, Bourassa "[a accepté] sans réserve l'autorité de l'Église" and felt obligated to "faire connaître la pensée de l'Église" while also informing the church "des opinions, des sentiments et des intérêts du peuple."
62 Bourassa, "Espoirs de paix."
63 Ibid.
64 Un Patriote [Joseph D'Amours], *Où allons-nous? Le nationalisme canadien* (Montréal: Société d'Éditions Patriotiques, 1916).
65 Ibid., 15–20.
66 Ibid., 29.
67 Ibid., 42.
68 Ibid., 43–44.
69 Henri Bourassa, "A nos lecteurs," *Le Devoir*, 9 December 1916, 1; "Ce n'est pas lui qui chantera notre libera."
70 L.O. Maillé, *Réponse de M. L. O. Maillé aux articles "Où allons nous?" et a M. l'Abbé D'Amours* (Montréal: n.p., 1917), 10.
71 Ibid., 11–13.
72 J. Castell Hopkins, *Canadian Annual Review War Series 1917* (Toronto: Canadian Annual Review, 1918), 286.
73 Canada, *House of Commons Debates*, 12th Parliament, 7th Session (22 January 1916), vol. 1, 6–7 (Robert Borden).
74 Henri Bourassa, "Sir Robert Borden et les conditions de paix: Indemnités de guerre – colonies allemandes," *Le Devoir*, 17 February 1917, 1.
75 Ibid.
76 Ibid.
77 Ibid.
78 Henri Bourassa, "Sir Robert Borden et les conditions de paix II: L'affranchissement des peuples," *Le Devoir*, 19 February 1917, 1.
79 Ibid.
80 Pope Benedict XV, "Exhortation Allorchè Fummo to the Belligerent Peoples and to Their Leaders," in *Principles for Peace Selections from Papal Documents Leo XIII to Pius XII*, ed. Reverend Harry C. Koenig (Washington, DC: National Catholic Welfare Conference, 1943), 181. It was originally written in Italian.
81 Bourassa, "Sir Robert Borden et les conditions de paix II."
82 Henri Bourassa, "Sir Robert Borden et les conditions de paix III: La Russie à Constantinople – la Russie et le Japon," *Le Devoir*, 20 February 1917, 1.
83 Ibid.; "on voit que de tout temps / Les petits ont pâti des sottises des grands." The line is from La Fontaine's poem "Les deux taureaux et une grenouille," about the impossibility of tiny frogs succeeding against large bulls.
84 Ibid.
85 Ibid.
86 Bourassa translated it as follows: "assurer à tous les États *leur libre développement*, dans de conditions d'égalité, et *conformément à leur génie propre*" (his emphasis). Henri Bourassa, "Sir Robert Borden et les conditions de paix IV: Le triomphe de la démocratie," *Le Devoir*, 22 February 1917, 1. Bourassa quoted Grey's speech from 16 October 1916. See Viscount of Fallodon, Edward Grey, *Why Britain Is in the War and What She Hopes from the Future; A Speech by the Rt. Hon. Viscount Grey of Fallodon ... Addressed to the Representatives*

of the Foreign Press in London on the 23rd October, 1916 (London: T.F. Unwin, 1916), 10–11. However, Grey noted that the words belonged to Prime Minister H.H. Asquith addressing the House of Commons on 11 October 1916. See *War Speeches by British Ministers 1914–1916* (London: T.F. Unwin, 1917), 133. The mistake was probably made because Bourassa mentioned another source that he was reading and likely took the quotation from Herbert Adams Gibbons, "Constantinople: Principle or Pawn?," *Century Magazine*, February 1917, 517–26, who also incorrectly attributed it to Grey (521).

87 Bourassa, "Sir Robert Borden et les conditions de paix IV."
88 Ibid.
89 Henri Bourassa, "Sir Robert Borden et les conditions de paix V: Liberté des mers – destruction du militarisme," *Le Devoir*, 23 February 1917, 1.
90 Ibid.
91 For a brief summary of Butler's activity during the war, see Martin David Dubin, "The Carnegie Endowment for International Peace and the Advocacy of a League of Nations, 1914–1918," *Proceedings of the American Philosophical Society* 123, 6 (1979): 344–68, and 358 for Butler's use of the pseudonym Cosmos. For the book, see Cosmos, *The Basis for a Durable Peace* (New York: Charles Scribner's Sons, 1917).
92 Cosmos, *The Basis for a Durable Peace*, 61; Henri Bourassa, "Sir Robert Borden et les conditions de paix VI: 'Militarisme canadien' – conclusion," *Le Devoir*, 24 February 1917, 1.
93 Bourassa, "Sir Robert Borden et les conditions de paix VI."
94 Justus D. Doenecke, *Nothing Less than War: A New History of America's Entry into World War I* (Lexington: University Press of Kentucky, 2011), 267.
95 Woodrow Wilson, *In Our First Year of the War: Messages and Addresses to the Congress and the People, March 5, 1917 to January 6, 1918* (New York: Harper and Brothers, 1918), 10.
96 Henri Bourassa, "La crise américain: Paix ou guerre?," *Le Devoir*, 7 March 1917, 1.
97 Doenecke, *Nothing Less than War*, 233.
98 André Bergevin, Cameron Nish, and Anne Bourassa, *Henri Bourassa: Biographie, index des écrit, index de la correspondence, 1895–1924* (Montréal: Les Éditions de l'Action Nationale, 1966), xlix.
99 Henri Bourassa, "L'intervention americaine I: M. Wilson: Son succès, sa valeur, sa sincérité – force de l'opinion pacifiste," *Le Devoir*, 7 May 1917, 1.
100 Wilson, *In Our First Year of the War*, 8.
101 Henri Bourassa, "L'intervention américaine II: Opinion des Américains sur les belligérants – influences allemandes, françaises, anglaises – la religion démocratique," *Le Devoir*, 8 May 1917, 1.
102 Henri Bourassa, "L'intervention américaine III: Évolution des sentiments – invasion de la Belgique, héroïsme de la France, finance anglaise – Pierpont Morgan & Cie: Achat de la presse," *Le Devoir*, 9 May 1917, 1.
103 Henri Bourassa, "L'intervention américaine IV: Torpillage du 'Lusitania': Démission de M. Bryan – derniers efforts pour la paix: Message du président aux belligérants, son programme de paix," *Le Devoir*, 10 May 1917, 1. See Doenecke, *Nothing Less than War*, 83–85, for more details on this turbulent time.
104 Bourassa, "L'intervention américaine IV." The accusation that there was an insidious campaign by these "financiers" was reflected in the American press and by some politicians. See Doenecke, *Nothing Less than War*, 255–56, 269–75.
105 Bourassa, "L'intervention américaine IV"; "Rarement un chef d'État a montré un tel souci de ses responsabilités, une prévision si grande des conséquences de ses actes."
106 Henri Bourassa, "L'intervention américaine V: La révolution russe – haine des monarchies – influences des loges," *Le Devoir*, 11 May 1917, 1.

107 Henri Bourassa, "L'intervention américaine VI: Motifs de l'intervention – pensée personnelle de M. Wilson – conditions *nécessaires* ou *désirables* de la paix – 'affranchissement, des peuples," *Le Devoir*, 12 May 1917, 1.
108 Ibid.
109 Henri Bourassa, "L'intervention américaine VII: Mode et valeur de l'intervention – intelligence et force du sentiment national – mesures pratiques – les 'bêtises' de l'Angleterre," *Le Devoir*, 14 May 1917, 1.
110 Ibid.; "c'est le triomphe du militarisme sous sa forme la plus dangereuse et la plus bête"; "c'est l'assujettissement de l'organisation militaire aux intérêts suprêmes de la nation."
111 Henri Bourassa, "L'intervention américaine VIII: Guerre par les armes et par l'or – partisans de la 'grande armée – demandes de la France et de l'Angleterre – la part du lion – puissance de l'Angleterre," *Le Devoir*, 15 May 1917, 1.
112 Ibid. La Fontaine's poem is titled "La génisse, la chèvre et la brebis, en société avec le lion" and used a cow, a goat, and a sheep to accompany the lion. The lion in his version symbolizes the king, making Bourassa's reference to Britain all the more apt.
113 Henri Bourassa, "L'intervention américaine IX: Conséquences de l'intervention – la guerre sera-t-elle abrégée? – saignée d'argent, arrêt des industries, retour à la terre," *Le Devoir*, 15 May 1917, 1.
114 Henri Bourassa, "L'intervention américaine X: Militarisme et révolution – l'Angleterre et les États-Unis, pourvoyeurs de révolutions – châtiment et rédemption – le pape et le président – la 'société des nations' sera-t-elle chrétienne ou païenne?," *Le Devoir*, 19 May 1917, 1.
115 Alberto Spektorowski, "Maistre, Donoso Cortés, and the Legacy of Catholic Authoritarianism," *Journal of the History of Ideas* 63, 2 (2002): 293. Spektorowski also outlines Cortés's understanding of an apocalyptic revolution, worth noting given the context of Bourassa in 1917: "Donoso's apocalyptic vision was defined in three stages. The first occurs when revolution dissolves permanent armies; the second takes place when socialist expropriation extinguishes the sense of patriotism, and finally, Donoso prophesizes that a new federation of Slavic nations led by Russia will punish the world for its sins" (294).
116 Hervé Serry, "Littérature et religion catholique (1880–1914): Contribution à une socio-histoire de la croyance," *Cahiers d'histoire: Revue d'histoire critique* 87 (2002): 22.
117 Brian Fox, "Schmitt's Use and Abuse of Donoso Cortés on Dictatorship," *Intellectual History Review* 23, 2 (2013): 165. Fox continued his explanation with "the final result was the existence of a morally superior spiritual order which spoke with authority upon the first principles of moral and social life that the separate political, temporal order must take into account in fulfilling its task of directing the commonwealth towards the common good materially considered. Authority speaks and Power acts" (165–66). Fox's article deals primarily with the link between the views of Cortés and fascism, a subject of much academic study but not worth exploring here.
118 Juan Donoso Cortés, *Essays on Catholicism, Liberalism, and Socialism: Considered in Their Fundamental Principles*, ed. William McDonald (Dublin: M.H. Gill and Son, 1879), 267, 344.
119 Bourassa, "L'intervention américaine X."

Chapter 6: The Wall of Deceit
1 R. Matthew Bray, "'Fighting as an Ally': The English-Canadian Patriotic Response to the Great War," *Canadian Historical Review* 61, 2 (1980): 157–59.

2 J. Castell Hopkins, *Canadian Annual Review War Series 1916* (Toronto: Canadian Annual Review, 1918), 320–24. Laurier was also vocally opposed to conscription, noting in January 1916 that "we must repel at once the impression which has been sought to be created that [expanding the army to 500,000 men] is a preliminary step to conscription. There is to be no Conscription in Canada" (410).
3 J.L. Granatstein and J.M. Hitsman, *Broken Promises: A History of Conscription in Canada* (Toronto: Oxford University Press, 1977), 40–45. Granatstein and Hitsman mention resistance to registration on p. 45.
4 Ibid., 45–46; John English, *The Decline of Politics: The Conservatives and the Party System, 1901–20* (Toronto: University of Toronto Press, 1993), 124.
5 Granatstein and Hitsman, *Broken Promises*, 48–49.
6 John Kendle assesses the influence of the Round Table movement in forming an Imperial War Cabinet but concludes that the movement intended to disseminate its ideas after the war and had not planned for the sudden shift in sentiment. For that discussion and about Lloyd George as the primary instigator, see John Kendle, *The Round Table Movement and Imperial Union* (Toronto: University of Toronto Press, 1975), 214–15. Lloyd George was not likely the hero of the imperialist movement, and Brock Millman writes that "what the Imperial War Cabinet really meant to Lloyd George, however, was that an executive body had emerged, amenable to his strategies, possessed of the authority to force them on recalcitrant British military establishment and which served, further, to drive a wedge between the generals and the leadership of the Unionist Party." See Brock Millman, *Pessimism and British War Policy, 1916–1918* (London: Frank Cass, 2001), 141.
7 Robert Craig Brown, *Robert Laird Borden: A Biography*, vol. II, *1914–1937* (Toronto: Macmillan, 1980), 80–81.
8 Henri Bourassa, "Aurons-nous la conscription?," *Le Devoir*, 26 March 1917, 1; "La conscription ... n'est que le moyen extrême ... de racheter l'engagement pris par le parlement tout entier de consacrer toutes les ressources du Canada au 'salut' de l'Empire."
9 Bourassa first mentioned this in Henri Bourassa, "Conscription et banqueroute," *Le Devoir*, 9 December 1914, 1. He was referring to Meighen's speech before the Canada Club in Winnipeg on 6 November 1914. The words were often evoked in Bourassa's articles throughout the war.
10 Bourassa, "Aurons-nous la conscription?" He expressed his ire to Bishop Élie-Anicet Latulipe in April 1917 at the bishops' refusal to admonish Abbé D'Amours for his pro-war (and to Bourassa pro-imperialist) writing in *L'Action catholique*. See René Durocher, "Henri Bourassa, les évêques, et la guerre de 1914–1918," *Canadian Historical Association Historical Papers* 6 (1971): 268.
11 Bourassa, "Aurons-nous la conscription?"
12 Henri Bourassa, "Aurons-nous la conscription? II," *Le Devoir*, 27 March 1917, 1; "par le Droit Naturel, ... le Canada a l'obligation morale et même légale de combattre pour l'Angleterre, même contre le gré de ses citoyens"; "les Canadiens, pris individuellement, ont le droit de se soustraire à cette obligation."
13 Ibid.
14 Ibid.
15 Ibid.
16 For a brief review of its reception in Canada, see Jonathan Vance, "Battle Verse: Poetry and Nationalism after Vimy Ridge," in *Vimy Ridge: A Canadian Reassessment*, ed. Geoffrey Hayes, Michael Bechthold, and Andrew Iarocci (Waterloo, ON: Wilfrid Laurier University

Press, 2007), 265–66, and throughout his chapter for how Vimy was remembered in the interwar period. The collection remains one of the best overviews of Vimy Ridge.
17 Gary Sheffield, "Vimy Ridge and the Battle of Arras: A British Perspective," in *Vimy Ridge: A Canadian Reassessment*, ed. Geoffrey Hayes, Michael Bechthold, and Andrew Iarocci (Waterloo, ON: Wilfrid Laurier University Press, 2007), 24–27.
18 Desmond Morton and J.L. Granatstein, *Marching to Armageddon: Canadians and the Great War, 1914–1919* (Toronto: Lester and Orpen Dennys, 1989), 143. In a strange accent on the Canadians' colonial relationship, King George V's message was delivered through the British general commanding the Canadian forces, Sir Douglas Haig. See Canada, Dominion Bureau of Statistics, *The Canada Year Book 1936* (Ottawa: King's Printer, 1936), 59.
19 J. Castell Hopkins, *Canadian Annual Review War Series 1917* (Toronto: Canadian Annual Review, 1918), 287–89; LAC, Borden Papers, M02611, Diary, 10 April 1917.
20 Hopkins, *Canadian Annual Review War Series 1917*, 359.
21 Henri Bourassa, "Apres la guerre, la révolution I," *Le Devoir*, 23 April 1917, 1. Bourassa believed that rich financiers had a role in intensifying and prolonging the war, such as American millionaire J.P. Morgan's efforts to push the United States into the war, as he would write about in his articles on the American entry in May.
22 Ibid.
23 Ibid.; "ils peuvent à leur gré aveugler le bon sens populaire et déguiser toujours la vérité sous la duperie des formules creuses et des arguments à côté."
24 Ibid.
25 Henri Bourassa, "Apres la guerre, la révolution II," *Le Devoir*, 24 April 1917, 1.
26 Ibid.; "Les protagonistes de la révolution sont les dénonciateurs les plus ardents de toute tentative de paix"; "ils comptent sur les souffrances et l'exaspération des masses populaires, énervées et aigries par la guerre à outrance, pour faire triompher leur projets."
27 Ibid.
28 Ibid.; "pour assurer le triomphe de la plouto-démocratie armée dont ils se sont constitués les cornacs." *Cornacs*, translated into English as mahouts, is a term for elephant drivers in India.
29 Ibid.
30 Ibid.
31 Quoted in Granatstein and Hitsman, *Broken Promises*, 62–63n12. Granatstein also claims that Borden's experience in Europe changed his mind on conscription. J.L. Granatstein, "Conscription," in *Canada and the First World War: Essays in Honour of Robert Craig Brown*, ed. David Mackenzie (Toronto: University of Toronto Press, 2005), 67.
32 English, *The Decline of Politics*, 129. English quotes Borden's diary from 17 May 1917. The question has been raised whether conscription was a matter of political expediency given the election that had to be held in 1917 after the Liberals rejected a further extension of the government past 1916, though Borden's diary suggests that nobody believed that to be true. See A.M. Willms, "Conscription 1917: A Brief for the Defence," in *Conscription 1917*, ed. Carl Berger (Toronto: University of Toronto Press, 1969), 8–11. In another work, English argues that the phrase "equality of sacrifice" fuelled the calls for conscription so that everyone served the country equally. John English, "Political Leadership," in *Canada and the First World War: Essays in Honour of Robert Craig Brown*, ed. David Mackenzie (Toronto: University of Toronto Press, 2005), 92.
33 Ramsay Cook and Robert Craig Brown, *Canada 1896–1921: A Nation Transformed* (Toronto: McClelland and Stewart, 1974), 268. Brown similarly emphasizes the push

toward a coalition government in his biography of Borden. Brown, *Robert Laird Borden*, vol. II, 84–94. So did J.W. Dafoe, according to Ramsay Cook, "Dafoe, Laurier, and the Formation of Union Government," *Canadian Historical Review* 42, 3 (1961): 194–96. English examines the early beginning of union government in greater detail in *Decline of Politics*, 129–60.

34 Henri Bourassa, *La conscription* (Montréal: Éditions du Devoir, 1917), 4.
35 For a concise and revealing overview of the extent of those demonstrations, see Béatrice Richard, "Le Québec face à la crise de la conscription (1917–1918): Essai d'analyse sociale d'un refus," in *Le Québec dans la Grande Guerre: Engagements, refus, héritages*, ed. Charles-Philippe Courtois and Laurent Veyssière (Québec: Septentrion, 2015), 116–21; also see Serge Marc Durflinger, "Vimy's Consequences: The Montreal Anti-Conscription Disturbances, May to September 1917," in *Turning Point 1917: The British Empire at War*, ed. Douglas E. Delaney and Nikolas Gardner (Vancouver: UBC Press, 2017), 160–87.
36 Bourassa, *La conscription*, 8.
37 A Canadian soldier received $1.10 a day. Ibid., 11–12.
38 Ibid., 16.
39 Ibid., 16–17.
40 Ibid., 17.
41 Ibid., 20–21.
42 Ibid., 21.
43 Ibid., 22.
44 Ibid., 22; "[entraîne] d'acrimonieuses explications, d'amères désillusions et surtout de fort périlleuses réactions."
45 Ibid., 23; "la muraille de duperie qui [les] sépare."
46 Ibid., 26–27.
47 Ibid., 31–33. Interestingly, Bourassa did not see Borden's participation in the Imperial War Cabinet as having any impact on his decision to enact conscription (34). Bourassa wrote that thousands of Americans joined the Canadian army but provided no source for his claim, though General James Moore wrote to the *Toronto Press* on 18 April noting that about 7,500 Americans had joined the Canadian forces. Hopkins, *Canadian Annual Review War Series 1917*, 355.
48 Bourassa, *La conscription*, 38–39.
49 Ibid., 40–41; "Toute coalition des partis, à l'heure actuelle, serait inutile, dangereuse et immorale ... Le parlement actuel ou futur ne doit pas voter la conscription ... l'opinion du peuple ne peut s'exprimer librement que par un plébiscite."
50 Hopkins, *Canadian Annual Review War Series 1917*, 553–60.
51 English, *The Decline of Politics*, 134–35. Réal Bélanger makes a similar point in *Wilfrid Laurier: Quand la politique devient passion* (Québec: Presses de l'Université Laval, 2007), 396. Laurier also believed that there was an undercurrent of opposition to conscription, suggesting that he might win an electoral contest against a pro-conscription government. See his letter to Ontario Liberal leader Newton Rowell in Oscar Douglas Skelton, *Life and Letters of Sir Wilfrid Laurier*, vol. II (London: Oxford University Press, 1922), 514–16.
52 Skelton, *Life and Letters of Sir Wilfrid Laurier*, vol. II, 512.
53 Durflinger, "Vimy's Consequences," 167.
54 Hopkins, *Canadian Annual Review War Series 1917*, 564.
55 English, *The Decline of Politics*, 136–39.
56 Wilfrid Laurier to Sir Allen Aylesworth, in Skelton, *Life and Letters of Sir Wilfrid Laurier*, vol. II, 518. Blair Neatby argues that Laurier's willingness to accept different points of

view on conscription, even when it meant Liberals joining a coalition government, was one of the leadership characteristics that would allow the Liberals to thrive in the postwar period. No one was shamed or attacked by the Liberal leader, and "Laurier had a genuine and sympathetic understanding, the positive quality of Christian love." H. Blair Neatby, *Laurier and a Liberal Quebec* (Toronto: McClelland and Stewart, 1961), 226–28.
57 Henri Bourassa, "Le cinquantenaire," *Le Devoir*, 4 July 1917, 1.
58 Ibid.; "une nation plongée dans une guerre dont les causes, la direction et le règlement échappent totalement à l'action immédiate de son gouvernement."
59 Ibid.
60 Ibid.; "La langue française ... c'est la langue de la vérité, de la justice, du courage, de la probité, de la logique ... Ne pas l'inviter [de] rendre hommage [aux dupeurs et aux dupes]."
61 Robert Rumilly, *Histoire de la province de Québec*, vol. XXII (Montréal: Fides, 1940), 99.
62 Archbishop Paul Bruchési, "L'opinion de son Eminence," *L'Action catholique*, 28 July 1917, 1.
63 René Durocher, "Henri Bourassa," 269; "sur la conscription je pense absolument comme vous. Et je ne crois pas manquer de logique parce que j'ai admis la participation du Canada à la guerre actuelle."
64 Yvan Lamonde, *Histoire sociale des idées au Québec 1896–1929*, vol. II (Québec: Fides, 2004), 42.
65 Hopkins, *Canadian Annual Review War Series 1917*, 318.
66 English, *The Decline of Politics*, 125–26; Hopkins, *Canadian Annual Review War Series 1917*, 483–86. See also Réal Bélanger, *L'impossible défi: Albert Sévigny et les Conservateurs fédéraux (1902–1918)* (Québec: Presses de l'Université Laval, 1983), 163–65, 244–47. After his victory, his reputation was tarnished when furniture from the speaker's house was found in his new residence.
67 Bélanger, *L'impossible défi*, 263.
68 Ibid., 294–95.
69 Ferdinand Roy, *L'appel aux armes et la réponse canadienne-française* (Québec: J.P. Garneau, 1917). It was translated into English and published in February 1918; Ferdinand Roy, *The Call to Arms and the French Canadian Reply*, trans. J. Squair and J.S. Will (Québec: J.P. Garneau, 1918).
70 Roy, *L'appel aux armes*, 8–14.
71 Ibid., 14; "cette foi en un prophète qui n'a pas la fatuité de réclamer l'infaillibilité n'est pas une foi aveugle, et la raison maintient son droit d'examiner avec soin sa thèse, qui n'est pas un dogme, et de juger si sa doctrine, toute logique qu'elle soit, captivante et dangereuse à la fois par l'appel qu'elle fait à nos haines de races, n'a pas pour base une erreur."
72 Ibid., 20; "ne plus lever les yeux, à courber le front."
73 Ibid., 25–27.
74 Ibid., 34; "Il nous faut, par des actes, par un changement d'attitude manifeste, sortir du remous d'incohérence où l'on nous a poussés, prendre pied sur le fond solide qui est là, ne plus nous laisser aller, éperdus, indécis et inertes, à la dérive."
75 Ibid., 32–33.
76 Hopkins, *Canadian Annual Review War Series 1917*, 475.
77 Durflinger, "Vimy's Consequences," 167–69.
78 Robert Rumilly, *Henri Bourassa: La vie publique d'un grand Canadien* (Montréal: Éditions Chantecler, 1953), 584–85; see also Réal Bélanger, *Paul-Émile Lamarche: Le pays avant le parti (1904–1918)* (Québec: Presses de l'Université Laval, 1984).

79 Originally published in the *New York Evening Post*, it was reprinted for a Canadian audience in Henri Bourassa, "Why Canada Should Not Adopt Conscription," *Le Devoir*, 12 July 1917, 1. The articles by Bourassa, Lamarche, and Montpetit were republished a few months later as the first three volumes of a series of English-language brochures that included other anti-conscription arguments. See *The Case against Conscription*, 6 vols. (Montreal: Éditions du Devoir, 1917). Montpetit's article was titled "Canada's Economic Destruction," and Lamarche's was "The Free American and the Canadian Flunkey."
80 Bourassa, "Why Canada Should Not Adopt Conscription."
81 Canada, *House of Commons Debates*, 12th Parliament, 7th Session (10 July 1917), vol. 4, 3191 (Arthur Meighen). For the long discussion about what national interest entailed exactly, see 3187–3260.
82 Canada, *House of Commons Debates*, 12th Parliament, 7th Session (17 July 1917), vol. 4, 3487 (Wilfrid Laurier).
83 Canada, *House of Commons Debates*, 12th Parliament, 7th Session (24 July 1917), vol. 4, 3736 (Arthur Meighen).
84 Henri Bourassa, "La fin du débat," *Le Devoir*, 26 July 1917, 1.
85 Ibid.
86 Ibid.
87 Ibid.
88 Canada, *House of Commons Debates*, 12th Parliament, 7th Session (24 July 1917), vol. 4, 3729 (Wilfrid Laurier).
89 Granatstein and Hitsman, *Broken Promises*, 69.
90 Enn Raudsepp, "Graham, Hugh, 1st Baron Atholstan," in *Dictionary of Canadian Biography*, vol. 16 (Toronto: University of Toronto; Laval: Université Laval, 2003–), http://www.biographi.ca/en/bio/graham_hugh_1848_1938_16E.html.
91 Durflinger ably recounts newspaper coverage of the trial in "Vimy's Consequences," 176–83.
92 Hopkins, *Canadian Annual Review War Series 1917*, 496–97.
93 Henri Bourassa, "Steriles violences," *Le Devoir*, 11 August 1917, 1.
94 Ibid.; "se sont appliqués systématiquement à boucher les yeux et oreilles du peuple," while preaching "servilisme abject et un loyalisme outrancier," and those who sought to avoid the consequence of the first group's faulty doctrine by "l'émeute, le meurtre et les déprédations."
95 Ibid.; "Pour ma part je ne prendrai jamais la responsabilité de conseiller la résistance passive à la loi de conscription: et ceux qui n'ont pas ce scrupule ont le strict devoir d'en faire envisager toutes les conséquences."
96 Ibid.
97 Ibid.

Chapter 7: Silenced
1 Pope Benedict XV, "Exhortation *dès le début* to the Belligerent Peoples and to Their Leaders," in *Principles for Peace: Selections from Papal Documents Leo XIII to Pius XII*, ed. Reverend Harry C. Koenig (Washington, DC: National Catholic Welfare Conference, 1943), 229. Originally written in French.
2 Henry E.G. Rope, *Benedict XV: The Pope of Peace* (London: Catholic Book Club, 1940), 33.
3 John F. Pollard, *The Unknown Pope: Benedict XV (1914–1922), and the Pursuit of Peace* (London: Geoffrey Chapman, 1999), 64.

4 This is concisely reviewed in Charles R. Gallagher, "The Perils of Perception: British Catholics and Papal Neutrality, 1914–1923," in *The Papacy since 1500: From Italian Prince to Universal Pastor*, ed. James Corkery and Thomas Worcester (Cambridge, UK: Cambridge University Press, 2010), 180–81. Pollard's work outlines Benedict's accomplishments, which included 82 million lire donated to the war's victims, helping 26,000 POWs and 3,000 civilian detainees to convalesce in Switzerland, and even formally protesting the ongoing Armenian genocide in Turkey. Pollard, *The Unknown Pope*, 112–39.

5 The publication of the Treaty of London by the Russians after the fall of the czar in 1917 certainly encouraged this view. See Oliver P. Rafferty, "The Catholic Church, Ireland, and the British Empire, 1800–1921," *Historical Research* 224, 84 (2011): 305–7. Pollard has an excellent chapter on Pope Benedict XV and Italy's relationship during the war in *The Unknown Pope*, 85–111.

6 One such example is Rudolph Gerlach, the papal secret chamberlain, accused of being the lead spy in an Italian espionage ring and allegedly linked to German and Austrian intelligence. He was discovered following an investigation into the destruction of the Italian battleship the *Leonardo Da Vinci* in August 1916. Benedict XV was convinced of Gerlach's innocence, and there is little evidence of his guilt in the historical record. Gerlach was quietly sent to Switzerland but eventually had several public and embarrassing meetings with the king of Bavaria, the German and Austrian emperors, and General Hindenburg. See David Alvarez, "Vatican Communications Security, 1914–1918," *Intelligence and National Security* 7, 4 (1992): 443–53; David Alvarez, "A German Agent at the Vatican: The Gerlach Affair," *Intelligence and National Security* 2, 2 (1996): 345–56; and Pollard, *The Unknown Pope*, 103–7.

7 Henri Bourassa, "L'appel du pape," *Le Devoir*, 18 August 1917, 1. His first footnote also remarks on some of the offending papers, which included Montreal's *La Patrie* and New York's *Evening Post*.

8 Ibid.

9 Ibid.

10 François-Albert Angers, "Le problème de la paix selon Bourassa," in *La pensée de Henri Bourassa*, ed. François-Albert Angers (Montréal: L'Action Nationale, 1954), 83.

11 Sylvie Lacombe, *La rencontre de deux peuples élus: Comparaison des ambitions nationale et impériale au Canada entre 1896 et 1920* (Québec: Presses de l'Université Laval, 2002), 276. For a succinct yet detailed examination of Bourassa's combination of political and religious ideology, see Sylvie Lacombe, "Entre l'autorité pontificale et la liberté nationale: L'anti-impérialisme britannique d'Henri Bourassa," in *Le Devoir: Un journal indépendant (1910–1995)*, ed. Robert Comeau and Luc Desrochers (Québec: Presses de l'Université du Québec, 1996), 274–77.

12 Mark G. McGowan, "'To Share in the Burdens of Empire': Toronto's Catholics and the Great War, 1914–1918," in *Catholics at the "Gathering Place,"* ed. Mark McGowan and Brian Clarke (Toronto: Canadian Catholic Historical Association, 1993), 188. Duff Crerar argues that English-speaking Catholic priests who served in the army "fought to establish a public identity as both Catholics and Canadian nationalists." Duff W. Crerar, "Bellicose Priests: The Wars of the Catholic Chaplains, 1914–1919," *Canadian Catholic Historical Association Historical Studies* 58 (1991): 21. See also Mark G. McGowan, "Harvesting the 'Red Vineyard': Catholic Religious Culture in the Canadian Expeditionary Force, 1914–1919," *Canadian Catholic Historical Association Historical Studies* 64 (1998): 47–70.

13 Gallagher, "The Perils of Perception," 169.

14 M.M. Abbenhuis, "'Too Good to Be True?' European Hopes for Neutrality before 1914," in *Small Powers in the Age of Total War, 1900–1940*, ed. Herman Amersfoort and Wim Klinkert (Leiden: Brill, 2011), 28.
15 John English, *The Decline of Politics: The Conservatives and the Party System, 1901–20* (Toronto: University of Toronto Press, 1993), 141–44.
16 English, *The Decline of Politics*, 151–59. English provides a comprehensive explanation of the trials and tribulations behind the formation of Union government between July and October (136–85). Also, a detailed if unsurprisingly bland narrative is found in J. Castell Hopkins, *Canadian Annual Review War Series 1917* (Toronto: Canadian Annual Review, 1918), 569–86.
17 Henri Bourassa, "La comedie parlementaire II: Savante manoeuvre de M. Laurier," *Le Devoir*, 25 August 1917, 1; "se doit à lui-même, il doit à ses partisans fidèles, il doit à ses compatriotes, il doit au pays tout entier, de sortir de la brousse et de se placer sur un terrain solide pour livrer à découvert la bataille électorale."
18 English, *The Decline of Politics*, 154–56.
19 J.L. Granatstein and J.M. Hitsman, *Broken Promises: A History of Conscription in Canada* (Toronto: Oxford University Press, 1977), 71–73. In a footnote on page 72, they recount a letter to Borden that explained how the "foreign vote" negatively affected Conservative support and the necessity of allowing only "loyal citizens" to participate in future elections.
20 J. Castell Hopkins, *Canadian Annual Review War Series 1917* (Toronto: Canadian Annual Review, 1918), 332. Hopkins devotes a mere four pages to the bill (330–34). A clear supporter of the war and Union government, he spends little time examining either piece of legislation in detail. Although he offers details on Liberal opposition to it, it is portrayed as a patriotic measure, not electoral manipulation.
21 Canada, *House of Commons Debates*, 12th Parliament, 7th Session (10 September 1917), vol. 6, 5567 (J.H. Sinclair).
22 Hopkins, *Canadian Annual Review War Series 1917*, 333.
23 Henri Bourassa, "Le dernier accès: La loi électorale," *Le Devoir*, 11 September 1917, 1.
24 Bourassa was no fan of women's rights or suffrage. See Susan Mann, "Henri Bourassa and the 'Woman Question,'" *Journal of Canadian Studies* 10 (1975): 3–11. He had a firm conception of the idea of family within a Catholic order that offered a limited role to women. See Joseph Levitt, *Henri Bourassa – Catholic Critic* (Ottawa: Canadian Historical Association, 1976), 11–12.
25 Henri Bourassa, "Le dernier accès: La loi électorale II," *Le Devoir*, 12 September 1917, 1.
26 Ibid.; "par son inspiration, ses motifs, ses conséquences immédiates, sa portée lointaine, cette législation est infiniment plus criminelle et dangereuse que la loi de conscription. Elle suinte par tous les pores l'iniquité, le mensonge, la fourberie, le despotisme lâche."
27 Réal Bélanger, *Wilfrid Laurier: Quand la politique devient passion* (Québec: Presses de l'Université Laval, 2007), 399.
28 Robert Rumilly, *Henri Bourassa: La vie publique d'un grand Canadien* (Montréal: Éditions Chantecler, 1953), 587. Rumilly does not offer any citation for his story, but it is likely to have been drawn from interviews with Bourassa or his *Memoirs* speeches during the Second World War. Rumilly quotes from an article by Bourassa on 20 October following his account of the meeting, suggesting that the meeting occurred between 12 September and 20 October. Bourassa confirmed that he met with Laurier in 1917 in a speech to the House of Commons in 1935 (see Conclusion, this volume), but

Bélanger's biography of Laurier makes no mention of that meeting. Bélanger does discuss a meeting between them in August 1918, though it was hosted by L.A. David's father, L.O. David. Bélanger, *Wilfrid Laurier*, 415–16.

29 Hopkins, *Canadian Annual Review War Series 1917*, 584–85; English, *The Decline of Politics*, 162–63.
30 Henri Bourassa, "Le pot-pourri du grand ministère," *Le Devoir*, 20 October 1917, 1.
31 Henri Bourassa, "La guerre de l'or," *Le Devoir*, 27 October 1917, 1. Bourassa never really described these financiers, other than the super rich such as J.P. Morgan. He implied that they were the industrialists in charge of war industries and investors making money off the war, but he rarely addressed this category in detail.
32 Frederick C. Howe, "Financial Imperialism," *Atlantic Monthly* 120 (1917): 477–84. Bourassa and the article both spell Howe's first name as Frederick, but it was actually Frederic.
33 Kenneth E. Miller, *From Progressive to New Dealer: Frederic C. Howe and American Liberalism* (University Park: Pennsylvania State University Press, 2010), 279–80. Howe was a progressive reformer and lawyer who wrote prolifically about financial topics and American democracy in the early twentieth century. There is no major literature on the League for Small and Subject Nationalities, so it is difficult to ascertain its impact on the formation of the League of Nations after the war. There is no evidence that French Canadians were represented there in any way.
34 Ibid., 256. Howe's work *Why War* was published in 1916 and elaborated many of the points in his article. Frederic C. Howe, *Why War* (New York: Charles Scribner's Sons, 1916). Howe cites Hobson, Brailsford, and other writers critical of imperialism.
35 Howe, "Financial Imperialism," 477.
36 Ibid., 484.
37 Henri Bourassa, "L'impérialisme financier," *Le Devoir*, 29 October 1917, 1.
38 Ibid.
39 Ibid.
40 Ibid.
41 Henri Bourassa, "Le Canada vendu: Le ministère de la trahison nationale – que fera M. Laurier?," *Le Devoir*, 31 October 1917, 1.
42 Ibid.
43 Ibid.
44 Ibid.
45 Ibid.
46 Ibid.; "Les partis – comme le peuple lui-même, vont se refaire dans la norme des courants nouveaux, des idées de demain, selon l'antagonisme des principes qui correspondent à la dure réalité des choses nées de la guerre et de l'après-guerre."
47 Ibid.; "suprême effort pour rendre à la nation canadienne conscience d'elle-même, de ses devoirs réels, de ses droits positifs pour l'arracher aux faux dieux de l'impérialisme, pour l'arrêter dans sa course au suicide, pour fermer ses plaies béantes et lui préparer une nouvelle vitalité."
48 Michael Bliss, *Right Honourable Men: The Descent of Canadian Politics from Macdonald to Mulroney* (Toronto: HarperCollins, 1995), 84.
49 Hopkins, *Canadian Annual Review War Series 1917*, 593.
50 Ibid., 597–99.
51 English, *The Decline of Politics*, 188–89. English cites Oscar Douglas Skelton, *Life and Letters of Sir Wilfrid Laurier*, vol. II (Oxford: Oxford University Press, 1922), 511, for Laurier's thoughts on the campaign, and he examines the reasons why the December

election focused on conscription. Until recently, his chapter on the election (186–203) was one of the most comprehensive historical examinations of its results. In 2017, Patrice Dutil and David Mackenzie offered an superb overview of the election; Patrice Dutil and David Mackenzie, *Embattled Nation: Canada's Wartime Election of 1917* (Toronto: Dundurn, 2017).

52 Hopkins, *Canadian Annual Review War Series 1917*, 592.
53 It is less clear how uniform opposition to conscription and Union government was across the whole of French Canada. Although it is probably reasonable to assume that Franco-Ontarians, Franco-Manitobans, and most French Canadians had no love for English-speaking Canadians after their experiences with bilingual schooling, there is not much work examining their reactions. English, *The Decline of Politics*, 197, points out that of sixty-seven ridings with French Canadian majorities sixty-five voted for the Liberals. Other work has examined aspects of French Canadian rejection of Union government, such as Andrew Theobald's novel work on Acadians, who supported conscription. Andrew Theobald, "Une loi extraordinaire: New Brunswick Acadians and the Conscription Crisis of the First World War," *Acadiensis* 34, 1 (2004): 80–95. Also see Tarah Brookfield's exploration of women in Montreal. Tarah Brookfield, "Divide by the Ballot Box: The Montreal Council of Women and the 1917 Election," *Canadian Historical Review* 89, 4 (2008): 473–501. Meanwhile, some Franco-Americans responded to the conscription crisis by advocating the annexation of Quebec by the United States. See Robert G. LeBlanc, "The Franco-American Response to the Conscription Crisis in Canada, 1916–1918," *American Review of Canadian Studies* 23, 3 (1993): 343–72.
54 For an excellent exploration of anti-Catholicism and the Unionist Party, see Kevin P. Anderson, "'This Typical Old Canadian Form of Racial and Religious Hate': Anti-Catholicism and English Canadian Nationalism, 1905–1965" (PhD diss., McMaster University, 2013), 67–72. English, *Decline of Politics*, 199–201, reflects on the lack of a French Canadian presence among Unionists. Since this work was prepared publication, Anderson's thesis has been published: Kevin P. Anderson, *Not Quite Us: Anti-Catholic Thought in English Canada since 1900* (Montreal and Kingston: McGill-Queen's University Press, 2019).
55 Hopkins, *Canadian Annual Review War Series 1917*, 607–610.
56 This was an attitude reflected throughout the province. See Béatrice Richard, "Le Québec face à la crise de la conscription (1917–1918): Essai d'analyse sociale d'un refus," in *Le Québec dans la Grande Guerre: Engagements, refus, héritages*, ed. Charles-Philippe Courtois and Laurent Veyssière (Québec: Septentrion, 2015), 124.
57 Henri Bourassa, "Le 'Devoir' et les partis actuels," *Le Devoir*, 8 November 1917, 1; "Le programme unioniste, c'est antithèse de tout ce que nous aimons, de tout ce que nous croyons, de tout ce que nous voulons. C'est la synthèse de tout ce que nous détestons, de tout ce que nous avons conspué – hommes, idées et tendances – dans les deux partis."
58 Henri Bourassa, "Pas de lutte à trois," *Le Devoir*, 12 November 1917, 1. Bourassa also favourably reviewed Laurier's platform earlier. Henri Bourassa, "Le programme de M. Laurier I: Les droits du peuple – le nord-canadien – loi électorale – cherté des vivres," *Le Devoir*, 9 November 1917, 1; Henri Bourassa, "Le programme de M. Laurier II: La conscription reste – plébiscite – que deviennent les conscrits?," *Le Devoir*, 10 November 1917, 1.
59 Bélanger, *Wilfrid Laurier*, 405.
60 Rumilly, *Henri Bourassa*, 591–92.

61 Union Government Publicity Bureau, *Plain Facts for English-Speaking Electors: Facts which Should Be Digested and Taken Seriously to Heart* (Toronto: W.S. Johnston, 1917), 3–14. It also quotes extensively from *La Croix*, a Catholic and *nationaliste* Montreal newspaper with a limited readership of 3,500 and edited by Joseph Bégin, son-in-law of *nationaliste* journalist Jules-Paul Tardivel. See James Kennedy, *Liberal Nationalisms: Empire, State, and Civil Society in Scotland and Quebec* (Montreal and Kingston: McGill-Queen's University Press, 2012), 232.
62 Hopkins, *Canadian Annual Review War Series 1917*, 601; Rumilly, *Henri Bourassa*, 592.
63 Skelton, *Life and Letters of Sir Wilfrid Laurier*, vol. II, 537. Skelton includes other examples of the scorn directed at Laurier.
64 P.B. Waite, "Petty-Fitzmaurice, Henry Charles Keith, 5th Marquess of Lansdowne," *Dictionary of Canadian Biography*, vol. 15 (Toronto: University of Toronto; Laval: Université Laval, 2003–), http://www.biographi.ca/en/bio/petty_fitzmaurice_henry_charles_keith_15E.html.
65 Lansdowne's biographer, Lord Newton, suggests that the memorandum split the cabinet and helped to break up Britain's coalition government, allowing David Lloyd George to come to power in December, though more recent studies have questioned its influence. See Thomas Wodehouse Legh Newton, *Lord Lansdowne: A Biography* (London: Macmillan, 1929), 449–50. One of the most recent works on Lansdowne rejects Newton's conclusion. See Frank Winters, "Exaggerating the Efficacy of Diplomacy: The Marquis of Lansdowne's 'Peace Letter' of November 1917," *International History Review* 32, 1 (2010): 32–33.
66 From a letter that Lansdowne wrote to Wilson's adviser, Colonel Edward House, in early November, as cited in Winters, "Exaggerating the Efficacy of Diplomacy," 36.
67 Ibid., 26.
68 This work draws from the copy of the letter in "Letter of Lord Lansdowne to the London *Daily Telegraph*, November 29, 1917," in *International Conciliation: Documents of the American Association for International Conciliation, 1918* (New York: Carnegie Endowment for International Peace, 1918), 5–10. The quotation is from page 8.
69 Ibid., 6.
70 Ibid., 9.
71 Newton, *Lord Lansdowne*, 469–73. For a review of British newspapers' response to Lansdowne's letter, see Winters, "Exaggerating the Efficacy of Diplomacy," 37–39.
72 Newton notes the influence that it had on President Wilson and quotes his adviser, Edward M. "Colonel" House, who credited it in encouraging them to create Wilson's Fourteen Points, which would shape the peace conference of 1919. Newton, *Lord Lansdowne*, 481. For a longer view of the impact of the Lansdowne letter over the winter of 1917–18, see Douglas Newton, "The Lansdowne 'Peace Letter' of 1917 and the Prospect of Peace by Negotiation with Germany," *Australian Journal of Politics and History* 48, 1 (2002): 16–39.
73 Brock Millman offers a nuanced discussion of this epithet and Lansdowne. Brock Millman, *Pessimism and British War Policy, 1916–1918* (London: Frank Cass, 2001), 1–2, 29–32, 112–29.
74 Bertrand Russell, "Lord Lansdowne's Letter [1917]," in *Pacifism and Revolution, 1916–18*, ed. Richard A. Rempel (New York: Routledge, 1995), 371.
75 One was published on 5 March 1918 in response to a speech by German Chancellor Count Hertling, who in turn had been replying to Wilson's Fourteen Points, and another on 31 July 1918 in response to a parliamentary motion to suppress pacifism. Newton, *Lord Lansdowne*, 475–76.

76 Although many papers reported on the letter, few offered any editorial commentary, as Bourassa did. A notable exception was the *Globe*'s editorial condemning the peace proposal and suggesting that Lansdowne's argument and attitude were reactions to the economic impact on Britain's aristocratic upper-class society. *Globe* [Toronto], 1 December 1917, 6.

77 Henri Bourassa, "Le manifeste Lansdowne," *Le Devoir*, 1 December 1917, 1.

78 Ibid.

79 They are as follows: "(1), That we do not desire the annihilation of Germany as a great power; (2), That we do not seek to impose upon her people any form of government other than that of their own choice; (3), That, except as a legitimate war measure, we have no desire to deny to Germany her place among the great commercial communities of the world; (4), That we are prepared, when the war is over, to examine in concert with other powers the group of international problems, some of them of recent origin, which are connected with the question of 'the freedom of the seas'; (5), That we are prepared to enter into an international pact under which ample opportunities would be afforded for the settlement of international disputes by peaceful means." "Letter of Lord Lansdowne," *International Conciliation*, 9.

80 Bourassa, "Le manifeste Lansdowne"; "les exploiteurs de chair humaine gagneront ... la partie cette année, en Allemagne, comme ils l'ont gagnée l'an dernier, en pays alliés."

81 Ibid.

82 Henri Bourassa, "Comment voter?," *Le Devoir*, 15 December 1917, 1.

83 Ibid.

84 English, *The Decline of Politics*, 191–95, 200. For a complete list of results, see Hopkins, *Canadian Annual Review War Series 1917*, 638–42.

85 English, *The Decline of Politics*, 191. English is quoting Charles G. Power's memoir, *A Party Politician: The Memoirs of Chubby Power* (Toronto: MacMillan, 1966).

86 Henri Bourassa, "L'alignment des forces politiques: De quoi demain sera-t-il fait?," *Le Devoir*, 20 December 1917, 1.

87 Ibid.

88 Ibid.

89 Henri Bourassa, "'L'isolement' des Canadiens-français: Fausses manoeuvres de conciliation," *Le Devoir*, 26 December 1917, 1.

90 Ibid.

91 Ibid.; "à rompre les énergies de leur compatriotes, à endormir leur vigilance, à leur faire consentir d'humiliantes concessions, toujours sous le prétexte facile de concilier la majorité, de conserver leur influence dans le cabinet et d'obtenir pour la province de Québec sa part de dépouilles."

92 Ibid.; "A tout le moins, la délégation de la province de Québec au parlement fédéral n'a aucune raison de se lier à aucun gouvernement, à aucun parti, avant d'avoir obtenu les conditions d'association absolument honorables pour elle-même, avantageuses sans excès pour la nationalité canadienne-française, profitables à toute la nation canadienne."

93 David Lloyd George, *British War Aims: Statement by the Right Honourable David Lloyd George, January Fifth, Nineteen Hundred and Eighteen* (New York: George H. Duran, 1918), 14–15.

94 Andrew G. Gregory, "'They Look in Vain': British Foreign Policy Dissent and the Quest for a Negotiated Peace during the Great War with Particular Emphasis on 1917" (PhD diss., McMaster University, 1997), 216–19. Gregory summarizes the speech and reviews historians' thoughts on it.

95 Henri Bourassa, *Le pape: Arbitre de la paix* (Montréal: Le Devoir, 1918), 128. Two editorials on Lloyd George's speech were published and then inserted into the book. See Henri Bourassa, "Le discours de Lloyd George I," *Le Devoir,* 8 January 1918, 1, and Henri Bourassa, "Le discours de Lloyd George II," *Le Devoir,* 9 January 1918, 1.
96 Bourassa, *Le pape,* 134. Bourassa is quoting the pope.
97 Arthur Ray Leonard, ed., *War Addresses of Woodrow Wilson* (New York: Ginn and Company, 1918), 18.
98 Recently, historians have questioned how much national self-determination was an aim of Wilson's Fourteen Points and whether Wilson was proposing self-government instead. That is, as Trygve Throntveit argues, Wilson advocated self-government, which meant the "participation, by all constituents of a polity, in determining its public affairs" and not the right of separate self-determination by nationalities. Trygve Throntveit, "The Fable of the Fourteen Points: Woodrow Wilson and National Self-Determination," *Diplomatic History* 35, 3 (2011): 446. In a similar vein, Borislav Chernev argues that the principle of self-determination owed as much to Lenin and the Treaty of Brest-Litovsk as it did to President Wilson, and ultimately "the historical origins of the concept of self-determination had less to do with Woodrow Wilson than with the specific circumstances during the last phase of the Great War." Borislav Cherney, "The Brest-Litovsk Moment: Self-Determination Discourse in Eastern Europe before Wilsonianism," *Diplomacy and Statecraft* 22, 3 (2011): 383.
99 The term "Wilsonian moment" has been used to describe the period between January 1918, when Wilson published his Fourteen Points, and the conclusion of the Treaty of Versailles in June 1919, though some historians argue that it began only in November 1918 alongside the formal peace process. The first use of the term that I could find was in Frank Ninkovich, *Modernity and Power: A History of the Domino Theory in the Twentieth Century* (Chicago: University of Chicago Press, 1994), 60. Tony Smith used it in his analysis of the future of America's global influence in "Morality and the Use of Force in a Unipolar World: The 'Wilsonian Moment'?," *Ethics and International Affairs* 14 (2000): 11–22. It was also used in James Chace, "The Wilsonian Moment?," *Wilson Quarterly* 25, 4 (2001): 34–41, but its most-well-known use is probably in Erez Manela, *The Wilsonian Moment: Self-Determination and the International Origins of Anticolonialism Nationalism* (New York: Oxford University Press, 2007), and his article on the topic, Erez Manela, "The Wilsonian Moment and the Rise of Anticolonial Nationalism: The Case of Egypt," *Diplomacy and Statecraft* 12, 4 (2001): 99–122.
100 Bourassa, *Le pape,* 136–37; Leonard, *War Addresses of Woodrow Wilson,* 18. Bourassa's analysis was published in *Le Devoir* as well. Henri Bourassa, "Le message du président I," *Le Devoir,* 10 January 1918, 1, and Henri Bourassa, "Le message du président II," *Le Devoir,* 11 January 1918, 1.
101 Bourassa, *Le pape,* 137.
102 Ibid., 139.
103 Ibid., 140.
104 Ibid., 142; "Il la convie à se joindre à ce programme de réfection mondiale, sans rien sacrifier de sa grandeur, de ses aspirations, de son régime même, pourvu qu'elle renonce à toute idée de domination et se contente d'une 'place égale parmi les nations du monde.'"
105 Ibid.
106 Ibid., 145; "Que tout cela était vrai, fort, juste et infiniment plus pratique que tous les conseils de la haine, les efforts de la force brutale et les roueries de l'astuce diplomatique!"

107 Ibid., 146; "Que la paix se fasse demain, ou que les nations, obstinées à leur perte, poursuivent leur œuvre de suicide et de dévastation, ce n'est ni la paix allemande, ni la paix française, ni la paix anglaise, ni la paix américaine, ni la paix impérialiste, ni la paix démocratique, qui mettra fin au massacre: ce sera la paix chrétienne, ou la révolution sociale."

108 The influence of the Protestant faith on the war effort has been explored by numerous historians, notably Jonathan Vance, *Death So Noble: Memory, Meaning, and the First World War* (Vancouver: UBC Press, 1997), Chapters 2 and 3; Ian Miller, *Our Glory and Our Grief: Torontonians and the Great War* (Toronto: University of Toronto Press, 2002), Chapters 2 and 3; Michael Bliss, "The Methodist Church and World War I," *Canadian Historical Review* 49, 3 (1968): 212–33; and Michelle Fowler, "'Death Is Not the Worst Thing': The Presbyterian Press in Canada, 1913–1919," *War and Society* 25, 2 (2006): 23–38.

109 Some French Canadians, just like Protestants, fought the war for religious reasons. This was most evident among the soldiers of the French Canadian 22nd Battalion. See Geoff Keelan, "'Il a bien mérité de la patrie': The 22nd Battalion and the Memory of Courcelette," *Canadian Military History* 19 (2010): 28–40.

110 Bourassa, *Le pape*, x. The introduction was printed in *Le Devoir* as well. Henri Bourassa, "Le pape: Arbitre de la paix," *Le Devoir*, 26 January 1918, 1.

111 Neil McNeil, *The Pope and the War* (Toronto: W.E. Blake, 1918), 1. See also McNeil's biography by George Boyle, *Pioneer in Purple* (Montreal: Palm Publishers, 1951).

112 For a concise overview of the anglophone Catholic (predominantly Irish) wartime experience and the continuing hostility toward French Canadians, see Adrian Ciani, "An Imperialist Irishman: Bishop Michael Fallon, the Diocese of London, and the Great War," *Canadian Catholic Historical Association Historical Studies* 74 (2008): 73–94. One of the most stringent opponents of Bourassa was Father Alfred Edward Burke, who frequently and venomously denounced Bourassa and French Canadians. Mark G. McGowan, "Burke, Alfred Edward," in *Dictionary of Canadian Biography*, vol. 15 (Toronto: University of Toronto; Laval: Université Laval, 2003–), http://www.biographi.ca/en/bio/burke_alfred_edward_15E.html.

113 René Durocher, "Henri Bourassa, les évêques, et la guerre de 1914–1918," *Canadian Historical Association Historical Papers* 6 (1971): 248–75.

114 Henri Bourassa, "Vers la paix, partie 1," *Le Devoir*, 29 January 1918, 1.

115 Henri Bourassa, "Vers la paix, partie 2," *Le Devoir*, 30 January 1918, 1.

116 F. Seymour Cocks, *The Secret Treaties and Understandings* (London: Union of Democratic Control, 1918), 9.

117 David Stevenson, *With Our Backs to the Wall: Victory and Defeat in 1918* (New York: Penguin, 2011), 25–26.

118 Henri Bourassa, "Diplomatie secrete," *Le Devoir*, 21 February 1918, 1. Articles published between 22 February and 18 March 1918 detailed the contents of the treaties. In Canada, printing the secret treaties was banned, though Bourassa avoided falling foul of the censorship laws, not in place until later in the spring. Some labour activists were not so lucky. See Benjamin Isitt, *From Victoria to Vladivostok: Canada's Siberian Expedition, 1917–19* (Vancouver: UBC Press, 2010), 67.

119 Martin F. Auger, "On the Brink of Civil War: The Canadian Government and the Suppression of the 1918 Quebec Easter Riots," *Canadian Historical Review* 89, 4 (2008): 508–12.

120 Ibid., 519–20.

121 Henri Bourassa, "L'ordre public doit être maintenu," *Le Devoir*, 5 April 1918, 1.

122 Henri Bourassa, "Le suffrage des femmes I: Désarroi des cerveaux – triomphe de la démocratie," *Le Devoir*, 28 March 1918, 1.
123 Henri Bourassa, "Le suffrage des femmes II: Le 'droit' de voter – la lutte des sexes – laisserons-nous avilir nos femmes?," *Le Devoir*, 30 March 1918, 1; "les esprits superficiels et courts, incapables de saisir les relations des causes et des effets, les insouciants et les opportunistes, toujours prêts à concilier le bien et le mal, le faux et le vrai." Bourassa published one more editorial on the issue. Henri Bourassa, "Le suffrage des femmes III: L'influence politique des femmes – pays avancés – femmes enculottés," *Le Devoir*, 1 April 1918, 1.
124 Bourassa, "L'ordre public doit être maintenu."
125 Ibid.
126 Castell Hopkins lay blame firmly on the nationalists and "a continuous stream of vituperative argument presented to men who knew nothing of Europe and little of the Empire and little of the War." J. Castell Hopkins, *The Canadian Annual Review War Series 1918* (Toronto: Canadian Annual Review, 1918), 640; see also the discussion on 462–64. The vehemently anti–French Canadian and anti-Catholic book *The Tragedy of Quebec*, by Robert Sellar, continued to sell well throughout 1917–18, and Kevin Anderson argues that Sellar's 1917 publication *George Brown: The* Globe, *Confederation* continued this trend: "For Sellar the sinister influence of the Church had manifested itself most clearly in the cowardly refusal of French Catholics to go to war at the behest of their priests, allowing good English Protestants to die in a just cause." Anderson, "'This Typical Old Canadian Form of Racial and Religious Hate,'" 71, 113n98.
127 Béatrice Richard, "Henri Bourassa and Conscription: Traitor or Saviour?," *Canadian Military Journal* 7, 4 (2007): 80.
128 E.J. Chambers to T. Mulvey, 5 December 1917, quoted in Jean-Noël Cossette, "La censure fédérale et les principaux journaux canadiens-français du Québec, 1915–1918" (MA thesis, University of Ottawa, 1972), 133. A month earlier Chambers noted that "such action would be impolitic and would give Mr. Bourassa and his friends a chance to pose as martyrs and to misrepresent the action taken as being due to political persecution." E.J. Chambers to M. Burrell, 2 November 1917, quoted in ibid., 97.
129 Ibid., 99, 115.
130 Ibid., 116–18.
131 A description of the law is in Canada, *Sessional Papers of the Dominion of Canada*, vol. 53, 1 (1918): 23. The French text of the law is in Cossette, "La censure fédérale," 141. Otherwise, the text of the order-in-council can be found in LAC, RG 2, Reel T-5034, Order-in-Council PC 915, 16 April 1918. For one of the most recent discussions of censorship during the war, see Jeffrey A. Keshen, *Propaganda and Censorship during Canada's Great War* (Edmonton: University of Alberta Press, 1996). Keshen cites Order-in-Council PC 1241 of May 1918 (77), which forbade any individual from persuading or inducing any person to resist or impede the Military Service Act (66), as the reason for the silence of Bourassa. However, he wrote in his paper a month earlier, on 18 April, about the new censorship laws in place and their impact on *Le Devoir*, and after that he published only one article until October, which makes it seem likely that PC 915 was the reason. Cossette, "La censure fédérale," explains as much on 141–43.
132 Henri Bourassa, "Nouveau régime de presse," *Le Devoir*, 18 April 1918, 1; "qui porte l'entière responsabilité des mesures de guerre ... le moment venu d'interdire toute expression d'opinion qu'il jugera propre à créer des discussions ou à alimenter des divergences d'opinion sur l'objet ou la conduite de la guerre." "Il nous reste qu'à nous

soumettre à cette décision des autorités et à laisser à l'avenir le soin de démontrer si elle est conforme aux meilleurs intérêts du pays."
133 Rumilly, *Henri Bourassa*, 603.
134 Henri Bourassa, "Hommage au délégue du pape," *Le Devoir*, 25 October 1918, 1.
135 Henri Bourassa, "Les preliminaires de paix: M. Borden et le Parlement," *Le Devoir*, 9 November 1918, 1.
136 Henri Bourassa, "Paix et revolution: Le doigt de Dieu – le devoir de la prière," *Le Devoir*, 11 November 1918, 1; "Remercions Dieu d'avoir fait taire la voix meurtrière des canons, c'est-à-dire la voix de l'orgueil, de la haine, de la force brutale et aveugle. Demandons-lui de faire parler plus haut que jamais la voix de l'humilité, du repentir, de la raison éclairée par la foi, de la vraie charité sociale. Supplions-le d'éclairer la conscience des peuples et l'esprit des gouvernants."
137 Ibid.

Conclusion

1 Robert Rumilly, *Henri Bourassa: La vie publique d'un grand Canadien* (Montréal: Éditions Chantecler, 1953), 606–8; André Bergevin, Cameron Nish, and Anne Bourassa, *Henri Bourassa: Biographie, index des écrits, index de la correspondance publique 1895–1924* (Montréal: Les Éditions de l'Action Nationale, 1966), li.
2 Henri Bourassa, "M. Laurier," *Le Devoir*, 18 February 1919, 1:

> Dans la vie d'un chef d'état et de parti, l'historien consciencieux a le devoir de rechercher les multiples facteurs de son influence et de son action publique, de distinguer entre les actes volontairement posés et les causes subies ou simplement acceptées. Toujours difficile, cette tâche est particulièrement ardue dans un pays et à une époque où il n'existe à peu près pas d'opinion libre des passions de parti. Elle est presque impossible tant que vivent les contemporains d'un homme éminemment sympathique et charmeur, dont la force et l'influence tenaient plus à l'affection des coeurs qu'aux convictions raisonnées de l'intelligence.

3 Canada, *House of Commons Debates*, 17th Parliament, 6th Session (22 January 1935), vol. 1, 106–7 (Henri Bourassa). This was partially quoted by Omer Héroux, "Sir Wilfrid Laurier et Henri Bourassa," in *Hommage à Henri Bourassa* (Montréal: Le Devoir, 1952), 73.
4 Other than Bourassa in *Le Devoir*, the argument could be made that the *Winnipeg Free Press* and the work of its editor, John Dafoe, were one such example. See Ramsay Cook, *The Politics of John W. Dafoe and the Free Press* (Toronto: University of Toronto Press, 1963). Still unexamined are the articles that appeared in *Maclean's* and *Saturday Night*, two of Canada's prominent national magazines. Agnes Laut is an excellent example of this lacuna in Canadian First World War history. Laut was one of Canada's foremost women writers in the early twentieth century who regularly published articles in *Maclean's* on the United States during the war as well as a book on Canada's political situation. Agnes C. Laut, *The Canadian Commonwealth* (Indianapolis: Bobbs-Merrill, 1915). To date, Laut has received a single serious article on her work, from a scholar of Canadian literature, Valerie Legge, "Agnes C. Laut: High Ideals and Dreams of Unity," *Studies in Canadian Literature* 42, 1 (2017): 1–25, though Laut is mentioned in Carole Gerson, *Canadian Women in Print, 1750–1918* (Waterloo, ON: Wilfrid Laurier University Press, 2011); John Elgin Foster, R.C. Macleod, and Theodore Binnema, *From Rupert's Land to Canada* (Edmonton: University of Alberta Press, 2001), 15; Beverly Boutilier and Alison Prentice, *Creating Historical Memory: English-Canadian Women and the Work*

of History (Vancouver: UBC Press, 1997); and Glenda Riley, "'Wimmin Is Everywhere': Conserving and Feminizing Western Landscapes, 1870 to 1940," *Western Historical Quarterly* 29, 1 (1998): 4–23. The few articles that do examine Canadians' perceptions of themselves on the world stage during the war tend to focus on the private and public thoughts of elites, not on the public understanding as conceived in popular media. For a recent example, see Graeme Thompson, "Reframing Canada's Great War: Liberalism, Sovereignty, and the British Empire c 1860s–1919," *International Journal* 73, 1 (2018): 85–110. Admittedly, my book also falls prey to the same impulse considering Bourassa's small readership.

5 Sylvie Lacombe, *La rencontre de deux peuples élus: Comparaison des ambitions nationale et impériale au Canada entre 1896 et 1920* (Québec: Presses de l'Université Laval, 2002), 124.

6 "Total war" in the Canadian context deserves further study, and Bourassa spoke to but a single facet of it, about which I have written elsewhere. See Geoff Keelan, "Canada's Cultural Mobilization during the First World War and a Case for Canadian War Culture," *Canadian Historical Review* 97, 3 (2016): 377–403. I believe that there is value, as Alexandre Dubé noted, in examining the "totality" of war to help push historians to escape the "silo" of Canada's current literature on the war. See Alexandre Dubé, "Construire la guerre totale par l'image au Canada (1914–1918): Acceptation différenciée d'un discours de guerre 'totalisé'" (MA thesis, University of Montreal, 2017), 161.

7 Historian John Keiger reviewed the distinction between "structuralist" and "intentionalist" causes of the war, calling for future research to "be replaced by a more integrated analysis that brings together long-term and immediate causes so that a clearer picture of causality emerges from the given conditions with which governments necessarily live at various moments and the actions that they and individual decision-makers take." See John F.V. Keiger, "The War Explained: 1914 to the Present," in *A Companion to the First World War,* ed. John Horne (Oxford: Wiley-Blackwell, 2010), 21.

8 This point is made in Richard Rempel's introduction to Bertrand Russell, *Pacifism and Revolution, 1916–18,* ed. Richard A. Rempel (New York: Routledge, 1995), xlvi. Rempel points to Russell's 1917 pamphlet for the No-Conscription Fellowship as proof of his anti-militarism (493–94).

9 Bertrand Russell, *Justice in War Time,* 2nd ed. (London: Open Court, 1917), 3.

10 Ibid., 105, 112.

11 Richard Rempel terms Russell's views "guild socialism" in his introduction to Bertrand Russell, *Roads to Freedom,* ed. Richard Rempel (New York: Routledge, 1996), vii.

12 Réal Bélanger, "Bourassa, Henri," in *Dictionary of Canadian Biography,* vol. 18 (Toronto; University of Toronto; Laval: Université Laval, 2003–), http://www.biographi.ca/en/bio/bourassa_henri_18E.html.

13 Rumilly, *Henri Bourassa,* 637.

14 Ibid., 692–93.

15 Bélanger, "Bourassa, Henri."

16 For the impact of the war on Quebec nationalism, see Charles Philippe Courtois, "La naissance d'un nouvel indépendantisme Québécois," in *Le Québec dans la Grande Guerre: Engagements, refus, héritages,* ed. Charles-Philippe Courtois and Laurent Veyssière (Québec: Septentrion, 2015), 160–79, and Catherine Pomeyrols, "Les intellectuels nationalistes québécois et la condamnation de l'Action française," *Vingtième siècle: Revue d'histoire* 73 (2002): 92–94.

17 For a more detailed examination of Quebec nationalism in the 1920s, see Susan Mann, *Action française: French Canadian Nationalism in the Twenties* (Toronto: University of

Toronto Press, 1975). Groulx still acknowledged in 1952 that Bourassa played the "rôle de semeur, rôle de redresseur," as a foundational influence on the nationalist movement. Lionel Groulx, "Rumilly, Robert, *Henri Bourassa: La vie publique d'un grand Canadien*. Les Éditions Chantecler Ltée, Montréal, 1953. In-8. 792 pages," *Revue d'histoire de l'Amérique française* 7, 3 (1953): 450.

18 Lionel Groulx, *Mes mémoires, tome 2* (Montréal: Fides, 1971), 260:

> Entre lui et ses compatriotes, un mur de solitude se dressa. Il entrait vivant dans un demi-oubli. Son mal lui avait-il enlevé quelque chose de ses prestigieuses facultés? Il semble bien. Au parlement d'Ottawa, après quelques fulgurantes apparitions, l'orateur qui, autrefois, emplissait invariablement les tribunes, finit par parler presque dans le vide. Au *Devoir*, où il n'écrit que rarement, il ne signe plus guère d'articles vrahnent marqués de la griffe du maître. Jamais plus il ne retrouva sa veine ni ses triomphes des grands jours. Ce n'est pas encore le couchant; c'est déjà le crépuscule.

I discovered these descriptions thanks to Béatrice Richard, "Henri Bourassa and Conscription: Traitor or Saviour?," *Canadian Military Journal* 7, 4 (2007): 81n57.

19 Hélène Pelletier-Baillargeon, *Olivar Asselin et son temps: Le volintaire* (Québec: Fides, 2001), 98.
20 René Durocher, "Henri Bourassa, les évêques, et la guerre de 1914–1918," *Canadian Historical Association Historical Papers* 6 (1971): 252–53.
21 Henri Bourassa, "Après la guerre," *Le Devoir*, 2 September 1914, 1.
22 Yvan Lamonde, *Histoire sociale des idées au Québec 1896–1929*, vol. II (Québec: Fides, 2004), 272–73.
23 Henri Bourassa to J.S. Ewart, 18 January 1918, LAC, Henri Bourassa Fonds, MG27-IIE1, Reel M721. Bourassa uses the term "imperialist revolution" a sentence above to describe his perspective on how Canadians reacted to the war in the fall of 1914 and afterward.
24 Pelletier-Baillargeon, *Olivar Asselin et son temps*, 145–46.
25 Ibid., 182–83.
26 It was one that endeared Asselin to French Canadian soldiers. At one point, his friend and fellow 22nd Battalion officer Joseph Chaballe urged Asselin to take over *Le Devoir* from Bourassa. Asselin refused, knowing that the newspaper's readers would never accept his position on the war, nor could he see himself betraying Bourassa in such a way. See ibid., 246–47.
27 Ferdinand Roy, *L'appel aux armes et la réponse canadienne-française* (Québec: J.P. Garneau, 1917), 34 and throughout.
28 Oscar Douglas Skelton, *Life and Letters of Sir Wilfrid Laurier*, vol. II (London: Oxford University Press, 1922), 467. Laurier wrote to Quebec Premier Lomer Gouin about handing Quebec to the extremists (512).
29 LAC, Borden Papers, M02611, Diary, 30 May 1915.
30 The two most-well-known studies of English Canadian and French Canadian memories of the war are Jonathan F. Vance, *Death So Noble: Memory, Meaning, and the First World War* (Vancouver: UBC Press, 1997), and Mourad Djebabla, *Se souvenir de la Grande Guerre: La mémoire plurielle de 14–18 au Québec* (Montréal: VLB, 2004).
31 Elizabeth Armstrong, *The Crisis of Quebec, 1914–1918* (Toronto: McClelland and Stewart, 1937), 53.
32 One only has to read Hopkins in the *Canadian Annual Review* to see this distinction. For example, in the 1917 volume, Hopkins wrote that Bourassa was engaged in "bitter

and unscrupulous denunciation of Great Britain and the British people and soldiers in the War with the reiteration of every possible misconception as to Allied policy and action" while "no man could die more gallantly for his country and Empire than Major Talbot Papineau." J. Castell Hopkins, *Canadian Annual Review War Series 1917* (Toronto: Canadian Annual Review, 1918), 477, 474.

33 Vance, *Death So Noble*, 253–54.
34 Ibid., 228–30.
35 Armstrong, *Crisis of Quebec*, 242–45.
36 Rumilly, *Henri Bourassa*, 7.
37 Ibid., 597.
38 It appears throughout Rumilly's history of Quebec as well, for instance "Henri Bourassa, en qui frémissait l'atavisme des Papineau." Robert Rumilly, *Histoire de la province de Québec*, vol. IX, *F.G. Marchand* (Montréal: Montréal-Éditions, n.d.), 117. Another example is "Bourassa, personnalité complexe aux atavismes contradictoires, curieux mélange de doctrinaire réaliste et de mystique chrétien." Robert Rumilly, *Histoire de la province de Québec*, vol. XX, *Philipe Landry* (Montréal: Montréal-Éditions, n.d.), 86. Allegations of atavism were also used to criticize Bourassa. In 1911, a pamphlet denounced his position against Laurier during the election that, like Rumilly, cited Bourassa's atavism as following in the footsteps of Papineau, though it argued that Papineau had failed to recognize the changing nature of the times. See *L'œil ouvert! Bourassa et l'anti-Laurierisme. Prétention – haine et impuissance, lâcheté et ingratitude* (n.p: n.p., 1911), 8–9.
39 Rumilly, *Henri Bourassa*, 784.
40 Henri Bourassa, *Que devons-nous à l'Angleterre? La défense nationale, la révolution impérialiste, le tribut à l'empire* (Montréal: Imprimerie du Devoir, 1915), viii; "Toutes les évolutions d'un peuple sont la résultante, harmonieuse ou incohérente, de ses mouvements antérieurs, de ses instincts ataviques."
41 Frédéric Boily, *La pensée nationaliste de Lionel Groulx* (Sillery, QC: Septentrion, 2003), 21–50.
42 Rumilly, *Henri Bourassa*, 791.
43 Admittedly, Rumilly's relationship with Quebec nationalism was far more complex than can be discussed here. See Jean-François Nadeau, *Robert Rumilly, l'homme de Duplessis* (Montréal: Lux Éditeur, 2009).
44 Claude Ryan, "Henri Bourassa devant l'histoire," *Le Devoir*, 31 August 1968, 4.
45 On British Canadian identity in the 1960s, see Phillip Buckner, *Canada and the End of Empire* (Vancouver: UBC Press, 2004); José Eduardo Igartua, *The Other Quiet Revolution: National Identities in English Canada, 1945–71* (Vancouver: UBC Press, 2006); and C.P. Champion, *The Strange Demise of British Canada: The Liberals and Canadian Nationalism, 1964–1968* (Montreal and Kingston: McGill-Queen's University Press, 2010). Each examined the "disappearance" of a British Canadian identity and its consequences, though Buckner and Champion suggest that it was transforming instead of disappearing.
46 The well-known debate between the Montreal and Laval schools of historians on the character of Quebec's history has been explored in detail by many, notably in English by Ronald Rudin, *Making History in Twentieth Century Quebec* (Toronto: University of Toronto Press, 1997). Ramsay Cook has also examined the influence on Quebec nationalism of Quebec historians such as Maurice Séguin and Michel Brunet. Ramsay Cook, *Canada and the French Canadian Question* (Toronto: Macmillan, 1966), 119–42.
47 Ryan, "Henri Bourassa devant l'histoire."

48 Robert Craig Brown and Ramsay Cook, *Canada 1896–1921: A Nation Transformed* (Toronto: McClelland and Stewart, 1974), 274.
49 Ramsay Cook, *The Maple Leaf Forever: Essays on Nationalism and Politics in Canada* (Toronto: Macmillan, 1971), 74–75; Cook, *Canada and the French Canadian Question*, 122. Cook is never negative toward Bourassa, but the greater thrust of his arguments regarding the problems of Canadian nationalism (and French Canadian nationalism) is against both its existence and its justifications. Throughout his many essays on the subject, Cook does not investigate the First World War other than as the context of problems related to Canadian unity and the cultural and linguistic divides of the 1960s. Bourassa's role as an international commentator is entirely ignored.
50 For an excellent and recent overview, see Mark Osborne Humphries, "Between Commemoration and History: The Historiography of the Canadian Corps and Military Overseas," *Canadian Historical Review* 95, 3 (2014): 384–97.
51 Mourad Djebabla, "Historiographie francophone de la Première Guerre Mondiale: Écrire la Grande Guerre de 1914–1918 français au Canada et au Québec," *Canadian Historical Review* 95, 3 (2014): 407.
52 See Paul-André Comeau, *Le Bloc populaire 1942–1948* (Montréal: Éditions Québec/Amérique, 1982); or, in comparison to Bourassa, see Michael Oliver, *The Passionate Debate: The Social and Political Ideas of Quebec Nationalism 1920–1945* (Montreal: Véhicule Press, 1991), 198–204.
53 Scott Staring, "'Not Heaven-Endowed to Run the World': The British Empire in the Early Thought of George Grant," *Journal of Canadian Studies* 45, 1 (2011): 52n17. A recent master's thesis also explores the extent of Bourassa's influence among English Canadians. See Benoit Longval, "Au-delà des 'jingos' et des 'coquins': Henri Bourassa et ses relations avec le Canada anglais (1896–1935)" (MA thesis, University of Ottawa, 2014).
54 Gabriel Martin, *Dictionnaire des onomastismes québecois: Les mots issus de nos mots propres* (Sherbrooke: Éditions du Fleurdelysé, 2013), 35–36. *Bourassisme* follows *papineauisme* and precedes *groulxisme*.
55 Oliver, *The Passionate Debate*, 208, makes this distinction.
56 Canada, *House of Commons Debates*, 17th Parliament, 6th Session (22 January 1935), vol. 1, 105 (Henri Bourassa).
57 Ibid., 107.

Selected Bibliography

Anctil, Pierre, ed. *Fais ce que dois: 60 éditoriaux pour comprendre* Le Devoir *sous Henri Bourassa (1910–1932)*. Québec: Éditions du Septentrion, 2010.

Anderson, Kevin P. "'This Typical Old Canadian Form of Racial and Religious Hate': Anti-Catholicism and English Canadian Nationalism, 1905–1965." PhD diss., McMaster University, 2013.

Angers, F.A., ed. *La pensée de Henri Bourassa*. Montréal: Éditions de l'Action Nationale, 1954.

Armstrong, Elizabeth. *The Crisis of Quebec, 1914–1918*. Toronto: McClelland and Stewart, 1937.

Asselin, Olivar. *'L'Action catholique,' les évêques et la guerre*. Ottawa: n.p., 1915.

Bélanger, Damien-Claude. *Prejudice and Pride: Canadian Intellectuals Confront the United States, 1891–1945*. Toronto: University of Toronto Press, 2011.

Bélanger, Damien-Claude, Sophie Coupal, and Michel Ducharme, eds. *Les idées en mouvement: Perspectives en histoire intellectuelle et culturelle du Canada*. Québec: Presses de l'Université Laval, 2004.

Bélanger, Réal. *Henri Bourassa: Le fascinant destin d'un homme libre (1868–1914)*. Québec: Presses de l'Université Laval, 2013.

–. *L'impossible défi: Albert Sévigny et les conservateurs fédéraux (1902–1918)*. Québec: Presses de l'Université Laval, 1983.

–. *Paul-Émile Lamarche: Le pays avant le parti (1904–1918)*. Québec: Presses de l'Université Laval, 1984.

–. *Wilfrid Laurier: Quand la politique devient passion*. 2nd ed. Québec: Presses de l'Université Laval, 2007.

Berger, Carl, ed. *Conscription 1917*. Toronto: University of Toronto Press, 1969.

–, ed. *Imperialism and Nationalism, 1884–1914: A Conflict in Canadian Thought*. Toronto: Copp Clark, 1969.

–. *The Sense of Power: Studies in the Ideas of Canadian Imperialism, 1867–1914*. Toronto: University of Toronto Press, 1970.

Bergevin, André, Cameron Nish, and Anne Bourassa, eds. *Henri Bourassa: Biographie, index des écrits, index de la correspondance publique 1895–1924*. Montréal: Éditions de l'Action Nationale, 1966.

Bourassa, Henri. *The Case against Conscription*. Montreal: Éditions du Devoir, 1917.

–. *La conscription*. Montréal: Éditions du Devoir, 1917.

–. *The Duty of Canada at the Present Hour*. Montreal: Le Devoir, 1915.

–. *The Foreign Policy of Great Britain*. Montreal: Le Devoir, 1915.

–. *French and English Frictions and Misunderstandings*. Montreal: Imprimerie du Devoir, 1914.

–. *Grande-Bretagne et Canada: Questions actuelles.* Montréal: Imprimerie du Pionnier, 1901.
–. *La langue française au Canada: Ses droits, sa nécessité, ses avantages. Discours prononcé au Monument National, le 19 mai 1915, sous les auspices du Comité régional de Montréal de l'A.C.J.C.* Montréal: Imprimerie du Devoir, 1915.
–. *Le Pape: Arbitre de la paix.* Montréal: Le Devoir, 1918.
–. *"Le problème de l'Empire": Indépendance ou association impériale? Étude critique du livre de M. Lionel Curtis:* The Problem of the Commonwealth. Montréal: Éditions du Devoir, 1916.
–. *Que devons-nous à l'Angleterre? La défense nationale, la révolution impérialiste, le tribut à l'Empire.* Montréal: Imprimerie du Devoir, 1915.
–. "Why Canada Should Not Adopt Conscription." *Le Devoir*, 12 July 1917, 1.
Bourne, Randolph Silliman. *Towards an Enduring Peace: A Symposium of Peace Proposals and Programs.* New York: American Association for International Conciliation, 1916.
Bray, Robert Matthew. "The Canadian Patriotic Response to the Great War." PhD diss., Laurentian University, 1977.
Brown, Robert Craig, and Ramsay Cook. *Canada 1896–1921: A Nation Transformed.* Toronto: McClelland and Stewart, 1974.
Cardinal, Mario. *Pourquoi j'ai fondé* Le Devoir*: Henri Bourassa et son temps.* Montréal: Libre Expression, 2010.
Coates, Colin, ed. *Imperial Canada 1867–1914: A Selection of Papers Given at the University of Edinburgh's Centre of Canadian Studies Conference, May 1995.* Edinburgh: University of Edinburgh, Centre of Canadian Studies, 1997.
Cole, Douglas L. "Canada's 'Nationalistic' Imperialists." *Journal of Canadian Studies* 5, 3 (1970): 44–49.
–. "John S. Ewart and Canadian Nationalism." *Historical Papers* 4, 1 (1969): 62–73.
–. "The Problem of 'Nationalism' and 'Imperialism' in British Settlement Colonies." *Journal of British Studies* 10, 2 (1971): 160–82.
Comeau, Robert, and Luc Desrochers, eds. Le Devoir*: Un journal indépendant (1910–1995).* Québec: Presses de l'Université du Québec, 1996.
Cook, Ramsay. *Canada and the French-Canadian Question.* Toronto: Macmillan, 1966.
–. *Canada, Quebec, and the Uses of Nationalism.* Toronto: McClelland and Stewart, 1986.
–. Review of *La rencontre de deux peuples élus: Comparaison des ambitions nationale et impériale au Canada entre 1896 et 1920*, by Sylvie Lacombe. *Revue d'histoire de l'Amérique française* 56, 4 (2003): 557–60. https://doi.org/10.7202/007791ar.
–. *The Maple Leaf Forever: Essays on Nationalism and Politics in Canada.* Toronto: Macmillan, 1971.
–. *Watching Quebec: Selected Essays.* Montreal and Kingston: McGill-Queen's University Press, 2005.
Cook, Terry. "George R. Parkin and the Concept of Britannic Idealism." *Journal of Canadian Studies* 10, 3 (1975): 15–31.
Corcoran, James I.W. "Henri Bourassa et la guerre sud-africain (suite)." *Revue d'histoire de l'Amérique française* 19, 1 (1965): 84–105. https://doi.org/10.7202/302441ar.
Cosmos. *The Basis for a Durable Peace.* New York: Charles Scribner's Sons, 1917.
Cossette, Jean Noël. "La censure fédérale et les principaux journaux canadiens-français du Québec, 1915–1918." MA thesis, University of Ottawa, 1971.
Courtois, Charles-Philippe, and Laurent Veyssière, eds. *Le Québec dans la Grande Guerre: Engagements, refus, héritages.* Québec: Septentrion, 2015.
Curtis, Lionel. *The Problem of the Commonwealth.* London: Macmillan, 1915.

Desjardins, Louis Georges. *England, Canada and the Great War*. Quebec: Chronicle Print, 1918.

Drolet, Jean. "Henri Bourassa: Une analyse de sa pensée." In *Idéologies au Canada français 1900–1929*, edited by Fernand Dumont, Jean Hamelin, Fernand Harvey, and Jean-Paul Montminy, 223–50. Québec: Presses de l'Université Laval, 1974.

Durflinger, Serge Marc. "Vimy's Consequences: The Montreal Anti-Conscription Disturbances, May to September 1917." In *Turning Point 1917: The British Empire at War*, edited by Douglas E. Delaney and Nikolas Gardner, 160–87. Vancouver: UBC Press, 2017.

Durocher, René. "Henri Bourassa, les évêques et la guerre de 1914–1918." *Canadian Historical Association Historical Papers* 6 (1971): 248–75.

–. "Un journaliste catholique au XXe siècle: Henri Bourassa." In *Le laïc dans l'Église canadienne-française de 1830 à nos jours*, edited by Pierre Hurtubise et al., 185–213. Montréal: Fides, 1972.

Dutil, Patrice, and David Mackenzie. *Canada 1911: The Decisive Election that Shaped the Country*. Toronto: Dundurn, 2011.

English, John. *The Decline of Politics: The Conservatives and the Party System, 1901–20*. Toronto: University of Toronto Press, 1993.

Fournier, Jules. *Mon encrier*. Edited by Thérèse Fournier. Montréal: Fides, 1965. First published 1922.

Hopkins, J. Castell. *Canadian Annual Review War Series: 1914–1918*. Toronto: Canadian Annual Review, 1918.

Jones, Richard. "La perspective nationaliste d'Henri Bourassa, 1896–1914: Commentaire." *Revue d'histoire de l'Amérique française* 22, 4 (1969): 582–86.

Kennedy, James. *Liberal Nationalisms: Empire, State, and Civil Society in Scotland and Quebec*. Montreal and Kingston: McGill-Queen's University Press, 2013.

Keshen, Jeffrey A. *Propaganda and Censorship during Canada's Great War*. Edmonton: University of Alberta Press, 1996.

Lacombe, Sylvie. "French Canada: The Rise and Decline of a 'Church-Nation.'" *Québec Studies* 48 (2009–10): 135–58.

–. "Un prophète ultramontain: Henri Bourassa (1868–1952)." In *Les visages de la foi: Figures marquantes du catholicisme québécois*, edited by G. Routhier and J.-P. Warren, 133–46. Québec: Fides, 2003.

–. *La rencontre de deux peuples élus: Comparaison des ambitions nationale et impériale au Canada entre 1896 et 1920*. Québec: Presses de l'Université Laval, 2002.

Lamonde, Yvan. *Histoire sociale des idées au Québec*. Vol. 1, *1760–1896*. Québec: Fides, 2004.

–. *Histoire sociale des idées au Québec*. Vol. 2, *1896–1929*. Québec: Fides, 2004.

Laurendeau, André. "Henri Bourassa." In *Our Living Tradition*, edited by R.L. McDougall, 140–58. Toronto: University of Toronto Press, 1962.

Le Devoir. *Le 5e anniversaire du* "Devoir." Montréal: Le Devoir, 1915.

LeBlanc, Robert G. "The Franco-American Response to the Conscription Crisis in Canada, 1916–1918." *American Review of Canadian Studies* 23, 3 (1993): 343–72.

Leland, Marine. "Quelques observations sur le nationalisme d'Henri Bourassa." In *Report of the Annual Meeting/Rapports annuels de la Société historique du Canada* 30, 1 (1951): 60–63.

Levitt, Joseph. *Henri Bourassa – Catholic Critic*. Ottawa: Canadian Historical Association, 1976.

–. "Henri Bourassa: The Catholic Social Order and Canada's Mission." In *Idéologies au Canada français 1900–1929*, edited by Fernand Dumont, Jean Hamelin, Fernand

Harvey, and Jean-Paul Montminy, 192–222. Québec: Presses de l'Université Laval, 1974.

—. *Henri Bourassa and the Golden Calf: The Social Program of the Nationalists of Quebec (1900–1914)*. Ottawa: Éditions de l'Université d'Ottawa, 1969.

—. *Henri Bourassa on Imperialism and Bi-culturalism, 1900–1918*. Toronto: Copp Clark, 1970.

—. "La perspective nationaliste d'Henri Bourassa, 1896–1914." *Revue d'histoire de l'Amérique française* 22, 4 (1969): 567–82.

Mackenzie, David, ed. *Canada and the First World War: Essays in Honour of Robert Craig Brown*. Toronto: University of Toronto Press, 2005.

Maillé, L.O. *Réponse de M. L.O. Maillé aux articles "Où allons nous?" et à M. l'Abbé d'Amours*. Montréal: n.p., 1917.

Mann, Susan. *The Dream of a Nation: A Social and Intellectual History of Quebec*. Toronto: Gage, 1983.

Martin, Jean. "La participation des francophones dans le Corps expéditionnaire canadien (1914–1919): Il faut réviser à la hausse." *Canadian Historical Review* 96, 3 (2015): 405–23.

Mayeur, Jean-Marie. "Les Catholiques français et Benoît XV en 1917: Brèves remarques." In *Chrétiens dans la première guerre mondiale: Actes des journées tenues à Amiens et à Péronne les 16 mai et 22 juillet 1992*, edited by Nadine-Josette Chaline, 153–65. Paris: Cerf, 1993.

McNeil, Neil. *The Pope and the War*. Toronto: W.E. Blake, 1918.

Murrow, Casey. *Henri Bourassa and French-Canadian Nationalism: Opposition to Empire*. Montreal: Harvest House, 1968.

Neatby, H. Blair. *Laurier and a Liberal Quebec*. Toronto: McClelland and Stewart, 1961.

O'Connell, Martin P. "Ideas of Henri Bourassa." *Canadian Journal of Economics and Political Science* 19 (1953): 361–76.

Oliver, Michael. *The Passionate Debate: The Social and Political Ideas of Quebec Nationalism, 1920–1945*. Montreal: Véhicule Press, 1991.

Prince, Robert S. "The Mythology of War: How the Canadian Daily Newspaper Depicted the Great War." PhD diss., University of Toronto, 1998.

Robertson, Susan Mann. "Variations on a Nationalist Theme: Henri Bourassa and Abbé Groulx in the 1920's." *Historical Papers* 5, 1 (1970): 109–19.

Roy, Ferdinand. *The Call to Arms and the French Canadian Reply*. Translated by J. Squair and J.S. Will. Quebec: J.P. Garneau, 1918.

—. *L'appel aux armes et la réponse canadienne-française*. Québec: J.P. Garneau, 1917.

Rumilly, Robert. *Henri Bourassa: La vie publique d'un grand Canadien*. Montréal: Éditions Chantecler, 1953.

—. *Histoire de la province de Québec*. Vols. 1–41. Montréal: Valiquette, 1940–69.

Smith, V.C. "Moral Crusader: Henri Bourassa and the Empire, 1900–1916." *Queen's Quarterly* 76 (1969): 635–47.

Trofimenkoff, Susan Mann. "Henri Bourassa and 'The Woman Question.'" *Journal of Canadian Studies* 10 (1975): 3–11.

—. "Henri Bourassa et la question des femmes." In *Les femmes dans la société québécoise: Aspects historiques*, edited by Marie Lavigne and Yolande Pinard, 109–24. Montréal: Boréal Express, 1977.

Index

22nd Battalion, 50–51

Action catholique, 146, 157. See also *Action sociale*
Action sociale, 51, 58, 101. See also *Action catholique*
Armstrong, Elizabeth, 9–10, 202–3
Asselin, Olivar, 30, 62–63, 93–94, 200

Bégin, Cardinal Louis-Nazaire, 51, 69, 123
Belcourt, Senator Napoléon-Antoine, 86–87, 122–23
Benedict XV (pope), 68, 106–7, 123, 166–67; on peace, 81–82, 183–84
biculturalism, 34, 78–79, 194, 205
bilingualism, 34, 78–79, 194, 205
Boer War, 25–26, 120
Borden, Sir Robert: and the 1911 election, 38–40; and the 1917 election, 179; on Bourassa, 200–1; Canadian autonomy, 145; on coalition government, 155, 169–70; on conscription, 150–51, 156; criticism of, 71–73, 132–33; on increasing size of Canadian army, 96, 144; support for the war, 49, 96
Bourassa, Henri: and the 1917 election, 173–76; on Benedict XV, 81–82, 168–69, 181–85; on British imperialism, 26; on Canadian identity, 44–45; on Canadian nationalism, 194; on Catholicism in Quebec, 100–1; censorship of, 188; comparison to Bertrand Russell, 195–96; on conscription, 145, 151–56, 171; correspondence with Talbot Mercer Papineau, 112–17; criticism of, 60–61, 114–17, 130–31, 158–60, 176, 200–1; criticism of English Canada, 88–89; on death of Laurier, 191–92; duty to dissent, 53–55; on the Easter Riots, 187–88; education of, 23; failure of international system, 127–28, 193; on French language, 44, 78–79, 109; on French war effort, 46–47; hierarchy of beliefs, 12–13, 194–98; historians' views of, 9–13; on imperialism, 71–73, 101–4, 121–22, 148–49; international criticism of the war, 82–85; and international critics of the war, 64–65; legacy, 206–10; as a Member of Parliament, 24–25, 191–92; memory of, 204–6; on militarism, 104–5, 114–16, 135–36, 195–96; and national unity, 4–6, 157–58, 173–74, 179–81; on naval issues, 38–39; on neutrality, 168–69; on patriotism, 74–75; on peace, 124–29, 177–78, 182–84; and Quebec bishops, 51–53, 101; Quebec nationalism, 196–98; reconciliation with Laurier, 171–72, 190–91; on Russia, 75, 126, 134; support for the war, 48, 52–55, 88–89, 93; ultramontane beliefs, 23, 89–90; and the Union of Democratic Control, 84–85, 104; on the United States, 137–41, 173; on violence, 164–65
Bourassa, Henri, publications of: *La Conscription*, 151–56; *The Pope: Arbiter of Peace*, 181–84; *The Problem of Empire*, 120–22; *What Do We Owe England?*, 87–90; *Yesterday, Today, Tomorrow*, 100–6
Bourget, Bishop Ignace, 22
Brailsford, Henry Noel, 63–64, 75, 83

Britain: conscription, 95–96; foreign policy, 75–76; naval issues, 76; on peace, 181–82; and peace proposals, 124–29; rule over Quebec, 21; war aims, 85–86; war effort, 55–57
Butler, Nicholas Murray (pseud. Cosmos), 136

Cahan, Charles Hazlitt, 61–62
Canada: autonomy from Britain, 99; coalition government, 169–70; relationship with the United States, 25
Canadian nationalism: compared to imperialism, 28–29, 130–31, 64–65; and danger of Quebec nationalism, 10; and the war effort, 47–48
catholicism, in Quebec, 21–22, 32–33, 44
Chamberlain, Joseph, 27–28
Chase-Casgrain, Thomas, 50, 59, 79–80
conscription: in Britain, 95–96; in Canada, 96, 145–47; enactment of, in Canada, 150–51, 156–57, 160–61, 170–71
Cortés, Donoso, 141–42
Cosmos. *See* Butler, Nicholas Murray
Courcelette, Battle of, 118
Curtis, Lionel, 120–21

D'Amours, Abbé Joseph Prio Arthur, 51, 130–31
Le Devoir, founding of, 6, 37–38, 70
Drummond-Arthabaska by-election, 39

Easter Rising, Ireland, 107–8
election (Canadian, 1911): 6, 39–40, 174–75, 179
English Canada: actions against Franco-Ontarian minority, 40–41, 86–87, 108; criticism of French Canada, 41, 152–54, 157, 176; identity, 28–29; newspaper reaction to war, 59–60; support for the war, 105–6, 125
enlistment: in the Canadian Army, 96, 144; in Quebec, 50–51
Eucharistic Congress, Twenty-First (Montreal), 44
Ewart, John S., 64–65, 199

federal election. *See* election
Fournier, Jules, 30, 62, 94–95, 198–200

France, 46–47
French Canada: conscription, 158–60, 163–64; Franco-Ontarians, 86–87; identity, 21–22, 42–44; nationalism, 196–98; newspaper reaction to war, 58–59; religion, 32–33; support for the war, 153–54

Garneau, François-Xavier, 43
Germany: and peace proposals, 124–29; relationship with the United States, 77–78; submarines, 76–77; war aims, 85–86
Gladstone, William, 36
Grey, Sir Edward, 56–57, 75, 85–86, 97, 135
Groulx, Abbé Lionel, 197–98

Héroux, Omer, 30, 62, 95
House of Commons. *See* Parliament, Canadian
Howe, Frederic C., 172–73

imperialism: in Britain, 27, 63; in Canada, 28–30, 120–22, 149; compared to nationalism, 28–29; revolution, 88, 100–5, 148–49, 199–200; and the war effort, 49–50
Ireland, and the Easter Rising, 107–8

Laflèche, Bishop L.F., 22
Lansdowne, Lord (Henry Petty-Fitzmaurice), 176–78
Lapointe, Ernest, 108–9
Lartigue, Bishop L.L., 22
Laurier, Sir Wilfrid: on Bourassa, 200–1; as Bourassa's mentor, 24; on coalition government, 155–56; and conscription, 155–56, 169–71; criticism of, 97–99, 148, 176; death, 190–91; and liberalism, 35; on Louis Riel, 24; on Quebec, 108–9; reconciliation with Bourassa, 171–72, 190–91; supporting the war, 49
Lavergne, Armand, 30, 62, 69, 93–94
Law, Andrew Bonar, 119
Lemieux, Rodolphe, 50
liberalism, as part of nationalism, 35–36
Ligue nationaliste, 30
Lusitania, 76–78

Maillé, L.O., 131–32
Manitoba School Crisis, 24–25
McMaster, Andrew, 112
McNeil, Archbishop Neil, 184
militarism, 114, 135–36, 193–96; in Canada, 5, 80, 99–101, 105–6, 159–60; in Germany, 83–84
Morel, E.D., 84–85

nationalism, 133. *See also* Canadian nationalism
nationalisme, 30–36, 200, conflict within, 93–95
Naval Service Bill, 38–39

Papineau, Louis-Joseph, 21, 108, 111
Papineau, Talbot Mercer, 110–17
Parliament, Canadian: criticism of, 73–74; extension of, 80–81, 97–98
La Patrie, 25, 58

Quebec: bishops, 51–52, 145–46, 157–58; and the Easter Riots, 186–88

recruitment. *See* enlistment
Regulation 17: court case against, 69, 78–79, 86–87, 122–23; repeal of, 40–41, 48, 62, 108–9
Riel, Louis, 23–24
Roy, Ferdinand, 158–60
Rumilly, Robert, 10–11, 203–4
Russell, Bertand, 195–96
Russia, 75–76

Sellar, Robert, 41, 108
Sévigny, Albert, 158
Siegfried, André, 43–44
Somme, Battle of the, 112
South Africa, and the Boer War, 25–26, 120

Tardivel, Jules-Paul, 31–32, 45
Tarte, Joseph-Israël, 31
The Tragedy of Quebec (Sellar), 41, 108

ultramontanism: and Henri Bourassa, 89–90, 168, 206–7; in Quebec, 22–32, 32–33, 141–42
Union Government, 169–72, 174–76
Union of Democratic Control, 63, 68, 82–85; on peace, 104, 177
United Kingdom. *See* Britain
United States: election of 1916, 123–24; entry into the war, 77–78, 136–37; neutrality, 77–78; and peace proposals, 124–29; relationship with Canada, 103–5; relationship with Germany, 77–78

Vatican. *See* Benedict XV
Vimy Ridge, Battle of, 147

Wetterlé, Abbé Émile, 46
Wilson, Woodrow, 123–24; on peace, 181–82

Ypres, Battle of, 76